PROSTHETIC CULTURE

The power of the photographic image to redefine the relations between consciousness, the body and memories is such as to produce a prosthetic culture. The manipulation of photographic images and ways of seeing make it possible for memories to be implanted in the individual while others are stored in 'banks'; advertising imagery holds open the moment of exposure for personal experimentation; and the powers of cartoon super heroes promise not only an inhuman extension of physical capability in space but also the ability to outwit time itself. From photographic events and seeing photographically thus emerges a self-identity that is no longer simply defined by the edict 'I think therefore I am' but by an extended agency of the body in prostheses both mechanical and perceptual. In this technological enhancement of 'potential', the self is defined by the relation 'I can therefore I am'.

In prosthetic culture, what have previously been seen as relatively fixed social and natural attributes of self-identity are reconstituted as modifiable by deliberate transformation, opening up new spheres of decision-making and choice. At the same time, however, apparently voluntary actions are redefined as the effect of previously invisible determinations, thus offering new grounds for the denial of individual responsibility, posing new ethical dilemmas. In this redrawing of the line between character and personality, questions of gender continue to prove troublesome. Photo-therapy, family albums, Benetton advertising, the phenomenon of false memory syndrome and the lives of cartoon characters illustrate how the 'eyes' made available by contemporary visual technologies involve not only simply specific ways of seeing but also ways of life.

Celia Lury is a Lecturer in Sociology at Goldsmiths College, University of London.

PROSTHETIC CULTURE

Photography, memory and identity

CELIA LURY

ROUTLEDGE

LONDON AND NEW YORK

First published 1998
by Routledge
11 New Fetter Lane, London EC4P 4EE

Simultaneously published in the USA and Canada
by Routledge
29 West 35th Street, New York, NY 10001

Transferred to Digital Printing 2002

Routledge is an imprint of the Taylor & Francis Group

Typeset in Baskerville by Routledge
Printed and bound in Great Britain by Biddles Short Run Books, King's Lynn

British Library Cataloguing in Publication Data
A catalogue record for this book is available from the British Library

Library of Congress Cataloguing in Publication Data
A catalogue record has been requested for this title

ISBN 0–415–10293–6 (hbk)
ISBN 0–415–10294–4 (pbk)

CONTENTS

FIGURES

ACKNOWLEDGEMENTS

I would like to thank the very many people who have contributed to this book. Chris Rojek gave me the opportunity to explore these issues, and encouraged me to follow up on the idea of experimental individualism, while Mari Shullaw had sufficient confidence in the project to make me hand over the manuscript. Lisa Adkins, Heather d'Cruz, Jeanette Edwards, Sarah Franklin, Penny Harvey, John Law, Stephanie Lawler, Rebecca Leach, Rolland Munro, Lynne Pearce, Peter Rush, Rob Shields, Jackie Stacey, John Urry and Alison Young all offered criticism, encouragement and ideas, while Mariam Fraser, Liz Greenhalgh, Scott Lash, Karen Lury, Stephen Pope and Beverley Skeggs helped me out when it mattered most. I am grateful to them all.

The author and publisher wish to thank the copyright holders for their kind permission to reproduce illustrations. Figure 2.1 The two functions of feedback © Jossey-Bass, Inc., Publishers; Figure 2.2 'We've included your brain in our System...' © Hasselblad (UK) Limited; Figure 3.4 Aids Faces and Figure 3.5 The Twins © United Colors of Benetton; Figure 5.1 Thurston County Sheriff's Office: the formal investigation of ritual abuse © Alfred A. Knopf, first published in *The New Yorker*; Figure 8.1 Superman or the tree of eyes © Keystone View Co., London. Every effort has been made to obtain permission to reproduce copyright material. If any proper acknowledgement has not been made, we would invite copyright holders to inform us of the oversight.

1

IDENTITY AND PROSTHETIC CULTURE

> Only the future has developers at its disposal that are strong enough to bring forth the image in all of its details.
>
> (Walter Benjamin, quoted in McCole, 1993: 290)

Conceptions of the person, self-identity, the individual and human nature are neither self-evident nor immutable building blocks of which societies are built (Stolcke, 1993). Moreover, there is no natural one to one correspondence between the person, self-identity and the individual. This is illustrated by Marilyn Strathern (1988), among others, who explicitly contrasts the partible, multiply constituted person of Melanesia, from whom aspects of identity may be detached, with the ideal construct of the self-determined, free-standing, integral individual of what she calls Euro-American societies. This notion of the unique, free, self-determining and responsible individual is, moreover, historically specific even within Euro-American societies, dating from the Renaissance and undergoing consolidation with the Enlightenment. Furthermore, the individual is by no means an identity that has been made available to all, even in contemporary Euro-American societies. Rather, the self-determined individual has been an enabling myth of such societies, a myth whose apparent universalism obscures its dependency upon practices of exclusion and principles of hierarchical classification.

In this book, I will consider some of the changing ways in which self-identity is constituted as a possession of the individual (and thus of some more than other people) in contemporary Euro-American societies. The idea that liberal democratic societies have encouraged a kind of *possessive individualism*, in which a free, self-determining and self-responsible identity is constituted as a property, is not new.[1] However, I will suggest that the terms of such self-possession are currently being renegotiated in a process of *experimentation* in what will be called a *prosthetic culture*. In the chapters that follow I argue that the adoption of experimentation as a technique of the self makes possible a relation to the individual so produced (including the previously defining characteristics of consciousness, memory and embodiment) in which aspects that have previously seemed (naturally or socially) fixed, immutable or beyond will or self-control are increasingly made sites of strategic decision-making, matters of technique or experimentation. Through

1 See, for example, Macpherson (1962); MacFarlane (1978, 1994); Abercrombie *et al.* (1986); Pateman (1988); Butler (1993); Diprose (1994).

experimentation, then, the previously automatic is converted into the volitional, the unconscious is brought into view, the forgotten is recalled and lack of control or responsibility over the self is converted into intentions, subject to calculation, risk-taking and the apparently never-ending exercise of will.[2] The tendency towards experimentation thus has widespread implications for contemporary understandings of agency, responsibility, the allocation of guilt, blame and virtue, the ascription of rights to the individual (and the exclusion of some people from this identity), and for recognitions of belonging, collective identification and exclusion. Transformations in these attributes of character and belonging both draw upon and refigure the modern category of the legal personality. Prosthetic culture thus provides a novel context for understandings of the person and of self-identity.

The focus of this analysis of prosthetic culture is photography and its subject-effects. Photography was chosen because of a wish to redress, to some small degree at least, the extent to which the significance of the visual image for understandings of the person in Euro-American societies has been tainted by what Jay (1994) calls the 'denigration of vision'.[3] While there is a long-standing and growing literature on the subject-effects of *narrative*,[4] the significance of the *image* for understandings of the self in modern Euro-American societies still remains somewhat under-developed, tending to become subsumed within more general discussions of postmodern culture. And this despite the recent proliferation of technologies of visualisation and the widely accepted claim that visibility is an imperative of contemporary life.[5] However, one of the starting-points of this book is that vision and self-knowledge have become inextricably and productively intertwined in modern Euro-American societies; photography – itself not a static apparatus – thus offers one way into an exploration of the historically specific and dynamic relations between seeing and knowing.[6] More specifically, the book asks how the photographic image may have contributed to novel configurations of personhood, self-knowledge and truth. It does so by examining specific photographs and their uses, by discussing a number of commentaries by photographers and critics, and by identifying and elaborating some of the

2 See Leys (1992) and Sedgwick (1994) for further discussion of the changing relations between consciousness, will and responsibility.

3 In this, as in many other respects, this book was prompted by Walter Benjamin, for whom, as Abbas puts it, 'In the relation between the image and reason, the image critiques reason and not the other way round' (1989: 52).

4 See, for example, Ricoeur (1984–1985); Carr (1986); Giddens (1991).

5 There is, of course, a long-standing engagement with questions of the visual from a psychoanalytic point of view. In addition, there has recently been increasing interest in this question: see Foster (1988); Virilio (1994); Jenks (1995). In her book, *The War of Desire and Technology at the Close of the Mechanical Age* (1995), Alluquère Rosanne Stone describes the emergence of social systems that arise in phantasmatic spaces enabled by and constituted through communication technologies as prosthetic communication, but she does not focus on the role of the image.

6 As Paul Stoller notes, this has meant that 'the guiding metaphors of the humanities and the social sciences have been visual ones'. He goes on to note, more specifically,

> Throughout the history of anthropology, ethnographers have been participant *observers* who *reflect* on their *visual* experiences and then write *texts* that *represent* the Other's *pattern* of kinship, exchange or religion.

⇒

subject-effects of *seeing photographically* in contemporary culture. The assumption here, then, is that the photograph, more than merely representing, has taught us a way of seeing (Ihde, 1995), and that this way of seeing has transformed contemporary self-understandings.

Chapter 2 seeks to outline a theoretical framework within which some of these transformations might be located, and introduces the idea that a *prosthetic culture* is beginning to emerge in Euro-American societies. The suggestion put forward here is that in this culture the subject as individual passes beyond the mirror stage of self-knowledge, of reflection of self, into that of self-extension, what Barthes calls 'the advent of myself as other' (1981: 12). The prosthesis – and it may be perceptual or mechanical – is what makes this self-extension possible. In adopting/adapting a prosthesis, the person creates (or is created by) a self-identity that is no longer defined by the edict 'I think, therefore I am'; rather, he or she is constituted in the relation 'I can, therefore I am'. In the mediated extension of capability that ensues, the relations between consciousness, memory and the body that had defined the possessive individual as a legal personality are experimentally dis- and re-assembled.

The photographic image plays a key role here in that it is one of the techniques that enables a refiguring of the conventional relations through which the previous self-understanding of the possessive individual had been secured. It does this through its abilities to *frame*, *freeze* and *fix* its objects. The framing of the image, it is argued, does not simply change the context of the object seen, but encourages a view of the object as if it could be seen from all positions at once, as if in a spatial continuum (Kracauer, 1995). This is described here as a process of *outcontextualisation*, as contexts are multiplied and rendered a matter of apparent choice or selective framing, while the photograph's ability to freeze and fix its objects is seen to have contributed to a process of *indifferentiation*, that is, the disappearance or infilling of the distance between cause and effect, object and subject. These processes have a distinctive temporality; more specifically, the freezing of time creates a dimension in which the *future perfect* of the photographic image – this will have been – may be suspended, manipulated and reworked to become the *past perfected* (Tyler, 1994). Retrodictive prophecy is thus identified as a key aspect of the power of the image in prosthetic culture. Together the processes of outcontextualisation and indifferentiation are seen to have encouraged an experimental individualism in which the subject is increasingly able to lay claim to features of the context or environment as if they were the outcome of the testing of his or her personal capacities.

> Recently a number of anthropologists and sociologists have challenged the interconnected paradigms of visualism and textualism. One of the most vocal critics, David Howes, has written, '. . . that it is only by developing a rigorous awareness of the visual and textual biases of the Western episteme that we can hope to make sense of how life is lived in other cultural settings'.
>
> (1995: 15)

Stoller himself goes on to explore what it would mean to 'sense ethnography' through an application of the notion of mimesis to ethnography. This involves the recognition of 'multisensorial perception'.

Chapters 3 and 4 explore some aspects of the history of photography and raise some points about the use of the photograph in defining self-identity in general terms. They look at the ways in which the photograph has been used to map humankind, as individuals, as types or genres of humans, as well as a species. Chapter 3 focuses on a shift in portraiture from representations of human difference in terms of *variety* to those of *diversity*, ending with an analysis of the continuities and contrasts between the 1955 photographic exhibition 'The Family of Man' and the contemporary advertising campaigns of the fashion clothing company Benetton. Diversity, it is argued, is represented in the latter not as a form of variation within a social and/or natural type, but as the containment of difference through the alienation of type, the estrangement of genre. The privileging of diversity is thus part of what Baudrillard (1994) describes as the move from generic to genetic man and results in what has elsewhere been called the serial or substitutable individual but is described here as the transparent individual. This is the ideal of an individual without the narrative continuity of memory, lacking interiority and depth, who is instead flexibly constituted across contexts through a strategic display or performance of the effects of indifferentiation, adopting motives and claiming effects without regard for the conventional requirements of narrative coherence. In chapter 4, the notion of a *prosthetic biography* is introduced to describe such performative self-understandings. The photographic portrait, with its distinctive invitation to 'become what you are', is seen to offer an important source for such biographies. However, the chapter also suggests that at the same time that prosthetic culture encourages a belief in the individual's right to be recognised as unique (Taylor, 1989, 1992) and thus is a further stage in the consolidation of possessive individualism, the prosthetic device of the photographic image is simultaneously able to make evident 'a kind of intractable supplement of identity' (Barthes, 1981: 109). This supplement – what Benjamin calls 'the image's lack of appearance, its inability or refusal to shore up appearance' (Abbas, 1989: 54) – thickens and renders murky the assumed transparency of the self-identity of the possessive individual.

Chapters 5 and 6 are concerned with the phenomenon of false memory syndrome. The aim here is to explore a specific instance of how the conventional narrative techniques of the self involved in the authorship of a continuous biography – including those of memory – are currently being refigured in relation to the power of the image. False memory syndrome is thus approached as an index of the ways in which seeing photographically does not just inform the use of photographs in representations of the individual and human difference, but also informs – indirectly – transformations in self-identity that appear, at least initially, to have nothing to do with photographs or images. These transformations are explored through a comparison of the technics of anaesthetics (Buck-Morss, 1992) of the early twentieth century with the prosthetic culture that characterises its end. The goal, it is argued, is now not simply to numb the synaesthetic system (or bodily logic of sense) but simultaneously to numb and animate it anew, both to deaden the senses and also to reawaken them, to repress memory and also to recover it. Prosthetic culture is thus seen to have ambivalent implications for self-identity, disturbing relations between the body, memory and consciousness, leaving them open to multiple refigurings and redrawing the lines of sexual difference.

The impact of digitalisation on the power of the image in self-understandings is the subject of chapters 7 and 8. Through a consideration of the biographies of non-dimensional personalities, the movement of cartoon figures and the memories of cyborgs, the question of the existence of an optical unconscious (Benjamin, 1970) is addressed. The concern here is to identify whether or not the potential of prosthetic culture has been entirely recuperated with the contemporary proliferation of visual technologies. In particular, attention is focused on the capacity to intervene in the time of exposure (Virilio, 1994) offered by digitalisation and computer-aided photography. The question at issue is whether the *reversal* of the relations of motivation between the referent and the signifier made more persuasive by digitalisation have rendered the distinctions between the human and the inhuman, the material and the immaterial, life and art, redundant. It is argued that while this reversal facilitates outcontextualisation and indifferentiation and feeds the ambition of the signifier to replace or reincarnate the thing it represents, the outcome of the process of reversal of motivation is not always already given, and that seeing photographically continues to make possible an optical unconscious that disturbs the functioning of this reversal.

Central to the arguments in each chapter is the notion of *mimesis*. The term is adopted and adapted from the writings of Walter Benjamin, in which it refers to the compulsion 'to become and behave like something else'. It is a relation of 'making oneself similar to the environment'; the 'nature that culture uses to create second nature, the faculty to copy, imitate, make models, explore difference' (Taussig, 1993: xiii). The book argues that mimesis is central to the changing role of aesthetics in the shift outlined above from a technics of anaesthetics to a culture of prosthetics. More specifically, the mimesis involved in seeing photographically is understood as provoking a bodily mediation in immediacy, a mediation that is both metamorphosis and coincidence. It is a metonymic relation operating both within and outside representation, within and outside the frame, and has the potential to enable a dissociation of the senses that disturbs the coherence of the individual for it is concerned with sensation that escapes the subject of representation.

As described above, the book explores how this potential to disturb is taking shape in the context of contemporary visual technologies: as Buck-Morss notes, they provide 'a new schooling for our mimetic powers' (1991: 267).[7] In particular, it identifies some of the political implications for self-identity and understandings of nature and society of the emergent options of *perfection-seeking homeostasis* (or autopoiesis) and *blind imitation*. In the former, it is argued, mimesis is reduced to the imitation of versions of itself, a stylistic reduction that is made possible by the belief that representation can replace its referent, producing a closed, textually inclusive self that is a development of the possessive individual.

7 Similarly, Stone describes what she calls the technosocial, a mode 'of reinvention and encounter in a technological space viewed as itself a social and physical environment, as a kind of nature' (1995: 42).

In the latter, mimesis continues to be understood as a relation of adaptation, affinity and reciprocity between self and context in which personhood is not limited to the confines of the individual. The rise of the former tendency, as has been widely noted, is supported by the convergence of scientific and visual technologies in the pursuit of total recall, complete transparency or what Barbara Stafford (1993) describes as the modern quest to make visible the unseen. However, so it is suggested, the second possibility ensures that mimesis continues to trouble prosthetic culture.

2

THE EXPERIMENTAL INDIVIDUAL

> Trauma is the key word, the abstract, specialized, but perfectly empowering and generalizing word, the word that captures a whole lot of seemingly unlikely events.
>
> (Ian Hacking, 1994: 45)

INTRODUCTION

In order to explore the historically changing relationship between conceptions of the person, self-identity and the notion of the individual as they have developed in Euro-American societies, let me start by introducing the notion of the possessive individual. Abercrombie *et al.* (1986) provide a valuable summary of the historical criteria by which individuals have come to be recognised as such. These include *embodiment*, that is, individuals are constituted as such through the recognition of their possession of *a unique body*. The recognition of embodiment has been achieved in modern society through the application of numerous techniques, from visual classification (including photographic portraiture) and finger-printing to genetic coding. The significance of embodiment in relation to the creation of the individual is well illustrated by the changing aims of these techniques. For example, taking the case of portraiture, Abercrombie *et al.* claim that 'in the contemporarily accepted sense of conveying the individuality of the sitter [it] is a relatively recent phenomenon' (1986: 61). They point out that in representations of the face in the pre-modern period, the artist's purpose was not necessarily to convey a likeness of the individual but to achieve other goals, such as the depiction of office, of religious symbolism, or even of pattern and colour. This they contrast with the importance, from the Renaissance onwards, of representing the uniqueness of the individual and the significance of individual experience in a new realism of visual representation.[1]

However, having a (recognisable) body has historically not been sufficient to define an individual. Continuity of *consciousness* and *memory* are also necessary for a person to claim separate status as an individual. Underlying this claim has been a foundational understanding of identity and difference in which the sameness of the self is fixed through the attribution of a set origin in time and space. So, for example, according to Locke, an entity is identical with itself if it has the same

1 Further changes in the significance of the portrait for the self-identity of the individual will be discussed later, especially in chapters 3 and 4.

origin in time and space 'and that which had a different beginning in time and place from that is not the same but divers' (Locke, quoted in Diprose, 1994: 10). The ability to identify this origin via a continuity of consciousness legitimated by memory has provided the foundation for the authority and validity of the story that makes the individual, that is, his or her biography. Abercrombie *et al.* write,

> To make a claim to separate status as an individual, we need a plausible history of ourselves, which recounts our past in such a way as to confirm our identity. This commitment is taken to be validating evidence of whom we are. Our memory of this intimate story is a form of authorization. We are the author and topic of this story, which makes us an authority on our past. (1986: 33)

Especially important in the maintenance of this authority has been the development of a set of *narrative* techniques by which continuity of consciousness and its memory are established. These, in turn, are part of what has secured the notion of the contract as the basis of modern social relations for they provide the basis for the *moral responsibility* the individual is recognised to have for his or her actions.[2] An individual, when defined in this way, is a legal personality.

As Abercrombie *et al.* argue, however, there are a number of contradictory discourses of the individual in Euro-American societies. Despite the complexities these multiple discourses produce, they argue, there is a long-running process, what they call the Discovery of the Individual, which results, in a very general way, in individuals being given greater and greater importance. Out of this process have developed more specific discourses of the individual, which identify particular qualities of individuals as important. The most historically significant discourse of this kind is said by Abercrombie *et al.* to be *individualism.*

Abercrombie *et al.* define individualism as a doctrine of human nature, with four interconnected aspects – freedom, action, rationality and self-motivation. Briefly, then, individualism consists of a conception of human liberty as the natural state of humankind: the individual is sovereign in matters concerning his or her self. This sovereignty is expressed in the capacity that individuals have for action and the transformation of the natural world. The capacity to act is ordered by planning, calculation and rationality; and through the exercise of self-motivation the individual is assumed to take responsibility for him- or herself. In Hobbes, for example, the sovereign individual is a man in whom

> the senses, which receive the pressure of outside bodies, transmit them through the nerves to the brain and heart, which then deliver a counter-pressure; the imagination, or memory, which can recall past sense impressions and store up experience of them; the mechanism of 'Trayne of Thoughts' or 'Trayne of Imaginations', which hunts 'the causes, of some effect, present or past; or . . . the effects of some present or past

2 The claim is that the individual has a self-contained identity (based on the continuity of consciousness and/or the body) prior to their relations with others. A contract with another is held to establish a social relationship without affecting the respective identities of the different parties involved.

> cause', and which thus enables the mechanism to forecast the probable result of various possible actions it might take; language, which enables the machine to communicate and receive communications and to order its own reckonings; and reason, which by adding and subtracting names and the consequence of names can reach general propositions or rules for its own guidance.
>
> (Quoted in Macpherson, 1962: 31–32)

The general direction or goal built into this notion of the human is that it seeks to continue its own movement.[3]

In a broadly Weberian vein, Abercrombie *et al.* locate the emergence of the discourse of individualism in relation to the modern challenge to the authority of tradition and a celebration of the freedom of the economic actor in the marketplace. The success of this challenge is held to be a consequence of a functional relationship with capitalism (although they argue that there is no necessary affinity between the two, and that the nature of this relationship has been subject to historical change). Other writers[4] have provided supplementary accounts of the rise of individualism, pointing to the centrality of categories of gender to the historical emergence of the possessive individual and the constitution of the spheres of society and nature. In particular, some of these writers highlight the ways in which it has only been through the subordination of women as a socio-natural grouping that men have been able to aspire to be (unique) individuals. These writers' concern with the importance of the categories of gender to the emergence and consolidation of the notion of the individual will be maintained throughout this book, with the aim of providing a counterpoint to the history that Abercrombie *et al.* propose.

The individualism which begins with Hobbes and extends to Locke is seen by Abercrombie *et al.* to have had an expansionary and confident view of human achievements and potentialities. This confident individualism had a number of dimensions. For example, it was closely associated with the rationalist tradition, which saw human beings emerging out of the dark age of magic and superstition and the rational individual as a new force who would shape society to enhance liberal values. It enshrined rational procedures and atheistic optimism. In the political sphere the new individualism was associated with the confident belief that constitutionalism would guarantee the autonomy and freedom of the individual against tyranny, while, in the public economic domain, it was assumed that the struggle of individual wills in the marketplace would lead ultimately and inevitably to shared economic accumulation. However, in the second half of the nineteenth century, a more pessimistic view of the future of the individual gathers force.

Writers in all fields – in economics, politics, philosophy, sociology and art certainly, but also in feminist political, philosophical and literary works – express

3 The development of this mechanical model of the individual will be explored in chapter 6, especially in relation to contemporary adaptations of homeostasis and systems theory.

4 Especially Pateman (1988); Riley (1988); Butler (1992); Wittig (1992); Irigaray (1993); and Diprose (1994).

increasing disquiet and anxiety about not merely the safety but also the legitimacy of individualism. The sanctity of the individual as an ideal is both under threat and called into doubt at the same time that a systematic, anonymous and effective system of surveillance of the individual is put in place. This is a process full of paradox and contradiction. Abercrombie *et al.* write,

> We see that the very process that we have called the Discovery of the Individual not only gives importance to individuals, it also makes it meaningful to tell individuals apart, to identify them, to register them and ultimately to control them; the uniqueness of the individual is his or her subordination. At the most fundamental level, the importance, and even dignity, of individuals is conveyed by giving them names, but the custom of unique names gave the state a powerful means of control.
>
> (1986: 151–152)

This process of subordination they call *individuation.* Moreover, over the course of the twentieth century, individuation has been complicated by the ways in which the individual has come to apply it to him- or herself through the adoption of techniques of self-surveillance in relation to prescribed norms of behaviour.

Important in the processes of individuation has been the social ordering of the sense of sight as vision. An important analysis of this is provided by Michel Foucault, notably in the studies *Madness and Civilisation* (1971) and *The Birth of the Clinic* (1976), in which he elaborates the inter-relationship of developments in scientific ways of knowing and the ordering of vision. On the one hand, there is the emergence of a heightened faith in medical evidence vested in the 'sovereign power of the empirical gaze' which has 'marvellous density of perception, offering the grain of things as the first face of truth' (1976: xiii); as a consequence, 'madness no longer exists except as *seen*' (1976: 250). On the other hand, Foucault points to shifts in the subject of vision so developed. He argues that the ocular discipline associated with the architectural geography of the panopticon creates a specific kind of subjectivity for the individual: the subject interiorises the gaze 'to the point that he is his own overseer, each individual thus exercising this surveillance over and against himself' (1980: 155). In this way, the subjectivity of the individual is developed by self-surveillance or *reflection* upon his or her own appearance, as if it were a mirror of the soul (N. Rose, 1989). As Jay (1994) notes, however, Foucault often writes ironically of 'self-evidence' to emphasise the artificial in visual experience; for Foucault, what was self-evident – that is, evident to the self and taken for granted as natural or objective – is precisely what has to be called into question. Indeed, Foucault remained unremittingly hostile to the power of vision. The account offered here, while acknowledging the force of this power, is concerned to identify some of the ambivalencies for the subject and self-identity – artificial or otherwise – of visual sensation.

Individuation operates in contradistinction not only to the discourse of individualism, but also to that of *individuality*, the central point of which is the need for the expression of each person's uniqueness. Individuality is concerned with the interior qualities of the person, with expressivity, and subjective conscience, personality and will. The cultivation of these qualities is what marks one person off from the other. Self-development is thus a prime virtue in the discourse of individuality. For doctrines of this kind, nature should be managed and society should be arranged so that individual qualities and differences can be recognised and individual talents cultivated. In an immediate way, then, individuation can be seen as a threat not only to individualism but also to individuality. However, as a consequence of what have been described as the cultural contradictions of modernity (Lasch, 1978), individuation and individuality can also be seen to have joined forces in paradoxical ways: the exercise of self-surveillance (the modern extension of individuation mentioned above) is linked to, or, indeed, rendered an aspect of, self-development or self-actualisation (conventionally part of the cultivation of individuality).[5]

A pertinent example of the processes of this paradoxical intermingling of individuation and individuality and the anxieties it produced for both individual and society is provided by Ian Hacking's study of the historical development of 'the sciences of memory' (1994, 1995). Hacking describes the emergence in Europe, in the period 1875–1895, of a science of memory which was concerned with how memory constituted the individual.[6] He argues that this science developed as a 'knowing that' by means of which knowledge of the interior of the individual could be acquired. Indeed, Hacking suggests that since there could not be a science of the soul, the sciences of memory provided a 'surrogate'.[7] As a consequence of the development of a body of knowledge concerning 'memory' acquired through medical and psychological surveillance, then, the individual comes to possess *interiority*, *dimensionality* and *depth.*

5 The continuing centrality of categories of gender to this revised conception of the possessive individual can be seen not only in the problematisation of the growth of the supposedly feminine phenomenon of narcissism and discourses of interiority, but also in the prevalence of anxieties relating to the integrity, univocity and authority of the (masculine) self produced by the increasingly intertwined discourses of individuation and individuality, such as the maladies of the will discussed by Seltzer (1993) and Sedgwick (1994).

6 For an interesting study that provides a valuable complement to Hacking's, see Laura Otis (1994). Otis argues that the period 1870–1918 was the age of organic memory. This term – which was ultimately deemed to be scientifically incorrect – is related by Otis to what she describes as a deep-seated anxiety in Europe about identity, both personal and national, and a determination to look at the past as the basis for self-determination (1994: ix). She writes,

> By redefining the process by which people stored information as a single unknown biochemical mechanism, writers created a feeling of progress. By envisioning history as something accumulated by a race and stored within an individual, they rendered it potentially accessible. . . . If the individual inherited his or her ancestors' memories, as one inherited facial features, a feeling of continuity, even of immortality, could be achieved.
>
> (1994: xi)

Her analysis indicates the ways in which questions of personal and national identity were closely bound together during this period, and highlights continuities between the belief in organic memory and the contemporary phenomena of ethnic cleansing and the human genome project, both of which are concerned with issues of heredity, memory and race.

Sigrid Schade (1995) provides another useful strand in the history of the sciences of memory in her discussion of the art historian Aby Warburg's notion of 'cultural memory'. For further discussion of this, see chapter 5.

7 As Hacking points out, it is no coincidence that this development occurs in the same period as the rapid growth of technologies of transport, including the railway, and the early stages of time–space ⇒

Significantly, in the emerging sciences of memory, it is not the remembered but the forgotten that provides the key to the 'rewriting of the soul'. Hacking writes, 'What is really powerful is not what is remembered but what is forgotten. It is powerful because the very fact that something is forgotten makes it a secret that works on us' (1994: 45). Hacking thus suggests that the science of memory defined itself as the investigation not of how remembering constitutes the individual but of the subject-effects of the forgotten. In this project, he believes,

> Trauma is the key word, the abstract, specialized, but perfectly empowering and generalizing word, the word that captures a whole lot of seemingly unlikely events . . . it means wound, and entered the psychology of the soul via anatomy, as what we now call whiplash injury, or the old railway spine.
>
> (1994: 45)

More specifically, the development of the notion of trauma provided the point of entry into the soul by which the techniques of the science of memory came to individuate *and* individualise the subject. That is, in its elaboration of techniques for the investigation of the subject-effects of trauma, the science of memory ordered and classified the subjectivity of the individual in relation to the pathologies of memory it uncovered. Simultaneously, however, the trauma, as a secret wound, provided the basis for the expression of individuality, to be recovered in a process of self-examination, confrontation, discovery, healing and survival. Some of the contradictory implications of this ambivalent process are at issue in the contemporary phenomenon of false memory syndrome which will be discussed in chapters 5 and 6. The fact that the memories designated false in this phenomenon are typically those of sexual abuse confirms that the categories of gender continue to be at the heart of the conception of the individual at issue here.

THE POSSESSIVE INDIVIDUAL, SOCIETY, NATURE AND SYNTHETIC CULTURE

A very different, but similarly thought-provoking, account of the fortunes of the possessive individual is provided by Marilyn Strathern in *After Nature* (1992). In this book, Strathern offers a way of exploring the contemporary implications of the paradoxical relationship between what have so far been called individuation and individualisation in Euro-American societies. More precisely, she considers the relationship between the discourses of individualism, individuation and individuality in contemporary society in a way that highlights the foundational role of culture. This consideration will be prefaced here by way of a detour through the more general argument she proposes, not least because of the way in which her analysis of the individual is inter-related to changing understandings of

distantiation. He describes how notions of depth, distance and perspective were simultaneously undergoing profound changes in relation to both the interior and the exterior of the individual and collective political body of the nation state. Hacking pays less attention to the significance of the First World War in the development of this term; for a literary approach to this question, see Pat Barker's trilogy *Regeneration* (1991, 1995, 1996).

nature and society, and thus provides a basis from which to begin to think the conceptions of the individual and of humanity, and of what links them together, that is, concepts of relationality.

To summarise, Strathern argues that in what she calls a plural society relations are in the nature of things, including in the nature of personhood. The inherent naturalness of relations to things is a consequence of what she calls the merographic capacity, the capacity to make partial analogies. These analogies are partial not only in the sense that they imply perceived difference as well as similarity in the making of comparisons between wholes and in that sense are not complete or total, but also in that they make wholes (including persons) out of parts in particular kinds of ways. In this making, while parts of a person are part of that person as a whole or a system (such as the individual), they are also, from another perspective, conceived as parts of other wholes, such as, for example, society and nature. In this sense, things (including the individual, nature and society) are seen to be *constructed* or *determined* and to be inhabiting what might be termed a *synthetic culture*[8] or a *culture that constructs*.[9]

As constructs, things are by their very nature partial, and the necessarily contextual knowledge of them is also always full of gaps and spaces. Indeed, for Strathern, partial analogies have profound implications for how the members of society 'see' any particular whole:

> Society is telescopically distinct from its individual members, in the same way as the foetus is microscopically distinct from its mother. In either case, what is seen fills the field of vision, but the field of vision *is never taken as all there is to see*: one can always alter scale and whether on the 'inside' or 'outside' always see more.
>
> (1992: 131)

Every threshold, between inside and outside, private and public, past and present, is the boundary of a domain, a domain given depth by the perspective of merographic capacity. In so far as the analogies are partial, each domain – the individual, society, nature – also participates in or extends into another.

So, for example, the person becomes an individual by means of partial analogy to society and nature: he or she is both more and less than, similar to and different from, more or less determined by both society and nature, which themselves are similarly, partially, related to each other. Indeed, the sovereign individual in liberal political theory is a paradigmatic case of personhood so conceived. According to Macpherson, the individual in this theory is 'essentially the proprietor of his or her own person or capacities, owing nothing to society for them' (1962: 3). Although, in this formulation, the individual might not appear to satisfy Strathern's definition of the plural self, Macpherson's analysis of the specific formulations by which the 'relation of ownership . . . was read back into the nature of the individual' (1962: 3) by Hobbes and Locke, among others, reveals that the conception of 'man' presented here was created in a series of

8 I am grateful to Scott Lash for suggesting this term.

9 And I am grateful to Jeanette Edwards for this phrase and for pointing out that the use of verbs might help me to avoid the reification of what I aim to describe.

inter-related partial analogies with nature and society. So, for example, Macpherson shows that Hobbes's writings demonstrate a complex shift from natural to social analogies, and concludes that 'even Hobbes's physiological postulates are about the physiology of socialized men' (1962: 69). Furthermore, for Hobbes, Macpherson argues, the state of nature is a logical abstraction drawn from the behaviour of men in civilised society. Crucially for the argument to be developed here, it is the use of what Strathern calls partial analogies that enables Hobbes both to argue that the individual is essentially the proprietor of his own person and capacities and owes nothing to society for this, and to argue that while he may alienate his capacity to labour, he cannot alienate the whole of the property in his own person. The partial analogy is thus what both enables a conception of the individual as entirely self-determined and sets necessary natural and/or social limits to his or her potential for self-dispossession.

Partial analogy is thus what both enables and constrains self-determination and helps explain the centrality of the notion of free will to modern political and moral debate. Furthermore, it is the 'more or less' nature of determination that is an important source of the tensions between individuation and individualisation. On the one hand, the person is individuated by his or her membership of the categories of determination, of social and natural classification; on the other hand, he or she is able to express his or her self by whether and how this determination is taken up and adapted as a source of individuality through the exercise of will.[10] As a consequence, the more or less nature of this determination explains how it is that not all persons have the same relationship to individualisation, individuation or individuality: the classifications of genre – of gender, class, race, sexuality, age or other natural, political and social categories or types – and other aspects of the individual come to inhere in different bodies in different ways.

In principle, the merographic capacity was what made the individual incommensurable: more than the sum of the parts, whole, but never totalisable. At the same time, partial analogy is the technique by which variation between individuals was subsumed within a natural and/or social understanding of humanity, and conversely, provided the means whereby the basis of humanity could be identified in the natural and/or social capacity of all individuals to be unique. The concepts of what I will call *generic* classification – in the social as well as the natural fields – have been fundamental to these mutually enhancing analogies. As Foucault (1989) and others have traced, the principles of generic classification, initially developed in natural science disciplines but then elaborated in the human sciences, were related to the laws held to be operating at the level of deep structure.[11] The abstraction of principles of organisation were then reconstituted in standardised relationships of *cause and effect*, thus both introducing a notion of parity between domains and simultaneously rendering natural and

10 See Stephanie Lawler (1995a) for an analysis of a contemporary exemplification of these processes in the contradictory construction of 'mother' as a self-identity.

11 As Nikolas Rose notes, the positive knowledges of clinical medicine, psychiatry, criminology, statistics, pedagogy and sociology sought to govern domains in terms of their 'internal' laws and truths rather than in terms of external virtues: 'for such authorities of conduct truth appears to teach itself in relation to the person and the ways of managing the person' (1996: 317).

social processes *technological.*[12] Significantly, however, in these techniques of generic classification (or variations of kind or type), the merographic capacity was generally itself implicit: in plural society relationality was held to be an attribute of things, it was in their nature.

However, the status and functioning of this relationality was always in doubt; it could never simply be taken for granted but was always being questioned and refined, even – or rather especially – in the philosophical and scientific procedures of reflection and experimentation themselves. So, to continue the example offered by Hacking, Locke's discussion of personal identity reveals the tensions of what is being described here as the plural individual. The individual as proprietor of himself is held by Locke to be modulated by three kinds of relationships, one involving the body, one involving collectivities, and one involving memory. These relationships did not always cohere:

> Locke's celebrated discussion of personal identity was struggling with the pull of these poles, the body and the memory. He made 'person' what he called a forensic concept, having to do with memory and responsibility. He made 'man' a concept based in part on bodily continuity.
>
> (Hacking, 1994: 41)

The result was an awareness of both the instability of the individual and the precariousness of the self-evidence he or she was able to draw upon in authorising his or her biography. However, so both Hacking and Strathern argue, this conception of the forensic individual – in which personal identity is constituted by continuities of memory and a person is not responsible for what he or she does not remember – is now not simply unstable, but beginning to falter, revealing its dependence on the merographic capacity, which itself is becoming explicit in the ongoing problematisation of the truth claims of contemporary (natural and social) science.

Indeed, while the relationship between the 'part' of memory and the individual has been continually under revision, Euro-American societies are now contending with the possibilities that memories may exist independently of the individual and that the individual may be defined or authorised by more than one set of memories. So, for example, as Hacking[13] notes, the defence of not remembering, or at any rate, not being aware, is being reworked as courts face a rash of multiple personality cases:

> The no-memory defence is being gradually turned into a non-starter, although, for some time to come, dissociation will perplex lawyers. In South Carolina law, an adulterous woman cannot collect alimony; one plaintiff claims it was her alter that was unfaithful, she, the non-alter, should still collect. The issues have almost nothing to do with memory or Locke's faltering idea of the forensic person.
>
> (1994: 42)

12 This formulation of Foucault's argument draws heavily on that provided in Harvey (1996).

13 Stone (1995) discusses a case in which a woman diagnosed as having Multiple Personality Syndrome brought a charge of rape against a man who she claimed deliberately drew out one of her personalities, a naive young woman, who he thought would be willing to have sex with him.

The sciences of memory – in which it is the forgotten and not the remembered that constitutes the individual – are turning in upon themselves, and are contributing to a shift from a plural to a *postplural society*.

In a postplural world, Strathern believes, relationality (or a relational view) will be lost; as it becomes explicit in a process of *literalisation*, it will no longer be deemed to be inherent in things. The power of partial analogy – the facility to calibrate difference and similarity – is being cancelled. As the naturalness of relationality to things disappears, wholes, including individuals, are disassembled into parts in such a way that they can only be reassembled as (multiple) parts, not as parts of a whole. As a consequence,

> The individual is judged by no measure outside itself. It is not to be related to either nature or society . . . . It is not analogous to anything. The individual is all there is of society . . . . It does not appear as a 'society' composed of relationships, as an organisation, but a composite or collage of human nature and processed convention, a kind of auto-socialised body.
>
> (1992: 152, 159)

For Strathern, the postplural individual is no longer imagined merologically, but is instead a constellation of implanted elements, parts without social or natural depth.

In this scenario, the individual in postplural society is made up not of parts of other domains, but of parts accreting with other parts, strategic assemblages, adjacent, coeval parts within the frame of a single form: memories substituted for one another, organs transplanted from one body to work alongside those of another's,[14] hues of cloth juxtaposed with colours of skin, hair and eyes. This is no longer a culture of *synthesis*, but one of *prosthesis*. While Baudrillard writes of '[h]uman cuttings *ad infinitum*', Strathern suggests,

> We move from the unique amalgam of elements drawn from different domains to a literal assemblage of parts perceived as substitutable or replaceable for one another. The relationship between these components cannot be conceptualised in other than terms of self-management.
>
> (1992: 183)

In Strathern's view, the individual is in danger of being sucked into hyper-individuality, although not without a struggle: on the one hand, there is a nostalgia for the individuality of *variation*, for whole forms, for purity, where elements are intrinsic and parts are non-detachable, while, on the other, there is a desire for the ideal (hyper-)individuality of *diversity*, the endless multiplication of new forms, through strategies of generic estrangement and combination. More grandly, Baudrillard (1994) speculates that we are seeing a move from *generic* man to *genetic* man, in which difference between people is not perceived through partial analogies (and by the individual's positioning within a genre or type), but is held to be a consequence of the articulation of combinatory codes of information (such as genes are said to be).

14 Rosi Braidotti, for example, argues that 'the new reproductive technologies, by officializing the instrumental denaturalization of the body, also institutionalize dismemberment as the modern condition, thus transforming the body into a factory of detachable pieces' (1994: 60).

DIS(AS)SEMBLING SELVES AND PROSTHETIC CULTURE

For some this move is 'another giant leap for Mackind'; however, for others its implications for personhood, self-identity and the individual are still uncertain. Consider, for example, how to answer the question 'how old are you?' if you know that your transplanted organs age at a different rate to their host body. Alternatively, consider the question of the colour of skin, or 'tanning', as it is somewhat euphemistically termed by Baudrillard:[15]

> The stage of the body changes in the course of an irreversible technological 'progression': from tanning in the sun, which already corresponds to an artificial use of the natural medium, that is to say making it a prosthesis of the body . . . – to domestic tanning with an iodine lamp (yet another good old mechanical technique) – to tanning with pills and hormones (chemical and ingested prosthesis) – and finally to tanning by intervening in the genetic formula (an incomparably more advanced stage, but a prosthesis nonetheless, that is, it is simply definitively integrated, it no longer even passes through either the surface or the orifices of the body), one passes by different bodies. It is the schema of the whole that is metamorphosed. The traditional prosthesis, which serves to repair a failing organ, changes nothing in the general model of the body. But what should be said of mental modeling via psychotropic agents and drugs? It is the *stage of the body* that is changed by them. The psychotropic body is a body modeled 'from inside', no longer passing through the perspectival space of representation, of the mirror and of discourse.
>
> (1994: 101)

In the place of the power of partial analogy, Baudrillard identifies the enabling power of technology in the form of the prosthesis. The suggestion is that the classifications of genre – of gender, class, race, sexuality and age or other natural and social categories – no longer inhere in the individual as they did in plural or synthetic culture; instead, they are seen as the effects of (mechanical and perceptual) prostheses.[16] And it is in this sense that postplural society, after nature, is described here as a *prosthetic culture*.

15 Adorno provides a related analysis of sun-tanning; he writes,

> In the sun-tan, which can be quite fetching, the fetish character of the commodity lays claim to actual people; they themselves become fetishes. The idea that a girl is more erotically attractive because of her brown skin is probably only another rationalization. The sun-tan is an end in itself, of more importance than the boy-friend it was perhaps supposed to entice.
>
> (1991: 165)

16 In making this claim, I don't want to pass over the centrality of power relations to both synthetic and prosthetic culture. It is not that older forms of classification have disappeared; rather, so I am suggesting, the meanings and the practices that constitute them are changing. In complicated ways, the older categories or genres may even be taking on renewed force, leading to more intense forms of exclusion. My point is just that older classifications are being joined by an array of new ones – including the construction of difference as diversity – which cross-cut and remake the older categories.

To describe this shift in terms of the emergence of a prosthetic culture is to imply that there is a certain force to the transformations discussed here; however, it is not to imply that all the members of Euro-American societies participate equally or on the same terms in this culture; nor is it to ignore the contradictions, hierarchies and exclusions that are an integral part of this shift. Nor, indeed, is it intended to imply that prosthetic culture has, in any simple sense, displaced synthetic culture. Furthermore, the notion of prosthetic culture is not meant to imply that the notion of prosthesis is specific to contemporary Euro-American societies for the extension of the human body in technology is frequently identified as part of what is understood as humanity. As Rosi Braidotti writes, '*homo sapiens* was never more than a crafty *homo faber* . . . all tools are . . . products of the creative human imagination, copying and multiplying the potencies of the human body' (1994: 43–44); while, as David Crossley (1995) notes, the capacity 'I can' forms Merleau-Ponty's definition of human nature. Similarly, David Wills in his book *Prosthesis* speaks of prosthesis as an apparently universal capacity of the body, 'being about nothing if not placement, displacement, replacement, standing, dislodging, substituting, setting, amputating, supplementing' (1995: 9). For Wills, prosthesis is the agency of the body in the operation of 'a transfer into otherness, articulated through the radical alterity of ablation as loss of integrity' (1995: 13). These are important recognitions; however, what makes it helpful, I think, to speak of a prosthetic culture is that experimentation is now taking on a specific and defining form. In relation to the individual, for example, the gaps between cause and effect, motivation and action, subject and object – the deficiencies and distortions in self-evidence as it were – are remedied through an artificial extension of capability, resulting in a transferable potential.[17]

More and more, *Homo faber*, the subject of experimentation, is able to make use of not only objective or reflective thought (the image as mirror of the truth of the self), but also the 'thought' of the reflective object – the prosthesis.[18] So, for example, genetic engineering makes possible the display of the effects of variation in human type or genre through a process of individual internalisation of genetic information or perceptual prosthesis. Baudrillard writes,

> It is the whole traditional world of causality that is in question: the perspectival, determinist mode, the 'active', critical mode, the analytic mode – the distinction between cause and effect, between active and passive, between subject and object, between the end and the means.
>
> (1994: 30)

In prosthetic culture, the distance between cause and effect, between subject and object – 'precisely the distance of meaning, the gap, the difference, the smallest possible gap' – disappears: 'It is this gap which vanishes in the process of genetic coding, in which indeterminacy is not so much a question of molecular randomness as of the abolition, pure and simple, of the *relation*.' In prosthetic culture there is an '*indifferentiation* of the active and the passive' (1994: 30–31; my

17 See Zygmunt Bauman (1991) for a discussion of the increased significance of technology in contemporary society and its implications for personal and collective morality.

18 And in this process reflection is reconstituted as reflexivity.

emphasis), as, through the adoption of prostheses, the previously naturally or socially fixed or determined aspects of self-identity are increasingly brought within the remit of choice or, better, selection.

At the same time that there is this process of indifferentiation, there is also a process of *outcontextualisation.* In the latter process, the previously naturally or socially determined aspects of self-identity are taken out of context and refashioned. This is not simply a process of de- and re-contextualisation, but a reconstitution or regrouping in order to make visible *the ability of a thing, an object, a part to be taken out of context.* An example is provided by Paul Rabinow: he notes that, through the use of the computer, individuals sharing certain traits can be grouped together in a way that not only decontextualises these traits from their social and/or natural environment (that is, the individual) but is non-subjective in a double sense: 'it is objectively arrived at, and does not apply to, a subject in anything like the older sense of the word (that is, the suffering, meaningfully situated integrator of social, historical and bodily experiences)' (1992: 243). These parts may then be subject to regrouping; indeed they are constituted *so* that they may be endlessly recombined. As a consequence, individuals, if they are acknowledged as units of analysis at all, are seen not as wholes but as the sum of diverse factors amenable to analysis and manipulation by specialists. They have been outcontextualised.

What was naturally or socially determined or constructed in the individual self-identity of plural culture is thus no longer a given in prosthetic culture, but is rather a matter of potential or technologically assisted choice or selection, a question of indifferentiation and outcontextualisation. The synthetic principles of social and natural determination of the individual have, as it were, been technologised and interiorised, and are now made available through prosthetic extension as extra-individual features of a self that may be continually dis- and re-assembled across contexts. Thus placed within the grasp of choice, natural and social attributes of the self may be constituted as modifiable by deliberate, voluntary transformation, thereby leading to the multiplication of new spheres of decision-making in the arenas of health, leisure, sexuality and work. At the same time, however, apparently voluntary actions are redefined as the effect of previously invisible determinations, thus offering new grounds for the denial of individual responsibility. The confusion this has brought about in relation to pre-existing understandings of the accountability of the legal personality for his or her actions is illustrated in the following complaint against what is called the 'molestation of normality':

> Large areas of ordinary behaviour hitherto considered benign have had their threshold radically redefined up, so that once innocent behaviour now stands condemned as deviant . . . . As part of this project of moral levelling, entirely new areas of deviancy – such as date rape and politically incorrect speech – have been discovered. And old areas – such as child abuse – have been amplified by endless reiteration in the press and validated by learned reports of their astonishing frequency . . . . The rationalisation of deviancy reaches its logical conclusion. The deviant is

> declared normal. And the normal is unmasked as deviant. That, of course, makes us all that much more morally equal. The project is complete. What real difference is there between us?
>
> (Krauthammer, 1993: 16)

As this quotation from a newspaper article indicates, with the disappearance of the gap between cause and effect and the blurring of the boundary between self and context, the question of how to identify the truth or validity of self-evidence is posed in an urgent form. Is interpretation meaningful at all in a culture of indifferentiation and outcontextualisation, in which there are apparently no fixed variables? 'Is there no real difference between us?' If consciousness of the self is both the means and the end of experimentation, if relationality has been cancelled and potential is immanent in the individual, the question posed is whether truth has become a personal affair, a matter of taste or individual preference. In considering this question in relation to the example of the validity of the knowledge claims of contemporary psychoanalysis for the subject, Deleuze suggests that there has been a transition from the signified to the signifier:

> if we no longer look for a signified or supposedly significant symptoms; if we look, on the contrary, for the signifier or symptoms which would be no more than its effect; if interpretation gives way to significance – then a new shift takes place.
>
> (1993: 111)

He goes on to suggest that 'Psychoanalysis then has, in effect, its own references and has no more use for external "referent." If this is so more widely, then there would be no more uses for the external referents of society or nature as the determinants or guarantors of truth (and thus of the truth of the subject's self-knowledge), and the will to know would have outstripped itself.'[19] But is it so?

NOW YOU SEE IT, NOW YOU DON'T

According to Cecil Helman, we are seeing the emergence of 'a new type of society, and new types of social relationships':

> The creation of implants or prosthetic organs, for example, requires an elaborate social organization of production, distribution, marketing, maintenance and repair of the artefacts. The individual's body is now

19 See Penny Harvey's analysis of technology as cultural artefact for a further illustration of this. In her discussion of the 1992 Expo in Barcelona, she suggests that

> By far the most popular exhibits at the Expo were those which offered sensation or experience with little or no specific cultural referent. . . . [For example,] Working with the theme of art in technology, Fujitsu stunned Expo visitors with the computer-generated graphics of the process of photosynthesis and glycolysis, the basis of all life in Earth. . . . We are in the presence of a technology that is not simply reproducing originals but generating idealised and imaginary forms, concrete versions of scientific abstractions which nevertheless can simulate the movements and the relationships of the original forms.
>
> (1996: 157)

> part-industrial. His implants link him permanently to the world of industry and science. He is also the ultimate *consumer*, incorporating the products of industry into his very body, as a living, walking advertisement for their efficacy. The new parts of his body are mass-produced, impersonal, replaceable . . . . The parallel for replaceable body parts is . . . replaceable people, particularly in the workforce. However, this new society – like the new body – is a collage of different elements: some living and contemporary, some artificial and industrial, and some ancient and traditional.
>
> (1988: 15–16)

Strathern, who quotes Helman, suggests that in the new types of social relationships of postplural society perspectives are constituted by the choices that resources afford, and anything – relationships, institutions, persons, even society – can be a resource ('We invest in relationships' is the advertising claim of the stockbroking firm PaineWebber), and choice requires no external regulation. Indeed, so effective may this literalisation be that not only the individual but also nature or society will disappear. Strathern takes as an exemplary instance of this the statement by Margaret Thatcher that 'There is no such thing as society. There are individual men and women and there are families' (1992: 158). Baudrillard himself says something similar: writing about the technologies of cloning and the hologram, he claims, 'This is how one puts an end to totality. If all information can be found in each of its parts, the whole loses its meaning' (1994: 97).

However, sometimes the disappearance of society is so unsettling to its erstwhile members that it is, all too explicitly and rather unbelievably, brought back in – the gap between cause and effect is reinstated – but only so that the act of its indifferentiation can lead to a reattribution of the ownership of effect. This is the case in John Major's plea for active citizenship, or as in the case of some recent marketing theory which suggests that 'Advertisers do not persuade consumers; they create societies around their brands to maintain power in the marketplace' (Verbeke, 1992). In this theory, advertising is no longer intended to cause changes in consumer attitudes (for this, apparently, would be a reductive, *reflective*, single-stage model of the consumer), but rather to shape consumer environments by creating 'massive parallel effects' in the marketplace, giving rise to 'societies' or business systems in which 'business' and 'the consumer' participate:

> a firm, by means of a marketing communications campaign, can create 'coupling mechanisms' between the consumer and the trade. Because of these mechanisms a 'society' (also called 'third-order system' or 'business system') is created.
>
> (Verbeke, 1992: 7)

'Coupling' in this discourse means that behaviours of one subsystem (such as 'the consumer' and business or 'the trade') can affect behaviours of another subsystem; furthermore,

> These interactions, when they reoccur over time, lead to the emergence of a new system which then creates its own dynamic or drift. In systems

> theory, these systems are called 'autopoetic' [*sic*] (Maturana & Varela, 1984) or dissociative (Prigogine & Stengers, 1984).
>
> (Verbeke, 1992: 7)

Marketing, in this view, should be concerned with the management of this drift:

> But because this system can, in the course of time, fluctuate into other states, the firm's marketing communication process must seek to protect this third-order system against fluctuation. In other words, the firm must be prepared to deal with unwanted interactions that might emerge between subsystems.
>
> (Verbeke, 1992: 7–8)

In this case at least, then, rather than a return to plural society, what seems to be happening is that disaggregated parts of individualism come to provide the resources for technologically extended, complex systems, the ownership and running of which is a matter of dispute.

Similar possibilities are opened up for the individual. One especially important relation in plural society was that between what is internal to the self and that which is external; this was a relation which had been defined, in various ways, by partial analogies with society and nature in, for example, conceptions of the body, mind and matter, the private and the public, and the subjective life of the interior and the external forces of nature and society. However, in postplural society or prosthetic culture, stable or reproducible context has disappeared and is no longer a natural part of every experience, but an artefact that can be altered at will. Indeed, as Hayles (1987) notes, an arbitrary relation to context *is* our context.[20] In this scenario of outcontextualisation and indifferentiation, the environment (nature and/or society) disappears, and the figure of the individual (including the boundaries of embodiment) becomes difficult to perceive.

However, a successful individual may emerge who can adapt to its context or environment (including the information that makes up a large part of it) or even, experimentally, take on certain characteristics of that environment as its own. In short, while it is possible that the individual will vanish from the exercise of its own individuality as it is possessed by the environment, it may re-emerge through the presentation of its relationship with this space as a strategic coupling of choice. The alternatives here, then, are either that things, including persons, will be put into contexts, or contexts will be put into things,[21] including persons.

20 Hayles points to the role of information theory in this shift. She argues that it made information quantifiable by removing it from the context in which it made meaning and, instead, defining it through its own internal relations. She writes,

> Never before in human history had the cultural context itself been constituted through a technology that makes it possible to fragment, manipulate, and reconstitute informational texts at will. For postmodern culture, the manipulation of text and its consequently arbitrary relation to context is our context.
>
> (1987: 26)

21 See my 'The objects of travel' (1996) for a discussion of how contexts are put into objects in the practices of travelling and dwelling of global cosmopolitanism.

The question is whether, in either case, the individual as a form of self-identity will survive, and for whom (it should not be forgotten that the individual was an identity that was only ever available to a minority). As Hayles points out, citing Luhmann, '"context control" is crucial' (1987: 30).

In the second case described above – in which contexts are put into people – both nature and society may be internalised in the individual as contexts or causes for action; in prosthetic culture, then, the *flexible* individual may be able to choose his or her ground or context for motivation, select his or her cause as the basis of asserting the significance of a specific effect, for accepting or declining responsibility for his or her actions. As indicated by my choice of adjective here, one instance of the individual who emerges as a consequence of this selection has already been documented. This is the individual with the 'flexible body' identified by Emily Martin. In *Flexible Bodies* (1994) Martin looks at the emergence of flexibility as an ideal in the discourse of immunology, and considers its uses in the worlds of computer software, economics, new age philosophy, feminism, government organisations and psychology, charting its take-up and effectivity across a range of social domains. In line with (but not explicitly discussing) Rose's study of the psy-complex (1985), she identifies the work of two psychologists, Mihaly Csikszentmihalyi and Kenneth Gergen, as especially influential in defining flexibility as an ideal. Both write about a flexible, ever-shifting self, that some people are 'lucky' enough to have.

For Csikszentmihalyi, some people, those born with a 'more focused and flexible neurological environment', are able to achieve an 'autotelic self', a self in which the goals that one pursues *arise from within and are not fixed*:

> On the one hand, having a feel of ownership of her [*sic*] decisions, the person is more strongly dedicated to her goals. Her actions are reliable and internally controlled. On the other hand, she can more easily modify her goals whenever the reason for preserving them no longer makes sense. In that respect, an autotelic person's behavior is both more consistent and more 'flexible'.
>
> (1990, quoted in Martin, 1994: 157)

For Kenneth Gergen, a self is emerging whose 'persistent identity cannot seem to be fixed': 'One swims in ever-shifting, concatenating and contentious currents of being' (1991, quoted in Martin, 1994: 157). Although the flexible self is seen, in part, to be a matter of neurological endowment, flexibility can also, it is held, be enhanced through training, leading to a kind of evolutionary adaptation (towards the species of Mackind perhaps), culminating in a belief in 'earnable competence'. As Martin notes, this is the emergence of an ideal individual for whom the capacity to put *all* the parts of the person to work is at a premium (not simply those parts that had been subject to wil(l-)ful modification, but also those previously a matter of social and natural determination), an individual for whom the possession of a resource-ful self is something to be worked at in the very serious role-play of what might be called *experimental individualism*. It is an individual who in looking in the mirror of the technological order no longer sees a reflection, but looks *through* the mirror to what he or she could be.

For Baudrillard, this ideal of the flexible self is already defining our lives. He writes that we have reached

> the last stage of the social relation, ours, which is no longer one of persuasion (the classical age of propaganda, of ideology, of publicity, etc.) but one of deterrence: 'YOU are information, you are the social, you are the event, you are involved, you have the word, etc.' An about-face through which it becomes impossible to locate one instance of the model, of power, of the gaze, of the medium itself, because *you* are always already on the other side. No more subject, no more focal point, no more center or periphery: pure flexion or circular inflexion.
>
> (1994: 29)

The primary capacity of the individual with a flexible body (and an about-face!) is the ability to be disembodied and then re-embodied at will, that is, to be disembedded from specific social relations, to be deracinated, without gender, class, sexuality or age, and then to display a combination of such natural and social characteristics as required through an assertion of a claim to the significance of their effects: to turn the substitutability of the customised individual in a postplural society into the individual art of colouring by numbers (to adapt Baudrillard's example of suntanning). If successful, the individual may be reconstituted as such through the possession of individuality as a set of cultural or stylistic resources, the proprietor of a technologically mediated or *prosthetic auto/biography*. As Mark Seltzer notes, in many ways this is not a radical disrupture but merely an extension of possessive individualism, for, as he notes,

> the discourse of possessive individualism posits a world animated through and through with intentions, a pan-intentionalism that appears in the understanding of things as prosthetic extensions of the self and its desires: the promiscuous personifications of 'living property'.
>
> (1993: 102)

However, it will be argued in later chapters, the prosthetic biography requires significant new forms of authorisation and, in this respect, the *image* is combining with *narrative* to produce techniques of the self in new ways. Moreover, as Hayles points out, what I have called outcontextualisation is not always controllable: as she writes,

> As crucial decisions come to rely more and more on information that has been processed and reconstituted in ways that decision-makers do not understand, the gap between text and context will increase.
>
> (1987: 30)

PUTTING PEOPLE INTO CONTEXTS AND CONTEXTS INTO PEOPLE

The acquisition and possession of a prosthetic biography by the person as individual is by no means an uncontested process, as is illustrated by, for example, the practices of the management specialism 'cultural diversity training'. (In other words, as noted above, contexts are not always put into people, but people into contexts.) This is a specialism that seeks to produce a work environment in which the diverse parts of the culturally 'different' self-identities of workers are constituted as occupational resources that can be managed for the benefit of the organisation or 'context'. According to the advocates of this specialism,

> The problem is not getting [women and 'ethnic minorities'] in at the entry level; the problem is making better use of their *potential* at every level, especially in middle-management and leadership positions. This is no longer a question of common decency, it is a question of business *survival*.
>
> (Thomas, 1990: 108; my emphasis)

This unexploited potential[22] is defined in terms of a specifically cultural identity or cultural difference. The issue for diversity managers is how what are called 'horizontal differences' (the flexible, or, perhaps better, malleable, bodies of those already 'in at the entry level' of the flat world of personal difference) can be better managed to serve the protection and enhancement of 'vertical differences' and the quest for profit. (Here 'horizontal differences' are those of cultural identity and 'vertical differences' are those of the organisational hierarchy.) The questions diversity managers seek to address are 'How do we create a work environment that fully utilizes all members in pursuit of organizational objectives?' or 'Can we get maximum corporate power from the diverse workforce we're now drawing into the system?' (Thomas, 1990: 109).

A key mechanism through which struggles between managers and employees are negotiated would appear to be performance review and feedback. One example of how these notions are being conceptualised is provided by a recent article in *Human Resource Development Quarterly* in which Fred W. Nickols aims to 'revisit the technical view of feedback and to stimulate its broader, better application' (1995: 289). He does so by returning to his first encounter with the term 'as a young US Navy technician working on complex shipboard naval weapons systems' (1995: 289). On the basis of this experience (described in conjunction with Figure 2.1), he identifies two key characteristics of feedback:

> First, the purpose of feedback is *control*. Feedback is used to control the gun mount's position and its movement. Said somewhat differently, feedback is used to obtain results and to shape behavior. Second, feedback is an integral element of the system itself, not information from outside the system. As the example shows, feedback occurs in the gun mount, not between the gun mount and the computer. And, as we shall see, this self-contained, self-governing aspect of the technical view of feedback has its counterpart in human performance systems.
>
> (1995: 298–299)

Nickols's assertion of the self-contained and self-governing nature of human performance systems is central here for it reveals the defining characteristics of

22 Strathern discusses the issue of claims of ownership to this potential in 'Potential property: intellectual rights and property in persons' (1995).

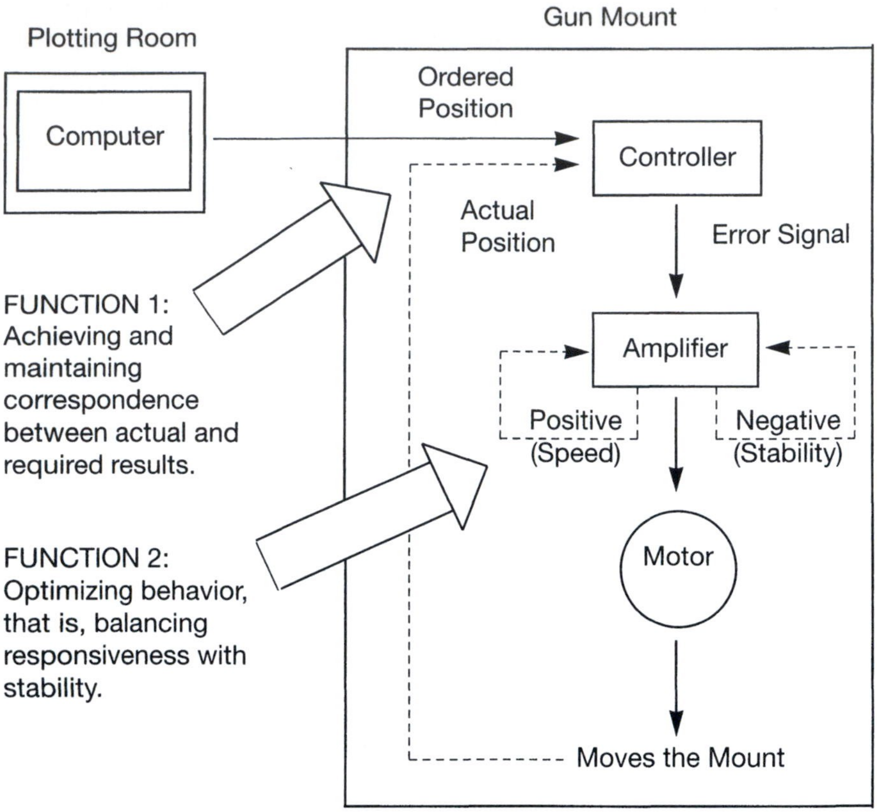

Figure 2.1 The two functions of feedback
Source: *Human Resource Development Quarterly*, © Jossey-Bass Inc., Publishers

the flexible or transparent individual constituted in practices such as feedback. However, struggles over the ownership of the effects of this identity is obscured by the phrase 'as we shall see' and the three further claims that Nickols makes. The first of these is that feedback 'occurs naturally. Contrivance is unnecessary' (1995: 292). The second is that 'Unlike gun mounts, people have minds of their own. Their behavior is exactly that – *their* behavior' (1995: 291), while the third, somewhat more complicated, is that while performance is often confused with behaviour, 'it pays to keep the two straight' (1995: 293).

In the first of these claims, Nickols posits the naturalness of feedback, so ignoring the different ways in which reflection on the self has been socially organised and encouraged in Euro-American societies, making self-reflection the abstract ability of the universal individual rather than the outcome of specific social relations. In the second claim, he assumes behaviour (or rather 'performance) not only to be the personal possession of the individual, but also to be conscious and voluntary in so far as the performative individual is assumed to be able to set his or her own goals. The assertion given above continues,

Although the gun mount or technical model of feedback cannot be applied

> directly to people, the modification required of it is surprisingly simple. About all that is necessary is to move the computer into the gun mount, to think of people as smart or self-directing gun mounts, as gun mounts with minds of their own. That includes memory and the ability to learn.
>
> (1995: 292)

As this quotation indicates, he does this by assuming that it is possible to merge the computer with the gun mount. One of the many questions he thus ignores is whether a computer can or should be used as a stand-in for the mind or consciousness. That there is no widespread agreement on this issue – even in the rhetoric of promotional culture – is indicated by the advertisement for a Hasselblad camera illustrated here (Figure 2.2) which suggests – albeit with the apparent intention of flattering the artistic aspirations of potential consumers – that the merger of which Nickols speaks is not so straightforward.

The third assertion makes visible how the notion of perfomance contributes to the creation of occupational resources, a key focus of many disputes between employees and employers in the contemporary workplace. As noted above, Nickols makes a distinction between performance and behaviour; crucially, performance includes 'a complex mix of goals, expectations, behavior *and the effects of behavior*' (1995: 293; my emphasis). In claiming certain effects as part of one's performance by means of naturalised self-reflection ('Feedback is information about my performance' [1995: 29]), the worker is held to be able to make use of his or her relation to an extended notion of self-identity as an occupational resource. In this way, he or she is able to make use of feedback to put 'effects', that is, some part of the (social or natural) context, into his or her self-identity as a worker to enhance his or her position within an occupational hierarchy. Feedback can thus be seen as a tactical mechanism by which the participants in a workplace negotiate who is able to lay claim not simply to behaviour but also to its effects, including effects that are collectively produced or are the outcome of contexts or technologically mediated networks of interaction.

In his account Nickols asserts that feedback is natural. For Nickols, each individual is at liberty to define this feedback as either positive or negative, as the following 'little story' from his Navy days is intended to illustrate:

> While in seminar with other organization development specialists, I had several testy exchanges with one of my colleagues. At the end of the day, he, in the company of some of his friends, confronted me in the hallway and announced, 'Nick, I am really bothered by your behavior in the seminar earlier today. As a matter of fact, I am quite angry.' Technically speaking, his feedback was correct; he had 'owned' his feelings and was apprising me of my effect upon him. His assumption, of course, was that I did not wish to anger him. I was of the opinion that he was taking no responsibility for his reaction to me and that what he ought to be confronting were the underlying reasons for his anger. To his surprise, I replied, 'Gee, thanks for the feedback, Dick. I've been trying to pull your chain for weeks now and I had no idea until this very minute that I was being so successful.'

Figure 2.2 'We've included your brain in our System . . .'
Source: © Hasselblad (UK) Limited

> His 'feedback' was indeed feedback, but not of the kind he thought or to the end he hoped for.
>
> (1995: 295)

In this account, Nickols presumes and prescribes a subject whose practice of feedback makes available *all* aspects of the self for experimentation in terms that are, apparently, set by the individual himself.

However, not many people could (or would) lay claim to all behaviours and their effects as occupational resources, some perhaps not at all and others not without feeling insincere or unethical. In other words, what Nickols does not address is whether all workers are able to adopt these notions of performance equally successfully, nor to what extent the management of these claims is informed by specific workplace practices (for further discussion of this issue, see Adkins and Lury, forthcoming).[23] He presumes the subject who is the outcome of the practices he describes. Nor, indeed, does he seem concerned by the disappearance of the ethical values associated with interiority of the self, such as authenticity and sincerity. This disappearance is, however, addressed by some commentators, including Stanley Bing in *Fortune*, who asks:

> Are you a master of (in)sincerity? If not, get with the program. Only losers show their true feelings in business. Test your bogus-sincerity quotient. Take our quiz.
>
> (1995: 49)

The quiz that follows is a multiple-choice quiz in which a correct reply enables you to move up the hierarchy from 'compulsory acquiescence' to 'noble weasling' to 'bogus frankness (a.k.a. superficial candor)' to 'lying right into people's face' to the 'most important level . . . cruelty'. (Perhaps the 'humorous' tone of this piece indicates *some* degree of anxiety about this ethical retooling.)

What this and the other analyses of workplace practices presented here suggest is that the proliferation of parts in postplural society or prosthetic culture does not straightforwardly lead to persons becoming either more individuated or being better able to express individuality;[24] rather they suggest that the two processes become entwined in *a prescriptive experimentation in which the individuality of the person is strategically disassembled and reassembled* with uncertain consequences for the possessive individual (and society and nature).[25] In prosthetic culture, then,

23 As Rabinow notes, 'Performance is a relative term. Practices make the person; or rather, they don't – they just make practitioners' (1992: 243).

24 Or, as Stanley Bing puts it,

> Do you want your peers saying what they actually think of your performance at a budget review? Do you want your subordinate's real opinion of your new haircut? And do I really want to hear another unvarnished word from Zukofsky at this time?
>
> No. I do not. I've heard enough. Real unmodulated thoughts and feelings have no place in business. They're exhausting and take up too much personal space. The effort to produce false sincerity among a group of people is a binding covenant, a commitment to keep things civilised.
>
> (1995: 50)

25 Strathern writes,

> Technology enables; it is a resource. Although it may take the form of property, it elicits ⇒

the issue of laying claim to the effect or outcome of the application of technical or earnable competence or the effects of prostheses as if they were one's own is paramount for the 'survival' of the individual (and, indeed, 'business', as Thomas notes). This is thus not simply a society or culture of technology – an operational culture which informs its members 'how to do so and so' – but one in which the member is constituted as such by claims to the possession of *performance, the effects of having done so, the ownership of the significance of experimentation.* However, so I wish to suggest, the question of whether or not the outcome of any claim to the ownership of the effects of drawing the boundary between inside and outside, subject and object, the self and nature and or/society, present and past, *here* rather than *there*, will produce a reconfigured possessive individual is still uncertain. As Donna Haraway notes, 'Siting (sighting) boundaries is a risky practice' (1991: 201). The multiple possibilities of the contemporary revision of the processes of siting and sighting, of putting people into contexts and contexts into people, and the risks they engender are the concern of the following chapters, but this chapter will now turn to the question of seeing itself.

IMITATION AFTER NATURE

In a final twist in her argument in *After Nature*, Strathern concludes that 'Choice becomes conventional and conventions are for the choosing' (1992: 152). Moreover, what is reproduced by these conventions, she claims, are not persons, but auto-enabling choice itself, a construct which is its own construction. What fuels this auto-construction is style, which itself emerges from within culture according to a principle of *imitation* or replication. Strathern writes,

> Styles appear to imitate other styles, replicating them by an inner momentum that is contained in the very notion that style itself is an imitative act. Not the imitation of nature or of more noble ages, as it might have been seen a century before, but imitation of versions of itself . . . . It would seem that Culture emerges as the new totalising concept that can gather all human enterprise to itself, including its own capacity for regeneration.
>
> (1992: 171)

What notion of imitation is she implying here? If it is not an imitation *of* nature in what sense is it *after* nature?

It is clear, I hope, that the contemporary domains in which experimentation is employed as a technique of self-identity are subject to intense contestation, and are constantly being reworked. This is not surprising – but, rather, predictable – especially given that the capacity for reflection on the self is one of the defining features by which the specifically modern character of self-identity is recognised as such by its members. Indeed, the characteristic of many contemporary Euro-

neither the old proprietorial sense of a given identity or possession nor the constraints of social class or position. Rather, anything – relationships, institutions, persons, minerals – may be assimilated to the idea of a resource.

(1992: 136)

American understandings of culture that enables (specific kinds of) experimentation is that it is held to be a construct (Clifford, 1988; Strathern, 1992; Harvey, 1996), a reserve of resources to be set to work. But surely Strathern is implying something more specific here?

Certainly there is a great deal more that might be said about the notion of imitation: from Plato onwards, an inter-related complex of terms – imitation, copying, originality, mimicry and mimesis – have been the focus of anxiety, prohibition and enticement. They have also been the subject of much definitional wrangling, but the understanding that will be adopted here is broadly that proposed by the writers of the Frankfurt School, especially Walter Benjamin.[26] He writes,

> Nature creates similarity. One need only think of mimicry. The highest capacity for producing similarities, however, is man's. His gift of seeing resemblances is nothing other than a rudiment of the powerful compulsion in former times to become and behave like something else. Perhaps there is none of his higher functions in which his mimetic faculty does not play a decisive role.
>
> (1985: 160)

For Benjamin, mimesis is a relation of adaptation, affinity and reciprocity; it is the unlimited tendency to represent the position of everyone else, 'every animal, every dead thing in the cosmos', the promiscuous projection into everything and everyone, a relation of 'non-sensuous similarity'. In Taussig's provocative formulation of Benjamin's writings, mimesis is 'the nature that culture uses to create second nature' (1993: xiii).

Benjamin's emphasis on the *non*-sensuous nature of this similarity may seem somewhat surprising (and is certainly difficult to interpret), but is taken here to be an attempt by Benjamin to indicate a mode of perception that is not already divided amongst pre-given senses, a perception in which the ratio between the senses is not already fixed in the subject.[27] In the case of vision, for example, it refers to an unstoppable merging of the object of perception with the body of the perceiver, not just the mind's eye. Indeed, it is this line of thought that leads Taussig (who is drawing on Benjamin) to the claim that 'a first step' is 'to insist on breaking away from the tyranny of the visual notion of the image' (1993: 57), towards a notion of 'the active yielding of the perceiver in the perceived – the

26 In the interpretation of Benjamin's use of this term, I have been guided by the commentaries of Susan Buck-Morss (1991), Andrew Hewitt (1992), Miriam Hansen (1993a, 1993b) and Michael Taussig (1993). I do not seek to produce an exhaustive mapping of the multiple meanings of mimesis (see Jay, 1993), but rather to put the term to work in understanding the contemporary self.

27 Benjamin writes,

> During long periods of history, the mode of human sense perception changes with humanity's entire mode of existence. The manner in which human sense perception is organized, the medium in which it is acccomplished, is determined not only by nature but also by historical circumstances as well.
>
> (1970: 224)

perceiver trying to enter into the picture and become one with it, so that the self is moved by the representation into the represented' (1993: 61). The very concept of knowing is displaced here by 'relating to' or 'yielding into': as Benjamin writes, 'Every day the urge grows stronger to get hold of an object at very close range by way of its likeness, its reproduction' (1970: 225).

This is an understanding of mimesis as a relation of being similar to the environment, not similar to anything or anybody in particular, just a relation of 'being similar'.[28] As such, it is a relation which might inform synthetic *and* prosthetic culture. But what happens when the individual *is* its own context or environment?; this is the scenario described by Strathern. The 'imitation' at work in contemporary style, Strathern says, is not 'the imitation of nature or of more noble ages, as it might have been seen a century before, but imitation of versions of itself'. How, then, should mimesis be understood 'after nature', that is, in prosthetic culture?

Benjamin is aware of the importance of looking at the historical changes that inform the workings of mimesis. He writes,

> we must suppose that the gift of producing similarities – for example, in dances, whose oldest function this was – and therefore also the gift of recognizing them, have changed with historical development.
>
> (1985: 160–161)

28 This definition of mimesis has resonances with that put forward by Roger Caillois in a fantastic essay, 'Mimicry and legendary psychasthenia' (published in the Surrealist magazine *Minotaure* in 1935 [reprinted 1988], and discussed at length by Krauss [1986b, 1994] and rather briefly by Taussig, 1993). Caillois argues that the phenomenon of mimicry in the praying mantis is in fact a kind of insectoid psychosis – the psychasthenia of his title referring to the psychologist Pierre Janet's notion of a catastrophic drop in energy. The life of any organism is seen to depend on the possibility of its maintaining its own distinctness, a boundary within which it is contained, the terms of its self-possession. Mimicry, Caillois argues, is the loss of this possession: the animal that merges with its setting becomes dispossessed, derealised. Recognising the oddness of applying psychological terms to this occurrence, he draws a parallel with primitive sympathetic magic, in which, as he describes it, an illness is conceived of as a possession of the patient by some external force, one that can be combated by drawing it off from the patient through the mimicry performed by a shaman in a rite of repossession.

Describing the behaviour of schizophrenic subjects, Caillois elaborates the effects of 'being tempted by space',

> 'I know where I am, but I do not feel as though I'm at the spot where I find myself.' To these dispossessed souls, space seems to be a devouring force. Space pursues them, encircles them, digests them in a gigantic phagocytosis. It ends by replacing them. Then the body separates itself from thought, the individual breaks the boundary of his skin and occupies the other side of his senses. He tries to look at himself from any point whatever in space. He feels himself becoming space, *dark space where things cannot be put*. . . . He is similar, not similar to something, but just *similar*. And he invents spaces of which he is 'the convulsive possession'.
>
> (1988: 72)

This astounding description of what Taussig calls 'an ineffable plasticity' (1993: 34) may be seen to indicate why photography might be a privileged medium in relation to mimesis. Following the example of the representational space of drama, in which 'the living being, the organism, is no longer the origin of co-ordinates, but is one point among others', photography can be seen to present a visual field within which the subject is dispossessed, is 'tempted by space' and 'no longer knows where to put itself'.

However, while he states that the direction of this change seems definable as 'the increasing decay of the mimetic faculty', he also suggests that the 'question is whether we are concerned with the decay of this faculty or with its transformation' (1985: 161). He, it seems, is concerned with the latter.

In the short quotation from Benjamin given above, his identification of mimesis with 'the primitive' and his fascination with its resurgence in modernity is evident. In this respect, he shows similarities with Adorno and Horkheimer's thinking on the subject: for example, the latter write,

> On the magical plane, dream and image were not mere signs for the thing in question, but were bound up with it by similarity or names. The relation is not one of intention but of relatedness. Like science, magic pursues aims, but seeks to achieve them by mimesis, not by progressively distancing itself from the object.
>
> (Quoted in Hewitt, 1992: 159)

Indeed, as both Miriam Hansen (1992) and Andrew Hewitt (1992) have pointed out, Adorno and Horkheimer elaborate a genealogy of mimesis in *Dialectic of Enlightenment* (1982), in which the reversal of Enlightenment to myth has come full circle, as 'ancient hieroglyphics', deriving from a time in which word and image still converged, have returned in the service of mass culture as a repressed presence.[29] For Adorno and Horkheimer, this is the absorption of artificially revived mimetic capabilities by monopolistic practice, and results in the ever more effective subjection of the individual *in representation*. They write,

> If mimesis makes itself like the surrounding world, so false projection makes the surrounding world like itself. If for the former the exterior is the model which the interior has to approximate [*sich anschmiegen*], if for it the stranger becomes familiar, the latter transforms the tense inside reality to snap into exteriority and stamps even the familiar as the enemy.
>
> (Quoted in Hewitt, 1992: 160)

They thus point to the central role of mimetic representation or what they call false projection, the organisation of mimesis, in modern society; perhaps then perversion of mimesis, rather than mimesis as such, is imitation or style in Strathern's sense.

Baudrillard too emphasises the significance of the technologies of mass culture in transforming the effects of representation and mimesis; indeed, he extends the argument by pointing to the contribution of such technologies to changes in the standing and significance of the prosthesis through the inauguration of the age of the simulacrum.[30] He writes,

29 Taussig (1993) too provides a genealogy of mimesis; his account is informed by a special emphasis on the colonial mirror of production and alterity.

30 Indeed, Baudrillard writes that

> It is no longer a question of imitation, nor duplication, nor even parody. It is a question of substituting the signs of the real for the real, that is to say of an operational double, a programmatic, metastable, perfectly descriptive machine that offers all the signs of the real and short-circuits all its vicissitudes.
>
> (1994: 2)

> It is necessary to revisit what Walter Benjamin said of the work of art in the age of mechanical reproducibility. What is lost in the work that is serially reproduced, is its *aura*, its singular quality of the here and now, its aesthetic form . . . . The most advanced, the most modern form of this development, which Benjamin described in cinema, photography, and contemporary mass media, is one in which the original no longer even exists, since things are conceived from their beginning as a function of their unlimited reproduction.
>
> This is what happens to us with cloning, no longer only at the level of messages, but at the level of individuals . . . . It is the irruption of technology that controls this . . . . The prostheses of the industrial age are still external, *exotechnical*, those that we know have been subdivided and internalized: *esotechnical*. We are in the age of soft technologies – genetic and mental software.
>
> (1994: 99–100)

In doing so, he makes explicit the significance of technology – specifically technologies of cultural reproduction – in the transformation of mimesis into style, the 'imitation of versions of itself' (Strathern), the precession of simulacra (Baudrillard). He writes,

> As long as the prostheses of the old industrial golden age were mechanical, they still returned to the body in order to modify its image in order to modify its imaginary and this technological metabolism was also part of the image of the body. But when one reaches a point of no return (deadened) in simulation, that is to say when the prosthesis goes deeper, is interiorized in, . . . as soon as it is imposed on the body itself as the 'original,' model, burning all the previous symbolic circuits, the only possible body the immutable repetition of the prosthesis, then it is the end of the body, of its history, and of its vicissitudes. The individual is no longer anything but a cancerous metastasis of its base formula.[31]
>
> (1994: 100)

Thus, it is developments in the uses of cultural technologies, or so Baudrillard suggests, which mean that *aesthetics* is being simultaneously subsumed and extended within a *prosthetic* culture in which a range of supplementary techniques fantastically extend the range of the senses, consciousness and memory, 'supplying deficiencies as by artificial limbs, teeth, etc.'. But they do so not only by extending 'things perceptible by the senses', but also by extending 'things

31 In a footnote, Baudrillard comments,

> One must take into account that cancerous proliferation is also a silent disobedience of the injunctions of the genetic code. Cancer, if it fits with the logic of a nuclear/computer science vision of human beings, is also its monstrous excrescence and negation, because it leads to total disinformation and to disaggregation.
>
> (1994: 102)

For a more nuanced interpretation of the cultural significance of cancer in contemporary society, see Jackie Stacey (1997).

thinkable or immaterial', by means of 'soft technologies' or perceptual, sentient prostheses. And they do so not, or so Baudrillard claims, by modifying the image of the body, but by their imposition as the 'original model'.

In this respect, consider the following description of one of the recent performances of the French performance and multimedia artist Orlan, in which she works on her self-portrait through its literal inscription in her flesh according to a model created by a computer montage of Diana, Europa, Psyche, Venus and Mona Lisa:

> In New York on 21 November 1993, . . . Orlan underwent her seventh facial operation. Her meaningful title Omnipresence suggested that the world public could be a part of this event, which would normally take place behind closed doors. Several art institutions were connected with the operating room via satellite and televised the surgery in all its detail. Like all previous and subsequent operations, this one was staged as an artistic performance following a carefully planned, well calculated choreography. The room is always appointed with strongly referential props and photographs, while the surgeons are clothed by fashion designers or by the artist herself. Orlan also wears costumes, chosen to suit the particular operation and its significance. She is fully conscious, supervises and observes the procedures, reads aloud psychoanalytical texts and willingly answers questions from the public.
>
> The pictures we are confronted with are shocking for non-medical viewers, all the more so because Orlan's facial operations are not to be understood as cosmetic surgery. The goal of her project, entitled The Reincarnation of St. Orlan, is the gradual transformation of her body and her person at the intersection of private and public concerns, of art and life. The artist studies the female body, its appearance and its manipulability – and our idea of corporeality and beauty on the eve of the second millennium.
>
> (Ermacora, 1994: 15)

Self-possessed of her new identity after the final surgery, Orlan intends to commission an advertising firm to create a new name for her, as it would for a new product.[32] This name is to appear legally on her passport.

The question such an example raises is whether the technical extension of perceptibility in a prosthetic culture should be seen as a destruction of the capacity of nature and society to become culture, of the decline of the power of the partial analogy in the era of the hyper-real.[33] Does the perversion of

32 A related example is that of the Pammy, the name given to the bottle designed to hold Virgin Cola. The shape of the bottle is said to be a rendering of Pamela Anderson's figure, itself the result of plastic surgery.

33 John O'Neill writes,

> To the extent that modern societies destroy nature, with its capacity to become culture, we naturalize our own culture – but at the level of barbarism from which our myths had once delivered us.
>
> (1992: 267)

mimesis mean that the organic and the technological no longer complement and become adapted to one another but that the technological has brought about a 'dematerialisation' of the body, and of reality itself?[34] As will be noted later, Lyotard, among others, is not as pessimistic in this regard as either Adorno and Horkheimer or Baudrillard; the rest of this book too seeks to explore some of the ambivalencies of prosthetic culture. By taking the example of photography, the possibilities of mimesis for personhood, self-identity and the individual are explored within *and* outside representation. In other words, the study of photography is presented as a way of considering transformations in the constitution of the possessive individual, including changes in the relations between memory, embodiment and the relation between the individual, consciousness and presentations of self including (auto)biography, character and personality, and understandings of human nature.

Photography was chosen as the focus for this exploration of transformations in part because it is an early example of the mass culture of which Adorno and Horkheimer speak. It was also chosen because of my view, prompted by reading Benjamin and his critics, that 'a crisis of experience is also a crisis of the image' (Abbas, 1989: 64). At the same time, the photographic focus is also intended to further the consideration of mimesis through an exploration of the *indexicality* of the photograph. This is especially illuminating in respect of the general argument proposed here since an indexical sign, in the terms defined by Peirce (1991), is bound to its referent, with which it is either physically contiguous (that is, of which it is an extension, as when a part is related to a whole) or causally connected (as with symptoms, outcomes or antecedents).[35] Photography is thus a useful test-case with which to explore the notion that the partial analogy has been cancelled through the processes of outcontextualisation and indifferentiation.

The focus on photography also provides a way of exploring Benjamin's notion of the flash in which, he argues, the recognition of similarity or mimesis necessarily occurs: 'It slips past [and] can possibly be regained, but cannot really be held fast, unlike other perceptions. It offers itself to the eye as fleetingly and transitorily as a constellation of stars' (1979, quoted in Taussig, 1993: 40). The flash, the 'now of recognisability', illuminates the past in the present; for Benjamin, 'to articulate the past historically does not mean to recognize it "the way it really was" (Ranke). It means to seize hold of a memory as it flashes up at a moment of danger' (1970: 255). The analysis of the flash of photography thus provides a means of considering whether, in the move to a postplural society and the development of experimental individualism in which the gap between cause and effect, part and whole, is in-filled and withdrawn into the individual, mimesis is now only a utopian category – whether snap-shots are also snap-shuts

34 Baudrillard describes the hyper-real as 'the generation by models of a real without origin or reality' (1994: 1).

35 Seltzer identifies what he calls 'an insistent, at times desperate, conversion of analogy into cause' in contemporary 'melodramas of uncertain motive and vexed agency'. He argues that this desperation is a consequence of the logic of destruction *for* fuller possession, a logic driven by what he calls the body–machine complex (1993: 100).

(as, has already been hinted, is indicated by the adoption of autopoietic ways of thinking and organising in postplural society[36]).

THE MAGIC OF MIMESIS

In considering the transformations in mimesis, the question of gender will be highlighted. Already in the genealogy proposed by Benjamin and Adorno and Horkheimer, the question of the relationship between mimesis and the category of gender is crucial for understandings of the individual. Benjamin and Adorno may disagree about whether or not redemptive qualities are to be found in the contemporary resurgence of mimesis, but both locate its origins in the primitive ('former times') or in the magic of myth. This mythic mimesis is grounded in a feminine nature characterised by its inexhaustibility and unending renewal, its fecundity or powers of *reproduction.* Yet for Adorno at least, interest in the feminine and the primitive is not an interest in the experience of women or 'the other' as such, but only in the possibility of liberation they offer for philosophy.[37] Moreover, as Hewitt remarks, in *Dialectic of Enlightenment* (1982) Adorno and Horkheimer repeat the exclusionary practices of the individualism they critique, for they deny women the 'honour' of individualisation by subsuming singular women within the generic category 'woman', albeit while describing that very process. He suggests that their denial of the capacity of mimetic practices to redeem contemporary life can be seen to be motivated by philosophy's fear of 'becoming woman', of collapsing back, regressing into prehistoric myth or magic.

As Hewitt points out, this is not to deny Adorno and Horkheimer's awareness that it is precisely this fear that impelled the historical move from mimesis to metaphysics:

> One after the other, mimetic, mythic, and metaphysical modes of behavior were taken as superseded eras, any reversion to which was to be feared as implying a reversion of the self to that mere state of nature from which it had estranged itself with so huge an effort, and which therefore struck terror into the self.
>
> (Quoted in Hewitt, 1992: 158)

36 Tyler's discussion focuses on the politics of passing and coming out; she writes,

> 'I am out, therefore I am' cannot close the gap between performance and utterance, performative and constative, subject and T-shirt, the one who is 'outing' and the one who is out. 'I' will have been out only at the end of the 'outing', which is not in its beginning, except retroactively. Being 'out' is a moebius movement of deferral without end and renewal without beginning – the future perfect as past perfected. The subject of the enunciation must pass through the statement in which his 'I' is uttered. All subjects therefore are *passing* through the signifiers which represent them for an other, to whom a demand for recognition and a question about being is addressed: '(Do you) Hear what I'm saying!? (Do you) See what I am!?'
>
> (1994: 221)

37 In the repressive identification of woman with nature is bound up the utopian instrumentalisation of woman as the means of a reconciliation with nature.

Indeed, they describe this move as a sacrifice, but, so Hewitt argues, what they do not admit is that what is sacrificed in the very notion of sacrifice is the specificity of a mimetic relation, for what replaces a particular relation of being similar is the abstract, disembodied subject in/of representation. This specificity is displaced onto the natural or social context, the archaic, the primitive, the magic of myth. To put this another way, in woman's identification with nature, her closeness to the context, to nature, is not simply the absence of her visibility as a subject of representation but also the loss of the specificity of the mimetic relation. In short, the reduction of mimesis to imitation is tied to the emergence of the modern individual as a subject of representation and the invisibility of the specificity of mimesis. In this appearance and disappearance occurs the gendering of the modern individual as masculine, the generic subordination of 'women' as the feminine and the invisibility of the mimetic specificity of women in nature.

At the same time (and this is something Hewitt does not remark upon) what is also lost is the specificity of those other groups that are defined as 'the primitive' or 'the other'. Here I would agree with Anne McClintock, who notes that mimesis (she uses the term mimicry) and ambivalence 'are less powerful if reduced to a single, privileged social category [whether that be either gender or race]' (1995: 65). For this reason, it is necessary in addressing issues of genre or type (of gender, of race, of sexuality or class) to also consider questions of difference. Indeed, the importance of doing this has been demonstrated by many feminist, poststructuralist and post-colonial writers who have pointed to the dangers of reifying and universalising the genre or category of 'women' as if it were all there is to gender; the argument here is that a sensitivity to difference makes possible a recognition of the simultaneous multiplicity of subject identifications. To this, I would add that in addressing questions of difference it is also important to acknowledge genre, for there are also dangers of reification arising from the abstraction of difference as a universal concept without relation to its historical uses in the implementation of generic categories or types.

This latter point is especially clear in relation to any analysis of the contemporary reversal of myth to Enlightenment that produces the totalising Culture of which Strathern speaks. Here, styles imitate other styles, replicating them by 'an inner momentum that is contained in the very notion that style itself is an imitative act'. This is a conception in which culture 'can gather all human enterprise to itself, including its own capacity for regeneration' (Strathern, 1992: 171). It is a notion of culture in which reproduction itself is apparently no longer tied to the feminine, the primitive or indeed to nature, since for the hyper-individual there is no 'outside', neither social nor natural, only, apparently, (in-)difference. How is this possible?

As Strathern writes, when nature becomes a question of cultural style, and culture the exercise of natural choice, the one ceases to be contextualised by the other. The grounding function of nature disappears (and with it women and the primitive as natural and social categories), and ground and figure are replaced by a system constituted in the strategic, technologically mediated couplings of the auto-reproducing individual with its environment (in a version of the game of 'snap' of which Adorno and Horkheimer speak). These are the processes of indifferentiation and outcontextualisation mentioned earlier.[38] In this account of the transition to prosthetic culture, the specificity of the mimetic relation is not displaced onto context (as in the move from myth to Enlightenment), but rather is incorporated into the system or individual. In this process, the feminine has been outcontextualised and indifferentiated in the universalised 'becoming woman' of contemporary culture (Jardine, 1985; Braidotti, 1991), while the primitive becomes a matter of style, as in the cultural practices of 'modern primitives', the aesthetics of neo-tribalism or the playful tribal face-painting of the fashion company Benetton's iconography; both the feminine and the primitive are subject to abstracted in-difference. To preserve a critical perspective on in-difference in this culture, then, it may be helpful to hold on to the problematic of genre or type.

However, while not wanting to isolate mimesis from this Culture in an effort to preserve its ambivalence,[39] this book will offer an analysis of specific examples of specific practices to show that indifferentiation and outcontextualisation do not exhaust the possibilities of mimesis in a postplural society. As Strathern notes, although nature no longer functions as a model or analogy for context,[40] and has been replaced by the environment, it is not surprising that contemporary crises are frequently presented as ecological ones. Neither should it seem unlikely, then, that although reproduction no longer functions in relation to sex and gender (or nature and society), and has been replaced by generation and the hyper-individual or clone, the question of gender will emerge to 'trouble' (Butler, 1990) prosthetic culture.

38 In her discussion of the emergence of the contemporary definition of information that defined it internally (that is, by reference to relational differences between elements of a message ensemble) rather than externally through its relation to the context that invests it with a particular meaning, Hayles (1987) argues for the importance of the gendered metaphors that helped secure its acceptance. She writes,

> Warren Weaver . . . argued that the separation of information from meaning was a regrettable but necessary price to pay if man was to subdue the information channel he likened to a discreet 'office girl' who processes all that comes to her desk without regard for its meaning.
> (1987: 25)

39 As McClintock points out, 'In the compulsion to repeat, the everywhere of the ambivalent becomes the scene of the same' (1995: 65).

40 Luhmann similarly identifies a new ecological consciousness in the systems-theoretical consciousness of system and environment. This consciousness, according to Luhmann, has its roots in a theoretical turn that began in the nineteenth century when the terms '*Umwelt*' and 'environment' were first used, and 'has reached its culmination today' in the view that 'systems define their own boundaries' (1989: 6). In this understanding, systems differentiate themselves and thereby constitute the environment as whatever lies outside the boundary.

> The environment is not a system of its own, not even a unified effect. As the totality of external circumstances, it is whatever restricts the randomness of the morphogenesis of the system and exposes it to evolutionary selection. The 'unity' of the environment is nothing more than a correlate of the unity of the system since everything that is a unity for the system is defined by it as a unity.
> (1989: 6)

⇒

However, what explains the power of ecological thinking is a belief in the absolute complexity of ecology as societal environment: the conviction that it can always change in more ways than society itself. As Luhmann writes,

> Statements concerned with complexity become productive only when they are turned from unity to difference. The distinction of system and environment can be used to do this. It enables one to make the statement with which we will introduce the following discussion: that for any system the environment is always more complex than the system itself.
>
> (1989: 11)

This is the belief that sustains ecological thinking after nature. However, this belief rests upon a paradox, which Luhmann knows only too well:

> there is inevitably a paradox because the unity of the whole is not outside or above the parts but is identical and not identical with the sum of them at the same time.
>
> (1989: 134)

However, he is sceptical of any attempt to resolve this paradox; indeed, he claims that

> we know that it is not possible (or only for specific purposes) to resolve this paradox through a differentiation of levels or a hierarchy of types. One can also show that in modern society every claim of a part to be the whole or to represent identity is subject to observation and contradiction since, for reasons of social structure, there are no longer any non-competitive positions, for example, the apex of the hierarchy or a center *vis-à-vis* a periphery. It is ill-advised and leads to a peculiar Utopianism and hopelessness if one does not recognize these restricting conditions or any attempt at rationality but persists in a belief in direct access to it.
>
> (1989: 134–135)

3

THE FAMILY OF MAN

> To pry an object from its shell, to destroy its aura, is the mark of a perception whose 'sense of the universal equality of things' has increased to such a degree that it extracts it even from a unique object by means of reproduction. Thus is manifested in the field of perception what in the theoretical sphere is noticeable in the increasing importance of statistics. The adjustment of reality to the masses and of the masses to reality is a process of unlimited scope, as much for thinking as perception.
>
> (Walter Benjamin, 1970: 225)

THE PORTRAIT AS AN INTRODUCTION TO THE INDIVIDUAL

The sheer range and volume of photographic practices offer ample evidence of the paradoxical history and status of photography within Euro-American societies: as John Berger notes, within three decades of its invention, photography

> was being used for police filing, military reconnaissance, pornography, encyclopedic documentation, family albums, postcards, anthropological records (often, as with the indigenous peoples in the United States, accompanied by genocide), sentimental moralizing, inquisitive probing (the wrongly named 'candid camera'), aesthetic effects, news reporting and formal portraiture.
>
> (1980: 52)

A primary concern in this chapter will be with the uses of photography to map humankind, specifically the ways in which photography has been put to use to define humankind, as individuals, as types or genres of humankind, and as a species. Even with this focus in mind, the range of uses to which photography has been put is enormous; nevertheless, it is possible to identify certain strands within a multiple and discontinuous history which give some indication of its part in the 'thickening' of modern life (Sontag, 1977: 3; see chapter 4). One such strand, as Berger notes, is that of the genre of portraiture, a genre that is widely recognised as having been profoundly influential in shaping the more general standing of photography in everyday life and in defining the self-identity of the individual (Abercrombie *et al.*, 1986; see chapter 2). Portraits were very popular when the camera was first invented as part of a cult of remembrance (Benjamin,

1985), and photography, in turn, has come to shape not only what we now understand as portraiture but also the individual and his or her relation to consciousness, memory and embodiment.

The emergence and popularisation of the photographic portrait took place in the middle and the second half of the nineteenth century and took on a broad cultural significance within a wider currency of contemporary images, in which the traditions of oil portraiture and the inventions of journalistic caricature were both of weight (Berger, 1980; Cardinal, 1992). In relation to the first of these, it has often been pointed out that the photographic portrait was employed to extend and popularise the function of the ceremonial presentation of the self which had been developed by the bourgeoisie in oil portraiture. So, for example, in 1854 André Adolphe-Eugène Disdéri became the proud owner of a patent of the *carte-de-visite* photograph (the name alludes to the photograph's similarity in size to a common visiting card: it was a paper print pasted on a mount measuring 4 × 2.5 inches). To take these small portraits, Disdéri first made a wet-plate negative with a special camera that had four lenses and a plateholder that could be slid from side to side. Four exposures were made on each half of the plate; thus eight negatives could be taken on one sheet. A single print from this negative could then be cut up into eight separate portraits. By the following year, Disdéri, had a team of no less than seventy-seven assistants, and was running a quasi-industrial operation with fixed poses and props. To accommodate card photographs of relatives, friends and celebrities, elaborately bound albums were introduced around 1860. The cards, of uniform size, were slipped into cut-out openings. Through these devices, the family album was made an ordinary possession and the portrait was made available as a commonplace document of identity, extending the social availability of the representation of self developed in oil portraiture.

However, while the influence of oil portraiture on the development of photographic portraiture should not be under-estimated, it is also important to point out the significance of caricature in the visual realism of the self that was emerging. Indeed, Cardinal argues that the practice of the *portrait-chargé*, a portrait sketch possessing an extra dose of verve and emphasis, 'formed the supportive context wherein, as technology advanced, the photographic portrait would discover its rationale and its characteristic idiom' (1992: 7). He identifies a complex mix of realism and allegorical caricature in the early stages of the development of the photographic portrait, a mix which has remained throughout its history (and will be explored in its contemporary manifestation through a consideration of cartoons in chapter 7).

And this history has had ambivalent implications for the representation of the individual in the photographic portrait. On the one hand, as John Tagg has noted,

> To 'have one's portrait done' was one of the symbolic acts by which individuals from the rising social classes made their ascent visible to themselves and others, and classed themselves amongst those who enjoyed social status.
>
> (1988: 37)

On the other, as Sekula records, from its beginnings, photography was recognised as a 'machine for providing small doses of happiness on a mass scale':

> Thus the photographic portrait in particular was welcomed as a socially ameliorative as well as a socially repressive instrument. Jane Welsh Carlyle voiced characteristic hopes in 1859, when she described inexpensive portrait photography as a social palliative:
>
> > Blessed be the inventor of photography. I set him even above the inventor of chloroform! It has given more positive pleasure to poor suffering humanity than anything that has been 'cast up' in my time . . . – this art, by which even the poor can possess themselves of tolerable likenesses of their absent dear ones.
>
> (1986: 8)

More generally, through the multiple uses of photography to document the human self, the very distinctions between suffering and pleasure, discipline and comfort, surveillance and self-expression, have come to be refigured. In what follows, the implications of photography for the self-identity of the individual will be explored by looking at this refiguring, with a focus on how these distinctions have been tied to the growth of other technologies for the mapping of human difference.

THE INDIVIDUAL AND THE HUMAN TYPE

As the quotation from Tagg above makes clear, at the same time that the honorific portrait tradition was giving 'positive pleasure' to the masses, it was also being adopted in medical, legal and administrative procedures 'to establish and delimit the terrain of the *other*, to define both the *generalized look* – the typology – and the *contingent instance* of deviance and social pathology' (Sekula, 1986: 7; Tagg, 1988). These procedures drew on the emergent sciences of phrenology and physiognomy. In claiming to provide a means of interpreting inner character from outward signs, these sciences promised a way of making sense in a social world where interaction was increasingly made through anonymised market transactions. Physiognomy, for example, promised to reveal the secrets of the individual; it promoted the belief that the surface of the body, and especially the face and head, bore the outward signs of inner character. It proceeded by means of the analytic isolation of the anatomic features of the head and face – forehead, eyes, ears, nose, chin, and so on – and the assignment of a significance to each. 'Character' was estimated through a linked series of these readings.

Significantly, however, this interpretive process required that distinctive individual features be read in conformity to a *type*. Photography appeared to promise to provide the evidence for such readings, and offered a documentary basis for formulating types in relation to which difference could acquire meaning as variation. Sekula writes,

> Here was a method for quickly assessing the character of strangers in the

> dangerous and congested spaces of the nineteenth-century city. Here was a gauge of the intentions and capabilities of the other.
>
> (1986: 12)

Indeed, Sekula argues that it is as a consequence of the application of these techniques that it becomes possible to identify a 'generalized, inclusive *archive*, a *shadow archive*' that encompassed *all* individuals within a social–national body. This all-inclusive archive is understood by Sekula as an enabling fantasy; it contains images of the bodies of the heroes, leaders and moral exemplars of society as well as images of its poor, diseased, insane, criminal, racially 'inferior' and female members. In relation to this shadow archive, every portrait implicitly took its place within a social and moral hierarchy of types or genres, themselves ordered in relation to a construction of humanity. As Sekula writes,

> The *private* moment of sentimental individuation, the look at the frozen gaze-of-the-loved-one, was shadowed by two other more *public* looks: a look up at one's 'betters' and a look down at one's 'inferiors'.
>
> (1986: 10)

In Strathern's terms, these looks were structured by the power of partial analogy and produced a visual rendering of human variation.

As Sekula further points out, these techniques for reading the body's signs contributed to both egalitarian and authoritarian outcomes:

> At the one extreme, the more liberal apologetic promoted the cultivation of a common human understanding of the language of the human body: all of humanity was to be both subject and object of this new egalitarian discourse. At the other extreme – and this was certainly the dominant tendency in actual social practice – a specialized way of knowledge was actually harnessed to the new strategies of social channeling and control that characterized the mental asylum, the penitentiary, and eventually the factory employment office.
>
> (1981: 18)

Similarly, Graham Clarke (1992) claims that it is always necessary to see the individual photographic portrait in relation to a larger, definitive classification to be able to identify the individual it depicts: the individual signifies only in relation to a hierarchy fixed through a series of representative figures or types. However, so Sekula argues, one of the features that distinguished the authoritarian from the egalitarian use of photography was that in the former there was an 'unmistakeable line between the professional reader of the body's signs – the psychiatrist, physiologist, criminologist, or industrial psychologist – and the "diseased", "deviant", or "biologically inferior" object of cure, reform or discipline' (1981: 18).

Nevertheless, underpinning the essential unity of this hierarchical archive, according to Sekula, is the dominance of a single hermeneutic paradigm. He writes,

> To the extent that bourgeois society depends on the systematic defence of property relations, to the extent that the legal basis of the self lies in prop-

> erty rights, every proper portrait of a 'man of genius' made by a 'man of genius' has its counterpart in a mug shot. Both attempts are motivated by an uneasy belief in the category of the individual.
>
> (1981: 16)

Through the operations of this shadow archive, then, photography tied self-identity to the cultural and legal construction of an ideal self modelled in property rights by presuming a particular conception of the individual and the individual's relation to humanity, within which the notion of the possessive individual had a special visibility. The very aesthetic conventions of portraiture enforced the individual's claims to assert his or her ownership of the self. For example, in the portrait, the frame provides a boundary of a discrete and coherent space inhabited by a 'unique' self, whose uniqueness lies in a knowable inscription of inwardness manifest across the body and, especially, the face. Trachtenberg writes,

> The frame designates closure, self-containment, an act which also signifies at the lower levels the alienation of the sitter's appearance from the sitter's being, the reification of pose and look as definitive possession, an apparatus of a piece with other props.
>
> (1992: 190)

In other words, in the confines of the photographic frame, the body, with its standardised pose acting as an expressive vehicle, is typically represented as belonging to the individual, and is as much its external and material possession as the objects which define the photographic space. Thus did the photographic portrait contribute to the necessity of embodiment for recognition as an individual.

Furthermore, as Eric Homberger (1992) notes, at the heart of the photograph portrait is a contract between the subject and the photographer, a contract in which the former negotiates the terms of the latter's appropriation of his or her property rights in the self. The conventional portrait photograph is never accidental, can never be something 'taken' by chance; rather it is necessarily arranged, agreed upon: the subject must consciously *consent* to the occasion. One consequence of this is that an element of self-awareness is an essential element of the contractual portrait. As Homberger writes,

> Portraits of infants and children, of the mentally retarded and of 'natives' – involuntary or culturally unequal portraits – lack that crucial element of self-awareness and understanding.
>
> (1992: 115)

The consumerist aspect of the contract in relation to the commercial portrait photographer makes especially clear the rights of the individual to self-possession created in portraiture: so, for example, the individual has the right to accept or reject the portrait, to purchase it for use for a specific purpose, for no purpose at all, or to throw it away as unacceptable and replace it by another. However, consent or contract does not necessarily imply a congruence of motives or sympathies between subject and photographer, and the subject may perceive the photographer as intent upon a hostile act, of attempting to steal the sitter from him- or herself. Moreover, this intent is not necessary for the sitter to be disconcerted by his or her self-image. Nathaniel Hawthorne wrote after seeing himself in a photographic portrait, 'I was really a little startled at recognising myself so apart from myself', and again, 'There is no such thing as a true portrait. They are all delusions' (quoted in Trachtenberg, 1992: 191). As Trachtenberg remarks, the relationship between likeness and self-awareness in the conventions of portraiture was by no means secure.[1]

In any case, the aesthetic and commercial conventions of the photographic portrait were frequently cross-cut by other epistemological and judicial principles, which on occasion provided the authority for the abandonment of the necessity of the contract and undermined the fiction of the uniqueness of the self as a possession of the individual. These epistemological principles were developed in a wide range of photographic portraiture practices: first, as already mentioned, in close relation with the disciplines of phrenology and physiognomy, and then, second, in conjunction with statistics and government bureaucracies. These principles were institutionalised in the principle of the archive; Sekula writes,

> In structural terms, the archive is both an abstract paradigmatic entity and a concrete institution. In both senses, the archive is a vast substitution set, providing for a relation of general equivalence between images.
>
> (1986: 17)

On the one hand, then, the portrait allowed for scrutiny of the person, the search for and depiction of character. It gave the belief in individualism full play, inviting the view that the individual is first and foremost a personality whose characteristics can be read from facial expression and gesture. On the other hand, however, the portrait might also communicate a type, whether that type be a sub-section of humanity or the whole of humanity itself, and thus provided a technique of individuation. Indeed, by the twentieth century, Cartier-Bresson,

1 The reputation of the photographer Diane Arbus is intimately bound up with these issues. In her own description of the marginal people who are the subjects of some of her best known work, she writes, 'Most people go through life dreading they'll have a traumatic experience. Freaks were born with their trauma. They've already passed their test in life. They're aristocrats' (quoted in Malcolm, 1996: 7). Here is an example of the elevation of trauma as the source of distinction in the era of experimental individualism. The publication of the posthumous book *Untitled* (1996), exclusively devoted to pictures of mentally disabled people at various 'residences', has produced further controversy about the ethics of her photographic practice. Critics explicitly evaluate her work in these terms: so, for example, in her own review of the book, the critic Janet Malcolm writes,

> In a peculiarly angry and completely misguided review of *Untitled* in *The New York Observer*, A. D. Coleman condemned it for violating 'the rights of the mentally challenged'.
>
> (1996: 7)

Malcolm then goes on to argue that Arbus's work is not unethical because in Arbus's images what is revealed is that the 'simple-minded' are also the 'pure-hearted: they will not betray themselves, because they have nothing to betray' (1996: 8).

for example, claims that portraits 'enable us to trace the sameness of man' (quoted in Lutz and Collins, 1993: 97). The portrait, then, has two faces: it individualises by highlighting the inner self or personality and yet constantly threatens individuation, the absorption of the individual into a taxonomic schema of humanity, the 'sameness of man'.

This oscillation between the individual and the social or natural type and their relation to human variation was at issue from very early in the use of photography in portraiture in both Europe and North America. So, for example, in the first American treatise on photography, *The Camera and the Pencil* (1864), the portrait maker Marcus Aurelius Root both spoke of photography as the supreme medium for achieving a unique likeness of an individual and advocated the adoption of conventions to indicate social roles or types. With regard to posing, for example, he suggested that those with primarily sedentary and private roles, such as poets and historians, should be photographed in a seated position, while 'statesmen, lawyers, clergymen, and public figures generally, should be taken in a standing posture' (quoted in Gidley, 1992: 139). At about the same time, Disdéri was also employing a set of practical conventions to depict types such as 'The Actor', 'The Painter', and so on. Pedagogic guides for both sitters and photographers were widely available. One example of these guides is a pamphlet written by Edward L. Wilson, permanent secretary of the American National Photographic Association, in 1871. In this guide, Wilson sought to establish the professional authority of the photographer in the minds of the potential subject:

> [The photographer] is entitled to the same respect and consideration from you as your minister, your physician or your lawyer, and it is just as essential that he should have *rules* for the best government of his establishment as it is for anyone else whom you patronize, consequently you should be quite as unwilling to trespass upon such reasonable regulations as he may make as you would apply fly-blister when your physician orders you to take soothing syrup.
>
> (Wilson, 1980: 129)

More generally, the guides prescribed costume and lighting ('The best materials to wear, for ladies, are such as will fold or drape nicely' [Wilson, 1980: 131]), studio props and bodily and facial expression ('Let your photographer pose and arrange you. He is responsible and will do his best' [1980: 133]), lacing their texts with citations from Lataver and Sir Charles Bell. According to Trachtenberg, in a comment which highlights the continuing influence of the caricature, these guides provided 'formulas for the *imitation* of inwardness, and resulted in stereotyped poses and in caricature, the underside of the bourgeois fetish of "character"' (1992: 189).

VARIATION IN THE REPRESENTATION OF THE INDIVIDUAL

The nature of the relationships of representation between the individual and the type developed in photographic convention is brilliantly described by Sekula in

'The body and the archive' (1986). He suggests that there have been two models of photographic meaning at work within the paradigm of visual or optical realism that underpinned the development of this archival *episteme*; these two models can be seen as exemplary instances of partial analogy. The first is the 'realist' approach, by which Sekula means the philosophical realism that insists upon the truth of general propositions, on the reality of species and types. The second approach is characterised as nominalist, that is, an approach which denies the reality of generic categories as anything other than mental constructs. He argues that these two approaches were variously combined in the positivist attempts of the nineteenth century to define and regulate social deviance by means of statistical and visual *variation* from the central conceptual category of social statistics, the notion of 'the average man'. They are evident in, on the one hand, the techniques of criminology, which hunted 'the' criminal body, and, on the other, criminalistics, which hunted 'this' or 'that' criminal body.

In the first, epitomised by Galton, the inferential reading of individual cases was the basis of establishing the reality of types, while in the second, represented by Bertillon among others, the type existed only as a means for refining the description of individuality. Sekula writes,

> Bertillon's nominalist system of identification and Galton's essentialist typology constitute not only the two poles of positivist attempts to regulate social deviance by means of photography, but also the two poles of these attempts to regulate the semantic traffic in photographs. Bertillon sought to embed the photograph in the archive. Galton sought to embed the archive in the photograph.
>
> (1986: 55)

In both, however, the power of partial analogy was made visible as variation.

Two inter-related axes of this variation were provided by the overarching orderings of time and space that organised the notion of the evolutionary development of humankind. These axes were especially clear in understandings of 'race' and culture. Under the ethnocentric assumption that the emergence of European cultures marked the pinnacle of human evolution, nineteenth-century white Euro-Americans speculated about explanations for the difference between their own cultures and that of others. Some commentators believed that other cultures had evolved along lines similar to those of European cultures, but had regressed to a level of 'savagery' according to the principles of physical and moral 'degeneration' after the 'fall'. Others believed that non-European cultures, by virtue of their supposed biological inferiority, simply evolved more slowly than whites. Ethnologists and ethnographers of the turn of the century tended towards the latter view, and incorporated it as a central premise in formulating their approach. So, for example, early ethnologists of the native American Indians theorised that change in Indian cultures was so slow as to be imperceptible. In his study of the photographer Edward Curtis, who sought to document 'the vanishing race', Lyman suggests that the fact that Indian cultures *had* changed since contact with whites was explained away in the following manner:

> Indians had changed since contact with Whites because of something – apparently due to White superiority – that made them acculturate or accept aspects of White culture.
>
> To the extent that they acculturated, Indians lost that vague quality of 'Indianness', in effect became less 'Indian'.
>
> Thus when Indians changed, they were no longer Indians, and the fallacy that Indian culture did not change remained sacrosanct.
>
> (1982: 50)

Lyman suggests that it was from this circular reasoning that the concept of the 'ethnographic present' emerged. Under this concept, particular cultures were studied in the context of the time when their ethnicity was thought to have last existed in a 'pure' form. In the early days of ethnology, this generally meant that researchers attempted to study Indian cultures in terms of what they were – or rather what they were *imagined* to have been – prior to contact with white peoples.

And photography was an important part of this imagining, not least as a consequence of the congruence between the photograph's defining tense of 'this will have been' and the anthropological nostalgia at work here; so, for example, Curtis retrospectively described his own project as an attempt to create 'a comprehensive and permanent record of all the important tribes . . . that still retain to a considerable degree their primitive customs and traditions' (quoted in Lyman, 1982: 51). And this aim was implicit in the conventions of the pictorialist genre studies of which *The North American Indian* is a famous early example. One volume opens with 'The Vanishing Race – Navaho', a nostalgic pictorial. In his caption to this image, Curtis described its intent in the following terms:

> The thought which this picture is meant to convey is that Indians as a race, already shorn of their tribal strength and stripped of their primitive dress, are passing into the darkness of an unknown future. Feeling that the picture expresses so much of the thought that inspired the entire work, the author has chosen it as the first of the series.
>
> (Quoted in Lyman, 1982: 79)

The shadow archive can thus be seen to be characterised by an evolutionary or natural ordering in time as well as a hierarchy in social space. It was how partial analogies, and the hierarchical classifications of genre or type to which they gave rise – specifically, what Anne McClintock (1995) describes as the triangulated analogy of race, class and gender – were made visible.

In exploring this triangulated analogy, McClintock points to the importance of the metaphor of the family and its use as 'a single genesis narrative for global history' (1995: 44). She suggests that the power and importance of the family trope – in, for example, the figure of the family tree and the classificatory device of 'the family of man' – was twofold. First, the family offered a figure for sanctioning social hierarchy within a putative organic unity of interests; because the subordination of woman to man and child to adult were deemed natural facts, the depiction of other forms of hierarchy in familial terms legitimated them as natural. Second, the family offered a trope for figuring historical time as progress or civilisation: 'Projecting the family image onto national and imperial progress enabled what was often murderously violent change to be legitimated as the progressive unfolding of natural decree' (1995: 45). Third, it might be added, the family also provided and continues to provide a powerful matrix within which the uniqueness of the individual – absent in the descriptions of Indian Americans above – has been represented.

This complex and highly nuanced understanding of the relationship of the individual and the social and natural types of race, gender and class is developed further during the first part of the twentieth century, although it is the social typology which begins to predominate. This is evident, for example, in the work of the German photographer August Sander, who claimed that 'the photographer with his camera can grasp the physiognomic image of his time' (quoted in Clarke, 1992: 71). His two best-known projects, 'Face of Our Time' and 'Citizens of the Twentieth Century', are intended to illustrate his claim that 'it is possible to record the historical physiognomic image of a whole generation and . . . to make that image speak in photographs' (quoted in Clarke, 1992: 71). In a radio talk in 1931, Sander explains the significance of his concern with physiognomy:

> Even the most isolated Bushman could understand a photograph of the heavens – whether it showed the sun or the moon or the constellations. In biology, in the animal and plant world, the photograph as picture language can communicate without the help of sound. But the field in which photography has so great a power of expression that language can never approach, is physiognomy.
>
> (Quoted in Sekula, 1981: 17–18)

Sander expresses here the common claim that the language of photography is universal, but with a special emphasis on the affinity between physiognomy and the universality of its language. In both of his major projects, however, each individual portrait is located in relation to a *social* order codified by the camera, that is, a biological anatomy of the collective body is subordinated to a social anatomy:

> The individual is viewed as a representative figure (of a group, of a profession, of a class) and figures are 'fixed' amidst a series of complex social codes. Identity is, therefore, insistently public.
>
> (Clarke, 1992: 71–72)

As Sander himself claimed, 'photography is like a mosaic that becomes a *synthesis* only when it is presented en masse' (quoted in Clarke, 1992: 71; my emphasis). Sander's own commitments were thus to a social, rather than a biological racial, typology, and he refused to link his belief in physiognomic science to biological determinism, preferring to construct a sociologically extended variant of formal portraiture.[2]

2 As Sekula notes, however, this impulse can be seen as part of the humanisation of the other that has been so central to modern projects of domination.

Moreover, typically, according to Clarke, while Sander sought to represent social types, he also celebrated the unique individual, in part by mobilising the (gendered) distinction between private and public in his portraiture.[3] So, even as the social typology displaced the natural, it was cross-cut by the unpredictable variation of the unique individual. Figures are consistently photographed in relation to their place within a social order, and grouped according to a vertical scale of significance, including, for example, The Farmer, The Woman, The Professions, The Artist, and so on. Yet the ways in which the subjects inhabit the space and the frame of the photograph, Clarke suggests, invokes a psychological register of an inner self which disturbs the authority of the social register of the image.

Indeed, Clarke argues that while a typology of the body as social index is basic to Sander's complex code of identity, what is important is that posture and stance reflect part of a larger mapping of the body in relation to *both* public status and inner self-confidence. Hands especially are key integers of the internal contradictoriness of social meaning. So, for example, in relation to the type 'small town citizens', hands are represented as accoutrements: 'The hand strikes a pose, a part of a larger pantomime in a series of gestures that seek an image of social importance' (Clarke, 1992: 78). In these representations, according to Clarke, both the aspiration to social status and the anguished embarrassment that goes along with it are made visible. Hands are not simply a part of the body but simultaneously a mark of the success or failure of a process of self-control and mastery. More widely, visual representations of the body – and especially the face – become 'a sign of a disquieting continuum between the somatic and the social' (Crary, 1994: 35).

THE INDIVIDUAL AND THE NUMBER

Photography can thus be seen as both the instrument and the object of a comparative taxonomy that seeks to encompass the entire range of human variation. It provides the visual evidence for the creation of a shadow archive as 'an encyclopedic repository of exchangeable images' (Sekula, 1986: 17), offering the possibility of a standard physiognomic gauge. For example, the French sociologist Gabriel Tardé argued in 1883 that 'a statistical bureau might be compared to an eye or ear', claiming further that

3 Gasché records Benjamin's view of Sander's photographs and Russian cinema in the following terms:

> if Benjamin celebrates the human face in these films or photographs, it is precisely because it is no longer auratic. The human face that appears on film 'with new and immeasurable significance . . . [is] no longer a portrait' he writes. It is the 'anonymous physiognomy' of people 'who have no use for their photographs'. No longer representative portraits, these pictures of human faces exhibit, on the contrary, the social provenance, role and function of the pictured, and train the beholder 'to read facial types', the ability for which, according to Benjamin, is 'of vital importance' given the 'sudden shifts of power such as are now overdue in society'.
>
> (1994: 193)

> each of our senses gives us, in its own way and from its special point of view, the statistics of the external world. Their characteristic sensations are in a certain way their special graphical tables. Every sensation . . . is only a number.
>
> (Quoted in Sekula, 1986: 24)

However, as Sekula notes, this archival promise of the Number was frustrated by the 'messy contingency' of the photograph and the sheer quantity of images. The problem of classification was enormous. The newly created entity of the average man might be effectively or comprehensively visualised, but the techniques of this visualisation created the conditions for new kinds of individuality and new modes of self-possession which raised problems of interpretation and classification.

So, for example, Tardé's model of individuality assumed an essential internal narrative coherence of the self: 'Identity is the permanence of the person, it is the personality looked at from the point of view of its duration' (Tardé, quoted in Sekula, 1986: 25). This model was also at work in Bertillon's procedures for the identification of *repeat* offenders, that is, criminals who were considered 'habitual' or 'professional' in their deviant behaviour:

> [The] task is always the same: to preserve a sufficient record of a personality to be able to *identify* the present description with one which may be presented at some future time. From this point of view signalment [the name given to Bertillon's system] is the best instrument for the *proof of recidivation*, which necessarily implies the *proof of identity*.
>
> (Bertillon, quoted in Sekula, 1986: 25)

However, this proof of identity was hard to come by, most obviously because of the professional criminal's mastery of disguises, false identities, multiple biographies and alibis. For Bertillon such problems could be circumvented by a series of procedures including the recording of eleven bodily measurements and the use of photographic portraits, in a judicial context in which consent was not required and self-awareness a positive hindrance. In relation to these portraits, Bertillon argued for an aesthetically 'neutral' standard of representation:

> In commercial and artistic portraits, questions of fashion and taste are all important. Judicial photography, liberated from these considerations, allows us to look at the problem from a more simple point of view: which pose is theoretically best for such and such a case?
>
> (Quoted in Sekula, 1986: 30)

To this end, he insisted upon the use of a standard focal length, even and consistent lighting, and a fixed distance between the camera and the sitter. A profile view was advocated to cancel the contingency of expression or the manipulation of self-understanding, while a frontal view was also taken on the grounds that it was more likely to be recognisable within the other, less systematised departments of police work. In these and other ways, the power of the image was framed to fit the requirements of a still predominantly narratively constituted conception of self-identity.

Sekula argues the classification of the criminal body involved a 'massive campaign of *inscription*, a transformation of the body's signs into a *text*, a text which pared verbal description down to a denotative shorthand, which was then linked to a numerical series' (1986: 33). The development of this set of photographic and statistical techniques for the textualisation of the body prepared the ground for the adoption of such techniques more generally, including the use of fingerprinting, although here the body did not have to be circumscribed, since the key to identity could be found in the merest trace of the body's tactile presence. Over time, Sekula claims, the adoption of such techniques led to the view that the individual only existed *as an individual* by being identified. He writes, 'Individuality as such had no meaning. Viewed "objectively", the self occupied a position that was wholly relative' (1986: 34). This is one aspect of the paradox which Abercrombie *et al.* and Strathern identify, in which the individual is itself displaced through the intensification of the 'Discovery of the Individual'.

At the same time, the representation of the relationship between the individual and the type in the shadow archive necessarily involved an adjudication of the terms of individual agency and responsibility for actions, through a mediation of the relationship between individual, society and nature. So, for example, according to Sekula, Tardé advanced a notion of 'criminal responsibility' based upon the continuity of individual identity within a shared social milieu, a milieu of 'social similarity'. This was in opposition to the biological determinism of the 'Italian school' of criminal anthroplogy, which centred on the anatomist–craniometrician Cesare Lombroso's quasi-Darwinian theory of the criminal as an 'atavistic being who reproduces in his person the ferocious instincts of primitive humanity and the inferior animals' (quoted in Sekula, 1986: 37). Within the environmentalist approach, there were a range of positions. Interestingly, Tardé insisted that crime was a profession that proliferated through channels of *imitative* behaviour, while others argued that the criminal suffered more than the non-criminal from the negative effects of urbanism.

In contrast, Galton had more in common with the Italian school of criminal anthropology and biological determinism in general. He argued that it was impossible to classify individuals by measuring differences between them; instead, he was more interested in identifying types. The technique of composite imagery was developed to this end (see Figure 3.1). Drawing on Herbert Spencer's prior proposal for a process of superimposition, Galton sought to mobilise the capacity of the mind to construct generic images from sense data. According to Sekula,

> Galton fabricated his composites by a process of successive registration and exposure of portraits in front of a copy camera holding a single plate. Each successive image was given a fractional exposure based on the inverse of the total number of images in the sample . . . . Thus, individual distinctive features, features that were unshared and idiosyncratic, faded away into the night of underexposure. What remained was the blurred, nervous configuration of those features that were held in common throughout the sample.
>
> (1986: 47)

Galton claimed that these 'pictorial statistics' constituted legitimate averages, and that the 'blur of the outlines' could be used to measure 'the tendency of individuals to deviate from the central type' (quoted in Sekula, 1986: 47–48). Furthermore, Galton drew analogies between the images produced by his optical process and 'mental images', which he claimed consisted of 'blended memories' or 'cumulative ideas'. He argued that his composites refuted nominalist approaches to the human sciences, demonstrating with certainty the reality of distinct human types. As Sekula notes, this 'amounted to an essentialist physical anthropology of race' (1986: 51).

What is significant for the argument being developed here is that in both the nominalist and the essentialist approaches of Bertillon and Galton, the indi-

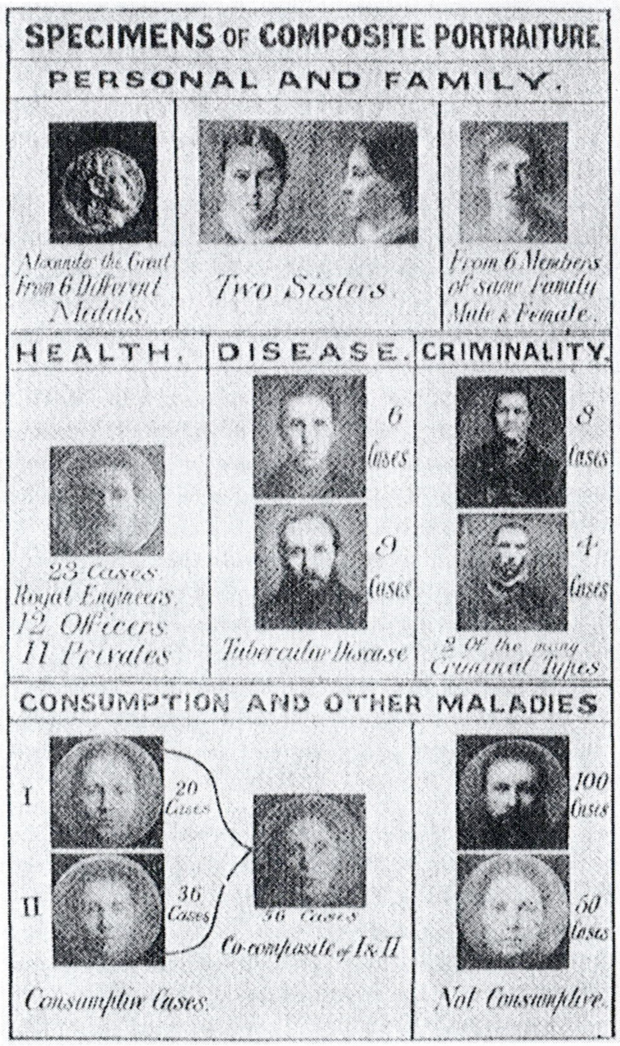

Figure 3.1 Composite portraiture by Sir Francis Galton

vidual's identity is held to be constituted in relation to either a socially or a biologically based type or genre. That is, in Strathern's terms, via the type or genre of classification, the individual is defined in terms of human variation through partial analogy to either society and/or nature. This process of partial analogy was the mechanism through which the responsibility for an individual's actions was divided and distributed by the law between the individual, society and nature. Moreover, as Sekula notes, this mutual definition was achieved, in part, through the use of photography, that is, photography, as a set of techniques of representation, was the medium through which partial analogies were calibrated, and thus, in part, the medium for the allocation of responsibility, and the mechanism by which the judgement of the innocence or guilt of the individual was reached.

However, as Sekula goes on to comment, a number of different photographic aesthetic principles were employed to order the semantic traffic in photographs. He writes,

> Bertillon, in taming the photograph by subordinating it to the verbal text of the *portrait parlé*, remained wedded to an *indexical* order of meaning. The photograph was nothing more than the physical *trace* of its contingent instance. Galton, in seeking the apotheosis of the optical, attempted to elevate the indexical photographic composite to the level of the *symbolic*, thus expressing a *general law* through the accretion of contingent instances.
>
> (1986: 55)

These possible uses of photography, that is, the use of photography as report or document or as symbol or metaphor, are seen by Sekula (1975, 1981) to be a consequence of photography's uneasy positioning between art and science. He writes,

> Photography is haunted by two chattering ghosts: that of bourgeois science and that of bourgeois art. The first goes on about the truth of appearances, about the world reduced to a positive ensemble of facts, to a constellation of knowable and possessable objects. The second specter offers us a reconstructed subject in the luminous person of the artist.
>
> (1981: 15)

However, he suggests that there is an underlying affinity between these two understandings. So in many photographic practices, a positivist scientism is yoked with a romantic metaphysics; while they might appear opposed, the 'ultimate goal of abstraction' appears in both, in one in positivist form while in the other in metaphysical and spiritualist guise.[4] Sekula asserts,

4 This oscillation between the use of the photograph as document and as symbol is also to be found in Curtis's photographic record of 'the vanishing tribe', which was explicitly intended to combine art with science. So, for example, in the general introduction to *The North American Indian*, Curtis wrote,

> Rather than being designed for mere embellishment, the photographs are each an illustration of an Indian character or of some vital phase of his existence. Yet the fact the Indian and his surroundings lend themselves to artistic treatment has not been lost sight of, for in his country one may treat limitless subjects of an aesthetic character without in any way doing injustice to scientific accuracy or neglecting the homelier phases of aboriginal life.
>
> (Quoted in Lyman, 1982: 62)

> both modern science and modernist art tend to end up worshipping in floating cathedrals of formal, abstract, mathematical relations and 'laws'.
> (1981: 16)

And, to illustrate the romanticism implicit in even the most formalistic applications of the photograph as document, Sekula provides a comment from Bertillon in which he declares that the problem of classifying the criminal is, 'at bottom', the same as that which forms 'the basis of the everlasting popular melodrama about lost, exchanged and recovered children' (quoted in Sekula, 1986: 34).

This romanticism continues to be a characteristic of photography during the course of the twentieth century, and is thrown into relief in a modernist aesthetic discourse, in which photographs are invested with a power that transcends the perceptual. In the work of the Photo-Secession group,[5] for instance, photographs are ascribed a *metonymic* power (as an encoding of the experience of the photographer, a phenomenonological equivalent of the photographer-being-in-that-place) that is so intense that it passes into *metaphor*. Consider, for example, the following acount of the taking of a photograph by Alfred Stieglitz, early in his career (actually before the Secession group had been established), by the editor of the magazine in which it appeared in 1888:

> The author of this very interesting photograph is well known as an excellent amateur. He has informed us that for some time he intended to capture by photography a gathering storm – a sight at once overpowering and of great potential beauty. One afternoon in August, 1887, he was sitting on the veranda of the place where he was staying in Bellagio and admiring in a half-doze the majesty of the beautiful lake. He did not notice that the sky was darkening and black clouds were gathering all around. A sudden clap of thunder woke him up. He was astonished by the change in scenery, and at once decided not to let the opportunity go by. He jumped up, got his camera, and quickly made an exposure. He used an azalin plate with an Aurantia yellow filter and exposed for a minute and half. The plate was developed in pyrogallol and to his delight Mr. Stieglitz obtained exactly what he wanted. Unfortunately, the accompanying illustration does not faithfully reproduce the splendor of the moment. All the atmospheric effect is lost; the picture is neither as brilliant, nor as rich, as the original platinum print made directly from the negative.
> (Quoted in Newhall, 1980: 168)

While the reproduction is deemed a failure, it is judged that in a successful photograph the faith of the viewer in the power of the image is so intense that the indexical level of the image will be displaced or denied and the claim for meaning made at the level of abstraction. This is a faith which uses from a

5 This was a group set up by the photographer Alfred Stieglitz at the turn of the century in New York to further the artistic recognition of pictorial photography. It was especially associated with the introduction of European modernism to the USA. The name 'Secession' was adopted because of its use by societies of avant-garde artists in Germany and Austria to denote their independence of the academic establishment.

photograph that which is indexical but interprets it in terms of a symbolism that is seen to exist on a conceptual level. It is in this emergent notion of form that the principle of the cause in the scientific experiment and the individually authorised arbitrariness of artistic expression came to be linked in photography,[6] although here, as in the related debates concerning the legal status of the photograph as a work of art, this combination was not easily held together (Edelman, 1979; Coombe, 1991; Saunders, 1992; Lury, 1993).

In relation to the use of photography in the modernist art movements that followed soon after, Sekula claims:

> All specificity except the specificity of form is pared away from the photograph until it stands transformed into an abstraction. . . . The romantic artist's compulsion to achieve 'the condition of music' is a desire to abandon all contextual reference and to convey meaning by virtue of a metaphorical substitution. In photography this compulsion requires an incredible denial of the image's status as report. The final outcome of this denial is [that the photograph] is reduced to an arrangement of tones. The gray scale, ranging from full white to full black, stands as a sort of phonological carrier system for a vague prelinguistic scale of affect.
>
> (1975: 42)

The use of photography as an arrangement of tones is, however, now no longer merely the province of photography-as-art, but is visible in contemporary commercial uses of photography, including the use of colour to represent the individual and to map human difference as diversity (rather than variation) in the recent advertising campaigns by Benetton, a fashion clothing company.

PAINTING BY NUMBERS

Before discussing these campaigns, however, I will consider 'The Family of Man', the 1955 photo-exhibition at the Museum of Modern Art in New York which collected together two million photographs from which 503 images were selected to represent humanity. Of this exhibition, which is an infamous representative in the tradition of mapping human variation outlined here,[7] Barthes writes,

6 Some indication of how the relationship between the claims of art and science on photography may be reconciled in more or less highbrow notions of form is elegantly elaborated by Montgomery in his discussion of the magazine *National Geographic*. In a description of how the natural world is depicted in *National Geographic*, he writes,

> The visibility of the natural world is therefore made to combine what is iconic with what is instrumental: every moment, every glance is as ordered into existence itself, planned, demanded, accomplished and offered. Beyond the most obvious meanings, this is a universe wholly without complexity and depth. It never lacks a centre, and thus a promise. Such an infinity of perfected moments, imposed upon the world, acts to recreate it in the image of a Science that will one day know everything.
>
> (1995: 25)

7 The viewing statistics associated with the exhibition are well documented and are part of its fame:

⇒

> the difference between human morphologies is asserted, exoticism is inherently stressed, the infinite variations of the species, the diversity in skins, skulls and customs are made manifest, the image of Babel is complacently projected over that of the world. Then, from this pluralism, a type of unity is magically produced: man is born, works, laughs and dies everywhere in the same way; and if there still remains in these actions some ethnic peculiarity, at least one hints that there is underlying each one an identical 'nature', that their diversity is only formal and does not belie the existence of a common mould.
>
> (1972: 100)

In his introduction to the book of the exhibition, the photographer and organiser Edward Steichen (1993) situates the exhibition in the practice of what he calls 'man explaining man to man'. Barthes seeks to explicate the terms of this explanation, and suggests that it is an instance of classical humanism which postulates that beneath veneers of difference one quickly reaches 'the solid rock of a universal human nature'. Barthes contends, however, that some people are represented without history; they are seated in the natural rather than the cultural realm, and have only a morphology, the surface of an identity, rather than a trajectory. In contrast to this, he hopes that a progressive humanism will constantly examine what is purported to be natural and universal 'in order to discover History there, and at last to establish Nature itself as historical'. In this way, ironically, Barthes himself can be seen to be in the tradition represented by Sander, replacing the natural body with a socio-historical anatomy.

Certainly, 'The Family of Man' represents the natural in a particular way through its adoption of 'life' as its organising principle, but this representation is both less and more than historical, both less and more than a teleological narrative, both less and more than a partial analogy. The exhibition, I suggest, stands at a threshold between the representation of human difference as *variation* and as *diversity*, of generic and genetic 'man'. The vital force of life is represented here, as in many other popular scientific discourses, in a mode derived from Darwinian theories of evolution, as 'an underlying connectedness of all living things' (Franklin, 1995: 4). This sense of life is widely accepted as a foundational term in the modern life sciences, yet life does not exist as a thing, as something either visible or tangible. Rather, so Sarah Franklin claims, 'Only its traces are accessible, through the forms in which life

> Between 1955 and 1962 'The Family of Man' was on the move. In several international editions it appeared in thirty-eight countries and was seen by over 9 million people. . . . The exhibition had made ninety-one stops in the thirty-eight countries visited by 1962. In Japan, 621,000 people saw one of the three versions, including 28,700 during a two-week stay in Hiroshima in October 1956. Over 1.5 million Indians filed past the photographs in the subcontinent. The stop in Belgrade brought 275,000, more than half the population of the city, to 'The Family of Man'. Head counts in the United States were similarly impressive: 37,600 in Minneapolis, 116,214 in Dallas, 113,991 in Cleveland, and a whopping 311,686 at the Museum of Science and Industry in Chicago.
>
> (Sandeen, 1995: 95, 96)

manifests itself' (1995: 5). The photographic image is mobilised in 'The Family of Man' as one such trace.[8]

In 'The Family of Man' the connectedness of life itself is represented through a number of devices.[9] These include the juxtaposition of images to invite analogies between the human and the natural; for example, between the figure and the landscape, the human face and the earth's crags and contours, and the weather and the expressions which cross the human visage. In his prologue to the book of the exhibition, Carl Sandburg reinforces this mode of interpretation:

> Often the faces speak what words can never say. . . . Some of them are worth a long look now and deep contemplation later. Faces betokening a serene blue sky or faces dark with storm winds and lashing night rain.
>
> (1993: 5)

The device that structures the book as a *cyclical* narrative, however, is that of the life-cycle, a trope that positions the origins of each life form in relation to the lives of those preceding it, the interconnectedness of the generations underscoring the inter-relation of life itself (Franklin, 1995: 12, *passim*).

In the book of the exhibition,[10] the photographs that occupy the first double spread introduced by one of the sayings, anecdotes or quotations which punctuate the text are, on the left, a full-page image of a river running through a mist-enshrouded valley, and on the bottom half of the right-hand page, a picture of an embracing couple (a man and a woman), lying on the ground, the curves of their bodies creating and shadowing the gap between them (see Figure 3.2). The valley is closed off in the background of the first image as the river disappears: its route is diverted by a massif of hills. The gap between the couple's bodies is blocked too, but this time in the foreground of the image, as each of the couple's arms reach over the other's body. The images are, then, in a formal sense, (vertically) reversed images of each other. In both cases, however, the image is a landscape of life, and the accompanying quotation from James Joyce confirms their originating status:

8 Edward Steichen himself described his intention in putting together 'The Family of Man' in the following terms: 'instead of making pretty pictures or technically perfect pictures, we are going out to get life' (quoted in Sandeen, 1995: 2). The photographer Barbara Morgan described the exhibition as if it were a life form itself: 'The scale shift from small-to-large, large-to-small, is a breathing rhythm – the systole and diastole of the organism – [and] keeps interest pulsing' (quoted in Sandeen, 1995: 51).

9 The romantic artist's compulsion to achieve 'the condition of music' noted by Sekula above provides one motivation for one such connecting device: the photograph of a Peruvian flute player that was displayed at several stations in the exhibition. It is described by Sandeen as the exhibition's 'missing accompaniment' (1995: 45).

10 In his study of 'The Family of Man' in its context of origin, 1950s America, Eric Sandeen (1995) points out that the book offers a very different experience to that provided by the exhibition. He points, in particular, to Steichen's use of exhibition techniques which exploited peripheral vision, three-dimensional collage and engineered perspectives to create an overwhelming effect on the viewer, as well as recognising that individuals had some degree of freedom of movement around the exhibition space. Unfortunately, I have only been able to view the book.

> . . . and then I asked him with my eyes to ask again yes
> and then he asked me would I yes . . .
> and first I put my arms around him yes
> and drew him down to me so he could feel my breasts all perfume yes
> and his heart was going like mad
> and yes I said yes I will Yes
>
> (Steichen, 1993: 7)

The natural crevice both images represent is the site of the origin of life, of positivity.

This double-page spread also opens the first section of images which are of 'the kiss' as a gesture of affirmation of life: in the images that follow, the kiss is represented as the human gesture which says 'yes', consents not just to love, but to life itself:

> Everywhere is love and love-making, weddings and babies from generation to generation keeping the Family of Man alive and continuing.
>
> (Sandburg, 1993: 4)

The kiss inaugurates the cycle of life, leading to sections on weddings, pregnancy and birth, in which an image of a newly born baby is accompanied by a quotation from Scriabin, 'The universe resounds with the joyful cry I am' (Steichen, 1993: 23). Sandburg uses this quotation to begin the prologue to the book, claiming that

> The first cry of a newborn baby in Chicago or Zamboango, in Amsterdam or Rangoon, has the same pitch and key, each saying, 'I am! I have come through! I belong! I am a member of the Family.'
>
> (1993: 4)

This assertion of the universality of the human is achieved here and elsewhere in the exhibition through the recognition and transcendence of natural and social difference (in this case, the difference of race, nation and place but not that of gender[11]). Time and time again, a moment in the life-cycle is represented through images of peoples who are visibly different, but who nevertheless are united by their shared participation in the cycle of life. So, to take one of the first examples, the mother–child relationship is represented through a vertically ordered series of 'American', 'Siberian' and 'Eskimo' mothers caring for a child, either drawing the baby into their arms, or engaged in a mutually satisfying gaze (Steichen, 1993: 28). The small section that follows, of fathers and

11 Sandeen describes the final stages of the selection of photographs in the following terms:

> Finally, having winnowed the ten thousand down to one thousand, Steichen made a decision: in order to reach the necessary number of five hundred, Wayne Miller was to select pictures having to do with men and men's work; Joan Miller was to make the final selection of photographs pertaining to women and children; Steichen would reserve for himself those pictures addressing larger themes. Such a practical division of labour was as commonsensical to the three as was the gender stereotyping that pervaded the images that they selected. Steichen assumed that the family functioned according to gender-specific roles.
>
> (1995: 45)

sons, leads into a series of the family (including a particularly striking series of an 'Italian', a 'Japanese', an 'African' and an 'American' family[12]), and then, almost indistinguishably, into the family at work on the land, and then on to images of work in urban sites and industrialised cities, to images of unrest, social and political conflict and war. (In this respect, it seems as if 'The Family of Man' follows the 'sociological arc' that orders the internal order of the social groups identified by Sander in 'Citizens of the Twentieth Century'. This begins with the 'earthbound man', moves upwards to the 'artist' and thence descends to the city and a series of increasingly 'marginal' types.) The juxtapositions are sometimes intended to provoke a smile through the naive ambition implied by their comparison, as in the juxtaposition of a picture of a small boy completing a simple sum on a blackboard next to a picture of Albert Einstein, caught with his hand to his mouth, as if in contemplation of a profound problem. On most occasions, however, the comparisons celebrate, with an air of wide-eyed wonder, without cynicism and without guile, the political and cultural differences of peoples across the globe, while ultimately recuperating those differences in the continuous, implacable sweep of the life-cycle. This cycle returns, via a detour in which political conflict and social disharmony are resolved in the representation of democracy embodied in the United Nations assembly ('We, the peoples of United Nations/ Determined to save succeeding generations from the scourge of war . . . '), to representations of childhood and the possibility of another chance, another life. The very last image is of a crashing wave.

What is significant about the representation of human variation in 'The Family of Man' is that the salience of the type is much less evident than in many earlier catalogues of humanity as the meaningfulness of the partial analogy declines. In the place of natural and/or social types, the family, and less visibly, but still notably, the nation, are the preferred intermediary terms, mediating between the individual and humanity. As Sekula argues, the exhibition universalises the bourgeois nuclear family, securing its taken-for-grantedness through the representation of a naturalised life-cycle. In these ways, a globalised utopian family album is created and a family romance is imposed on every corner of the earth in a cyclical narrative. Moreover, the familialism of the exhibition functions metaphorically as well as literally:

> If nothing else The Family of Man was a massive promotion for family photography as well as a celebration of the power of the mass media to represent the whole world in familiar and intimate form.
>
> (Sekula, 1981: 20)

In this way, the nuclear suburban family, which more widely was also increasingly a unit defined as a member of the nation rather than of an ethnic or racial type, provided the ordering principle for a model of a de-socialised and de-naturalised individual identity.

12 At the time, the critic Phoebe Lou Adamo remarked: 'A posed family photograph looks exactly the same whether it's African, Asian or European. The dog may be fat or thin, but the people have identical expressions of slightly apprehensive satisfaction' (quoted in Sandeen, 1995: 52).

Figure 3.2 ' . . . and then I asked him with my eyes to ask again yes'
Photographs: Dmitri Kessel (above) and Ralph Morse (opposite)

Furthermore, the trope of the family is extended to embrace relations between humankind and nature: 'With all beings and all things we shall be as relatives, Sioux Indian' (Steichen, 1993: 55); 'The land is a mother that never dies, Maori' (Steichen, 1993: 63). In these ways, comparison between individuals are not drawn by reference to either social and/or natural types or genres and the time and space of human evolution; instead, the cluster of values associated with the family in Western societies – the private, the domestic, and the emotions – are given symbolic expression through a lyricism of light, shade and tone which, in turn, legitimates the appropriation of these images as a document of life. In the conjoined processes of aestheticisation and emotionalisation, the relations between the individual, the family, the nation and humankind hold together not through the power of partial analogy, but by a process of scaled enclosure, containment, as in a family of Russian dolls, in which each is carried within the next in size in the series.

Significantly, however, this process of enclosure (in which questions of comparison are still relevant, albeit as a simple multiplication of scale) is cross-cut by the process of substitution, operating at the level of the individual.[13] The process of substitution is most clearly made explicit in a quotation attributed to Sophocles which accompanies the image of a soldier lying in a ditch, at the top of which is a rifle, stuck into the ground, some kind of marker in what seems to be no-man's land (Figure 3.3). The quotation, which is one of the few to be printed in white on black, and stands alone in the middle of the page, reads, 'Who is the slayer, who the victim? Speak' (Steichen, 1993: 180). The image which accompanies this question on the next page makes it impossible for the viewer to 'speak', for there is no enemy visible, the rights and wrongs of the conflict are impossible to uncover. (The image is of a soldier killed in the Korean war. This information is not easily ascertained from the minimal details provided for each image.) It seems as if it is not just impossible, but irrelevant, for the viewer to judge who is the aggressor, who the victim, who is the slayer, who the slain, for 'we' are all both.

This image of the soldier follows a series of photographs of pain and suffering, poverty and disease, interspersed with conventional sources of hope, such as religious imagery and the democratic rituals of debate and voting, and more symbolic images of hope, typically sacralised representations of 'human' emotions such as joy, struggle and wonder. Some of the images of people in distress can be located in relation to specific political conflicts, although sometimes, I imagine, only by reference to their captions, but others are simply decontextualised images of pain. Each figure is thus placed within a classification schema or archive within which the decontextualised pain of one individual is no less and no more than the pain of another; one individual can stand in for another in a universalism of painful substitutability.[14] In Sandburg's prologue to

13 Eric Sandeen quotes the critic Minor White's remark that the exhibition was like a Cecil B. DeMille extravaganza (1995: 40).

14 This abstraction from context was anticipated, even planned, by Steichen, who was not especially concerned with the effect of individual photographs, but with the impact of the exhibition as a whole. So, for example, he claims, ⇒

the book of the exhibition he catches the algebra of this emotional symbolism when he describes the exhibition as 'a multiplication table of living breathing human faces' (1993: 5). As Sekula says,

> Suddenly, arithmetic and humanism collide, forced by poetic license into absurd harmony . . . this is the aestheticised job of global accounting.
>
> (1981: 20)

The depiction of dispersed threat implies that the slayer and the slain are both equally at risk, one might stand in for, or substitute, the other, since both are representatives of *life itself* under threat.

However, while some of the quotations suggest that the universality of suffering is a feature of humankind throughout history – 'What region of the earth is not full of our calamities? Virgil' (Steichen, 1993: 150), ' . . . Nothing is real to us but our hunger. Kakuzo Okakura' (Steichen, 1993: 152) – others indicate the specific political context within which this invocation of a universal, substitutable subject, caught in the shadow of incipient disaster, is promoted.[15] The overarching context is that of the threat of nuclear war:

> . . . the best authorities are unanimous in saying that a war with hydrogen bombs is quite likely to put an end to the human race . . . there will be universal death – sudden only for a fortunate minority, but for the majority a slow torture of disease and disintegration . . . Bertrand Russell.
>
> (Steichen, 1993: 179)

(Interestingly, the single photograph from the exhibition that does not appear in the book was its single most important image, that of a hydrogen bomb explosion. It was the only colour photograph in the exhibition.) Yet, hope in the face of this threat is provided by the figure of the heterosexual couple which reappears once again in a series of photographs, and although this time the couples are elderly, the intimacy they share symbolises the intrinsic goodness of the sociability of life. Underneath each of the images is the phrase 'We two form a multitude.' They give way, following the photograph of the United Nations mentioned above and a rather ostentatiously out-of-place image of the lower half

> It is Photography (this medium that was born only a little over a hundred years ago) giving an account of itself. This is what it has done – it has made a record – a portrait of man. Feeling about people the way I do, I feel we have here an article of faith – an antidote to the horror we have been fed from day to day for a number of years.
>
> (Quoted in Sandeen, 1995: 57)

Moreover, just as details concerning the subjects of the photographs were left unclear – for example, it was not felt to be important that viewers should discern that one of the children featured in the triptych beginning the bomb sequence was a survivor of the Hiroshima attack – so also were the names and achievements of photographers. Indeed, the exhibition was perceived in some quarters as an undermining of American modernism in that its authorship clearly lay in the shape of space and the control of the materials – that is, in editorship, rather than the production of individual artworks. As a consequence, 'The Family of Man' has been subject to much criticism, the hostility of which has intensified as time has gone by.

15 Interestingly, the editorial stance of the magazine *National Geographic* has consistently been concerned to show 'The kindly nature of all that is' (quoted in Montgomery, 1995: 14).

Who is the slayer, who the victim? Speak.

Sophocles

Figure 3.3 'Who is the slayer, who the victim? Speak'
Photograph: Raphel Platnick

of a young woman's body, her nakedness half-hidden by a bouquet of flowers, to images of young children again. The life-cycle turns full circle, and another beginning is made possible.

The imagery of global accounting, and with it a decline in the power of the partial analogy and a rise in individual substitutability, is developed and extended in the apocalyptic publicity imagery of the clothing company Benetton.[16] Their use of images from the genres of photodocumentary and news journalism locates these campaigns as a self-conscious development in the tradition of photo-anthropology. These now familiar images – a duck covered in oil, its red eyes staring out from its polluted environment; an AIDS patient at the moment of his death; a black soldier holding a human femur behind his back with a Kalashinikov rifle hanging from his shoulder – show images of life itself, animal and human, in situations of apparent danger. As Back and Quaade note, the 'over-riding theme is the fetishisation of images of abject catastrophe' (1993: 74). The condensed-to-the-moment-of-catastrophe narrative space–time frame of these images disembeds them from their partial locations, their specific social, political and natural contexts (indeed such contexts would appear parochial), and re-embeds them in apocalyptic time, in the context of a planet facing global dangers. As such, they are a visible instantiation of outcontextualisation. The subjects of these images are, as in 'The Family of Man', representatives of a universalised life itself, a life in which types or genres have been superseded. In this case, however, rather than the United Nations, the United Colors of Benetton slogan, the caption they all share is what offers millenarian hope in the face of impending global catastrophe.[17]

The epistemological principle that makes possible the displacement of type or

16 Taussig argues that the capacity of 'mimetic machines' such as advertising 'to pump out contact-sensuosity encased within the spectrality of a commoditized world is nothing less than the discovery of an optical unconscious' (1993: 23). In 1948 the magazine *Life* (one of the precursors of 'The Family of Man') sponsored a series of Round Table discussions in which it was argued that the American urge to buy had to be contained by a moral leadership. In his interesting study of American society in the 1950s, Eric Sandeen quotes the following summary of one section of this debate:

> [A]dvertising cannot escape the moral and cultural implications of its deeds, some of which are deplorable. But it was also agreed that advertising cannot be expected to provide cultural leadership. This must be done by editors, educators, the clergy and various individuals and institutions immediately concerned with the enlightenment of the people. If such leadership is provided, however, so that people begin to get a better grasp of the principle that happiness is not to be found in mere pleasure and self-gratification, then advertising can help carry the load.
>
> (1995: 7)

17 Sandeen shows how the meaning of 'The Family of Man' shifted between its initial display in 1955 and its exhibition in Moscow in 1959. He writes,

> The anthropological appeal of 'The Family of Man', that all people are fundamentally the same, had been replaced by an economic assertion to which there was no acceptable rejoinder other than capitulation. The photographic exhibition had constructed a statement about common origins; the American exhibition in Moscow fought over the future. In this economic struggle, capitalism, aided by technology, would inevitably have the upper hand.
>
> (1995: 143)

genre in a new universalisation of life itself in Benetton campaigns is *diversity*, the ordering of the difference of life within what Homi Bhabha calls a grid of containment (1990: 208). Two apparently divergent Benetton images, neither of which is at least apparently in the disaster genre outlined above, illuminate the operation of this grid. The first is an image comprised of a multitude of different photographic portraits, images of individuals, all but one of whom is unknown (the exceptions that I have noticed are a couple of portraits of Olivero Toscani, the photographer son of a photographer who is the author of much of Benetton's publicity, one of whose images appears in the place often taken by the signature of the artist in a painting) (Figure 3.4). At first glance, there is no apparent ordering of these images, they jostle against each other, filling every corner of the public hoarding or magazine double spread. It is an image made out of images, a collective portrait that does not subordinate the individual to the type or genre, but rather bypasses the type and, through the form of its composition, suggests that the individual *is* the species, that is, the individual *is* what it is to be human. In one sense, this can be seen as the literal fulfilment of Sander's claim that 'photography is like a mosaic that becomes a synthesis only when it is presented *en masse*' (quoted in Clarke, 1992: 71), but it is a mosaic in which the position of individual fragments is apparently arbitrary.

Despite the arbitrariness of individual pieces of the mosaic, the viewer can slowly see that there is an order; in the midst of the image, the letters A I D S are just visible, themselves made out of photographs of unknown people, arbitrarily caught up in a spelling out of danger. This is a representation of universality in which the individual is no longer ordered in relation to a type, but in which the equality of the individual, the substitutability of one for the other, is made possible by the representation of a global threat in relation to which all are

Figure 3.4 United Colors of Benetton: spelling out global danger

represented as equally at risk.[18] That this is self-consciously one of a series in an 'at-risk' genre distinguishes this image from those in 'The Family of Man'; in the Benetton world, the distribution of risks is arbitrary: they are multiple, dispersed, random and unavoidable. Death is not simply a stage in a continuing life-cycle, a moment that leads to re-entry into life itself, but an exit (see chapter 4). This is an imaging of diversity in which the individual is a representative of life itself under threat of extinction, bereft of type or genre, whose only hope is the apocalyptic universalism of Benetton, purveyors of the prescriptive individualism of which Strathern speaks.[19]

The second image to be discussed here provides a way of colouring the mosaic, of decoding the message, of identifying the salvation that Benetton sells (Figure 3.5). However, it too displaces type or genre, but in this case, paradoxically, by drawing attention to it (and its [imputed] arbitrariness). It is an image of two white men, one in a green shirt, one in a pink shirt, their cheeks against each other's, their arms around each other, faces turned towards the camera, one smiling, one apparently more hesitant in his anticipation of the viewer's response. In the context of Benetton imagery, in which portraits of young people, in twos, groups of three, four or more are a familiar sight, the image is self-consciously ambivalent. At first glance it may be seen as a portrait of a gay couple in an intimate embrace; as such it both conforms to the Benetton convention of collective portraiture and to the aesthetics of pseudo-shock that characterises an alternate strand in the Benetton iconography (given the lack of visibility of gay men and lesbians in contemporary commercial culture). However, on a more prolonged inspection, the viewer may come to the opinion that the two men are remarkably similar in appearance; indeed, on second thoughts, it may seem more likely that they are twins. It is this second interpretation that is given legitimation by the appearance of the same image, without the ubiquitous green tag 'United Colors of Benetton' that appends all the firm's explicit advertisements, in a promotional catalogue (January 1994). This catalogue includes a number of pictures of two or more members of a family

18 This use of images of people is a characteristic of a number of advertising campaigns for what might be described as global products, including British Airways, one of whose most well-known advertisements shows groups of colour-coded people standing in for the coloured segments of a moving mosaic of the human face. Here the substitutable individual is colouring in the features of a human face, such as an eye or an ear. It seems then that Gabriel Tardé's claim in 1883 that 'a statistical bureau might be compared to an eye or ear', that 'each of our senses gives us, in its own way and from its special point of view, the statistics of the external world. Their characteristic sensations are in a certain way their special graphical tables. Every sensation . . . is only a number' (quoted above) has been brought to life as substitutable people are used to colour in the numbers of modern marketing techniques. As part of this campaign, a Cambridge University social anthropologist was hired to ensure a complete cross-section of the world's 'peoples' was represented. In another advertisement in the same series, these representatives were then brought together to be photographed in 'contrasting pairs and threesomes' (Burgoyne, 1995: 28). Perhaps the definitive use of people as fragments of a global mosaic was Coca-Cola's campaign, 'I'd like to teach the world to sing'; however, if Tardé is right, it may be challenged by Microsoft Corporation's use of the symbols of eye, ear and hand to promote its range of communications products.

19 For further discussion of the ethos of survivalism see chapter 4.

together, and the two men appear towards the end of the catalogue: they are given names – Fabio and Fabrizio Bogi – an age – 27 years old – and described as twins.

As a picture of twins, the image refers back to other photographic records of twins, including those discussed by Graham Clarke (1992), 'Farm Girls' (1928) by August Sander, and 'Identical Twins' (1967) by Diane Arbus. In his discussion of these images, Clarke argues that while Sander locates the twins in relation to their social position, Arbus makes the question of identity basic to the photograph. He further suggests that the Arbus photograph draws attention to the difference within identity. In the Arbus image, Clarke suggests, there is a portrayal of the uniqueness of the individual, and the (social) type is rendered irrelevant as difference is internalised in the representation of oddity, an individual that is not identical with itself.[20] In many ways, this can be seen as a

Figure 3.5 United Colors of Benetton: the art of estrangement

20 For Sontag, what the photographer Moholy-Nagy called an optical hygiene has purified, pacified, the individual and social body. The normal has been rendered perverse, but only in order that perversity can be classified, managed and even encouraged for effect, as eccentricity, innovation or style:

> The camera has the power to catch so-called normal people in such a way as to make them look abnormal. The photographer chooses oddity, chases it, frames it, develops it, titles it.
> (1977 : 34)

Making strange, she argues, has dissolved into a taste for the bizarre, and the desire for stylistic innovation is seen as an end in itself. For an alternative interpretation, see chapter 6.

continuation of the destabilisation of the social inaugurated by Sander. But this is not what happens in the Benetton image.

The Benetton image is a double image: even if the viewer has seen the catalogue, which most presumably will not, the image is of a gay couple *and* twins. This is a doubleness which would have confounded Bertillon – for his reliance upon continuity of consciousness underpinned by narrative makes it impossible – but is commented upon here in the photograph's formal structure: as the two men look outwards at the viewer, their similarity in pose gives the impression that the two of them are a single person reflected in a mirror. Their shirts too are of a similar style and material, only of a different colour. In whatever order, with whatever emotional or moral response, the viewer is invited to move from the green shirt to the pink shirt and back, from one interpretation to the other, and to consider the significance of this move. Containing the two images of the two men, one image located in relation to a typology of sexuality, the other a typology of kinship, each of which is understandable as the preferred reading in the context of a recognisable Benetton iconographic convention, the advertisement asks the viewer to consider which classification, which typology, is more relevant. Like Sophocles, it asks the viewer to 'speak'. As a self-consciously double image, the text itself does not presume to say which is correct. Or, perhaps, more accurately, in itself, the image of the advertisement suggests *both* that neither typology is correct *and* that both are.

This is not the repression of type to be found in the Arbus image, in which the type is internalised but still speaks, albeit as eccentricity. By making the two typologies or genres, of sexuality and kinship, formally analogous – they are both juxtapositions of colours, either green and pink, or pink and green – the advertisement requires the reader to move between the possibilities, to accord both possibilities the status of a choice. Simultaneously, the logo, 'United Colors of Benetton', positions the Benetton brand not as the mediator (as is the United Nations), but as the *medium* of movement between colours, between types, between genres, and sets itelf up as a quintessential exponent of *generic estrangement* (see Jameson, 1992, from whom this term is drawn, for an analysis of its relation to postmodern culture). In this kaleidoscopic vision in which the mosaic changes with each twist of the lens, Benetton represents itself as the disinterested exponent of generic estrangement, constantly shaking up the colours of the human mosaic, to make visible the sameness of the global individual.

Diversity is thus represented here not as a form of variation understood in relation to a social and/or natural type or genre, but as the containment of difference precisely through the alienation of type, the making strange of genre: it is a staging of the leap-frogging of the individual over the type in a play of difference, that is, as a matter of style or personal taste.[21] However, as Bhabha points out in his discussion of diversity, the viewer must assume a transparent

21 It is interesting to note that Norman Mailer penned 'The White Negro' just two years after 'The Family of Man' was first shown. As Eric Sandeen argues, this mimicry can be seen as a direct response to the threat of nuclear war and thus as an example of what, following Bauman, I have described as an ethos of survivalism. The essay begins:

⇒

norm – the disappearing or unmarked individual – in order that the addition of colour, of type, be seen as arbitrary, playful or stylish.[22] It is only the assumption of a transparent or white figure that would allow a colour to be added and remain pure, that allows the selection of colour, green or pink, to be understood as a choice. Which colour shirt shall I wear today? Which typology will I be defined by today?

While the social and/or natural type is put in question, culture itself – style – is given a new salience; as Strathern puts it, 'Culture . . . somehow seems at once less than real and larger than life' (1992: 36). Indeed, in many respects, culture becomes 'superorganic', as Friedman (1994) puts it. It is no longer clearly rooted in a place or a territory, and neither is it the outgrowth of a people. Instead, 'it becomes arbitrary with respect to those who possess it' (1994: 67), and those who possess it are individuals who are outside or move between (social and/or natural) types. In Benetton's flat world, the different agencies and determinations of the social and the natural are made coeval, both are mobilised, but both are understood as a question of style, and both are represented as a consequence of the exercise of choice. More generally, the arbitrary, unlimited but finite sets of possibilities and combinations opened up by this exercise of choice in the context of lifestyles has contributed to the emergence of a play of forces and forms that Deleuze (1986, quoted in Rabinow, 1992: 234) has called '*fini-illimité*', the creation of *diversity* by endlessly combining bits and pieces.

As an instance of what Strathern calls literalisation, the formal devices of juxtaposition employed by Benetton make culture visible as a construct, proliferating perspectives, and rather than acting as ground or foundation each new context of interpretation is rendered functional or instrumental. Pluralism is here represented as no more than the accumulation of a series of options and as such is a harbinger of the recognition that reality is haunted by a lack, because it

> Probably, we will never be able to determine the psychic havoc of the concentration camps and the atom bomb upon the unconscious mind of almost everyone alive in these years. For the first time in civilized history, perhaps for the first time in all of history, we have been forced to live with suppressed knowledge that the smallest facts of our personality or the most minor projection of our ideas, or indeed the absence of ideas and the absence of personality could mean equally well that we might still be doomed to die as a cipher in some vast statistical operation in which our teeth would be counted, and our hair would be saved, but our death itself would be unknown, unhonored and unremarked, a death which could not follow with dignity as a possible consequence to serious actions we had chosen, but rather a death by *deus ex machina* in a gas chamber or a radioactive city. . . .
>
> (Mailer, 1961: 282)

Mailer outlined a choice that, for him, was not a choice at all. Faced with a postwar world, one could either endure 'a slow death by conformity with every creative and rebellious instinct stifled' or one could 'divorce oneself from society' and 'set out on that uncharted journey into the rebellious imperatives of the self' (1961: 282). In this rebellion, the Negro hipster provided an example to follow.

22 Similarly, Seltzer (1993) describes diversity as a 'violent negotiation of the singularity or generality of persons' and suggests that it makes reference to 'a kind of serial individuality, in effect referring the individuality of the individual to his location within the system, series, and repetitive standardisation'. By this logic, he argues, 'the making of persons inhabits the logic of systematic management and its products' (1993: 97–98).

makes explicit that an alternative perspective is always possible. Culture itself is visible as a construct, acknowledged as artifice, a technological extension, that which can in-fill the gaps. At the same time, the relation between its parts and the whole does not inhere in the culture itself, but rather is a matter of (multiple) interpretation, a twisting of the kaleidoscope, what Strathern calls self-management, thus returning us to the question of style, and thence to imitation, which, so Strathern argues, is style's principle, not only of combination, but also of (re)generation. Much of the rest of this book will be taken up with the notion of imitation that is at issue here.

CODA: NATURE AND HISTORY

In many respects, this analysis of Benetton appears to provide evidence for the suggested (in-)difference of prosthetic culture and confirmation of Baudrillard's view (quoted earlier) that there has been

> An about-face through which it becomes impossible to locate one instance of the model, of power, of the gaze, of the medium itself, because *you* are always already on the other side. No more subject, no more focal point, no more center or periphery: pure flexion or circular inflexion.
>
> (1994: 29)

However (and despite the rather pessimistic tone of this chapter), perhaps it is worth suspending judgement for a bit longer. The Benetton iconography is an instance of what Siegfried Kracauer describes as 'the go-for-broke of history' that is inherent in photography. Kracauer, writing in 1927, argues, like Sekula, that the history of photography is tied to the symbol. However, he also argues that with what he calls the increasing domination of nature, the image loses its symbolic power:

> Consciousness, which disengages itself from nature and stands over against it, is no longer naively enveloped in its mythological shell; [although] it thinks in concepts that, of course, can still be used in an altogether mythological way.
>
> (Kracauer, 1993: 435)

In his definition of the symbol, what is thought is contained in the symbolic image, so, for example, he claims that even at the time of the daguerreotypes 'consciousness is so imbricated in nature that the faces bring to mind meanings that cannot be separated from natural life' (1993: 434). He quotes Bachofen: 'Symbolism, like language, sat in nature's lap' (Bachofen, 1954, quoted in Kracauer, 1993: 433). With the domination of nature, however, consciousness departs from its natural contingency, and as this happens, the natural foundation represents itself more purely. In the case of Benetton, the natural (or social) foundation or type is either rendered invisible (as in Figure 3.4) or is made not simply visible but depicted as resource, made available, precisely through its estrangement (as in Figure 3.5).

> The images of the stock of nature disintegrated into its elements are offered up to consciousness to deal with as it pleases. Their original order is lost; they no longer cling to the spatial context that linked them with an original out of which the memory-image was selected.
>
> (Kracauer, 1993: 435)

According to Kracauer, what is meant no longer appears to consciousness in images as such; rather, this meaning goes 'towards and through nature'.

However, rather than assuming only one outcome, as Baudrillard seems to, Kracauer predicts that this confrontation of consciousness with nature (itself now devoid of meaning), the go-for-broke of history, may turn out either of two ways. On the one hand, it may lead to a society that succumbs to mute nature, 'no matter how abstract its silence' – what would now be described as the global environmental catastrophe. This is the society that Kracauer believes is to be found in the images of his period's illustrated journals. Meaning is set free from nature, but only to find its own consciousness arbitrary and meaningless. In an apocalyptic tone anticipating that of Baudrillard, Kracauer prophesies,

> Were it to last, the consequence of the emancipation of consciousness would be its own eradication; nature that consciousness failed to penetrate would sit down at the very table that consciousness had abandoned.
>
> (1993: 434)

On the other hand, Kracauer can also see with an alternative vision which is that of a consciousness less enmeshed in the natural bonds than ever before – showing cities in aerial shots and bringing statues, angels and gargoyles down from Gothic cathedrals, able to prove its power by suspending the habitual relationships between consciousness and nature. In this view, it is precisely the disintegration of natural appearances promoted by the camera, and the ensuing exposure of the contingent aspect of every arrangment, that creates new political possibilities. This is photography as a technique of redemption:

> It is therefore incumbent on consciousness to establish the provisional status of all given configurations and perhaps even to awake an inkling of the right order of the inventory of nature.
>
> (1993: 436)

For Kracauer, the moment of suspension that is the arbitrary, split-second exposure of the camera's action is the moment around which the two alternatives of apocalyptic disaster and messianic redemption turn. Kracauer holds on to a moment of suspension not as a moment of choice, but as one of politics, and it is with this moment that this chapter will end.

4

BECOME WHAT YOU ARE

> Photographs are perhaps the most mysterious of all the objects that make up, and thicken, the environment we recognize as modern.
>
> (Susan Sontag, 1977: 3)

INTRODUCTION

Why are photographs, one of the most pervasive sources of imagery in contemporary culture, so mysterious? Perhaps because they endlessly invite deduction, speculation and fantasy about the self. What is the thickness they produce? Perhaps it is a consequence of the ways in which, as Barthes remarks, the photograph inaugurates 'the advent of myself as other', a cunning dissociation of consciousness, memory and the body from self-identity (1981: 12). But what is the nature of this advent-ure? What narratives of identity does the photographic image provoke? In considering how identity is informed by the image, this chapter explores the contradictory implications of the development of photography for the possessive individual in prosthetic culture: hyper-individuality, multiple personalities, loss of self, or the reconstitution of the individual in the exercise of choice that has been described here as experimental individualism.

THE ADVENT-URE OF MYSELF AS OTHER

As noted in the last chapter, the genre of portraiture has played a significant role in the development of the likenesses through which the self-understanding of the possessive individual has been secured. In the aesthetic conventions of this genre, the viewer is invited to transform him- or herself in anticipation of what he or she might look like as an image. This is part of a more general functioning of photography in which 'living beings [are turned] into things, things into living beings' (Sontag, 1977: 98). This merging of the subject and the object is both 'one of the perennial successes' and 'the pathos' at the heart of photography. Indeed, both Barthes and Sontag claim that it is by letting us see ourselves as things that photographs encourage a promiscuous empathy not only with other people but also with things.[1]

1 The phrase 'promiscuous empathy', however, is taken from Walter Benjamin (see chapter 1). Siegfried Kracauer, a fellow cultural critic, adopts a similar stance to the camera when he writes, ⇒

In this invitation, the ability of the photograph to *frame*, *freeze* and *fix* its objects – including the person – is of crucial importance, for with the acknowledgement of the arbitrariness of the frame comes a recognition of the inter-relationship of the properties and positioning of subject and object, of the difficulties of establishing cause and effect, the problems of separating out image and matter. More specifically, the photograph's invitation to the subject is to see him- or herself as an object by way of a model – a reflection in the mirror – that does not yet exist. As Barthes points out, the outcome of accepting this invitation is uncertain:

> I must ask myself: Who is like what? resemblance is a conformity, but to what? to an identity? Now this identity is imprecise, even imaginary, to the point where I can continue to speak of 'likeness' without ever having seen the model . . . . I can spontaneously call them 'likenesses' because they conform to what I expect of them.
>
> (1981: 100–102)

The questions that need to be addressed here thus include: Is this imitation in which likeness *anticipates* its own model the imitation of which Strathern speaks? Is it confined to the moment of being photographed or has it become generalised as a mode of self-presentation, as style? If self-identity is not only reflexively defined through resemblance to an image of a model self in a process of individuation, but imitation is also appropriated by the individual as a paradigm of self-expression and individualisation, then what does this mean for the possessive individual? Perhaps impostures (or vogueing) are not only what thickens the modern environment, but also a crucial component of the contemporary cultural essentialism of the self that occurs in the practices of lifestyle (Featherstone, 1991; Maffesoli, 1991).

In order to address these questions, an analysis of the open-endedness of the advent-ure of the self-as-other will be developed. But first it should be noted that while the photograph offers the possibility of the merging of subject and object, it sometimes – commonly – happens that the subject of the photograph is objectified in the conventions of possessive individualism. So, for example, Barthes himself argues that as the identity of the individual is increasingly defined through resemblance, it becomes an 'absurd, purely legal, even penal affair; likeness gives out identity "as itself"' (1981: 102–103), an object to be possessed. This claim – that the likeness of the photography is a penal affair, that portraiture is a disciplining of the subject – may seem extreme, yet while possession of self-likeness is the subject of legal dispute only in rare cases when stars contest the commercial exploitation of their image (Gaines, 1992), it is increasingly the implicit focus of disputes between employers and employees (as noted in chapter 2) and in struggles over the representation of indigenous peoples and their ways of life in tourist promotions (Coombe, 1993). More widely, it has become an

The archaic camera is indifferent vis-à-vis objects; while not excluding the consciously acting human being, it displays an equal interest in the 'holdings' or 'inventory' of the material world, be they factual or imagined, human or nonhuman.

(Quoted in Hansen, 1993b: 448)

explicit part of everyday life as individuals seek strategically to control the reception of their self-presentation through distinctive visual signatures. Indeed it sometimes seems, as Baudrillard (1995) claims, that since we now live in a culture in which we each have a video recorder in our head, we are constantly in the position of having to transform ourselves in the anticipation of what we might look like as an image. In other words, the invitation is more often than not a prescription; in Adorno's classic phrase, the invitation to 'become what you are' is one we cannot easily refuse.

What is at stake in this advent-ure is the regulation of a 'new social value', that is, the 'publicity of the private' (Barthes, 1981: 98). In his discussion of photography, Barthes writes that its emergence

> corresponds precisely to the explosion of the private into the public . . . : the private is consumed as such publicly . . . . But since the private is not only one of our goods (falling under the historical laws of property), since it is also the absolutely precious, inalienable site where my image is free (free to abolish itself), as it is the condition of an interiority which I believe is identified with my truth, or if you like, with the Intractable of which I consist, I must by a necessary resistance, reconstitute the division of *public and private*: I want to utter interiority without yielding intimacy.
>
> (1981: 98)

In participating in the regulation of this social value, the subject draws upon models of the private, the immediate, the interior, derived from the public, the mediated, the exterior. In doing so, he or she is drawn into a process of *stylised* repetition or iteration, a process which, as Miriam Hansen notes, Adorno and Horkheimer described as typical of the culture industry more generally:

> Horkheimer and Adorno ascribe the effectivity of mass-cultural scripts of identity not simply to the viewers' manipulation as passive consumers, but rather to their very solicitation as experts, as active readers. The identification *with* the stereotype is advanced by the appeal to a particular type of knowledge or skill predicated on repetition: the identification *of* a familiar face, gesture or narrative convention takes the place of genuine cognition.
>
> (1993a: 51)

Not even the unconscious can evade this prescriptive identification:

> Instead of paying tribute to the unconscious by elevating it to consciousness so as to fulfill its urges and at the same time pacify its destructive force, the culture industry . . . reduces human beings to their unconscious behaviour even more than the conditions of their existence do all along.
>
> (Adorno, quoted in Hansen, 1993a: 54)

For Barthes, the photograph typically discloses a dis-internalised countenance as the new truth of identity, and depicts that countenance in relation to profound changes, not by removing the boundary between the public and the private, but by making the traversal of that boundary productive. The public display of the private, the mediation of the immediate, the making external of the internal, both denies and depends upon the boundary between the two. It erases only to redefine this boundary, reconstituting the private within the public, making immediate the mediated and bringing inside what was outside, *blurring*[2] the distinction between individuation and individualisation, identification and dis-identification, combining them as 'a necessary resistance'. The force of the photographic image, then, is such that it sets up the advent-ure of my self-as-other as an obligatory choice,[3] making wilful artifice into a necessary contrivance (Wills, 1995).

2 A recent article in *Eye*, which quotes Lazló Moholy-Nagy to the effect that 'Every period has its own optical focus,' suggests that 'The focus of today's visual landscape is the indistinction between things. . . . The blur is the emblem of design in the 1990s.' It continues,

> We are living in a time of profound ambiguity, at once liberating and unsettling. The physical and institutional boundaries through which we have traditionally defined ourselves and against which we have rebelled – whether political, sexual or cultural – are in flux. We are not sure who we are or who we want to be, and there is no moral imperative to spur us toward a decision. What are we to do when we no longer recognise the culprit? And why bother, when the next upheaval, whether an act of political terrorism or of plastic surgery, can speedily reinvent us?
>
> In this boundary-free world, we can never be sure where responsibility lies. The chain of causality includes real and virtual acts, some of which can be reversed by a simple 'Undo' command, others which are indelible . . . mesmerised, we can scarcely formulate our response to what we see before the ground shifts, reframing us in yet another context.
>
> Whether blurring is about the promise of infinite possibilities or the decadence of digitally enhanced leisure, it epitomises the world we live in today – transmutable, mediated and ambiguous. As we reflect on the turn of yet another century, the blur raises the question: what exactly did we see anyway?
>
> (Staples, 1995: 6–7)

3 One outcome of this is that the stylisation of this choice may become a source of distinction. For example, a recent feature on fashion in a January edition of the American magazine *Interview* poses the question: 'What is the imaginary line dividing one year from another that has the power to make us reconsider our lives, come up with fabulous resolutions, and want to start with a clean slate?' The answer the feature provides to its own question is,

> It must be the same line that invented the fashion industry long ago. The one that leads designers to bring out new lines season after season, each one with the promise that the clothes will be part of making dreams come true. In many ways, fashion is the way you write the story of your life, line by line.

In this refiguring of personal (and collective) biographies, the writing of the experimental individual's life does not simply (or perhaps not at all) adopt the cause and effect of narrative realism (in which one line of prose leads to another), but rather emerges from the repeated reframing of the image, boundary marking, drawing lines between old and new, interior and exterior, self and other. The feature continues,

> Think about that line that divides beige from buff and the line that divides above the knee from below the knee. That line that divides short from too short and long from not long enough. And then think about that other kind of line, that newsy kind that heads the front-pages of the fashion press, pronouncing what's 'in' today that was 'out' the day before. Or think about that funny wrinkle-line of your best friend's forehead when you debut your new rubberized shorts. The ones you had to wait on line forever to purchase by signing on the all-too-real dotted line on your credit-card receipt. . . . We like fashion because we think it's a form of expression for everyone. It lets everyone decide: Is it time to step in line or time to step out of line? Which line should be crossed today? What line will be crossed that will make this day, this month, this year, unlike every other?
>
> (Pandiscio, 1996: 90, 92)

Indeed, Barthes suggests that photography has contributed to the development of a self-identity constituted in a continuous, repetitive dis-internalisation of subjectivity and a simultaneous affirmation of new modes of intimacy, individual affect and self-representation. Through the simultaneous breaching and reaffirmation of the public and private ('the private is consumed as such publicly'), the inter-relationship of these categories of social life is made visible, and in the form of personal style becomes a resource to be used in the display of 'interiority without intimacy', manipulated in projects of self-identity, and evaluated in terms of a/effectivity. Furthermore, Barthes suggests that as self-revelation becomes a continuous, evenly distributed process, conventional distinctions of aesthetic and ethical value are relativised and new categories of 'interest' – not only 'fashion' but also 'news', 'scandal' and 'information' – are created, and with them fresh responsibilities, novel spheres of decision-making arising from the newly seen. As a consequence, as Sontag notes, boredom is established as the flip side of fascination, for

> What is safe no longer monopolizes public imagery. The freakish is no longer a private zone, difficult of access. People who are bizarre, in sexual disgrace, emotionally vacant are seen daily on the newsstands, on TV, the subways.
>
> (1977: 45)

As has been widely noted, these are the conditions of the confession as a public genre, the talk show and the ordinary person as celebrity, but they are also, as the next section demonstrates, those of the family album.

FAMILY ALBUMS

Most people's most valued photographs are taken, shown and displayed in the intimate spaces the family album provides, whether these are to be found between the leaves of an album or in the nooks and crevices of domestic life – the mantelpiece, the pin-board, the bedside table, the wallet, the handbag or the old shoe box on top of the wardrobe. Indeed, so much a part of everyday life are these spaces that the rights of possession of the subject by the photographer (and/or the owner or keeper of the photograph) are not generally seen to require the necessity of a formal contract.[4] (An example of this assumption is provided by the copyline of a recent newspaper advertisement for the Handycam

4 See Patricia Holland's discussion of 'popular images of childhood' (1992) for a more detailed consideration of the role of photography in the Romantic association between childhood and innocence. The innocence of this privacy, she argues, is no longer respected; indeed, it was always a fiction. In his study of the relationship between the photographer and the subject in portrait photography, Homberger (1992) points out that intimacy has been a defining relation in the setting of aesthetic standards not only inside but also outside the family. However, Homberger also illustrates some of the fraught relations, sexual, political and psychological, within which intimate contact is achieved (or imposed). He argued that the conventions of intimacy were established, self-consciously, by photographers such as Edward Weston who documented their working practices in notebooks. The following extract from Weston's notebook records his thoughts on a session taking Tina Modotti's portrait:

⇒

videocamera by Sony: 'At last, a daddy that's easy to smile for.') Indeed, the very characteristics – innocence, spontaneity and naturalness – that define the child as a subject in a family snapshot are a consequence of the image's production as a copy which is believed to be motivated by intimate contact, not contract. (The advertising copy continues, 'You are now released from the confines of squinting down that viewfinder. Leaving both your eyes free to catch all those magical moments. And, who knows, one day you may even capture the most elusive of them all. Your baby, smiling.') This is what, in part, defines the special status of family snaps as the ultimate private good.[5]

However, the intensity of the 'magical moments', the encounters or intimate contact between members of a family made possible by looking through family albums and their attendant boxes of loose, assorted prints, has been little discussed, at least until recently (see Spence, 1986; Spence and Holland, 1991;

> she leaned against a whitewashed wall – lips quivering – nostrils dilating – eyes heavy with the gloom of unspent rainclouds – I drew close – I whispered something and kissed her – a tear rolled down her cheek – and then I captured forever the moment – let me see – f8 -1/10 sec. KI filter – panchromatic film – how brutally mechanical it sounds – yet really how spontaneous and genuine – for I have so overcome the mechanics of my camera with my brain that it functions responsive to my desires – my shutter coordinating with my brain is released in a way – as natural as I might move my arm – . . . .
>
> (Quoted in Homberger, 1992: 123)

The conventions in which the aesthetic value of the photograph is related to the extent to which the subject does not seem to give him- or herself but to be 'taken' by the photographer have been sustained and made public in biographies and commentaries that focus on the portrait as a record of the intimate relationship between photographer and subject.

Recognising the prevalence of these criteria, Homberger suggests that 'no portraits are more perplexing' than the nude photographs of Lee Miller taken by her father. He describes one of these:

> A stereoscopic photograph, taken in 1928, portrays Miller sitting with her head sharply turned to her right, and her arms interlocked behind her back. The pose, which pulled Miller's shoulders back and thrust her breasts forward, draws upon the provenance of images from fine art as well as from pornographic material. Theodore Miller's portrait is an 'Orientalist' image of the nude female in the tradition of Jean-Leon Gerome's painting, *Oriental Slave Market*. The 'bondage' content of his daughter's pose is equally obvious. Such pictures function within the male fantasy of absolute possession of women's naked bodies. Lee Miller's face is expressionless. She is displayed here before the man with whom she had the most intense ties. Yet the absence of expression is itself disturbing, for it embodies a narcissism, a disconnection from the fact, which everyone who looks at the image cannot forget, that she is posing here for her father.
>
> (Homberger, 1992: 126)

Homberger goes on to claim that 'family photographs' are almost always taken in family relationships such as that of father and daughter, but that Theodore Miller's portraits 'are much more disturbing for they calmly transgress the many other kinds of contract that normally govern relations between parents and their children' (1992: 127). But perhaps even the *punctums* of 'less disturbing' family photographs have the power to disturb even 'normal' moments of intimacy, for the *punctum* raises the question, '*whose* memories are being made of this?'

5 According to Don Slater (1995a), market research from 1982 suggests that 39 per cent of respondents rated their family photos as the possessions they treasure most and would least like to lose (out of a list which included jewellery and clothes).

Kuhn, 1995; and Slater, 1995a, for consideration of this phenomenon).[6] The lack of attention paid to the intensity of these encounters may perhaps be explained as a consequence of the difficulties associated with any discussion of the issue of 'consent' that is raised by the family album (and, indeed, families more generally). Yet the line between private and public is currently being redrawn in contemporary family albums, often without common agreement and sometimes with controversial results. At issue, I suggest, is the uneven availability of experimental individualism to subjects and their photographers as mothers, fathers and children, husbands and wives, that is, as members of families and the problems this new form of individualism poses for the visual regimes of copy and cont(r)act.

To consider these issues, let me turn first to some recent work by photographers exhibited at London's Barbican Centre in the exhibition 'Who's Looking at the Family?', in which our society's fantasies of the innocence of childhood are questioned. In the work displayed there, including that of Sally Mann in which her children are depicted, sometimes naked, sometimes clothed, it is as if the copy and cont(r)act of the portrait in the presumed intimacy of the family album is deliberately entered and reworked for aesthetic effect. In this process, the relationship of dependence of both taboo and innocence upon the existence of the boundary between public and private is made explicit. Indeed, critical evaluation of Mann's photographs hinges, somewhat nervously, on how well this is done; for example, one critic comments that while Mann is 'technically conservative' her work also exhibits a 'slimy daring' (Hilton, 1994: 26). Another writes of her work in *Immediate Family* that

> These children enter a theater created by themselves and a parent. Such a theater is not inherently innocent. . . . These are beautiful and self-possessed children. The lens opens their world and self-dramatizations to the intrusion of intent strangers they would not necessarily welcome. Theirs is a theater they, or Sally Mann, or all together make.
>
> (Miller, 1994: 64–65)

The uncertain listing of the possible participants in the photograph here indicates that both critical anxiety and praise are connected to the possibility that suggestion may be being reworked as suggestiveness, contact as contract.

Alternatively, consider the way in which the family album has been 'wired'. Diego Goldberg created *Cronicas Apasionados* (A Passionate Chronicle) on his Macintosh computer to celebrate his parents' 70th birthdays (Ziff, 1991). It is a digital picture book which traces the lives of the two main characters, his mother and father, Perla and Alberto. Most of the photographs were scanned from originals, and some were digitally manipulated (see chapters 7 and 8 for further discussion of digitalisation). In addition, however, Goldberg also created images which never existed – such as one of his mother at work as a young woman – to illustrate important moments in their lives. The book is divided into thematic

6 Jo Spence (1986) was one of the first photographers seriously to investigate the family album. While recognising the complexity and variety of the image practices that the family album encompasses, she also points to their role in the idealisation of the family.

chapters; in the last chapter, 'All of us', each family member's personal message is recorded. Goldberg says of the book, of which there are only two copies in existence,

> I prepared the graphics of each double page and everybody wrote their own words. The glossary at the back is a list of words which each trigger a personal memory.
>
> (Quoted in Ziff, 1991: 76)

Is this an example of a reproductive technology, in which technologically assisted reproduction can generate families of choice? Is it analogous with the legal precedent by which a child can bring 'divorce' proceedings against his or her parents (Strathern, 1995)? How are contact and contract superimposed here? What kind of family romance (Freud, 1953; Lawler, 1995b) does this technology make possible?

Then again, consider the use to which photographs are put in the practices of photo-therapy. In a feature on this subject in the women's magazine *Elle* (Montrose, 1993), we are invited to see family albums as a means of unlocking the secrets of family history, of 'speeding up the recovery of forgotten or repressed memories' (1993: 57). Photographs are described as a 'fast-track to the unconscious' 1993: 57); they are a 'testimony that can't be denied' (1993: 57). Although these images are coded, the person with the key – or rather the person with 'the credit card in the door' (1993: 60) – is the subject in therapy. The therapist who is the subject of the feature is quoted as saying, 'The only meaning lies inside the head of the person I am working with' (1993: 58); this is because, 'It's not what the photo is of that's important, it's what it's about.' Indeed, the therapeutic element is downplayed: 'the context is familiar – like showing holiday snaps to your colleagues or reminiscing with your friends' (1993: 58). The subject is invited to confirm possession of herself by uncovering the truth of the photograph and collecting the memories which it reveals:

> you are the keeper of secrets, not the therapist; she's there just to draw out and explore the things you already know. She may uncover the truth – and make it bearable – but it must be your truth, not hers.
>
> (1993: 60)

The do-it-yourself nature of the therapy described is further confirmed by the inclusion of a list of ten questions at the end of the feature which 'can be used to find hidden secrets in your own family album'. These range from 'Which are your favourites?' and 'Why?' via 'What is the story of each picture – how did it come to be?' to 'Is your family album a true representation of your childhood as you remember it? If not, what would you change to make it accurate?' (1993: 60).

The final question implicitly awards the reader the power to take the photographs again ('What are the differences between pictures of yourself that you like and dislike?' 'What would you have to change about the ones you don't like to make them more likeable?') and, in this way, to rewrite (to '(re)take') her own life history and that of her family on the basis of her own 'likes' (or likenesses). More specifically, she is encouraged to use photo-therapy to 'undo' the repression which is posited as the root of her (assumed) unhappiness. In this relationship to her past, she can make good a technologically mediated re-imaging of her life, making herself a better, happier person, more at one with herself. In the context of contemporary glossy women's magazines, which Winship (1987) argues are characterised by an ideology of feminine individuality, the retrodictive prophecy of self-discovery made possible by photo-therapy seems to interpellate a characteristically 'petit-bourgeois' feminine subject (Featherstone, 1991) and sustain the possibility of an imaginary mobility, provoking both ambition and fear: '[The therapist] interrupted, and my heart sank before slowly rising to my throat. Bull's eye – we both knew she'd pushed the right button' (1993: 60).

Or again, consider the phenomenon of 'the pinboard' on the bedroom or office wall as the contemporary manifestation – or displacement – of the family album (and, as such, a private form of the kaleidoscope of photographic portraits spelling AIDS created by Benetton discussed in the preceding chapter). According to Don Slater, instead of sticking photos into albums, arranged narratively into books and therefore into history, 'we rather pin and blu-tack them haphazardly onto surfaces and therefore into the moment, into the display and self-presentation of the present' (1995a: 139). Snapshots, bits of photobooth strips left over from passports or identity cards take their place alongside postcards sent by friends, newspaper paragraphs, a child's drawing, birthday cards, pictures of celebrities, notices and advertisements. In this way, Slater argues, the pinboard evokes a collage of affiliations, in which the representation of self is produced by and within the activities of the present. The collage displaces the narrative as the privileged technique of self. Indeed, Slater goes so far as to suggest that the image of self is always in the moment 'and need not take the form of representation at all' (1995a: 140). Instead, the image of self is subordinated within a flow of other images within 'whose image environments we may feel more practically at home than in our family album' (1995a: 130). In these environments,

> identity is produced through a presentation of self in the moment rather than in a reflective representation of it as (an imaginary) community over time. . . . In a developed consumerism, the image is the way we present ourselves in the heat of the moment rather than the way we represent that moment as an object of reflection.
>
> (1995a: 140)

Personal investment in these images may be intense, but is short lived; they gradually become invisible, either too familiar to be noticed or are simply replaced by newer images.

All these examples – eclectic though they may be – illustrate the ways in which the contemporary photographic practices of the family album are making it possible for an individual to discard old selves, to try on personae and compare the multiplicity of subject-effects of retrodictive self-transformation. For some, but not perhaps for all, this is an opportunity. Individuation and individualisation are intricately inter-twined here, but the individual does not necessarily disappear: rather, through a process of repetitive dis-internalisation, he or she may be reconstituted

– inside or outside a remade family – in the exercise of choice. In the examples discussed above, as more widely in what I have called experimental individualism, the subject may be dissociated from his or her biography – consciousness and memories – but may then, as an artefactual person (Seltzer, 1993), acquire a *prosthetic auto/biography*[7] or biographies, of his or her own choosing.

What these examples indicate is that the likeness or resemblance presented by the photograph is being adopted by the observer as an origin or a cause in complex and contradictory ways. The photograph's freeze-framing creates a loop in time from which a newly self-possessed individual may emerge. In this loop, the future perfect of the photographic image – this will have been – may be suspended, manipulated and reworked to become the past perfected (Tyler, 1994). Indeed, the loop is absolutely central to the photograph's invitation to the observer to 'become what you are': it is the photograph's distinctive contribution to the emergence of the potential of the experimental individual. The photograph's decisive moment – its freeze-frame – makes possible an instant of decision-making, an experimentation, in which the potential of prosthetic culture may be recognised. However, the loop is not employed in the same way by everybody: as the examples described above indicate, there are losses, conflicts and anxieties associated with experimental individualism in the family album.

It is not just that the subject who can make a choice is not always already given, but is, precisely, an effect of the reiteration of the practices just described (Butler, 1993), but also that such subject-effects are unevenly distributed and unequally enabling: not everyone is able to make choices or lay claim to their effects, to realise his or her potential, and not everybody who is able to chooses so to do. Indeed, the loop, while inviting, does not of itself incite such experimentation, nor does it foreclose the outcome; rather, so I suggest, the artefactual person requires not only what Slater (1995b) calls consumerism and Featherstone (1991) describes as lifestyle, but also a more widespread ethos of survivalism (Bauman, 1992) to emerge as a possessive individual. In order to explore the workings of this loop further, then, let me return to a more general discussion of Barthes and portraiture.

RETRODICTIVE PROPHECY

Barthes writes that the re-visioning of self-identity made possible by photography has a particular temporality:[8] it is retrodictive in its operation. He notes that photographs act as prophecies in reverse; they make possible a 'flow back from the presentation to retention' (1981: 90) or 'reverse the course of the thing' (1981: 119). Other writers too have made this point. Kracauer, for example,

7 The term 'prosthetic biography' has been developed by the psychologist Rom Harré.

8 In 'Rhetoric of the image', Barthes writes that the photograph establishes

> not a consciousness of the *being-there* of the thing (which any copy could provoke) but an awareness of its *having been there*. What we have is a new space–time category: spatial immediacy and temporal anteriority, the photograph being an illogical conjunction between the *here–now* and the *there–then*.
>
> (1981: 44)

claims that the viewer of old photographs shudders: this is because it is not the person who appears in his or her photograph, but 'the sum of what can be subtracted from him or her' (1993, 1995: 57). In this observation, Kracauer seems to anticipate Barthes's elucidation of the temporal technique by which the photograph comes to have the power to detach biography – not simply the ornamentation of the 'fashionably old-fashioned' surface details it depicts, but also the subject's very consciousness, memories and body – from him- or herself: as he writes, 'the smile is arrested yet no longer refers to the life from which it has been taken' (1995: 48).

For Barthes, however, while the deduction or detachment of biography from the individual coincides, in the instant of a photographic 'take', with the death of the subject, this death is simultaneous with the beginning of an after-life. On the one hand, Barthes holds that the subject of a photograph is always in the shadow of death: the photographic image is a testament to the what-has-been-but-is-no-longer. Even when the person photographed is still living, that moment when he or she *was* has for ever vanished. Indeed, strictly speaking, the person who *has been photographed* – not the ongoing person – is dead. Like any other prosthesis, then, the photograph is haunted by a phantom pain (Wills, 1995). For Kracauer, its 'ghost-like reality is unredeemed' (1995: 56). For Barthes, on the other hand, the subject also acquires an after-life – as a spectre[9] – in which his or her identity is reconstituted in the anticipation and reception of the image of what-was-but-is-no-longer. He writes,

> the Photograph (the one I intend) represents that very subtle moment when, to tell the truth, I am neither subject nor object but a subject who feels he is becoming an object: I then experience a micro-version of death (of parenthesis): I am truly becoming a specter.
>
> (1981: 15)

Moreover, while the artefactual individual whose after-life this is has no memories of his or her very own – the photograph cannot sustain memory for it leads to the 'cumulative decreation of the past (in the very act of preserving it)' (Sontag, 1977: 77) – he or she can acquire, indeed, is constituted as the subject-effect of, the counter-memory of the photograph. For Barthes, then, the fixed photographic image is not only a death but simultaneously another life, for it may activate an after-life. Moreover, this after-life is informed by the retrodictive prophecy of the image as much as if not more than the continuity of consciousness of narrative realism.

Nevertheless, the power that the photographic portrait has to detach the subject from his or her biography, memories and consciousness is sometimes seen to have frightening consequences. Barthes writes,

> In front of the photograph of my mother as a child, I tell myself: she is going to die: I shudder, like Winnicott's psychotic patient, *over a catastrophe*

9 Similarly, Donna Haraway writes, 'To make an exact image is to insure against disappearance, to cannibalize life until it is safely and permanently a spectacular image, a ghost' (quoted in Lutz and Collins, 1993: 87).

> *which has already occurred.* Whether or not the subject is already dead, every photograph is this catastrophe.
>
> (1981: 96)

Adorno too talks in terms of the living dead: he argues that the contemporary culture industry is the site of a perverted form of mimesis involving a slippage between life and death, the individual's assimilation to lifeless material, or a feigning of death for the sake of survival. For Adorno what Barthes describes as the disciplining of identity by likeness is the reduction of life to self-preservation. Hansen writes,

> In that sense, mimesis entails what Michael Cahn calls 'a deadly reification complex' that perpetuates the state for which Adorno likes to cite Kurnberger's apothegm, 'Das Leben lebt nicht' (life is not alive).
>
> (1993a: 53)

Kracauer puts it somewhat differently; he argues that the photograph 'annihilates the person by portraying him or her, and were person and portrayal to converge, the person would cease to exist' (1995: 57). (This is the feared moment of self-destruction in the looping narratives of time travel characteristic of science fiction: the contemporary formulation of the long-standing fear of being 'taken' by the camera is one in which becoming what you are leads to the annihilation of the self as the gap between inside and outside, image and matter, between then and now, here and there, is erased and leads to implosion.[10])

Barthes, however, does not seem to fear this possibility; instead, he seems to seek out the shudder which is for him a kind of photographic ecstasy. Indeed, he writes,

> What Marey and Muybridge have done as *operators* I myself want to do as *spectator*: I decompose, I enlarge, and, so to speak, I *retard*, in order to have time to *know* at last. The Photograph justifies this desire, even if it does not satisfy it. . . .
>
> (1981: 99)

For Barthes, the photograph justifies this desire by its 'air'; and although he claims that this 'air' is something inexpressible – 'evident (this is the law of the Photograph) yet improbable (I cannot prove it)' (1981: 107) – he goes on to define it as an expression, a look:

> a kind of intractable supplement of identity, what is given as an act of grace, stripped of any 'importance': the air expresses the subject, insofar as the subject assigns itself no importance. In this veracious photograph, the

10 As Christopher Pinney remarks in his discussion of the collapse of time and space in virtual reality,

> The removal of the outward journey and the return – the removal of the frame and the incarnated viewer – have indeed threatened the 'entire gridding of the system [which presupposes] that there is a *place* for every *figure*. . . . Virtual reality's distance-travel has blurred self and other.
>
> (1994: 423)

> being I love, whom I have loved, is not separated from itself: at last it coincides. And mysteriously, this coincidence is a kind of metamorphosis.
>
> (1981: 109)

How is it that this coincidence is not also an annihilation (as Kracauer predicts);[11] what is the mysterious process involved here by which coincidence is also metamorphosis, not convergence of person and portrayal? Is it possible to avoid becoming what we are?

STICKY REALISM: COPY AND CONTACT

First of all it is important to note that, for Barthes, coincidence is by no means also always metamorphosis;[12] indeed, as noted above, he recognises that, more often than not, it results in a disciplining of the subject: copy and contract. However, he also wishes to acknowledge the unpredictable effect of the *punctum* of the photograph: the unexpected 'small wound', sting or cut that disturbs the conventional intelligibility of the photograph. Anne Game provides a helpful explication of the *punctum*, and with it a reformulation of Barthes's shudder. Discussing his comments on a photograph by Alexander Gardner, 'Portrait of Lewis Payne' (1865), she argues that Barthes responds to this photograph with a combination of erotic affect and fear of death, a kind of mortal longing. For Game, the boy is Barthes' object of desire; in viewing the photograph, he puts himself in the place of the object who will die, has already died. But, she argues, the effect of the photograph is the depiction not so much of a death in life, as of a life in death: it points to 'the duration of the body; the effects of a particular individual's death on his, Barthes' body – the *shudder*' (1991: 143). In so far as the *punctum* of a photograph raises this shudder, Game suggests, it offers a way of seeing that does not simply displace and rework but radically disturbs the opposition between immediacy and mediation, presence and absence, subject and object, life and death. In the *punctum*, time 'is a bodily mediation in immediacy' (1991: 145); it offers an experience that 'need not be equated with presence' (1991: 147).

Barthes further distinguishes between the 'photographic shock' which

11 That this coincidence is not an annihilation might be seen to be a consequence of the fact that in this example from Barthes it is not a coincidence in which the viewer coincides with an image of his or her own previous self but with someone else; but as the following analysis suggests, this difference is unimportant from Barthes's point of view. What is important is the metamorphosis involved.

12 In some of his writings on photography, Barthes suggests that the possibility of coincidence also being metamorphosis is limited by what he calls the image-repertoire, which he compares to Lacan's *imaginaire*: 'What Lacan means by *imaginaire*', he told an interviewer in 1975,

> is closely related to analogy, analogy between images, since the image repertoire is the register where the subject adheres to an image in a movement of identification that relies in particular on the signifier and the signified. Here we reencounter the theme of representation, figuration, the homogeneity of images and models.
>
> (Quoted in Jay, 1994: 446)

In other writings, however, he gives less attention to the conditions of these limits, and more to the occasions in which coincidence is also metamorphosis.

'consists less in traumatizing than in revealing what was so well hidden that the actor himself was unaware or unconscious of it' and 'the *punctum*', the point of sudden and strong emotion, of small trauma, which wounds. He writes,

> I experience the Photograph and the world in which it participates according to two regions: on one side the Images, on the other my photographs; on one side, unconcern, shifting, noise, the inessential (even if I am abusively deafened by it), on the other the burning, the wounded.
>
> (1981: 98)

His project is to explore the experience of photography 'not as a question (a theme) but as a wound: I see, I feel, hence I notice, I observe and I think' (1981: 21). Perception and cognition are not separated in this experience, and the senses are not differentiated. It is made possible, so Barthes implies, following Merleau-Ponty, from the way in which the mirror (and by implication the camera)

> anticipates, within things, the labor of vision. . . . The mirror appears because I am seeing-visible, because there is a reflexivity of the sensible; the mirror translates and reproduces that reflexivity.
>
> (Merleau-Ponty, quoted in Jay, 1994: 315)

Here is a formulation of the power of the image to anticipate without aim; the intractable supplement of identity is made possible by a 'reflexivity of the sensible'. However, Barthes's perception of the *punctum* as the photograph's power to wound, to provoke 'tiny jubilations, as if they referred to a stilled centre, an erotic or lacerating value buried in myself' (1981: 16), mysteriously to bring together coincidence and metamorphosis, has often been dismissed as wishful thinking, as a subjective desire for presence, not experience.

This dismissal is most strongly voiced in relation to Barthes's discussion of a photograph from his own family album. For example, John Tagg writes that Barthes's account

> *must* be read against the death of his own mother, his reawakened sense of unsupportable loss, and his search for 'a just image' and not 'just an image of her'. His demand for realism is a demand, if not to have her back, then to know she was here: the consolation of a truth in the past which cannot be questioned.
>
> (1988: 1; my emphasis)

Notwithstanding Tagg's dedication of *The Burden of Representation* to his own mother ('In memory of my mother, Ethel Tagg, born 1922, died 1980'), he declares that photography 'cannot deliver what Barthes desires: the confirmation of an existence; the mark of a past presence; the repossession of his mother's body' (1988: 3). But Tagg's declaration is dubious not only because it is premised upon the psychoanalytic diagnosis of a subject who is a construct of Tagg's own reading of the text, but because he presents a reductive interpretation of the way of seeing photographically that Barthes elucidates. As noted above, Barthes claims that the photograph *justifies* the spectators' desire, not that it *satisfies* it.

Tagg quotes Barthes's belief that 'from a phenomenological viewpoint, in the

Photograph, the power of authentification or designation exceeds the power of representation' (1988: 1), but reduces this phenomenonological power of authentification to the photograph's objective guarantee of a corresponding pre-photogaphic existent, that is, to coincidence without metamorphosis. In doing so, he insists upon an opposition between subject and object, viewer and image, which Barthes undoes. As Annette Kuhn (1991) affirms, Barthes's *punctum* of a photograph seems to utter a truth that goes beyond the *studium*, the evidential, however intricately coded. Barthes himself is at pains to explicate this 'beyond' in precise terms; he writes,

> The name of Photography's noeme will therefore be: 'That-has-been', or again: the Intractable. In Latin . . . this would doubtless be said: *interfuit: what* I see has been here, in this place which extends between infinity and the subject (*operator* or *spectator*); it has been absolutely, irrefutably present, and yet already deferred. It is all this which the verb *intersum* means.
>
> (1981: 77)

Tagg's reduction ignores the emphasis that Barthes places on the relation – the irrefutably present, and yet already deferred – that exists between the photograph and the viewer. As Metz notes, the '*punctum* depends more on the reader than the photograph itself, and the corresponding off-frame it calls up is also generally subjective' (1990: 161). The metonymic power of the *punctum* is, for Barthes, what is able to make the viewer add something beyond what he or she sees, 'what I add to the photograph and *what is nonetheless already there*' (1981: 55). More generally, Barthes suggests that the *punctum* of the photograph is revealed as the viewer *looks away or closes his or her eyes*. It arises in the '*hors-champs subtil*', a subtle beyond-the-frame, 'as if the image launched desire beyond what it permits us to see' (1981: 59). It is a consequence of a relation of *suggestion* between the objectively mediated image that *anticipates* and the viewing subject who *hesitates*.

Tagg, however, transforms this two-way relation of suggestion into a one-way projection of (psychoanalytic) desire.[13] He substitutes Barthes's interpretation of the realism of photography with a naive illusionism, and interprets a relation of suggestion as a 'poignant' effect of Barthes's grief and his desire for wholeness. In his reading of *Camera Lucida*, Tagg seeks to evade the merging of the self and the other, subject and object, implicit in seeing photographically by interpreting the effects of the photograph as the product not of the relationship *between* the image and viewer, but (only) of the viewer's (repressed) desire. As a consequence, Tagg, paradoxically, reaffirms the depth, autonomy and uniqueness of the viewing subject as an individual (albeit an individual who is de-centred by the workings of an unconscious and the impossible aspirations of desire), an integrity that his critical project is apparently intended to disturb.

In contrast to Tagg's interpretation, the thesis put forward here is that Barthes's assertion of the power of the *punctum* to wound is related to an understanding of the photograph in terms of suggestibility and the powers of animation, that is, in terms of mimesis, at least in the sense that Taussig (1993)

13 For this formulation I am indebted to an article by Ruth Leys (1992) on mimesis and the subject of representation.

identifies. In this definition, mimesis is both a copying or imitation *and* a palpable, sensuous connection between the very body of the perceiver and the perceived, copy *and* contact, coincidence and metamorphosis. Taussig describes the mimetic faculty as the ability to copy, to imitate, to yield into, and become other in such a way that the copy draws power from the original. He writes that 'the model, if it works, gains through its sensual fidelity something of the power and the personality of that which it is a model' (1993: 21). It is this kind of understanding, I think, that underpins Barthes's belief in the action of the *punctum* by means of which he can enter 'crazily into the spectacle, into the image, taking into my arms what is dead, what is going to die' (1981: 117). This is not the feigning of death as a means of survival of which Adorno speaks; rather it is the recognition of a life in death that Game identifies. It is not the recognition of a likeness that conforms to liking, of likeness that 'gives out identity "as itself"': it is an imitation that is both coincidence and metamorphosis.

In developing his understanding of mimesis, Taussig draws upon J. G. Frazer's development of what he takes to be the two great classes of sympathetic magic in *The Golden Bough* (1911–1935): the magic of *imitation* and the magic of *contact*, imitation or sympathy *and sensuousness or contagion*. Mimesis involves a copying or imitation, and a palpable, sensuous connection between the very body of the perceiver and the perceived, making contact. This explication of mimesis comes close to explaining the magical, sticky or fairy-tale realism of photography that Barthes seeks to describe; it explains the difficulty of distinguishing a photograph from its referent that is commonly taken to be definitive of the camera's aesthetic.[14] It makes it possible to recognise the possibility of a relation of suggestion – of 'objective' motivation and 'subjective' intentionality, of anticipation and hesitation – which occurs before the subject and object of representation are fixed. It is in mimesis, then, that the photographic loop does not necessarily lead to annihilation.

However, the translation and reproduction of the sensibility of photography's reflexivity – its power of anticipation – are not static: developments in the apparatus of the camera – themselves informed by the multiple uses to which the technology has been put – continually transform the terms of its anticipation,

14 Barthes himself claims that 'it is reference which is the founding order of Photography'. He comments,

> the realists, of whom I am one and of whom I was already one when I asserted that the Photograph was an image without a code – even if, obviously, certain codes do inflect our reading of it – the realists do not take the photograph for a 'copy' of reality, but for an emanation of *past reality*: a *magic*, not an art.
>
> (1981: 88)

This is a sticky realism: as with a glue 'the referent adheres' (1981: 6); with the Instamatic, reality and image are bonded securely in seconds. For Barthes, this realism is not an illusionism; nevertheless, the fact that

> Photography never lies: or rather, it can lie as to the meaning of the thing, being by nature *tendentious*, never as to its existence . . . its force . . . is superior to everything the human mind can or can have conceived to assure us of reality.
>
> (1981: 87)

reconfiguring the terms of its powers of retrodictive prophecy as identified by Barthes. As the examples above indicate, these changes are nowhere more clear than in the case of the family album, hovering on and making visible as it does the border between the private and the public, the immediate and the mediated, the interior and the exterior, framing the boundaries between life and death.[15] In these examples, the effects of this loop are ambiguous. In the next section, a further example of a family album will be discussed, one in which, so it will be argued, the ethos of survivalism forecloses some of these ambiguities. However, this example – another image from Benetton's publicity – will be approached indirectly via a consideration of another critic of Barthes.

SURVIVAL AS A CHOICE IN GLOBAL CULTURE

In a recent interpretation of *Camera Lucida*, Neil Roughley argues that Barthes returns to phenomenology[16] and the explication of 'an affective intentionality' in this book. This is an interpretation that enables Roughley to highlight the importance of the affective, bodily dimension to Barthes's account of the metamorphosis effected in the *punctum* of the photograph.[17] For Roughley, however, while the return to phenomenology enables Barthes to demonstrate the embodied character of vision, it also means that Barthes tends towards an unwarranted individualism (and thus confirms rather than challenges the possessive individualism that is one of his targets). As Roughley points out,

> Within this enterprise a key role is played by the concept of intentionality, the directedness of consciousness which as such is always 'consciousness of something'. In line with this perspective, 'reality' comes to be reconceptualized as the correlate of sense-conferring intentional acts, 'real units' as 'units of sense'. Thus the analysis of the structure of consciousness appears to provide access to unmediated certainties.
>
> (1995: 112)

In this explication, Roughley identifies what he believes to be an underlying individualism and assumptions of a fixed structure of consciousness in Barthes's account of the *punctum*. But, so I will suggest, Barthes does not assume the nature of this structure; nor does he relate intentionality to the isolated, abstract indi-

15 The family is a key site in prosthetic culture for an examination of whether or not relationality has disappeared: David Wills writes,

> Haunting all questions of relation is the notion of proximity, the economy of the family, the oikos that is the family as a model for all economies. Prosthesis itself would seem to rely for its definition on such an effect of contiguity. It occurs first of all within the space of family ritual. There the codes are well nigh impossible to render explicit, so subtle are they, so attuned to an intricate and unspoken system of conditioned response.
>
> (1995: 20)

16 The book has as its dedication a homage to Sartre's *L'Imaginaire*.

17 For Roughley, Barthes's central question is 'what does my body know of Photography?' (1981: 9). See chapters 5 and 6 for consideration of gender and the body of photography in the phenomenon of false memory syndrome, and chapters 7 and 8 for a consideration of the relations between the body, movement and the image in what has been described as a post-photographic era.

vidual whose existence is defined teleologically by his or her death. For Barthes, the subject is not its own context; that is, the subject is not (only or necessarily) an individual, even in prosthetic culture. But nor does Barthes wish to avoid the presence of a life in death, even in a risk society (Beck, 1992).

Roughley argues that one of the ways that Barthes reveals his individualism is in his stated disinterest in what Roughley calls the socio-cultural determinants and intersubjective constitution of the experience of photography. But the ostentatious nature of Barthes's statement of disinterest suggests an alternative interpretation: namely that Barthes dismisses these determinants because they have themselves come to be strategically employed in contemporary photography for stylistic effect. Roughley contrasts Barthes with Walter Benjamin, whom he praises for insisting on the necessity of developing captions for photographs, since by this means single moments of human existence can be located in relation to their socio-historical and cultural determinations.[18] As Roughley notes, this is precisely what Barthes refuses to do. Perhaps this is a consequence, as Roughley suggests, of Barthes's awareness of the imminence of his own death, an awareness that forecloses interest in anything other than the inevitable end which gives life (individual and universal) meaning. Indeed, for Roughley, the disinterest in the contextualising caption is evidence of Barthes's assumption and privileging of a universalising ontology of consciousness tied to the (embodied, decaying) individual, for the subject's death is taken by Roughley to be the individualising teleology of Barthesian intentionality.[19] I would suggest, however, that Barthes is aware of the ways in which photographs are now taken to illustrate pre-given captions and contexts to which they are subsumed. In this view, Barthes's awareness of the extent to which the contexts or spaces of viewing of the photograph now precedes its taking is what leads him to be wary of the potential of the photograph to foreground its own status as social document, advertisement or legal evidence through the use of captions[20] or, indeed, any other kind of reflexive or self-positioning device. He thus shows some

18 While I have some sympathy with this view, as the discussion of 'The Family of Man' in the previous chapter indicates, the contrast between Barthes and Benjamin seems somewhat unfair, not only because, as the analysis which follows seeks to show, this is to miss Barthes's point, but also because it misrepresents Benjamin, who was cautious about the implications of the adoption of captions. In 'The work of art in the age of mechanical reproduction' he notes that

> For the first time, captions have become obligatory. And it is clear that they have an altogether different character than the title of a painting. The directives which the captions give to those looking at pictures in illustrated magazines soon become even more explicit and more imperative in the film where the meaning of each single picture appears to be prescribed by the sequence of all preceding ones.
>
> (1970: 228)

19 There is obviously much to support this view; for example, Barthes writes, 'By giving me the absolute past of the pose (aorist), the photograph tells me death in the future. What *pricks* me is the discovery of this equivalence' (1981: 96). However, as the following discussion hopes to demonstrate, this discovery of 'death in the future' is not necessarily tied to the individual, as Roughley seems to imply.

20 Similarly, Sontag argues that much contemporary photography suppresses social and political queasiness, the unease provoked by the strange, the difficult, oddity. This suppression, she argues, ⇒

apprehension about the ways in which the camera has come to anticipate the viewer's seeing through the process of outcontextualisation.

To come to the example: Roughley is scathing about the way in which a photograph of a dead child in Nicaragua provides the occasion for Barthes not to consider the 'western powers' implication in the daily mass slaughter of the Third World' (as Roughley presumably thinks he should do), but to reflect on the way in which photography depicts the way in which 'our time assumes death'.[21] Roughley remarks,

> It is worth recalling here the young Barthes' rhetorical question, 'Do we really have to sing [death's] essence once again and risk forgetting what we can do against it?'
>
> (1995: 119)

Yet, the photographs of catastrophe, disaster and death in the advertising campaigns adopted by the fashion clothing company Benetton – including that of a man about to die from AIDS – offer an example which demonstrates that the older Barthes might have been right to be sceptical for they show how the right caption – in this case, 'United Colors of Benetton' – illustrates how remembering what we can do against death does not necessarily preclude singing its essence. For the ethos of survivalism *is* now death's essence. For Barthes, then, the development of photographic vision has been informed by a process of what Strathern (1992) describes as literalisation, of making explicit the conditions of perception, including its socio-historical determinants, in such a way as to make even death seem, if not preventable, then at least a matter of choice. This, I suggest, is the basis for his unwillingness to caption the photograph, or rather, as he sees it, photograph the caption or somehow else in-fill the context of viewing in the image. Let me try to substantiate this claim.

The advertisement in question is one in which a documentary-style photograph of a man on his deathbed surrounded by what one assumes to be his family illustrates the caption 'United Colors of Benetton'. It is a snap from a family album that both depicts the contemporary assumption of death in contemporary global culture – as a risk that pervades the everyday and evades the normal probabilities of 'life' insurance – and mines the assumption itself to provide (consumerist) motives for 'doing something' against it: go shopping! In

> works out not as a liberation of but as a subtraction from the self: a pseudo-familiarity with the horrible reinforces alienation, making one less able to react in real life.
>
> (1977: 41)

Contemporary photography, she argues, possesses the immediacy of a shock, minus the shudder, which has become institutionalised and domesticated. In this sense, photographs act as what Buck-Morss (1992) describes as an an-aesthetic (Buck-Morss, 1992); perhaps, then, there is something more to the parallel (mentioned in chapter 3) which Jane Welsh Carlyle drew between photography and chloroform than their capacity to give 'positive pleasure to poor suffering humanity'.

21 Barthes argues that photography corresponds to the intrusion in modern society of an asymbolic death, 'a kind of abrupt dive into literal Death: *Life / Death*: the paradigm is reduced to a simple click, the one separating the initial pose from the final print' (1981: 92).

other words, the socio-historical determinants of death and disaster with which Roughley and the early Barthes are concerned are put to work in this image in the service of a creed of individualised survivalism.

The image speaks to a society in which, as Bauman notes, 'Death as such is inevitable; but each specific instance of death is contingent' (1992: 5). It is a society in which salvation is not to be arrived at through the 'entry' of death into an after-life, for death is now only an 'exit', but through the strategies of survival.[22] Bauman continues his analysis by arguing that what is significant about the contemporary notion of survival is that it is targeted on others, not on the self: 'We never live through our own death; but we do live through the death of others, and their death gives meaning to our success: we are *still* alive' (1992: 10). As such, the personal achievement of self-preservation can only be grasped as a social relation of survival, but this is a social relation that is made visible as a lifestyle, in this case as a style of life organised in relation to the mathematical modelling of catastrophe.

Bauman identifies a range of techniques or policies of survivalism in Euro-American societies: the religious belief in the transcendence of the limitations imposed by the body; collective designs, such as nationalism, that contemplate the introduction and management of a total order in exchange for a guarantee of the propriety of individual death; the quest for a partner in love who, as a mirror, can offer a space of transcendence; and contemporary techniques of self-care, lifestyle or experimentation. Benetton's iconography offers representations of all of these policies – in depictions of 'life itself' as a divine force, in images depicting the youthful uniformity of global subjecthood, and in endless combinations of people in smiling, (a)symmetrical harmony with each other – but it is as an aesthetic rendering of the last that the advertisement introduced here is most relevant.

As Bauman notes, the survival policies he presents are ordered so as to expose 'the gradual shrinking of the space in which the thrust to immortality is vested', but the last 'shows an amazing capacity for expansion' (1992: 18). (It is perhaps this amazing capacity for expansion that can explain how it is that the caption 'United Colors of Benetton' can be illustrated by almost any image.) Bauman continues,

> What is involved here is an attempt to belie the ultimate limits of the body by breaking, successively, its *currently* encountered, *specific* limitations . . . . By the same token, the impossible task of escaping the mortality of the body is never allowed to be encountered in its awesome totality, as it is split into a never-ending series of concrete challenges, reduced to a manageable, and hence realistic size. The time dimension of transcendence is turning here into a spatial issue: stretching the *span of life* is turned into the effort to stretch the *capacity to live.* Time all but disappears: it has been reduced and flattened out of existence, subjected to a process that 'narrows the present down to a chaos of evanescent events' (Redner, 1982: 280). . . .
>
> (1992: 18–19)

22 These strategies, like the photographic image, can act as the basis of an after-life or prosthetic biography.

In the terms of this last survival policy, the individual, forced by the fear of death to in-fill or fall in upon him- or herself, takes on the 'consuming task of transcending the technical capacity for living' (1992: 19); the individual is absorbed in the life-long labour of the defence of health, construing life as a process of self-constitution. S/He does so by stretching the capacity to live, abolishing the future, which can no longer be colonised by planning, probability and responsibility, perhaps not even by what has been the guardian of life itself, the family, and replacing time with a multitude of individual occurrences, each with its own cause, the locus of individual experimentation. As Bauman points out, the drawback of this survival policy is that the (experimental) individual is left alone – despite the visible presence of a family – to face the exigencies of surviving in what Roger Friedland and Deidre Boden (1994) have called now/here: 'loneliness is frightening and unbearable, because of my uncertainty as to how adequate are the weapons I deploy to fight off the threats to my body' (Bauman, 1992: 20). In the advertisement described here, however, Benetton is able to both represent and assuage this loneliness for the individual who is required/chooses to experiment with lifestyle for his or her own survival.

Like other images in Benetton's iconography of disaster, the advertisement seizes a moment of temporal transcendence, non-flowing time, time without continuation or consequence, as its own, transforming it into a global event, so giving it a spatial dimension in which private uncertainty may be lost in 'a shared audacity and temerity of numbers' (Bauman, 1992: 20–21). In these images, Benetton represents itself as the archangel of indifferentiation, holding back the future for the viewer until the past can be perfected. The condensed-to-the-moment of catastrophe narrative time frame of these photographs disembeds a death, a disaster, from specific spatial and temporal contexts and re-embeds them in an apocalyptic global space – in the context of a planet facing catastrophe – and invites the viewer to hold open the aperture of the camera by exercising his or her capacity to make survival a choice. This stylised process of outcontextualisation is a global instantiation of copy and contract, not copy and contact. As Bauman comments: 'Eschatology is dissolved into technology. It is "how to do it", not "what to do", on which survival concerns focus' (1992: 18–19). Benetton stages 'no time' and in so doing delays the closure of the feared moment in which the individual may be annihilated as person and portrayal converge, offering salvation in the after-life of the now/here made possible by the photograph captioned 'United Colors of Benetton'. Simultaneously, however, I suggest, the operation of this loop in this case forecloses the possibility of metamorphosis in its depiction of catastrophe, delaying annihilation but precluding change in the here and now by insisting upon the inescapability of now/here.

As noted in chapter 3, Sekula argues that there is an underlying affinity between a positivist scientism and a romantic metaphysics in modern photography, revealed in what he calls its pursuit of the 'ultimate goal of abstraction'. More specifically, Sekula argues, 'both modern science and modernist art tend to end up worshipping in floating cathedrals of formal, abstract, mathematical relations and "laws"' (1981 : 16). In the image of salvation described above,[23] these abstract laws are further redefined as the assumptions of the laws of probability and their relation to the norm(al individual) are challenged in the representation of an illness that, in popular discourse at least, shows no respect for these laws, for the probabilistic calculations of insurance, the precautions of the responsible individual or the fears of parents for their children, and tells young people that their parents cannot protect them. In their place, it provides an aestheticised representation of what Bauman calls chaos but might also be described as catastrophe, the mathematical 'art of models'.

In mathematics, catastrophe theory offers the possibility of mapping the discontinuous instance, the chance occurrence, without reducing its arbitrariness or indeterminacy.[24] Its aim is to provide a formal language for the description of jump behaviour, sudden discontinuities within a gradually changing system. Mary Ann Doane writes,

> The etymological specification of catastrophe as the overturning of a given situation anticipates its more formal delineation by catastrophe theory. Here, catastrophe is defined as unexpected discontinuity in an otherwise continuous system. The theory is most appropriate, then, for the study of sudden and unexpected effects in a gradually changing situation. The emphasis upon suddenness suggests that catastrophe is of a temporal order. . . .
>
> [It is] 'a theory about singularities. When applied to scientific problems, therefore, it deals with the properties of discontinuities directly, without reference to any specific underlying mechanism.' It is, therefore, no longer a question of explanation. Catastrophe theory confronts the indeterminable without reducing it to a set of determinations.
>
> (1990: 228, 234)

As a sub-discipline in mathematics, catastrophe theory has been developed in certain global applications, including meteorology, but Doane believes that television is also a catastrophic machine. So too is the image of salvation described above, for it depicts an image of catastrophe not as a danger that might portend change or metamorphosis (and thus the archangel of Benetton is not the Angelus Novus of which Benjamin writes), but as an event, that is, the aestheticised image of an unexpected discontinuity, both 'thrill and preclusion' (Doane, 1990), a traumatic event that does not wound (Barthes, 1981).

More widely, it seems the process of literalisation, of the increasing informedness of photography, is never ending, and brings with it the continual revision of private and public, inside and outside, life and death, the notion of the individual and his or her relation to context or, perhaps better, global environment: it is what shapes the copy and contract of experimental individualism in now/here.

23 The similarities between this Benetton advertisement and popular depictions of Christ did not go unnoticed in the British press.

24 Catastrophe theory is based on a theorem in topology discovered by the French mathematician Renè Thom in 1968, who described it as an 'art of models' (quoted in Mellencamp, 1990: 244–245).

That there were public debates about the tastefulness of Bennetton's use of this image – many of which focused on the issue of whether or not the subject (or his family) had consented to the use of his image in this way – indicates that these revisions are by no means acceptable to all. However, there are many other uses of photography and imaging devices – from video-recording to ultrasound, computer modelling and the mapping of the human genome[25] – which suggest that the process of literalisation is beginning to disturb the relationship between individual and self-identity, as consciousness, memory and life itself are increasingly dissociated from the individual and collective body.

ANTICIPATION AND HESITATION

More generally what this example suggests is that Barthes's dislike of captions, rather than a consequence of his location of the intentionality of the photograph in an individual whose embodied biography is predetermined by its inevitable end in death, indicates his caution about a contemporary photography that combines a pseudo-universal individualised intentionality with a knowing informedness of its own status as image.[26] (And thus Barthes can be seen to be critical of experimental individualism.) In opposition to this use of photography, I suggest, Barthes seeks to redefine seeing photographically in terms of the development of a techno-intuitive knowledge of a kind which has the potential to mark an interruption or suspension in the human relationship with time, memory and death. This knowledge is, for him, created in a relation of intentionality[27] *and* indexicality, of hesitation and anticipation: for Barthes, the viewer has the opportunity to confront in the photograph 'the wakening of intractable reality' (1981: 119).

As Roughley himself points out, Barthes uses Husserl's description of the phenomenological '*Einstellung*' – which means both 'attitude' and photographic 'focus' – to characterise 'photographic reduction': it is by this means – that is,

25 Barthes notes, alongside the penal use of the photograph as likeness, that it has also had a special value because of its ability to speak of lineage. He writes,

> But more insidious, more penetrating than likeness: the Photograph sometimes makes appear what we never see in a real face (or in a face reflected in a mirror): a genetic feature, the fragment of oneself or of a relative which comes from some ancestor. In a certain photograph, I have my father's sister's 'look'. The Photograph gives a little truth, on condition that it parcels out the body. But this truth is not that of the individual, . . . ; it is the truth of lineage.
> (1981: 103)

Here Barthes gives some forewarning of how the image might be employed to redefine the identity of lineage in terms of fragments or parcels of the body in genetic mapping techniques such as the human genome project, although, if the analyses of Rabinow (1992), Biddick (1993) and others are accepted, he was too confident that the photograph – and its descendants – would not be able to reduce what he calls 'the inhuman distance of the Stock' (1981: 105).

26 He writes, 'The photograph touches me if I withdraw it from its usual blah-blah: "Technique", "Reality", "Reportage", "Art", etc.: to say nothing, to shut my eyes, to allow the detail to rise of its own accord into affective consciousness' (1981: 55).

27 I use this term somewhat tentatively since there is much debate about whether or not Barthes is true to classical phenomenology; for a discussion of the phenomenological notion of intentionality see Hammond *et al.* (1991). According to Jay, Barthes himself describes his method as 'a phenomenological method, an entirely subjective one' (quoted in Jay, 1994: 451).

reduction not reflection – that Barthes suggests that the photograph breaks the '"constitutive style" [of experience]' (1981: 90). This is how the *punctum* of the photograph freezes the pure contingency of a singular, unrepeatable moment, interrupting or suspending the 'hermeneutic', 'proairetic' and 'cultural' codes which determine how we see the world, producing the possibility of metamorphosis. He writes, 'I am the reference of every photograph, and this is what generates my astonishment in addressing myself to the fundamental question: why is it that I am alive *here and now*?' (1981: 84). While Roughley appears to suggest that the astonishment is subsumed by Barthes in the biography of the observing individual (this seems to be one of the principal grounds for his critique of an 'individualism' underlying Barthes's account), I would suggest that the emergence of the *punctum* is a process that is neither simply that of an individual body (the viewer) nor that of a machine (the camera), but a combination of the two. Moreover, Barthes recognises that this combination is not itself fixed but is continually being revised. Roughley, like Tagg, criticises Barthes for an individualism which he himself reinscribes, for he confines intentionality to a teleological individual consciousness. For Barthes, in contrast, intentionality and indexicality are not to be understood in isolation from each other, and they cannot be located in either the individual or the camera but only in *seeing photographically*.

When Barthes writes that 'every photograph is somehow co-natural with its referent', this is not an assertion of the self-evidential function of the photograph, of the one-way incorporation of the natural within the cultural, the bringing inside the frame of the outside. Rather it can be interpreted as a statement of the equivalence of image and referent, of culture (or second nature) and nature, as media of mimesis. This is an equivalence, however, which is not given but has to be made in the two-way relations of suggestion, of hesitation and anticipation, between viewer and image. Simultaneously, however, it is also a recognition of transmutation in suggestion, of metamorphosis, in the superimposition, or interleaving, of nature and culture, culture and (second) nature, outside and inside, inside and outside. And if this is so, seeing photographically – and the possibilities it offers for mimesis – needs to be understood in relation to the specific contemporary spaces which the subject inhabits, what Barthes calls 'the here and now'. These clearly include those not only of the family album and promotional culture but also of the scientific attitude.[28] This is especially important since, so it is widely claimed, in the global space of contemporary science-as-culture, the boundary between inside and outside, the limit in relation to and against which mimesis acts, is itself continually being redrawn.[29]

In short, the image occupies spaces other than those of now/here, including those of the practices of situated knowledge (Haraway, 1991). And attention to the particular, the here and now, the situated, is especially necessary since it is

28 Roger Caillois claims, 'In the end, for science everything is milieu' (1988: 70).

29 Krauss makes this explicit. She points out that the 'spatial beyond' is not simply any space whatsoever (Deleuze, 1989), but exists in an anterior relation to a specifically modern formation of space, the space of modern vision, that which is 'the infinitely multiple on the one hand, and the simultaneously unified on the other' (Krauss, 1994: 6), in which 'the viewpoint and the vanishing point are symmetrical' (Krauss, 1994: 113).

only in relation to particular spaces and times that the question of difference and its significance in prosthetic culture can be reintroduced without flattening it in diversity. Moreover, just as the relation of mimesis to difference is not already given, but is, rather, always a matter of context, of the familiar and the global, it is the particular that makes possible an exploration of the reiterations, the inclusions and exclusions, the displacements and replacements, the erasures and substitutions of the now/here of experimental individualism. This inter-related set of concerns is the subject of the next two chapters (which also return to the familiar and the global) but some general remarks on gender and the force of vision – its powers of life and death – in the emergence of prosthetic culture will bring this chapter to an end.

THE FORCE OF VISION

> The Photograph is violent: not because it shows violent things, but because on each occasion *it fills the sight by force*, and because in it nothing can be refused or transformed.
>
> (Barthes, 1981: 91)

In this quotation, Barthes implies that the power of the image – its ability to raise a shudder – is a consequence not only of its inability to show anything other than what has been but no longer is, but also of its intransigence, its resistance to transformation. How, though, is this to be reconciled with the possibility of metamorphosis outlined above? I want to explore this by reflecting on the force – the ability to wound – that fills sight and makes visible a life in death.

In a fascinating article on 'Technology's body' (1993), Mary Ann Doane argues that the historical instrumentality and rationality of photography and cinema as technologies were predicated on a culturally specific assumption of their separability from the human body. As a consequence, she suggests, there has emerged both an almost fearful attitude to the idea that 'taking a picture' implies some kind of bodily loss *and* a fascination with the possibility of an imbrication of technology and the body. Moreover, while the body (and individual) at stake in the technology of the image appears to be universal, as sexually and racially unspecified, it has, Doane argues, historically been constituted as white and male. More particularly, she suggests that the specificity of this constitution is related to a dominant conceptualisation of modernity as shock or trauma, since, with its suggestion of a penetration or breach of an otherwise seamless body, trauma is premised upon and produces a masculine subjectivity. It produces both the wish for a superhuman body endowed with new organs,[30] and

30 This is a wish that is clearly visible in the writings of Ernst Jünger, who is one of the last surviving German members of the generation of 1914, and has been alternately celebrated as modernist and condemned as fascist. Jünger saw photography as a sign of the emergence of a cold, instrumental 'second consciousness'. He praised the camera as a new eye, devoid of feeling and thus able to contemplate the horrors of the modern world with an almost aesthetic detachment. For Jünger, the camera was both a shield for the sentiments, and an aggressive visual weapon. Defenders of Jünger, the stylist, have compared him to a seismograph of the crisis of his times. As Huyssen notes, however, the metaphor is not necessarily in Jünger's favour. ⇒

the denial of the body through the projection of contingency and embodiment on to the white woman or the racial other, the primitive. Both these wishes, she argues, have come to be satisfied in modern cinema: through the fantasy of identification with the male hero of adventure narratives, on the one hand (see chapter 8 for further discussion of the superhero), and the spectacularisation of the female and 'primitive' body of the other.[31]

Is this inscription of the masculinity of technology's body what prevents anything other than the reification of mimesis as a living death in contemporary uses of photography?[32] Do the historical links between the photographic image, trauma and modernity make it impossible for women to see themselves in contemporary culture? Has the possibility of a specifically feminine relation to mimesis been lost in the disappearance of context: does the individual who internalises the exterior, or makes immediate the mediated, necessarily construct a masculine self-identity? Is the global subject addressed by Benetton necessarily white and male? As the grounding function of nature disappears (and with it not just the singularity of women but also the mythological specificity of the feminine), and figure and ground are replaced by a system constituted in the strategic, technologically mediated couplings of the auto-reproducing or experimental individual with its environment, can there be any conception of context or space other than that of now/here?

As chapter 2 indicated, trauma is by no means a simple term; its emergence and development cannot be captured in a single, continuous historical narrative. Nor, indeed, can it simply be mapped onto modernity. What is useful about Doane's analysis is her attention to the multiple ways in which the historical development of cinema as a technology has come to be tied to the gendered assumptions of certain models of seeing and embodiment. She does not presume that this exhausts the image and its relationship to gender, embodiment and space; and she and many other writers have sought to explore these alternatives. For example, in her discussion of 'Photography in the service of surrealism'

Huyssen (1993, 1995) writes that Jünger's advocacy of the camera as an 'armoured eye' can be understood as part of his attempt to protect the human body against pain, and that his writings present increasingly aestheticised depictions of his experiences in the trenches in order to protect himself against the memory of these traumatic experences.

> I would suggest that this identification with the destructive forces of modernity that overwhelmed Jünger on the battlefield is a traumatic reaction formation, which resulted in a compulsive repudiation of his own body as organic and in a literary repetition compulsion which makes Jünger's texts of the 1920s so very similar to each other.
>
> (1993: 13)

31 In his 'Project for a glossary of the twentieth century', J. G. Ballard defines 'prosthetics' as 'The castration complex raised to the level of an art form' (1992: 271).

32 Doane argues that this has not always been the case in cinema. So, for example, she argues, cinema would seem to reinscribe the deficiency of the eye to exploit the notion of the after-image in order to transform a series of still images into an illusion of movement. She concludes:

> Hence, we are faced with the strange consequence that the cinema, as a technology of images, acts both as a prosthetic device, enhancing or expanding vision, and as a collaborator with the body's own deficiencies.
>
> (1993: 5)

(1986a), Rosalind Krauss suggests that surrealism created a photographic frame for 'an opening' in space:

> If we are to generalize the aesthetic of surrealism, the concept of convulsive beauty is at the core of its aesthetic, a concept that reduces to an experience of reality transformed into representation. Surreality *is*, we could say, nature convulsed into a kind of writing. The special access that photography, as a medium, has to this experience is photography's privileged connection to the real. The manipulations then available to photography – what we have been calling doubling and spacing as well as a technique of representational reduplication – structure *en abyme* – appear to document these convulsions. The photographs are not *interpretations* of reality. . . . Instead, they are presentations of that very reality as configured or coded or written.
>
> (1986a: 35)

Moreover, in surrealism, argues Krauss, the capacity of the photograph to depict a curious invasion of the body by space is given aesthetic form. This is exemplified by the use of techniques for the deliberate disintegration rather than the creation of form, what she calls the condition *informé* . She writes,

> a variety of photographic methods has been exploited to produce an image of the invasion of space: of bodies dizzily yielding to the force of gravity; of bodies in the grip of a distorting perspective; of bodies decapitated by the projection of shadow; of bodies eaten away by either heat or light.
>
> (1986b: 70)

Is this a way of seeing that does not require the masculine subject that Doane identifies? Krauss believes that rather than seeing this optical power in terms of a new mastery, as did some theorists of modernity, the surrealists and, later, Lacan[33] described this as a mastery from without, imposed on a subject who is, as Krauss puts it, 'trapped in a cat's cradle of representation, caught in a hall of mirrors, lost in a labyrinth' (1986b: 78).

My view is that this interpretation, while seductive, tends to describe no more than the distress of a (masculine) subject who aspires to mastery: the sense of the inevitablity of loss, lack and entrapment is palpable in the quotation above while it is the apparent inevitability of this sense of loss in psychoanalysis that makes predictable Tagg's transformation of suggestion into desire. A more pressing question for the argument being developed here, however, is: does *Barthes's* notion of the *punctum* provide an opening in space that is not subsumable in now/here? Or is his notion of the *punctum* as a wound necessarily tied to a masculine conception of the individual? To answer this it is worth returning to the distinction, noted above, that Barthes himself makes between the 'photographic shock' which 'consists less in traumatizing than in revealing what was so well hidden that the actor himself was unaware or unconscious of it' and 'the *punctum*', the

33 Psychoanalysis too, Krauss suggests, can be seen as a movement in which the invasion of the body by space is given expression.

point of sudden and strong emotion, of small trauma, which wounds. For Barthes, the *punctum*, which can be a tiny detail, 'has more or less potentially, a power of expansion', but this expansion is not that of which Bauman speaks. Rather, 'This power is metonymic' (Barthes, 1981: 45); it occurs because the photographer cannot '*not* photograph the part object at the same time as the total object' (Barthes, 1981: 47).

In many respects though, the notion of the *punctum* as a wound has strong similarities with the definition of trauma that Krauss arrives at in her discussion of surrealism. She writes,

> The structure of the trauma, then, is not just that it initiates a compulsion to repeat but that it institutes the gap of the trauma itself – the missed encounter – as the always-already occupied meaning of that opening onto a spatial beyond that we think of as the determining character of vision.
>
> (1994: 72)

Yet whereas the notion of trauma that Krauss identifies is tied to a sense of ineffable loss – the missed encounter – Barthes's notion of the *punctum* as a wound is not so tied, or at least not necessarily; for the *punctum* is the effect not only of metamorphosis but also of coincidence. This coincidence is an encounter that has not been missed but is waiting to happen.[34] In other words, whereas the psychoanalytic notion of trauma is tied to the past, that which Barthes identifies is still in the future. This future, while it has not yet happened, is held in anticipation by the image. The *punctum* that arises in the loop of seeing photographically thus offers a continuation of the possibility that, in Strathern's words, 'what is seen fills the field of vision, but the field of vision *is never taken as all there is to see*' (1992: 131; quoted in chapter 2).[35]

The possibility of this way of seeing photographically is explored in Barthes's discussion of looking at the film still (1977). Looking at a still, for Barthes, takes place at a divide, at a point where the perception, or, perhaps better, the invention, of the image is in the process of being transformed, is between the edge of things and their representation. It is free of the narrative or sequential impera-

34 Some recognition of coincidence is perhaps also visible in Krauss's acknowledgement of the gap of the trauma itself, but psychoanalysis determinedly insists upon the always already given nature of the in-filling of the gap, and tends not to allow that the filling in of vision may reproduce the gap without in-filling, nor acknowledge that the process of filling in may leave its own rem(a)inders. (See Strathern, 1991; Irigaray, 1993; and Baudrillard, 1994, for contrasting discussions of the notion of the remainder.) In this respect, psychoanalysis shares a more widely held distrust of the visual, assuming that the photograph cannot leave a gap, will not only fill the viewer's sight by force but fill it in completely. This, I suggest, is to reduce the photograph to a fetish (Metz, 1990). However, Sontag believes that the demand for an ethical response has been foreclosed in contemporary photography in what she sees as the prevailing prescription: do not blink (1977: 41), do not miss *anything*.

35 This is not to forget that while the photographer cannot not photograph the partial object, s/he may also be aspiring to capture the total object. In some interpretations, the part object does not extend outside the total object, but is a cut within it. Derrida, for example, writes that Barthes is 'right to protest against the confusion between that which was his mother and the Figure of the Mother' but that 'the metonymic power (one part for the whole or no name for another, etc.) will always come to inscribe both in this relation without relation' (quoted in Jay, 1994: 454).

tive of film while retaining its movement; the still is the 'possibility of configuration', the 'armature of a permutational unfolding'. It is in precisely this sense that the still is a prosthesis, 'the disposition that deals with inclusion and exclusion, with the boundaries between what remains and what is discarded, with the facts and functions of the cut-off or fragment' (Wills, 1995: 38). But the still does not in-fill the gap; rather the gap is reproduced, lies in waiting for the future, for the still carries marks or accents which designate the displacement of the centre of gravity, a centre of gravity which, so Barthes notes in his discussion of Eisenstein, is transferred inside the fragment, into the elements or parts included within the image itself. This displacement is an example of the filling or folding of sight by force to which the quotation with which this section begins refers.

As an example of such force, consider the photographic series of 'film-stills' (1994) by Cindy Sherman in which a woman's moment of response to the imminence of a harm unknown, to being 'taken', is the consistent focus. This series of photographs ('taken' from films that never existed) are representations of moments of response in which the most intimate expressions of femininity (vulnerability, fear and the uncertainty of waiting) are offered to the viewer as a gift. But this is an offering which can turn bitter in the mouth. The viewer, prompted by the framing which makes self-conscious each photograph's interruption of the stories of melodrama in which the woman's gestures belong, is required to acknowledge his or her complicity in the invention of a *mise-en-scène*, and thus in the constitution of femininity as response, as that which is done to, as something to be 'taken' (Williamson, 1983). The anticipation of the viewer's response in these images produces a moment of hesitation for the viewer, in which the sighting/siting of femininity is acknowledged as a risky business, a matter of life and death. This moment, while capable of filling sight as if by force, is not necessarily already occupied. In the future it anticipates, but does not predict, the possibility that prosthetic culture will not be entirely recuperated by the experimental individual and the spaces of now/here.

5

REMEMBER ME

> It is the technological order itself, that great mirror in which the growing objectifications of our life appear most clearly, and which is sealed against the clutch of pain in a special way . . . . We, however, stand far too deeply in the process to view this . . . . This is all the more the case, as the comfort-character of our technology merges ever more unequivocably with its characteristic of instrumental power.
>
> (Walter Benjamin, quoted in Buck-Morss, 1992: 33)

INTRODUCTION

Questions of memory have always been entwined with the construct of the individual. Indeed, as noted in chapter 2, the techniques of the self involved in the authorship of the memory of a continuous biography were central to the constitution of the modern possessive individual as such. And over the last century, memory has come to acquire an ever greater significance as one of the principal relays between interior life and exterior life, between private and public, the individual and society (Lyotard, 1991; Otis, 1994; Hacking, 1995). One of the most important ways in which memory has come to have this role is through the creation of narratives of self- and collective identity (Ricoeur, 1984–1985; Carr, 1986; Bhabha, 1993). Indeed, narrative is perhaps the principal trope that has enabled a continuity of consciousness organised on the basis of a concrete–qualitative sense of time and its manifestations: experience, subjective recollection and the individual. It thus crucially informs the development of distinctively modern understandings of personal and moral qualities such as self-knowledge, autonomy and responsibility. However, so it has been suggested here, the creation and pervasiveness of images has also had a profound – if often unrecognised – significance in modern self-understandings. This significance has increased as individuals have come to be subject to the processes of rationalisation and commodification (Adorno and Horkheimer, 1982) as the consciousness of a temporal continuum around which narratives of the individual were organised begins to disintegrate into discontinuous shock-like moments.

As the individual is surrendered to present-ness, the moment of transience and the instantaneous, techniques of narrativised self-identity have undergone considerable revision. Indeed, it is sometimes argued that the unified and stable ego constituted in narrative realism has been replaced by psychic discontinuity and incoherence, and subjectively varied and temporally differentiated modes of experiencing are being levelled out and neutralised in abstract, mechanical constructions of time. So, for example, Breuer summarises Theodor Adorno's analysis in the following terms:

> The predominant social character is thus a 'subjectless subject', which engages in 'self-preservation without a self', and is characterized by a 'scattered, disconnected, interchangeable and ephemeral state of "informedness" which one can see will be erased the very next moment to be replaced by new information'.
>
> (1985: 21)

Simultaneously, however, self-identity is continually being reconstituted in novel – technologically mediated – ways, including, for example, the development of the prosthetic (auto)biographies described in chapter 4.

In their constantly changing states of informedness, such (auto)biographies make use of novel ways not only of remembering, but also of forgetting. Indeed, as Hacking (1994) notes, the uniqueness of individuals is now held to be as much, if not more, a function of what they forget than of what they remember. What will be suggested here is that the transformation wrought by images, especially the mechanically reproduced image of the photograph, in the role of memory in prosthetic (auto)biographies simultaneously disturbs and reorders the conventional narratives of continuity of consciousness and self-identity. In other words, the cultural politics of memory are a site at which the conflicting processes of individuation and individualisation described by Adorno and others are played out in terms of the image and narrative.

In order to elaborate these claims, photography will once again be the focus of analysis here. However, rather than approaching photography, as in the preceding chapters, by means of a direct consideration of photographs and viewers, it will be addressed through a consideration of its subject-effects. In particular, two inter-related examples of contemporary identity politics, namely, the 'maladies of agency' (Seltzer, 1993; Sedgwick, 1994) known as multiple personality and false memory syndrome, will be presented in these terms. These phenomena will thus be investigated as illustrations of a cultural politics of memory and are introduced as a way of thinking about how the pervasiveness of the photograph in contemporary society may have contributed – indirectly but none the less powerfully – to transformations in self-identity. To this end, two scenes of (mis)identification from the beginning of the twentieth century will be compared with a third from its end. Here, multiple personality and false memory syndrome are taken to be (historically specific) examples of the implications of seeing photographically for understandings of the individual and self-identity. But, so this analysis will also seek to show, they are not random examples; rather they are at the heart of the complex, changing relationship between vision, technology and (self-)knowledge that defines the individual and modern societies as such to and for themselves. The questions of sexual difference they pose are not incidental but fundamental to how we know ourselves.

In pursuing these questions, I have adopted a somewhat unusual structure for this and the next chapter, according to which the reader is asked to adopt the perspective of the viewer of a photograph, seeing the object of investigation from multiple positions or points of view.[1] The aim is to involve the reader in understanding the specificity of this particular way of seeing; as Haraway (1991) says, this requires both a commitment to mobile positioning and passionate detachment. It may also require a degree of patience, since, as Haraway also notes, it involves (at least) double vision.

MULTIPLE PERSONALITIES

The first illustration in this series of scenes in cultural politics is taken from Rachel Bowlby's discussion of the relation between women and commodities at the dawn of consumer culture in the early part of the twentieth century. As part of this discussion, Bowlby notes the use of the phrase 'just looking' as an apology for the hesitation in a shop before a purchase, which

> expresses the suspended moment of contemplation before an object for sale – the pause for *reflection* in which it is looked at in terms of how it would look on the looker.
>
> (1985: 32)

Bowlby goes on to argue that consumer culture transforms the narcissistic mirror into a shop window, a glass which does not simply reflect but *anticipates* the idealised image of the woman who stands before it in the form of the model she could become: 'Through the glass, the woman sees what she wants and what she wants to be' (1985: 32). She further notes that, unlike Narcissus's reflection, the model in the window is

> something both real and other. It offers something more in the form of another, altered self, and one potentially obtainable via the payment of a stipulated price. But it also, by the same token, constitutes the looker as lacking, as being without 'what it takes'. . . . The window smashes the illusion that there is a meaningful distinction in modern society between illusion and reality, fact and fantasy, fake and genuine images of the self.
>
> (1985: 33–34)

Bowlby historically contextualises Freud's adaptation of the Narcissus myth in his conception of the ego, and suggests that his account of female subjectivity in terms of a feminine tendency to remain closer to the narcissism of childhood may have been appropriate in the early stages of the consumer period of capitalism, but requires revision as the

1 Before doing so, the reader might like to consider the following remarks by Virilio:

> In calling his first photographs of his surroundings 'points of view', around 1820, their inventor, Nicéphore Nièpce came as close as possible to Littré's rigorous definition: 'The point of view is a collection of objects to which the eye is *directed* and on which it *rests* within a certain distance.'
>
> (1994: 19)

> private solipsistic fascination of the lady at home in her boudoir, or Narcissus at one with his image in the lake, moves out into the worldly, public allure of *publicité*, the outside solicitations of advertising.
>
> (1985: 32)

This solicitation, however, is seen to lead to a new dance in which women and commodities,

> seducer and seduced, possessor and possessed of one another . . . flaunt their images at one another in an amorous regard which both extends and reinforces the classical picture of the young girl gazing into the mirror in love with herself.
>
> (1985: 32)

The second scene is drawn from a recent analysis of the text, *The Dissociation of a Personality: A Biographical Study in Abnormal Psychology* (1905), which is the account by a once well-known New England psychotherapist, Morton Prince, of his treatment of a young woman, Miss Beauchamp. The patient exhibits behaviour which is at first diagnosed as a typical if extreme example of neurasthenia[2] or hysteria, but which is later identified as multiple personality.[3] In a fascinating discussion of this once-famous text, Ruth Leys pays particular attention to Prince's presentation of a scene in which one personality, 'BIV, who has been locked in a "life and death struggle" with her hated rival, Sally, had a "very remarkable experience"' (1992: 179–180). While combing her hair, BIV looks at herself in a mirror and sees a

> curious, laughing expression – a regular, diabolical smile – come over her face . . . . [She] had a feeling of horror come over her at what she saw. She seemed to recognize it as the expression of the thing that possessed her. She sees herself as another person in the mirror and is frightened by the extraordinary character of the expression
>
> (1992: 180)

yet decides to interrogate this 'thing' – which, of course, is Sally – by using automatic writing to make it speak.

In both these scenes from the beginning of the twentieth century, then – in Europe and North America respectively – relations of looking are deemed central to the constitution of (feminine) self-identity and thus of self-knowledge. However, these relations are the locus of instability. In short, a woman recognising someone or something similar but somehow other than herself in her reflection is held to be indicative of a fundamental instability in all moments of

2 Susan Buck-Morss notes that neurasthenia was used to describe the disintegration of the capacity for experience in the nineteenth century: the disorder was caused by an 'excess of stimulation' (*sthenia*), 'and the incapacity to react to the same' (*a*sthenia) (1992: 19). Rabinach (1992) notes that the standard textbook on neurasthenia in *fin-de-siècle* France, *L'Hygiène de neurasthénique*, was co-authored by Dr Achille Adrien Proust, father of the greatest literary neurasthenic of the age.

3 For a more detailed account of the emergence of multiple personality, see Ian Hacking's *Rewriting the Soul*. Hacking describes his own account of multiple personality as 'a story about what I have called making up people' (1995: 6).

identification. The instability of this identification is related to a process of imitation of an-other mediated by a mirror, an instance of the technological order of which Benjamin speaks. How, though, was this process of mediation understood?

Leys offers a powerful interpretation of how mediation has been, as she sees it, fixed (and I use this term deliberately to draw an analogy between the fixing of identity and the fixing of the image in the photograph). She believes that there is a radical notion of the psyche linked to the notion of suggestion or imitation implicit in Morton Prince's text,[4] arguing that

> the notion of hypnotic suggestion as involving a somnambulistic, unconscious identification with the hypnotist so deep that the patient 'blindly' or unconsciously, without the possibility of subsequent recollection or narration, takes the place of or incarnates the other ('who at the same moment isn't an "other", but "myself", in my undecidable identity of the somnambulistic ego'), can scarcely if at all be distinguished from the phenomenon of multiple personality as it was experienced in the early twentieth century. Understood in this way, multiple personality is the mimetic idea *par excellence*.
>
> (1992: 173)

However, she goes on to show that this possibility is not realised in Prince's account: instead, he interprets

> the scandalous estrangement or splitting of the 'self' in hypnosis not as the effect of mimetic identification but as the sign of *another subject or personality* – that is, as the manifestation of a part of the self that has hitherto been latent or concealed . . . but that has now been revealed or 'dissociated' by a trauma or by suggestion.
>
> (1992: 173–174)

Her thesis is thus that Prince's analysis of the Beauchamp case simultaneously instantiates and suppresses what she calls the *mimesis-suggestion* paradigm through the fixing of the subject of/in representation.

In the suppression of this paradigm, so-called 'spontaneous phenomena' are taken as evidence that the multiple personalities displayed by Miss Beauchamp are neither the product of suggestion nor simply delusions, but rather the signs of representation, will and desire.[5] For example, in the scene described above,

4 Seltzer argues neurasthenia and other maladies of the will were 'in effect understood as maladies of mimesis, representation and writing'. He cites the description by Charcot of his neurasthenic patients by the name '*l'homme du petit papier*', a title adopted because they frequently appeared with 'slips of paper or manuscripts endlessly listing their ailments' (1993: 103).

5 Leys also discusses recent deconstructive readings of Freud's work which have stressed the extent to which his thought continually struggled to distinguish itself from a problematic of hypnosis or suggestion, understood as involving a kind of imitation or mimesis. One of these critics, Jacqueline Rose, argues that

> Telepathy appears and disappears in Freud's own writing . . . the transference of thoughts . . . exceeds the fact of any single and determinant event. But in doing so [it] also push[es] the yet-to-be-born neurotic science up to and even beyond the limits which it will later choose to set for itself.
>
> (1986: 190–191)

⇒

Prince's account presents the use of automatic writing as a means of the expression of a rival will and thus as the means of an 'independent' personality. As Leys notes, the scene 'converts the automatic into the volitional, BIV's loss of control into Sally's intentions'. Crucially, this interpretation is dependent on the framing context of the mirror, since the mirror, an inanimate technology, stands in as an apparently objective replacement for the analyst, and thus – through its powers of decontextualisation – assuages the anxiety that the distinct personality it reveals is an effect manufactured by the observer. What Leys's analysis highlights is not only the instability of identification, but also struggles to channel, stabilise and fix possession, ownership even, of 'the thing' of suggestion,[6] both real and other, the alter(ed) self that arises in the creation of a subject of representation.

While Leys is most concerned with the implications of this for self-identity, especially its role in the reification of subjectivity as a 'thing' to be owned, she also points to its implications for the reduction of meaning to representation through the insistence upon an obligatory distance between the self and the other depicted in the mirror. In the keeping of this distance, she suggests, the technological order and the knowledge it produces have been used, adapted and developed in such a way as to stabilise the process of mimesis in a notion of visual representation as *reflection*. Moreover, while the particular technology

She points out that

> Freud believed that telepathy was a danger to psychoanalysis because of the relationship of pure belief which it induced in relation to its object, and because he felt that the nature of any object (telepathic or otherwise) which fell into the realm of psychic life was irrelevant to the way it would operate according to the associations and psychic dynamic of individual subjects.
> (1986: 189–190)

According to these deconstructive readings, Freud sought to evade the radical dedifferentiation of self and other implicit in hypnotic suggestion by interpreting the effects of hypnosis as the product not of the relationship between the hypnotist and subject, but of the subject's sexual desire. In these writings, it is argued, what Freud found uncanny or scandalous about hypnosis/suggestion, and what therefore he struggled to suppress, is the idea that in suggestion the patient's thoughts do not come from her or his own mind or self but are produced by the 'imitation' or suggestion of another – in this case, the hypnotist or the analyst.

Some deconstructive critics argue that there is a double-logic at work in the Freudian subject – a primary mimesis by which the desiring subject is brought into being, and a violent suppression of all reference to identification and mimesis; as Borch-Jacobsen writes, 'it is as if the process of identification were regularly transformed into a claim of identity' (1988: 54).

6 Leys reports that the goal of therapy in cases of multiple personality has recently been described in the following way: 'It seems to me that after treatment you want to end up with a functional unit, be it a corporation, a partnership or a one-owner business' (1992: 199). There has also been a long-standing debate within what Hacking calls the multiple movement about whether the term personality should continue to be used at all. Indeed, the term Multiple Personality Disorder has just been replaced in the psychological profession by Dissociative Identity Disorder. One of the key psychologists involved in this redefinition is reported by Hacking as saying,

> I want in a sense to mainstream this disorder – I don't want it to be seen as some kind of circus sideshow. . . . I felt that the important thing was to emphasize that the main problem is the difficulty in integrating disparate elements of memory, identity and consciousness, rather than the proliferation of personalities.
> (1995: 19)

at issue in this case – a mirror – appears simple, historically it is only one surface in an ever-lengthening hall of cultural technologies: lighting, advertising, publicity, promotion, images, art, photography, cinema and – as Bowlby makes clear – psychoanalysis itself. Altogether, they may be said to comprise what Rodolphe Gasché (1986) terms the tain of the mirror of the modern subject.

Gasché argues that specular or reflective discourses of identity, in which images or words are held to mirror objects or thoughts 'without remainder', have forgotten the silver backing, the tain behind every image. In these discourses, when the tain is remembered, becomes, as it were, visible, the mirror is believed to lose its capacity to reflect. However, so he argues, this does not mean that the tain is without its subject-effects. Similarly, I will argue here that the tainted power of Benjamin's great mirror of the technological order – which is to be exemplified here by the photograph – has not always been and cannot always be confined in reflection, and disturbs and refigures the self that is subject-ed to its object-ivity. Indeed, so disturbing are its subject-effects that it does not seem inappropriate to reintroduce Barthes's claim that 'the photograph fills our sight as if by force'. The question I address is whether the image of the 'great technological order' necessarily uses the force of 'total recall' or whether it makes possible a perhaps still violent but none the less partial recollection.

FALSE MEMORY SYNDROME

Multiple personality disorder has recently undergone a revival in the United States (and, to a much lesser extent, elsewhere):[7] after virtually disappearing in the 1930s, reports of the disorder have now increased hugely.[8] Only two hundred cases of multiple personality were reported prior to 1980 in the United States, but one thousand were known to be in treatment by 1984 and four thousand in 1989 (Leys, 1992; Hacking, 1995). Contemporary estimates of the total number of cases in the United States go as high as three hundred thousand.[9] The number of personalities in a given case has also been growing rapidly; in 1989 the median was eleven, but as many as sixty-five or more 'alters' have been

7 Rabinach notes that

> In his pioneering work, *American Nervousness* (1881), Beard claimed that 'nervous diseases are far greater here than in any other nation of history'. . . . Beard believed, paradoxically, that because of their superior mental capacity, the scientific and technological genius of Americans made them less resilient to the shocks inflicted on them by their own mighty civilization.
>
> (1992: 178)

8 Hacking suggests that the influence of psychoanalysis 'may be responsible for the waning of multiplicity during the first half of the twentieth century', at least in the United States (1995: 44). Rather than challenging Leys's thesis, this can be seen as confirmation of the force of the need felt by those in the psychoanalytic movement to distance themselves from the hypnosis/suggestion paradigm.

9 This figure is taken from Leys (1992). Hacking reports the claim that 'Maybe one person in twenty suffered from a dissociative disorder' (1995: 8); however, he also notes that 'Multiple personality has become the most contested type of diagnosis in psychiatry' (1995: 9).

reported.[10] Now, as before, the majority of patients so diagnosed are women. Typical cases, involving splitting or dissociation, memory lapses, time distortions and the use of the third person, are attributed to emotional and physical trauma, especially childhood sexual abuse.[11] The therapy of choice is usually hypnosis. Multiple personality is also commonly associated with another syndrome of suggestion, recovered memory, or false memory syndrome. This syndrome will be the focus of investigation in the third scene of (mis)identification to be discussed here.

10 These figures are taken from a report in *The Independent on Sunday* (Schnabel, 1993) on the case of Donna Smith, an American woman diagnosed as having multiple personality disorder who brought charges of sexual abuse against her father.

11 Hacking argues that

> The multiple personality field has been solidified by the causal idea that multiplicity is a coping mechanism, a response to early and repeated trauma, often sexual in nature.
>
> (1995: 13)

However, he also notes Judith Herman's observation that 'every time we have taken trauma seriously, it has been "in affiliation with a political movement"' (1995: 55). The three movements she discusses are hysteria, shell shock and sexual and domestic violence.

Hacking himself defines his own approach to the relationship between sexual abuse, trauma and multiple personality in terms of the following interest:

> Child abuse, and repressed memories of child abuse, are supposed to have powerful effects on the developing adult. What interests me is less the truth or falsehood of that proposition than the way in which assuming it leads people to describe their past anew. Individuals explain their behaviour differently and feel differently about themselves. Each of us becomes a new person as we redescribe the past. I find the so-called social construction of child abuse a topic of limited interest. But I shall constantly return to the question of how that constructed knowledge loops in upon people's moral lives, changes their sense of self-worth, reorganizes and reevaluates the soul.
>
> (1995: 68)

Later he writes,

> My thesis is altogether consistent with what Herman writes, but it reverses the direction of her enquiry. She sees the study of trauma, especially forgotten trauma, as arising within three political movements. I see the way in which those movements latched on to trauma as part of a politics of memory legitimated by, indeed made possible by, the new sciences of memory.
>
> (1995: 213)

This approach has similarities with that adopted by Rabinach, who points out that at the turn of the twentieth century the chief sign of neurasthenia was 'the perpetual sensation of fatigue' (muscular, energetic or mental); neurasthenics frequently showed a distinctive but inexplicable 'aboulia' or lack of will, a lack of attentiveness and disturbances in memory. He further describes early twentieth-century neurasthenia as not simply 'a malady, but a kind of incessant orchestration of analogies to other maladies' (1992: 179), noting that as 'allegories of the real', neurasthenic symptoms derive their power entirely from 'the amplification of other illnesses' (1992: 180), and goes on to point out that these symptoms are elusive, fleeting and immediately lost 'unless invested with meaning by becoming part of a larger interpretive matrix – a phenomenon that Walter Benjamin once explained as the shock required by all allegorical representations' (1992: 180).

Stone too is concerned with 'how the phenomenon of multiple personality fits into a broader framework of cultural developments in which the abstract machine of multiplicity . . . is grinding finer and finer' (1995: 53). She wants to ask whether there is 'any room for nontraumatic multiplicity' (1995: 58).

False memory syndrome is the term employed by the psychology profession and adopted and adapted by the media to describe a complex of memories, typically of child sexual abuse recalled by adults (but also of abduction by aliens) through the use of psychotherapeutic techniques, which are described as false or untrue.[12] So, for example, the journalist and therapist Susie Orbach (who is critical of the term since she does not think it useful) writes,

> In this argument naive patients are said to be encouraged by psychotherapists to believe that the distress and anger they feel are consistent with childhood sexual abuse. The therapist is charged with reconstructing the patient's memory in such a way that the individual believes that they were abused when this was not the case.
>
> (1993: 15)

One particular account has been chosen as the focus of this analysis of the phenomenon.[13] It is the two-part feature, 'Remembering Satan', I and II, that appeared in *The New Yorker* (17 May and 24 May 1993) in which journalist Lawrence Wright reports on a case in which

> The small town of Olympia, Washington, was devastated when the Ingrams, one of its most respected families, suddenly self-destructed amid bizarre accounts of sexual abuse and satanic ritual. As the family unravelled, the allegations escalated into a landmark case in the national obsession with cults and 'recovered' memory.
>
> (1993a: 60)

The central protagonist is Paul Ingram, the father in this respectable family, and the feature delineates his response to the allegations of sexual abuse made by his two adult daughters.

What makes this feature especially interesting[14] for the argument being put forward here is that the explicit focus of Wright's discussion is the therapeutic function, repression and the recovery of memory in a media or information society.[15]

12 According to Frederick Crews, 'a conservative guess of the number of people in the US suffering from "false memory syndrome" would be a million persons since 1988 alone' (1994: 54).

13 The articles that appeared in *The New Yorker* were a serialisation of Wright's book (1994) of the same name. It does not have the same status as Prince's text, but is a notable example of media accounts of the phenomenon. At the same time that the feature was published, there was a whole slew of reports in the British and American press: including Gerrie (1993); Grant (1993, 1994); Jaroff (1993); Orbach (1993, 1994); Schnabel (1993); Bennett (1994); Butler (1994); Crews (1994); Lacey (1994); Morton (1994); Robson-Scott (1994); Cornwall (1995); Mihill (1995). The analysis of the articles by Lawrence Wright presented here is informed by an interpretation of all these writings and my viewing of a number of television accounts.

14 I have chosen to explore false memory syndrome through an analysis of a specific media representation. This is not to say that I see it as an exclusively representational phenomenon; rather I see it as an example of a phenomenon that emerges precisely through the blurring of the boundary between representations and practices (including techniques of the self) that is characteristic of what has been called reflexive modernisation (Beck *et al.*, 1994).

15 It is thus an instance of what Hacking describes as 'memory-thinking'. In *Rewriting the Soul*, Hacking is concerned with the question: 'why has it been essential to organize so many of our present projects in terms of memory?' (1995: 3).

More specifically, this function is taken to be an example of the many mechanisms by which, in Bowlby and Barthes's terms, the private is made into publicity in contemporary society. It is represented as the (unstable) mechanism by which an individually experienced hallucination is translated into a collective nightmare and is thus an example of what happens when the allure of publicity cannot be resisted, when the tain of the mirror becomes visible. The report ends,

> Whatever the true nature of human memory, the Ingram case makes obvious the perils of a fixed idea – in this instance, the fixed idea being that the truth of human behavior, and even of one's own experience, can be cloaked by a trick of the unconscious mind, which draws a curtain of amnesia over a painful past. Unfortunately, the theory of repression also permits the construction of imaginary alternative lives, which may contain some symbolic truth but are in other respects damaging counterfeits that corrupt the currency of real experience.
>
> (1993b: 76)

It thus takes as its explicit focus the 'growing objectifications of our life' as they are reflected in that 'great mirror', the 'technological order'.

THE INTERROGATION OF MEMORY

In Wright's account, when Paul Ingram was first officially asked about the sexual abuse charges that his two daughters, Ericka and Julie (then 22 and 18 respectively), had made, he replied that

> he could not ever remember having ever molested his daughters, but added, 'If this did happen, we need to take care of it.' He said, 'I can't see myself doing this,' but added, 'There may be a dark side of me that I don't know about.'
>
> (1993a: 60)

Several hours later, Wright reports, Ingram confessed:

> I really believe that the allegations did occur and that I did violate them and abuse them and probably for a long period of time.
>
> (1993a: 60–61)

When asked why he is confessing when he can't remember any specific incidents, Ingram replies,

> Well, number one, my girls know me. They wouldn't lie about something like this. And, uh, there's other evidence . . . . The way they've been acting for at least the last couple of years and the fact that I've not been able to be affectionate with them, uh, even though I want to be . . . . I have a hard time hugging them, or even telling them that I love them, and, uh, I just know that that's not natural.
>
> (1993a: 61)

According to Wright, Ingram would 'later recall . . . Vukich [one of the police investigators] having asssured him that, if he did confess, the memories would come back'. Wright thus sets out to uncover how the 'absurd' is generated by the 'not natural', to reveal 'where the hole in Ingram's memory' (1993a: 61) was to lead. To this end, the life-history of this apparently typical, small-town American family is laid out in detail for the readers so that they can appreciate the full implications of the forced recovery or filling in of Ingram's memory.

Wright describes the lives of Paul and his wife-to-be, Sandy – his hopes of being a priest, her desire to be a nun, their first meeting, courtship, marriage and the birth of their children – in matter-of-fact terms. We are told that Paul and Sandy had, or so they believed, a happy, stable and old-fashioned marriage: 'Paul's word was law. Because Sandy seldom disagreed with him, they almost never quarrelled' (1993a: 62). Their neighbours too believed them to be a hard-working Christian family: 'in fact, several later told the police that they had tried to model their own family on the Ingrams' (1993a: 62). The peak of the couple's happiness is reached when they are able to afford to build a house on some land of their own:

> At last, Paul and Sandy's hopes were realized. Their home was surrounded by fir, alder, ash, cottonwood, cedar, and hemlock. In the spring, the dogwoods bloomed and deer poked around in the bush. The woods were full of racoons and possums and grouse, and there was an occasional red fox. There were ducks and herons in the pond. Sandy expanded her garden, making room for fruit trees and flowering plants. In addition to the chickens and rabbits that Paul raised, there was enough land to graze a few cows. It felt like paradise to Paul and Sandy.
>
> (1993a: 63)

But this Garden of Eden is not as idyllic as it seems; it does not feel like paradise to the children: 'They thought of the place as remote and isolated, and felt as if the chores never stopped' (1993a: 63).

But these feelings are not expressed at the time: it is only as a consequence of the allegations made on the basis of memories recovered by the daughters as adults that Sandy and Paul are forced to confront the hollowness of their dream. When this happens, Wright suggests, it is not just the dreams of this single couple that are called into doubt. It is the land of the free itself which is threatened by the confusion wreaked by false memories: the contentment of individual lives, solidarity and trust amongst colleagues at work, the security of the community, and the health of the national psyche itself are all put at risk. Others implicated in the allegations recognise what is at stake:

> Even if he [Rabie] got off, the fact that he had been charged would mean that his reputation was destroyed, his lobbying career was finished, his Kiwanis work was over, his marriage was placed in peril, and he might not be allowed ever to see his granddaughters again . . . . In short, his life was ruined.
>
> (1993a: 73)

The seriousness of this threat is confirmed for the readers when they are told that the accused, including Ingram himself, are not only churchgoers and respected citizens of the community, but also members of the local police force. And, they learn,

> Even more disquieting to the investigators was a growing conviction that the Ingram case was, as they frequently said to each other, 'the tip of the iceberg' – the iceberg being a nationwide satanic conspiracy.
>
> (1993a: 77)

The filling in of the missing gaps in Ingram's memory, so the investigators seem to both hope and fear, will reveal the 'dark side' not only of Ingram, but also of the national psyche itself:

> When McClanahan hung up, it struck him that the Ingram case was much more important than anyone had realized – that it was the one case in America that could prove, finally, that satanic-abuse was real.
>
> (1993a: 81)

Yet it is the filling in of the hole in Ingram's memory[16] rather than whether or not satanic abuse is 'real', or indeed the implications of abuse for the individuals concerned or the society of which they are part,[17] that is Wright's principal concern. In this respect, what he as 'the reporter at large' finds most disturbing is that the standard investigative procedures by which the truth of allegations of abuse can be established are thrown into complete disarray:

> They were groping to understand what was going on in their community – and, indeed, in their own department. All the familiar road signs of a typical police investigation had been turned upside down. The investigators were investigating not just one but several colleagues and former co-workers. The alleged central perpetrator was admitting to more depraved crimes than the victims were alleging. It seemed nearly impossible to coordinate all the accusations into a coherent set of allegations. Jaded detectives who regularly visited the worst precincts of the human psyche were thoroughly shaken by the emerging revelations of the Ingram case.
>
> (1993a: 77)

16 In her discussion of the so-called Cleveland case, Bea Campbell writes of the media's response:

> the problem for most of the media was not society's crisis in confronting sexual abuse, but the tragedy of innocent parents wrongly accused. And so the issue was not the difficulty of prevention and detection of the most elusive crime, but the etiquette of intervention.
>
> (1988: 210)

17 This is important for the argument being developed here, since it suggests that what is involved in the construction of false memory syndrome is a series of displacements in which the question of 'what really happened' is continually deferred or mediated by various references to claims upon the natural, the real or the truth. In pointing to this process of displacement I do not mean to presume that displacement can or should be undone, but rather, simply, to point to the ways in which the lack of recognition of the displacement of the referent is constitutive of the very construction of recovering memory as a syndrome. As such it can be seen as a formulation of a problem – the syndrome – in a way that is characteristic of contemporary society and its reflexive self-understandings.

This confusion is what, Wright implies, leads the investigators to encourage Ingram, rather too forcefully, to search his memory.

For example, on the morning after his arrest, Ingram is reported to have met a psychologist, Richard Peterson, whom he asks,

> why, if he had committed these heinous acts, he had no memory of them. Peterson told him that it was not uncommon for sexual offenders to bury the memories of their crime, because they were simply too horrible to consider. He went on to say that Ingram himself had probably been abused as a child.
>
> (1993a: 69)

Once again, we are told that 'According to Ingram, Peterson assured him that, once he confessed, the repressed memories would come flooding back' (1993a: 69). And apparently memories did come flooding back to Ingram, memories of abusing his daughters, one of his sons, the participation of his friends and colleagues and his wife, and of their involvement in sacrificing animals and human babies in satanic rituals. In no time at all, an escalating spiral of confessions, memories and allegations is created by the protagonists, both accusers and accused. But the enigma that structures Wright's investigation is not whether Ingram is innocent or guilty, but rather:

> Where were all these memories coming from? Were they real or were they fantasies? If they were real, why couldn't any two people agree on them?
>
> (1993a: 73–74)

Thus, it is memory itself which is interrogated by Wright, specifically memories recovered in the act of confession prompted by that great mirror, the technological order.

Wright stresses that the process of recovering memories is neither easy nor natural for Ingram:

> The pauses in Ingram's statement sometimes lasted ten full minutes, intensifying the frustration on the part of the questioners. He would grab hold of his hair and lean forward, dead still, until his limbs went to sleep, while the investigators stood around, fuming with impatience . . . .
>
> (1993a: 70)

This impatience leads to 'prodding', 'extrapolations' and 'guesswork' on the part of the investigators. But it is not simply 'coercive police interrogations' which are at issue here for Wright; it is also religious 'fundamentalism' and the credulity of faith that are subject to Wright's investigations. He quotes from interviews with Ingram:

> 'Choose life over living death,' Peterson exhorted, lapsing into the religious language that seemed to reach Ingram. 'You are as alone as Jesus was in the desert when he was comforted.'
>
> 'God's given you the tools to do this, Paul,' Vukich said. 'You've got to show him by what you do and what you say as to whether or not you're worthy of his love and redemption and salvation.'

> 'Oh, Jesus!' Ingram cried in a frenzy. 'Help me, Lord! Help me, Lord!'
> (1993a: 70)

Wright records that Ingram comes to believe that he is possessed and asks his pastor to perform an exorcism. Most of his confessions are said to be delivered in the third person while he is in a trance-like condition, what Wright calls an auto-hypnotic trance.[18] Ingram is reported to have been encouraged to use visualisations and prayers to 'produce' more and more memories:

> Paul's memory, however, was becoming more and more active, aided by the visualizations that Peterson and the detectives encouraged and, he claims, by constant prayer and assurances from Pastor Bratun that God would not allow thoughts other than those which were true to come into his memory.
>
> (1993a: 73)

The daughters' memories too are interrogated by Wright. He concludes that they have also been artificially stimulated. This stimulation is held to derive from a number of sources. The principal of these is religion once again, specifically the 'fundamentalist' Pentecostalism adopted some years earlier by the whole Ingram family. Interestingly, this is a faith which is depicted by Wright as having been corrupted by the easy values of mass entertainment; so, for example, the Ingrams' church is described as projecting

> an atmosphere that is intended to be informal and inviting. The sanctuary is a windowless theatre called the Living Room, where the pastoral staff sits on a dais in easy chairs beside an artificial fireplace. It has the ambience of the set of a daytime television talk show.
>
> (1993a: 64)

And, we learn, it is at the church-sponsored annual two-day retreat for teenage girls, Heart to Heart, that the first allegation against Ingram was made by the elder daughter, Ericka, in 1988. '[A] woman from California', Karla Franko, a charismatic Christian who 'believes she has been given the Biblical gifts of healing and spiritual discernment', triggers the memory by describing her visions, including one which led her to declare to the gathering of young women that 'someone in the audience had been molested as a young girl by a relative'. It is immediately following this revelation that Ericka is said to have first alleged, 'I have been abused sexually by my father.'[19]

18 Discomfort with such techniques is also evident in other newspaper reports which criticise 'memory-enhancement techniques' such as 'guided imagery hypnosis' and 'body massage' (Jaroff, 1993).

19 This, according to Wright, is only one version of how the memory of sexual abuse is recovered: in another version, Franko has an even more directly suggestive role. Having been asked to pray over Ericka, she is supposed to have said,

> 'You have been abused as a child, sexually abused'. . . .At no time, says Franko, did Ericka utter a word; she was so devastated by Franko's revelation that she could do little more than nod in acknowledgement.
>
> (1993a: 66)

Initially, Wright tells us of Franko's past without comment: before 'going to Bible college, she had been a dancer and a standup comic as well as an actress, and had had parts in several sitcoms and TV commercials' (1993a: 65). But this description of Franko's past career in entertainment is later revealed to have a more disturbing significance as a result of Wright's presentation of the role of the mass media in the suggestion of 'fantastic' memories. He itemises a series of publications which, he implies, have provided models for allegations such as those made by the Ingram daughters. These include *Michelle Remembers*, a book, written by Michelle Smith and her husband (and ex-psychiatrist), which describes Smith's 'memories of black-magic ceremonies and of atrocities she was subjected to by a satanic coven, which counted among its members Smith's mother'. Wright comments that

> Smith recovered these previously buried memories while she was in therapy, and usually during a kind of self-induced trance. Her account became a model for the many survivor stories that would follow, although, characteristically, there was no evidence that any of her story was true.
>
> (1993a: 77)

He also mentions the book *Satan's Underground*, 'which purported to be a true account of abuse and sexual slavery' and refers to a prime-time Geraldo Rivera special on NBC entitled 'Devil Worship: Exposing Satan's Underground'. Wright does not explicitly claim that such media representations influenced either the Ingram daughters or Ingram himself (although he does indicate that one daughter, Ericka, had seen a copy of *Satan's Underground* and that the whole family watched the television special). He has no need: he is able to draw on long-standing and widely held anxieties about the media and its ability to influence the suggestible (and feminised) masses; so, he lets the protagonists speak for themselves:

> The little office where the interrogation took place became stale and overheated from the press of so many bodies. 'Boy, it's almost like I'm making it up, but I'm not,' Ingram said as the interview drew to a close. . . . He had produced several new memories of sexual abuse, one occasion as recent as the week before he left on vacation. He had also begun to see 'weird shadows' and tombstones. 'It's like I'm watching a movie', he said. 'Like a horror movie.'
>
> (1993a: 71)

The suggestive role of other technologies in the creation of these memories is seen to require greater explanation, however. Principal amongst these techno-mnemonic aids is the psychological profession and its promulgation of the therapeutic function.[20] Wright makes it clear that psychologists are themselves divided about whether memories of satanic ritual abuse are to be believed. On

20 A feature on false memory syndrome in *Time* states that critics of recovered memory cite two principal sources for such memories: popular culture and misguided or inept therapy. In one newspaper report, a commentator claims that 'What is really happening . . . is that conflicts are being generated by false memories. We have found something to make therapy easy' (quoted in Jaroff, 1993: 61).

the one hand, Bennett Braun is reported to claim that, 'of the two hundred thousand Americans that he estimated were suffering from M.P.D. [Multiple Personality Disorder], up to one-fourth could be victims of S.R.A. [Satanic Ritual Abuse]' (1993a: 78). On the other hand, George K. Ganaway is reported as arguing that dissociative disorders, such as multiple personality disorder, might account for the satanic ritual abuse phenomenon, because 'the alleged victims were highly hypnotizable, suggestible and fantasy-prone' (1993a: 78). What is problematic for Wright, the reporter at large, is not that some psychologists believe in the truth of recovered memories of satanic ritual abuse but that both those psychologists who so believe *and* those who do not hold that the difference between memory and fantasy is unimportant from a professional point of view. He quotes another psychologist:

> In the end, we (as clinicians) cannot tell the difference between believed-in fantasy about the past and viable memory of the past. Indeed, there may be no structural difference between the two.
>
> (1993a: 79)

It is not whether something is true or false that matters, Wright explicates, but its structural function, that is, whether or not it is 'relevant material' for the client's treatment.

The same inability (and unwillingness) to distinguish between memory and fantasy is attributed to feminists and other advocates of women's rights. Wright notes the claim made by Elizabeth S. Rose ('the pseudonym of a freelance writer who says she herself is an S.R.A. survivor') in a cover story in *Ms* that

> People would rather believe that survivors – particularly women survivors – are crazy. This keeps many survivors from coming forward. The cover line read, 'BELIEVE IT! CULT RITUAL ABUSE EXISTS.'
>
> (1993a: 80)

He finds other feminists who are willing to acknowledge doubts about the truth of claims of satanic ritual abuse, but concludes by stating that these doubts are irrelevant in this community because, as the co-ordinator of a rape-crisis centre is quoted as saying,

> We are already struggling against a tidal wave of disbelief – it's a tidal wave! Nobody wants to believe how bad it really is for women and children. Whoever walks in or calls us on the phone will tell us what she needs to tell us to survive this minute, this day. Our job is to help her survive through recovery. It's not our job to believe or disbelieve.
>
> (1993a: 81)

Significantly, in all these instances – in relation to religion, the media and political/professional activism – the unwillingness to discriminate between fantasy and memory is reified by Wright and represented as the inevitable consequence of a kind of fundamentalism. It is not shown to be a consequence of the widely acknowledged difficulty of making such discriminations, nor is it represented as an integral part of a specific set of therapeutic and/or political practices and, as such, not the basis on which accusations are made or legal cases brought to court.[21] Nor indeed is it understood to be a consequence of differences in epistemology, of differences between claims upon the natural, the real and the truth as guarantors of 'what really is'.[22] Rather it is represented as the inevitable outcome of the absolute need on the part of the professional advocate (political activist, therapist or religious functionary) to know, as if the quest to know the truth has displaced or somehow outstripped its subject, that is, the individual. From Wright's perspective, then, it is the professionals' need to know that makes them unwilling, or makes it impossible for them, to distinguish between true and false memory, that makes them detach memories from the subjectivity of the individual and replace them with an artificial substitute. This indeed is what underpins the 'fantastic' nature of their knowledge claims:

> two communities that normally have little to do with each other – fundamentalist Christians and a particular set of mental-health professionals – found common ground in the question dominating any consideration of satanic-ritual abuse: whether to believe that it actually exists. In the absence of evidence that these stories or memories of satanic-ritual abuse were real, one could reject them as absurd, withhold judgment until evidence appeared, or accept them on faith. The middle ground was rapidly shrinking as the proselytizers for both groups spread the word that S.R.A. was real and anyone who doubted it was 'in denial' or was part of the satanic underground.
>
> (1993a: 80)

It is the will to know the truth – to see oneself – which, according to Wright, extends the boundaries of the real beyond all limits – filling in all the gaps – with devastating consequences for the individual. He quotes the interrogator of Ingram's son:

> 'You want to believe it's dreams,' Schoening said. 'You don't want to believe it's real. It was real. It was real, Chad.'
>
> (1993b: 74)

21 One of the most contentious aspects of recovered memories in the newspaper reports analysed here is their status as legal evidence; for example,

> Nearly half the state legislatures in the US have responded to the widespread public acceptance of recovered memories by applying a strange twist to venerable statute-of-limitation laws. In general, the new legislation allows alleged victims of child abuse to sue the accused perpetrators within three to six years after the repressed memories emerge. This means that with little more than the recollection of the accuser, a parent or other relative can be hauled into court decades after the supposed crime. Taking advantage of the newly enacted legislation, some of the supposed victims have successfully brought civil and even criminal actions against members of their own families. Juries have awarded them damages, and in a few cases the accused parent has been sentenced to jail – based entirely on the recovered memory of his adult off-spring.
>
> (Jaroff, 1993: 59)

22 Significantly, Wright allows for no debate on what might count as the correct procedures for establishing the truth, and thus for no debate about the nature of truth itself. Furthermore, he allows for no debate about what the truth is for, that is, he simply assumes the usefulness of truth.

RECOVERY OF MEMORY IN THE SPATIAL CONTINUUM OF THE PHOTOGRAPH

But how does Wright believe this filling in has occurred? The suggestion that will be put forward here, as indicated earlier, is that it is a consequence of the force and pervasiveness of the image in contemporary society. The suggestion that the mechanically reproduced image has played a key part in the emergence of multiple personality syndrome and false memory syndrome is not new.[23] Hacking, for example, describes how the visual image has historically played a key part in understandings of multiple personality syndrome. He notes that

> The very first *multiple* personality – multiple meaning *more than two* – was photographed in each of ten personality states. . . .
>
> Photography was part of the initial rhetoric of multiplicity. Today quantitative tests of dissociation fill a similar role.
>
> (1995: 5)

He continues,

> Observers have always reported a different 'look' to different alters, and have sometimes included drawings or photographs in their reports in order to suggest the change. . . . Thus multiplicity was made visual from the very beginning, and faithfully followed new technologies. After movies had been invented, they were used to record switches [between alters]. And now there are innumerable videos. . . .

23 In a fascinating article, Sigrid Schade argues that in *fin-de-siècle* Paris the medical avant-garde of Charcot and Bernheim were in competition with the literary and artistic avant-garde, including Edmond de Goncourt, Daudet and Baudelaire, for 'influence over the unconscious'. She points out that

> Whereas the writers and artists were engaged in a 'cultivation of the nerves', by maintaining that they could produce vibrations of the senses through psychodynamic forms (of poetry or of ornamentation), i.e., texts and works of art, the medical scientists staged demonstrations of this kind of influence in spectacular presentations of hypnosis.
>
> (1995: 500)

She further demonstrates the two-way relationship between the two avant-gardes, identifying Charcot's significance in the field as a consequence of his mobilisation of 'all the aesthetic *and* medical means available to him' (1995: 500; my emphasis). So, for example, his insistence on viewing the patients medically – a procedure that Schade describes as comparative viewing – was matched by his obsession with producing and publishing proofs of his understanding of hysteria in the form of visual documentation, including not only traditional means such as drawings, plaster casts and wax models but also photography. He regarded his Salpêtrière clinic (where roughly five thousand women were accommodated) as a 'living pathological museum'. She further points out that the body, particularly the female body, was thus 'constructed as the scene of a competition between different types of knowledge' (1995: 502).

Schade also points to the parallels between the view held in artistic circles that women's achievements in handicrafts were a consequence of their ability to 'imitate with extraordinary sensibility' and the medical opinion that hysteria, a disorder closely associated with women, was related to an understanding of femininity as the ability to adapt, to conform and to imitate. She writes, 'In contrast to the women who acted out their mimic talent in handicrafts, the hysterical women expressed theirs in and with their own bodies' (1995: 508).

> Some really dysfunctional multiples going through a bad patch switch personalities very rapidly, each time assuming a new stock character. The effect is similar to that of switching TV channels by channel surfing. This impression is enhanced because patients with a great many alters often choose, for some of their personalities, the names of characters in sit-coms, soaps, and crime series. It happens that TV remote controls became widely available in America just about the time that today's florid multiples became abundant.
>
> (1995: 31–32)

As this last quotation indicates, however, Hacking shifts from commenting upon the contiguity or analogy between the developments in multiple personality and technologies of visual culture, to making use himself of this contiguity as if it were a cause, although he does so initially at least in an apparently casual manner. (As chapter 2 noted, this conversion of analogy into cause is a characteristic of prosthetic culture.) So, for example, at a later point in the book, he writes,

> There is no canonical way to think of our own past. In the endless quest for order and structure, we grasp at whatever picture is floating by and put our past into its frame.
>
> (1995: 89)

By the end of the book (pp. 238–257 *passim*), however, Hacking identifies what he calls 'semantic contagion', a term he says he is compelled to introduce because 'the imaginary camcorder in the sky, which records everything that happens in a particular scene, does not of itself suffice to record what people were doing' (1995: 248).

Similarly in nearly all the contemporary accounts I have studied, I found a parallel or analogy drawn between recovered memories and photographs or video-recorded images.[24] To take just one example, the journalist Frederick Crews writes,

> But this was no ordinary trial. Factually impoverished, it came down to

24 And in a reciprocal move, commentators on the rise of cyberspace have made use of the notion of multiple personality to describe the personae of the cyborg:

> Just as changes in complex 'real-world' political economies presage a radical simplification of biological diversity, the ramifications of complex social systems in the alter-space of communications technologies suggest a war between simplification and multiplicity . . . an explosion of actors and actants that includes the almost-living, the not-living and the never-living arising in the boundaries between technology, society and 'nature', in the architectures of multiple embodiments and multiple selves. . . .
>
> The actively multiple, situational and fragmented character of the online persona calls into question commonsense notions of the relationships between communities and the individuals that constitute them.
>
> (Stone, 1992: 611, 612)

Elsewhere Stone describes 'plugging a person with MPD into the MUDs [multiple user domains]' as 'the ultimate experiment' (1995: 59).

> little more than a twelve-person referendum on the photographic return of the repressed.
>
> (1994: 56)

Wright himself makes sparing use of metaphors of vision to describe the forced recovery of memories; however, he too, I will argue, also identifies the power of the image as the root cause of the phenomenon of false memory syndrome. This argument – while evident in his attention to self-induced visualisations by Ingram and the emphasis on the role of the media – is most explicit in his discussion of a chart commissioned by the investigators to provide a graphic representation of ritual abuse, drawing on the data that they gathered in the course of their investigation (Figure 5.1). Describing this chart, he writes,

> The chart . . . provided a visual framework for the investigators' growing conviction that the Ingram case was part of a national and international satanic conspiracy. One can also see it as an illustration of exactly how confused the investigators became as they tried to explain the case to themselves. 'It shows the links and how everything fits together. It isn't just a matter of people running around in robes and killing babies – it's much more complicated than that,' McClanahan says. 'When you look at the chart, don't you more or less go, like "Wow"?'
>
> (1993b: 55)

Yet, so I will go on to suggest, while both Hacking and Wright make use of the metaphors and models of vision as causes (and not only as analogies), neither comments upon how seeing is productive, simply noting that it is; that is, neither addresses explicitly the question of what it means to *see photographically*.[25]

Let me to try to substantiate this claim (in relation to Wright at least) by

25 In contrast, Schade is explicitly concerned with this question. She writes,

> The example of Charcot demonstrates that an iconographic sequence is initially constituted by the particular historical interest of the person who determines the sequence. It makes sense only in the context of this interest, which is, on the other hand, itself a constitutive moment of that which is designated cultural or social memory. In the course of a staging of (the master's) power, a 'truth' of hysterical behaviour patterns is produced in the framework of a medical setting. The meaning of this 'truth' consists solely in its spectacularity and in the demonstration of the mastery of the person who provides something to see, and on which depends his state of privilege (wealth, social recognition, being able to follow his own voyeuristic impulses undisturbed in institutionally legitimized forms). The idea of a 'collective unconscious' as a static repository of stored memory matter overlooks the fact that memory does not simply mean repetition, but rather a constant rewriting of the traces of memory in social processes.
>
> (1995: 512)

She also points out that although the observations that Freud made during his stay at Salpêtrière were the starting-point for his examination of hysteria, he 'removed his gaze from the patients and gave them his ear instead: Freud's psychoanalysis is predicated upon what the patients told him' (1995: 517). She thus provides an insight into the realisation of the French sociologist Gabriel Tardé's claim, in 1883, that 'a statistical bureau might be compared to an eye or ear'. As noted in chapter 3, he claimed further that 'each of our senses gives us, in its own way and from its special point of view, the statistics of the external world. Their characteristic sensations are in a certain way their special graphical tables' (quoted in Sekula, 1986: 24).

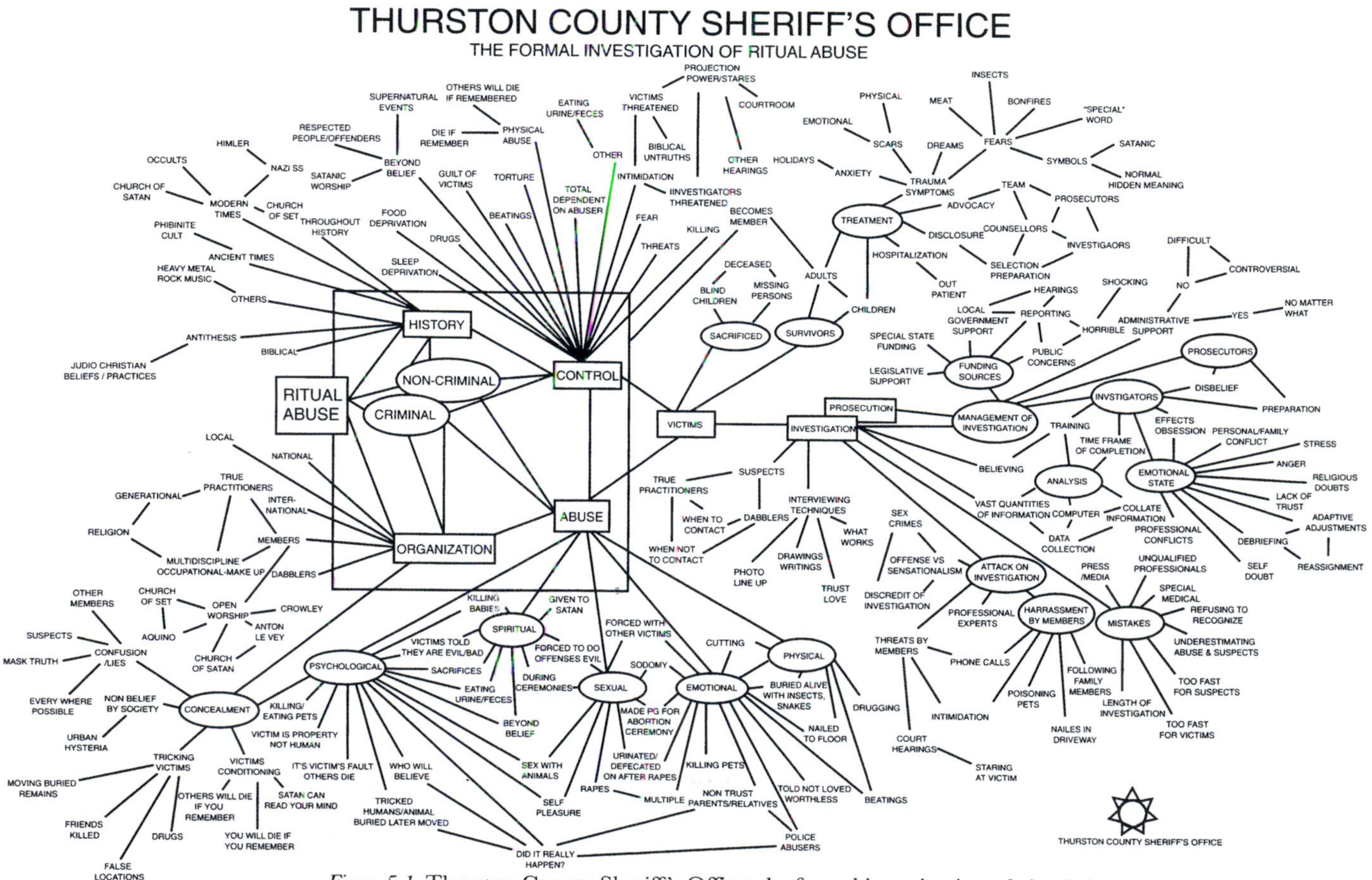

Figure 5.1 Thurston County Sheriff's Office: the formal investigation of ritual abuse

comparing Wright's discussion of the chart described above with Siegfried Kracauer's comments on photography. In these comments, Kracauer notes that, from the perspective of photographic representation, 'memory images appear to be without any gaps', while 'from the perspective of memory, photography appears as a jumble that consists partly in garbage' (1927, reprinted in 1995: 50, 51). He explains that this is because just as historicism, which arises at the same time as photography, seeks to explain phenomena 'in terms of their genesis' and aims to provide a 'temporal continuum', so photography provides a 'spatial continuum' (1995: 50). He writes,

> On the whole, advocates of such historicist thinking believe they can explain any phenomenon purely in terms of its genesis. That is, they believe in any case that they can grasp historical reality by reconstructing the course of events in their temporal succession *without any gaps*. . . . Historicism is concerned with the photography of time. The equivalent of its temporal photography would be a giant film depicting the temporally interconnected events from every vantage point.
>
> (1995: 49–50; my emphasis)

In considering the impact of the use of photographs in illustrated newspapers, Kracauer continues,

> If [photography] were offering itself as an aid to memory, then memory would have to determine the selection. But the flood of photos sweeps away the dams of memory. The assault of this mass of images is so powerful that it threatens to destroy the potentially existing awareness of crucial traits. . . . The phrase 'lie together, die together' applies to the multiply reproduced original . . . .The spatial continuum from the camera's perspective predominates the spatial appearance of the perceived object; the likeness that the image bears to it effaces the contours of the object's 'history'. . . . The *contiguity* of these images systematically excludes their contextual framework available to consciousness.
>
> (1995: 58)

Here Kracauer points to the destructive subject-effects of the photograph, in so far as it contributes to the erosion of the historical or narrative continuity of consciousness which he believes to have been constitutive of individual and collective self-identity. Moreover, he points directly to the significance of the photograph as a multiply reproduced original in this dispersal of continuity in a reconfigured space and time. In describing further the effects of what I have called outcontextualisation and indifferentiation, he writes,

> The photograph does not preserve the transparent aspects of an object but instead captures it as a spatial continuum from any one of a number of positions.
>
> (1995: 53)

Kracauer elaborates his position by arguing that in photography objects are not given order or meaning by the significance attached to them by a person, as they 'should be' in memory. Rather, in a photograph, 'a person's history is buried as if under a layer of snow' (1995: 51). He writes,

> As long as they are embedded in the uncontrolled life of the drives they are inhabited by a demonic ambiguity; they are opaque like frosted glass that hardly a ray of light can penetrate. Their transparency increases to the extent that insights thin out the vegetation of the soul and limit the compulsion of nature. Truth can only be found by a liberated consciousness that assesses the demonic nature of the drives.
>
> (1995: 51)

In some respects, Kracauer's analysis seems to provide grist for Wright's mill.[26] So, for example, Kracauer's conception of photography can be seen to be shared in Wright's understanding of the chart for it represents the information relating to the Ingram case as a spatial continuum from all of 'any one of a number of positions'.[27] The chart is depicted as an attempt to produce such a 'giant film' and is used, so Wright reports, to 'show the links and how everything fits together'. Indeed, it is precisely because it represents the information in this way that the phenomenon of recovered memory appears 'without any gaps'. It is

26 Kracauer writes that photography 'is a secretion of the capitalist mode of production' (1995: 61). In newspaper accounts of false memory syndrome, recovered memory is frequently described in the language of industrial mass production: for example,

> The thriving recovered memory industry dismays psychiatrist Ganaway. 'In some cases,' he says, the hospitals and clinics 'are memory mills with an almost assembly-line mentality. . . . A patient comes in with no memory but leaves with memories of childhood incest or ritual abuse.'
>
> (Jaroff, 1993: 61)

At other times, memory is described as faulty and is distinguished from commmunications technologies: so, for example, Professor John Morton (chair of the British Psychological Society's working group on false memory syndrome) warns,

> memory is fragile. Everything you recall is not likely to be correct. There is a danger that people will elaborate, fill in any incomplete bits to make a full story. The memory is not like a tape-recorder or a video; claims such as 'the body remembers what has happened to it' mean nothing.
>
> (Quoted in Lacey, 1994: 23)

27 Consider the following description of looking at photography by Régis Durand:

> Photography, then, echoes the unconscious process, not in its subject matters or in its affects, but in its very inchoative energy. Yet it cannot help but draw away from this original impulse even as it draws closer to it. That is because the images produced (contrary to the unconscious 'encounters' described by Freud [in his description of the unconscious as a mystic writing pad]) do not cancel themselves out. They remain in visible forms, which generate in turn other associations, other desires, and call up other images. It is like an infinite proliferation of small branching-outs, which end up covering completely the original trace and leading the mind astray in many directions. Hence the strange paradox of photography: its incessant quest for new subjects, but at the same time always the same subjects, ending up in an infinitely complex palimpsest, a subtle layering of images.
>
> (1995: 149)

For further discussion of photography and the (optical) unconscious, see chapter 8.

thus, I suggest, a representation of the causal effectivity of the photographic image, or, more precisely, seeing photographically.[28]

The chart is evidence of the opacity of modern life: Wright's investigation is to be the ray of light that penetrates its mystery. Or so it might seem. However, there is a crucial difference between Kracauer and Wright: the latter, while attributing a causal effectivity to the image, is not willing to see photographically himself. What is under scrutiny in his interrogation of memory is not the truth in Kracauer's sense, that is, whether or not the memories that are recovered via 'insights' or the technological order are adequate to the demonic ambiguity they reveal, but, rather, how to return to a society in which memory images are personal possessions, linked internally, within an individual subject-ivity, to 'truth content', and externally, by the representative techniques of investigative journalism to the truth or object-ivity of the public sphere and the liberal democratic nation state.[29]

In other words, I am suggesting that Wright's account (and the more general invention of the phenomenon of false memory syndrome) is motivated not by a concern for truth in Kracauer's sense, but by a desire to restore the relations that existed between memory, the individual and the object before the age of the photographic image, before we became so completely immersed in the 'great technological order'. His article is part of a fight for the survival of the subject of representation, the individual, a self-identity founded on the value of propriety, of property and properness, of the appropriation and reappropriation of the self made possible by a belief in the continuity and interior depth of subjectivity authorised by the narrativisation of memory. Wright represents false memory syndrome in the way he does in defence of a self and a society in which the obligation to know is out of control, in fear of a society in which information multiplies uncontrollably – like a cancer or a contagious disease.[30] He wishes to throw out the jumble as well as the garbage, because he cannot distinguish

28 I should like to make it clear at this point that I am not suggesting that the diagram is understood by Wright as if it were a photograph, but, rather, that he interprets it as if it were, as a consequence of the pervasiveness of what I have called seeing photographically in contemporary society.

29 As such, Wright's approach might usefully be contrasted with that adopted by Bea Campbell, who writes,

> Most crime is solved with the co-operation of the people. And yet many, if not most, sexual crimes against women and children have gone both unsolved and unreported because the people pessimistically expect little co-operation from the police. Detection is always contingent. It depends on co-operation and a consensus about what matters, what is wrong, what hurts, what is visible and what is knowable. Detection is above all about what is *evident* and what is *evidence*. But all this is dependent on political consciousness. Seeing is believing, we're told, and yet evidence, like beauty, is in the eye of the beholder. If you don't believe it is possible for children to be sexually abused *en masse* by the men in their lives, then you don't see the signs, even when they stare you in the face.
>
> (1988: 70–71)

30 Hacking draws attention to the relevance of Sontag's work on the morality of disease for the move to interpret multiple personality in relation to sexual abuse and trauma. He argues that redefining abuse as trauma has had significant moral implications: rather than inscribing judgement onto the person with the disorders associated with abuse, it 'exculpates, or passes the guilt up to the abuser' (1995: 15). He continues,

⇒

between them.[31] He is afraid, as Kracauer foresaw, that 'those who lie together, die together'. He, like Miss Beauchamp, is frightened of the thing that is reflected in that great mirror, the technological order. His account is written from the perspective of a reporter for whom the visual evidence offered by the chart can only be indicative of a state of confusion.

Furthermore, Wright's account is not only a critique of what happens to society when the individual's quest for self-knowledge is distorted, but is itself, in its techniques of investigation, an exemplification of what he suggests is in danger. This is a society that knows itself, that respects and reinforces its own boundaries, both internal and external, both imagined and real: that is, the nation state, a society in which both cultural and political representation assume and require an individual self-identity. ('A society that knows itself is at one with itself' would seem to be Wright's motto.) It is in the cause of the truth of this endangered society – and of the possessive individuals who are its subjects – that Wright deplores false memory syndrome. Indeed, as the next chapter hopes to make clear, it is not just the identity of the individual that is seen by Wright to be threatened here, but also the family and the nation. Sedgwick points to this in her discussion of the pervasiveness of the vocabulary of addiction: she notes that just as the 'integrity of (new and contested) national borders, the reifications of national will and vitality, were readily organised around . . . narratives of introjection' during the early stages of imperialism, so too 'the dramas of "foreign substances" and of the new imperialism and the new nationalisms have been quite inextricable' (1994: 135). In what is perceived by Wright and others as a threatening global cultural economy of semantic contagion, the boundaries between domestic and foreign are ill-defined as flows of ideas, images, people and illnesses seep through national borders, and the limits of the senses and their disorders are no longer so easy to categorise.[32]

> Not only is a person with multiple personality genuinely ill: someone else is responsible for the illness. Lest you think I exaggerate the emphasis on morality and metaphor, consider the opening words at the 1993 annual conference on multiple personality: 'AIDS is a plague which attacks individuals. *Child abuse* damages individuals and is the cancer of our society: all too often it flourishes unrecognized and metastatizes across families and generations.'
>
> (1995: 15)

As he goes on to point out, the advocates of false memory syndrome – of which Wright is one – make use of the same metaphors, but return the attribution of guilt to the abused.

31 In his description of the human genome project, Paul Rabinow writes,

> It is currently held, not without a certain uneasiness, that 90% of human DNA is 'junk'. The renowned Cambridge molecular biologist, Sydney Brenner, makes a helpful distinction between 'junk' and 'garbage'. Garbage is something used up and worthless, which one throws away; junk, though, is something one stores for some unspecified future use. It seems highly unlikely that 90% of our DNA is evolutionarily irrelevant – but what its precise relevance could be remains unknown.
>
> (1992: 237)

32 In her discussion of multiple personality syndrome, Stone quotes an 'expert' on Multiple Personality Disorder who, when asked in a court of law, 'How many psychologists actually have patients with MPD?', replied, 'There's a band of very intense believers who have all the sightings, where the rest of us never see any. . . . What I call the UFOs of psychiatry' (1995: 52–53).

THE THREAT TO THE POSSESSIVE INDIVIDUAL

In its concern to fix the individual and collective subject of representation, this account thus has many similarities with the scenes of (mis)identification from the beginning of the twentieth century described earlier. But there are also some important dissimilarities, perhaps the most obvious of which is that the Wright report takes as its central protagonist a man (the accused, Paul Ingram) rather than a woman. Wright himself notes the significance of this focus, which might otherwise be explained as nothing more than a consequence of the news value of the fact that this is one of the few publicised cases in which the accused parent, at least for a while, not only accepted the validity of the accusations, but even implicated himself further in confession. However, Wright self-consciously quotes from a paper which compares the growth of cases of recovered memory of child abuse to the witch hunts of several centuries ago:

> There are some parallels but the differences are just as striking. In terms of similarities, some of the stories today are actually similar to stories of earlier times (e.g., witches flying into bedrooms). In terms of differences, take a look at the accused and the accusers. In the most infamous witch-hunt in North America, 300 years ago in Salem, Massachusetts, three-fourths of the accused were women . . . . Today, they are predominantly (but not all) men. Witches in New England were mostly poor women over 40 who were misfits . . . . Today, the accused are often men of power and success.
>
> (1993b: 71)

The author of the paper, the psychologist Elizabeth Loftus, goes on to argue that there is 'a "great fear" that grips our society, and that is fear of child abuse', but this is not the fear that Wright stokes.

Neither, however, is he overly concerned with the identification of what Maureen McNeil (1991) has called the 'new oppressed', amongst whom McNeil includes fathers ('men of power and success'). She argues that a key component of Thatcherism in the United Kingdom and of the New Right in the United States is the process whereby oppressed groups who 'have demanded greater social justice have come to be seen . . . as agents in the oppression of other, more powerful groups' (1991: 230), pointing out that the cultivation of sympathies for the 'new oppressed', often through the identification of female or feminist trouble-makers, has been a crucial aspect of recent authoritarian politics and a key component of its gendered dimensions. Such a strategy is visible in a number of other journalistic accounts,[33] and is, I think, present in Wright's account of the Ingram case, but the new oppressed are not, at least apparently, his principal concern.

The elder daughter, Ericka, is identified as a trouble-maker (a description of her as a 'habitual liar' is cited), but her motives are not seen to be sufficiently

33 Ironically, another journalist describes false memory syndrome as part of a tradition which sees spirit-possession among women 'as a more or less routine and culturally sanctioned form of manipulation and protest in male dominated societies' (Schnabel, 1993: 13).

interesting to warrant investigation. Moreover, Paul Ingram is represented not as the innocent victim of a conspiracy, but as a willing because gullible participant in a national disaster (or, perhaps better, a disaster for the nation). Wright presents Ingram in such a way as to support the view of the only 'trustworthy' social psychologist mentioned, Richard Ofshe, who describes Ingram as 'a highly suggestible individual with a tendency to float in and out of trance states, and of having a patent and rather dangerous eagerness to please authority' (1993b: 69). Indeed, it is precisely Ingram's suggestibility (rather than his innocence or guilt) which makes him culpable in Wright's eyes, since what is at issue is self-control and individual responsibility.

Without exception, the issue of self-control is foregrounded in the reporting of false memory syndrome in the press: Crews, for example, writes in relation to another case that

> the cardinal point about all this self-destruction went completely unnoticed. Eileen Lipsker [the 'victim' of false memory syndrome in this case] did not *decide* to send her mind into a tailspin after making rational calculations about the opposing claims of justice and filial loyalty; she was progressively *encouraged* to do so by therapists who believed that full psychic health must wait upon a vomiting up of the repressed past. . . .
>
> The Franklin/Lipsker case . . . shows how a 'memory' originating in conscious hunches and resentments can be crystallized by protracted therapeutic *suggestion*, or the subliminal contagion of ideas between a dominant and a subordinate party. That is what we regularly find when missing elements of recovered memory stories are filled in; where repression was, there shall suggestion be.
>
> (1994: 58)

In the intense concern shown for the destabilisation of decision-making ('encouragement', 'a vomiting up', 'suggestion', 'subliminal contagion'), false memory syndrome can thus be seen as a reworking of the long-standing anxiety associated with what Leys calls the mimesis/suggestion paradigm. But what is especially interesting in this contemporary formulation of the anxieties of identification is how questions of sexual difference are simultaneously instantiated and suppressed at the same time as is the possibility of mimesis.[34]

It is the *masculine* individual's knowledge of himself, his distance from his self in the process of representation, his control of emotion and his autonomy, which are in danger here, yet the question of sexual difference is foreclosed. Wright's account is motivated by the desire to stem the dire consequences for society

34 Once again, a striking contrast can be drawn with Bea Campbell's account of the so-called Cleveland case for she foregrounds the issue of sexual difference. She writes,

> Faced with a stiff challenge to its resources and its procedures when Middlesbrough General Hospital escalated the rate of referral of suspected sexual abuse cases to the police and social services in spring 1987, Cleveland Constabulary responded with masculine panic, then tantrums and a reliance on 'masculine intuition', all of which became palpable in the police evidence to the inquiry.
>
> (1988: 73)

arising from the threat to masculine self-identity associated with the spread of the mimesis/suggestion paradigm and it is the danger that this paradigm poses to the masculine possessive individual that constitutes the news value that Wright finds in the phenomenon of false memory syndrome,[35] but there is a curious silence on the question of sexual difference. In place of a recognition of sexual violence is an account of the way in which 'we', the nation's citizens, are all potentially emasculated victims of the forced recovery of memory. Indeed, it is precisely this emphasis which is evident in the stress that is continually placed in Wright's feature on the harmful effects that false memory syndrome is seen to have had for 'families', as if, somehow, families were not comprised of gendered subjects, as if feminisation of identity were something that would be experienced in the same way by everyone, as if feminisation were indeed a threat. Yet this silence on the question of gender is not Wright's alone.

The account of false memory syndrome discussed here displays the three characteristics that Jacqueline Rose identifies as exemplifying a more general uncritical inflation of a psychic economy across the whole of social space: dramatisation, sanitisation and desexualisation:

> Dramatisation because it becomes precisely the drama of all modern subjects; sanitisation, since, despite the idea of a crisis, the model seems to become strangely divested of some of the most difficult aspects of the psychic itself; desexualization perhaps most oddly of all, although this is no doubt an effect of the first two, because of the glaring omission of any question of sexual difference.
>
> (1987: 31)

Rose remarks that it would be necessary to fill in this omission to 'bring terror back into the very centre of the definition of the social' (1987: 32). The response to the filling in of this omission described here, however, is to refuse to see the image photographically, to assume and reinstate the requirement that each person be answerable as a (masculine) self-possessing individual. In adopting this response, Wright refuses to acknowledge the existence of either sexual difference or prosthetic culture. Instead, he insists upon the need for the subject's actions to

35 In his discussion of serial killers, Mark Seltzer makes a related point in relation to the public anxieties associated with the construction of serial killing as a 'motiveless crime'. He writes,

> The commonplace description of serial killing as motiveless is therefore perhaps inseparable from the commonplace description of the serial killer as anonymous or, as one prosecutor of such cases concisely put it, as 'abnormally normal'. This abnormal normality is the 'complete disguise' of looking and being just like everybody else. The crime of anonymity makes for the utterly generic profile of the criminal: the nonidentification ('He didn't do it. He couldn't do it. I *know* him!') but also a fundamental nonidentity (the wisdom [LA County Sheriff's Sergeant] Sett learned from a quarter-century of chasing down murderers is that 'nobody knows anybody else' (McDougal)). Such failures of identity virtually register just how abnormal normality is premised on a primary imitation: 'To go unnoticed is by no means easy. To be a stranger, even to one's doorman or neighbors. If it is difficult to be "like" everybody else, it is because it is an affair of becoming' (Deleuze and Guattari). This is an affair of becoming or self-making premised on the self as an empty category and as an effect of imitation and not its cause.
>
> (1993: 97)

be the outcome of self-knowledge and of a responsible effort; even if the action is subordinate to the informed dictation of an other, then this alterity must be authentic and not factitious, neither simulated nor stimulated by artificial projections or prostheses,[36] or else both the masculinity of the individual and the authority of the nation of which he is part will be called into doubt. Yet, so the next chapter will suggest, this is not the only possible response to the power of the image in self-understandings, and the existence of these other responses brings the question of sexual difference more clearly into view.

36 In another report about an alleged sufferer from false memory syndrome, the mother is reported as saying that the daughter alleging abuse

> would just pick up everybody's habits . . . . She wasn't in there for anorexia, she was in there for bulimia. But the anorexic girls would cut up their food real small . . . she would watch them doing it so she would cut up her food real small.
>
> (Quoted in Schnabel, 1993: 11)

This contributes to a view of the daughter as suffering from 'sickness-imitating behaviour':

> The Smiths believe that their daughter has been heavily influenced by the suggestions of her various therapists, and may also suffer from a compulsive need for medical attention. Mrs Smith says she has wondered whether Donna has Munchausen's Syndrome, whose sufferers chronically present themselves at hospitals with a variety of invented or self-induced injuries or illnesses. (Munchausen's is disproportionately common among nurses and people with an early history of hospitalisation; it has often been compared with MPD.)
>
> (Schnabel, 1993: 15)

As this quotation indicates, a further new syndrome or disorder that disturbs the self-possession of the self is what is described as 'feigned illness' or 'factitious disorders'. The book *Patient or Pretender? Inside the Strange World of Factitious Disorders*, by American psychiatrists Marc D. Feldman and Charles V. Ford (1996), describes patients, most of whom are women, who 'fake' or 'falsify' the symptoms of disease, 'misapplying' medical knowledge. Feldman states,

> Factitious patients don't need a manual. They're so resourceful, going into medical libraries and doing wonderful research, that at times they're more knowledgeable about the illness they're faking than the doctor is.
>
> (Quoted in Robson-Scott, 1994: 5)

6

SEEING YOU, SEEING ME, SEEING PHOTOGRAPHICALLY

> The 'eyes' made available in modern technological sciences shatter any idea of passive vision; these prosthetic devices show us that all eyes, including our own organic ones, are active perceptual systems, building in translations and specific *ways* of seeing, that is, ways of life.
>
> (Donna Haraway, 1991: 190)

INTRODUCTION

In the last chapter, it was suggested that the journalist Wright's account of false memory syndrome is motivated by the desire to stem the dire consequences for society arising from the threat to masculine self-identity associated with the spread of the mimesis/suggestion paradigm. It was further argued that the fact that these representations occur at the site of some of the most contested issues in contemporary gender politics is an indication of the seriousness of what has been called a backlash to feminist political activity (Faludi, 1992). However, the fact that Wright is apparently critical of false memory syndrome does not mean that his account is not, at least in part, responsible for the classification of the syndrome as such: while it is declared to be *false* it is also given fixity (and is in this sense rendered a snap-shot that is also a snap-shut) as a syndrome through this account and other reports such as this. The allegations of sexual abuse which are made visible but unbelievable by this classification are made searingly real and, simultaneously, impossibly false (and, indeed, falsely impossible to judge). What this chapter will suggest is that Wright's account of this phenomenon contains not simply a backlash, a defensive response to the contemporary politics of identity, but also some indication of a more aggressive development in the gendering of cultural politics. In doing so, it employs what might be described as a perversion of mimesis: autopoiesis.

It was argued in the last chapter that Wright's interrogation of memory leads him to conclude that the great mirror of technology is tainted. This is identified by Wright as a fault that can and must be put right: the mirror can be repaired, the (s)tain removed. At the same time, however, so this chapter will suggest, Wright also sees that the tain of the mirror may be productive; specifically, he identifies the use of psychotherapy to bring 'repressed' material to consciousness as the principal technique with the power to reproduce something out of nothing.[1] It is the making visible of repression which for him results in the substitution of 'seen' memories for accurate recall, and of a simulated coin for the true currency of experience.[2] As the single trustworthy psychologist Ofshe[3] is reported as telling Ingram,

> Nobody can blank out as many events as you think you blanked out – it has never happened . . . . Paul, everything that you have told me this evening adds up to one thing. There exists a process that you have learned to use that allows you to invent images that are consistent with what you think should be happening.
>
> (1993b: 74)

Indeed, while Wright is apparently baffled by the phenomenon of false memory syndrome, since it confuses his distinctions between illusion and reality, fact and fantasy, false and genuine recollections of the self, his confusion should not mask his active role in its creation. Moreover, when Wright describes the confusion associated with recovered memory he does not only dismiss it as a feminising relation of suggestion, he simultaneously attributes a complex productivity to the phenomenon. This chapter will explore how recovered memory is identified in the account from this second point of view.

In this view from another position, recovered memory is defined as an unstable amalgamation of the voluntary memory of representation, characterised by abstract time and the operations of consciousness, and the involuntary memory of invention or generation, characterised by discontinuity and the operations of the unconscious. It is thus represented as a new phenomenon neither solely human nor wholly technological; recovered memory is 'wired':

1 In an analysis which parallels that of Wright, although developed from a different point of view, Deleuze argues that a version of psychoanalysis itself may claim to have filled the gap, as a consequence of the fact that, so he claims, psychoanalysis has stopped being 'in search of' family history and is now constitutive of the truth of the history of the family. He writes, 'The psychoanalyst has become like the journalist: he creates the event' (1993: 111). Deleuze argues that as long as psychoanalysis goes on interpreting, it returns desires and utterances to a condition which, while deviant by comparison with the dominant order,

> by the same token localizes them in the pores of this dominant, established body, like something which can be exchanged by virtue of a contract. . . . When it discovers the signifier, it appeals to a distinctively psychoanalytic order . . . , whose only need is itself, because it is statutory or structural: it is it which develops a body, a corpus sufficient to itself.
>
> (1993: 111)

There is here thus the suggestion that psychoanalysis *as a technique of interpretation* has created the oedipal unconscious as a stop-gap, the sufficient possession of its own corpus.

2 In Wright's account, it is the failure of the protagonists to have respected the true currency which precipitates their fall; as Ingram initially and retrospectively claims, 'the other evidence', aside from his daughters' allegations, was his own failure to act 'naturally' with his children: ' "I wasn't a good father, I know," he admits. "I wasn't there for the kids . . . " ' (1993b: 76).

3 In another newspaper account, Ofshe is recorded as being 'particularly disdainful of the concept of what he calls "robust" repression: the instantaneous submergence of any memory of sexual abuse'. Recovered memory therapists, he says, 'have invented a mechanism that supposedly causes a child's awareness of sexual assault to be driven entirely from consciousness' (quoted in Jaroff, 1993: 59).

> In the Ingram case, Ofshe [a social psychologist] was told, the reason the suspect couldn't remember raping his children repeatedly over seventeen years was that he had repressed the memories as soon as the abuse occurred. Even the prosecution was uncomfortable with the theory, and the idea of mind-control had arisen as an alternative to it. Perhaps the cult had interfered with the ordinary process of memory formation, either through drugs or through chronic abuse. Perhaps the reputedly brilliant Dr Ofshe could unlock the programming that had scrambled the memory circuitry of nearly everyone in the Ingram family.
>
> (1993b: 65)

There is here a momentary or instantaneous recognition of the existence of prosthetic culture. In what follows, I will illustrate some of the ways in which Wright instantiates and suppresses this construction of memory as wired by simultaneously bringing into being and distancing himself from the existence of false memory syndrome as a reflexively mediated technological extension of reality: that is, as a prosthetic device. In doing so, I hope to show how this recognition is channelled through a specifically masculine (re)construction of the self.

ANAESTHETICS AND PROSTHETICS

To explore this second point of view I will draw upon the theory of autopoiesis, a conjectural model developed by neurophysiologists for interpreting living processes. The inspiration for doing so comes from Susan Buck-Morss's compelling essay 'Aesthetics and anaesthetics: Walter Benjamin's artwork essay reconsidered' (1992), in which she shows how understandings of the individual in aesthetics, philosophy and neurophysiology converged in the creation of a technics of an-aesthetics at the beginning of the twentieth century. It will be suggested here that it is a similar convergence at the end of the century that has contributed to the emergence of a prosthetic culture.

Buck-Morss starts with Walter Benjamin's understanding of the neurological basis of modern experience. She notes that here, as seldom elsewhere in his writings, Benjamin relies on a Freudian insight, that is, the idea that consciousness is a shield protecting the organism against stimuli from without – 'excessive energies' – by preventing their retention, by resisting their impress as memory. Benjamin writes,

> The threat from these energies [that is, the excessive energies of the external world] is one of shocks. The more readily consciousness registers these shocks, the less likely they are to have a traumatic effect.
>
> (1970: 163)

Under extreme stress, the ego employs consciousness as a buffer or stop-gap, breaking innervation and excitation, blocking the openness of the synaesthetic system,[4] thereby isolating present consciousness from past memory: filling the

4 Buck-Morss uses the term 'synaesthetics' to describe the aesthetic system of sense-consciousness. It is open, not only in that it is open to the world through sensory organs, but also because the nerve cells within the body form a network that is in itself discontinuous. She adopts the term to⇒

gap by turning the 'incident into a moment that has been lived' (1970: 165), putting the event into the past.

As a consequence of the daily, routine nature of shock in modern life, technology subjects 'the human sensorium to a complex kind of training' (1970: 177), and response to stimuli *without thinking* becomes necessary for survival. Mimesis is adapted as one such defensive reflex: for example, 'The smile that appears automatically on passersby wards off contact, a reflex that "functions as a mimetic shock absorber"' (Buck-Morss, 1992: 17). This defensive adaptation, in turn, is absorbed, so Buck-Morss argues, into a specialised synaesthetic system developed to ward off stimuli in order to protect both the body from the trauma of accident and the psyche from the trauma of perceptual shock:[5] this is the technics of anaesthetics. She writes,

> the system reverses its role. Its goal is to numb the organism, to deaden the senses, to repress memory: the cognitive system of synaesthetics has become, rather, one of anaesthetics.
>
> (1992: 18)

She goes on to chart the growth of anaesthetics in the latter part of the nineteenth century, describing the abrupt increase in the use of drugs and therapeutic practices, from opium, ether and cocaine to hypnosis, hydrotherapy and electric shock. Whereas the body's self-anaesthetising defences are largely involuntary, what distinguished these methods was the conscious, intentional manipulation of the synaesthetic system.[6]

Buck-Morss further argues that, beginning in the nineteenth century, 'a narcotic was made out of reality itself' (1992: 22), and adopts Benjamin's term 'phantasmagoria' to describe the appearance of this new reality that tricks the senses through technical manipulation, not by numbing but by flooding the senses. She writes,

> These stimulated sensoria alter consciousness, much like a drug, but they do so through sensory distraction rather than chemical alteration, and – most significantly – their effects are experienced collectively rather than

stress this openness in contradistinction to the traditional conception of the human nervous system, which, as will be noted below, artificially isolates human biology from its environment.

5 As noted earlier, in *Rewriting the Soul*, Ian Hacking provides a powerful account of how the notion of trauma came to acquire a psychological as well as a physiological meaning as a 'lesion of the soul'. See his chapter 13 for a fascinating account of the complex association of ideas between the railway, the accident, the nervous system and trauma at the end of the nineteenth century. He ends this discussion by quoting Nietzsche:

> 'Psychological pain' does not by itself seem to me to be a definite fact, but on the contrary only an interpretation – a causal interpretation of a collection of phenomena that cannot be exactly formulated – it is really only a fat word standing in place of a skinny question mark.
>
> (Quoted in Hacking, 1995: 197)

6 As Schade (1995) points out, Charcot treated his patients with ether and other drugs and conducted experiments on himself with hashish. Charcot's discussions of the status of hypnosis also contributed to the development of the image of the neurasthenic, over-sensitive or hysterical artist who followed his or her inspiration in a kind of a trance, sometimes induced by the consumption of anodynes such as opium.

> individually. Everyone sees the same altered world, experiences the same total environment. As a result, unlike with drugs, the phantasmagoria assumes the position of objective fact.
>
> (1992: 22–23)

One consequence is that the subject's 'frame of mind is such that he cannot make much use of experience' (Benjamin, 1970: 180–181). What is it, then, that replaces experience? Buck-Morss suggests that

> In this situation of 'crisis in perception', it is no longer a question of educating the crude ear to hear music, but of giving it back hearing. It is no longer a question of training the eye to see beauty, but of restoring 'perceptibility'.
>
> (1992: 19)

The hypothesis proposed here is that prosthetic culture began to emerge and has continued to develop in order to do precisely this,[7] to restore perceptibility. And as Benjamin himself notes, certain simple technologies of comfort had a key role in this development: on the one hand,

> Comfort isolates; on the other hand, it brings those enjoying it closer to mechanization. The invention of the match around the middle of the twentieth century brought forth a number of innovations which have one thing in common: one abrupt movement of the hand triggers a process of many steps.
>
> (1970: 176)

He goes on to suggest that

> Of the countless movements of switching, inserting, pressing, and the like, the 'snapping' of the photographer has had the greatest consequences. A touch of the finger now sufficed to fix an event for an unlimited period of time.
>
> (1970: 176–177)

Once fixed, perceptibility is not simply restored but is made available for manipulation and intervention. In this process, the technics of anaesthetics is refigured as prosthetic culture and the 'experience' of shock is itself transformed: so, for example, Benjamin writes, 'The camera gave the moment a posthumous shock, as it were' (1970: 177).

Buck-Morss suggests that the common ground from which the technics of anaesthetics emerged in three apparently disparate discourses – biology, philosophy and aesthetics – was 'the motif of autogenesis' (1992: 7), the myth in which 'modern man, *homo autotelus*, literally produces himself, generating himself . . .

7 Durand suggests something similar when he writes,

> A defense against external 'unbinding', the photographic image is perhaps just as much and simultaneously its inverted figuration – that which, in ourselves, would unconsciously go out toward external stimuli, acting as their ready receptacle.
>
> (1995: 148)

"miraculously out of his own substance"' (1992: 8). She argues that autogenesis offers an illusion of total control. In the technics of anaesthetics, it emerges as the autoproduction of a (masculine) subject who purges himself of the senses which endanger autonomy and is given cultural form in the phantasmagoria of

> the individual as part of a crowd that itself forms an integral whole, – a 'mass ornament', to use Siegfried Kracauer's term, that pleases as an aesthetics of the surface, a deindividualised, formal and regular pattern.
> (1992: 35)

What I shall suggest is that Wright's representation of recovered memory as a wired circuit indicates that the latest reworking of the myth of autogenesis is given cultural form not in the mass ornament, but in the trope of autopoiesis or the self-referential organism. In prosthetic culture, the goal is now not simply to numb the synaesthetic system, but simultaneously to numb and animate it anew, both to deaden the senses and also to reawaken them, to repress memory and also to recover it. One of the forms this takes is an experimental individualism in which all the gaps in the biography of the individual are not simply filled in but are rather in-filled in the pursuit of total control, total recall.

What, then, is autopoiesis? As a biological theory, it is meant to answer 'what could well be the most important question about the universe. This is the nature of *potential* and the processes by which potential is realized' (Boulding, 1981: xiii; my emphasis).[8] This question is answered by asking two further questions: 'what is a living system?' and 'what is cognition?' (Zola, 1990–1991: 61). Its principal theorists, Humberto Maturana and Fransisco Varela (1980), argue that life is not defined by reproduction, heredity or adaptation, which only affect the species, and not the unity of the individual organism. Rather, what characterises life is the constancy of certain organisational elements. Furthermore, for them this organisation is *self-referential* in the sense that processes are organised in terms of 'the interaction of their own products'. Autopoiesis is thus a model which takes the mechanisms of homeostatic self-regulation in biological organisms as the basis of life itself.

More specifically, Maturana and Varela argue that not only are living systems cognitive systems but that living is a process of cognition. (Indeed, it is for this reason that autopoiesis is sometimes described as an epistemological constructivism.) Animal neurophysiology has for some time held that neuronal cells, like every other biological system, are organisationally 'closed';[9] that is, it is not possible to determine experimentally the difference between states of nervous

8 The grandeur of this claim serves well as an illustration of Rosi Braidotti's commentary on the ways in which biotechnologies have developed such that ' "bios" – the notion of "life" – has burst open to cover an immense variety of living organisms'. As she notes, 'our age as a whole is characterized by the calculating and rational management of *all* living matter' (1994: 43).

9 Benjamin's premise of an open synaesthenia is thus significantly at odds with this conception of the nervous system as closed. This difference raises the question as to why it is that the experimental finding that it is not possible to determine the difference between states of nervous activity whose cause is to be found within the nervous system and states caused by external stimuli should not mean that the nervous system be described as open rather than as closed by neurobiologists. Or why the issue itself – of openness or closure – should be seen as so important.

activity whose cause is to be found within the nervous system and states caused by external stimuli. It is not possible to distinguish 'between perception and hallucination in the operation of the nervous system' (Maturana and Varela, quoted in Zola, 1990–1991: 69). On the basis of this experimental epistemology, Maturana and Varela argue that any feature attributed by a living system to an observed object belongs only to the observing system's 'cognitive metadomain' and not to the observed object. For each living system the cognitive process 'consists in the creation of a field of behavior through its actual conduct in its closed domain of interactionism and not in the apprehension or the description of an independent universe'. And since what is valid for the neurophysiology of all living organisms is necessarily valid for the neurophysiology of *Homo sapiens*, human knowledge is itself internal to *Homo sapiens*' metadomain. Knowledge is an activity without a subject: it is simply 'to be able to operate adequately in an individual or cooperative situation' (Maturana and Varela, quoted in Zola, 1990–1991: 69). It is these self-productive interactions which, according to Maturana at least,[10] constitute the condition 'necessary and sufficient to characterize the organisation of living systems' and designate autopoiesis (quoted in Zola, 1990–1991: 64).

Some interpreters have found forerunners for this understanding of autoproduction in earlier theories in other disciplines.[11] Others, notably the social scientist Niklas Luhmann (1986, 1989, 1990), have generalised from the neurophysiological understanding of self-referential autopoietic organisms to psychic and social systems; he considers Maturana and Varela's work a decisive paradigm shift transcending Bertalanffy's General System Theory. For Luhmann, because of its ability to synthesise the new 'circular' categories emerging in physics, biology and the social sciences, autopoiesis provides the foundations of a new system theory, a new general sociology and a new epistemology .

In Luhmann's work, autopoiesis ceases to be inextricably related to biological life and becomes a general category of self-referential systems or 'the general form of system building using self-referential closure'. Circularity and self-production, Luhmann argues, characterise not only cells, nervous systems and biological organisms, but also psychic and social systems. However, the latter cannot strictly be considered living systems, but are, rather, 'meaning-using systems'. In these systems, self-reference, which entails 'self-observation' and 'self-description', is not only structural or intentional: it concerns the constitution of the elements of the system and as such it is basic. In this way, according to Luhmann, not only in biological but also psychic and social systems, 'openness' to the environment takes place through the self-productive 'closure' of self-observation and self-description.

10 While Varela believes that self-referential organisation is a necessary condition for autopoiesis, he does not accept that it is a sufficient condition (Zeleny, 1981).

11 Boulding, for example, writes,

> I would certainly argue as an economist that Adam Smith in *The Wealth of Nations* discovered the concept of autopoiesis in the 'invisible hand'. This is the concept of the development of the social order through the unplanned interactions of large numbers of individuals, each seeking their own gain through production and exchange, co-ordinated through the development of the system of relative prices.
>
> (1981: xii)

Luhmann (1990) and other reflexive law theorists go on to use the autopoietic model to uphold a 'neo-liberal' policy. For example, they interpret the crisis of the welfare state in terms of the loss of the law's regulating ability. Legislation invades private spheres as well as other functionally differentiated and autonomous subsystems. Unfortunately, however, the welfare state's interventionist strategy overloads the law to the point of distorting its regulatory function. This overload results in chaotic legislation which complicates the legal system and prevents its rational self-reproduction. Against this, Luhmann and the other reflexive law theorists defend what they describe as the autopoietic autonomy of social subsystems – particularly those concerning the economy, education and family life. In this way, the autopoietic paradigm is used to support deregulatory policies (Zola, 1990–1991: 62–63).

The autopoietic paradigm is, I suggest, also transposed from the biological to the social world in Wright's account, or at least it is visible as such when Wright does not turn away from what he sees in that great mirror, the technological order. In these moments, false memory syndrome is represented, in effect, as the outcome of a situation in which the individual's cognitive relation to the environment has gone awry, distorted by the technological order which has instituted a self-referential meaning-using system that is chaotic or out of control. So, for example, the chart discussed above, 'The formal investigation of ritual abuse' (Figure 5.1), is interpreted by Wright as an illustration of this chaos or confusion. It is, in his terms, characterised by self-reference, circularity and self-production, but the production is out of the control of the self which it produces. Nevertheless, false memory syndrome can be seen to have been interpreted by Wright as a mapping of autopoiesis or a graphic representation of a metaphysics of knowledge which, because it assumes self-reference as the structure of every basic element of knowledge, is 'simultaneously self-referential and realistic' (Zola, 1990–1991: 78).

Furthermore, in Wright's account, recovered memory functions without a subject as such (witness the emphasis on Ingram's characteristic dissociative use of the third person in his confessions): indeed, recovered memory is represented as a subjectless memory. But neither is recovered memory accorded objective facticity ('It's like I'm watching a movie . . . . Like a horror movie'); instead, it is made to appear to be internal to its own cognitive metadomain, operating through the techniques of prayer, visualisation, therapy and auto-hypnotic trance. Once again, the parallels with Luhmann's conception of autopoiesis are clear:

> the system maintains itself not by storing patterns but by producing elements, not by transmitting *memes* (units of cultural transmission analogue to *genes*) but by recursively using events for producing events.
>
> (Luhmann, 1990: 10)

As is the case with recovered memory, autopoietic systems do not create 'a material world of their own'. Rather, whatever input they use as identity and difference 'is of their own making' and not from the outside world. Self-referential systems are thus 'sovereign with respect to the constitution of identities and differences' (Zola, 1990–1991: 4). Luhmann writes,

> All structures of social systems have to be based on [the] fundamental fact of vanishing events, disappearing gestures or words that are dying away. Memory, and then writing, have their function in preserving – not the events, but their structure-generating power.
>
> (1990: 9)

Similarly, as noted above, Wright argues that the defining characteristic of recovered memory is the belief that there is indeed 'no structural difference' between 'believed-in fantasy about the past and viable memory of the past' (1993a: 79). Both, we are informed, are held to have structure-generating power.

Furthermore, the concept of autopoietic closure can be seen to underpin Wright's identification of the function of enforced binary choices in recovered memory ('In the absence of evidence that these stories of memories of satanic-ritual abuse were real, one could reject them as absurd, withhold judgment until evidence appeared, or accept them on faith. The middle ground was rapidly disappearing . . . ' [1993a: 80]), and his identification of his own (endangered) position with the mediating third position, that of the 'reporter at large'. Unfortunately for Wright, however, according to Maturana and Varela, the system can only either continue its autopoiesis or stop it. As Luhmann remarks, 'There are, with respect to autopoiesis, no third states. This is a powerful technical simplification' (1990: 13). Consequently, it leads to a kind of 'internal unity':

> To be or not to be, to continue the autopoiesis or not to, serves as an internal representation of the totality of possibilities. Everything that can happen is reduced for the system to one of these two states. The world, whatever this is, may be indifferent to this question. The system emerges by inventing this choice, which does not exist without it. . . . This is not a question of preference, nor a question of goal attainment. Rather, it has to be conceived as a 'code' of existence, code taken as an artificial duplication of possibilities with the consequence that every element can be presented as a selection.
>
> (1990: 13–14)

The systematicity of recovered memory is identified by Wright when he declares that it requires the choice of whether to believe in the reality of sexual abuse or not. However, the statement in which the daughters' recovered memories of sexual abuse are first given credibility is seen by Wright to be the moment in which the self-possession of the individual is eradicated and the autopoietic system can be seen to have spun out of (the) control (of the self).

As noted above, Ingram himself is reported as saying,

> 'If this did happen, we need to take care of it.' He said, 'I can't see myself doing this,' but added, 'There may be a dark side of me that I don't know about.'
>
> (1993a: 60)

For Wright, this statement marks the interruption of the therapeutic code by an arbitrary choice, inaugurating a tainted process of confession leading to the emergence of 'unplanned order out of randomness'. It is the moment when 'an uncertain or probabilistic event actually comes off'; this

> changes the probabilities of all potential events around it. This change itself, of course, has to have a certain order, and where this order comes from is something of a mystery. We might call it order of the second kind.
>
> (Boulding, 1981: xii)

But Wright cannot interpret this order with any certainty; he has not learned how to see photographically.

RE-ENTRY: THE EXPERIMENTAL INDIVIDUAL AND THE STYLISATION OF LIFE ITSELF

According to Luhmann, components of any autopoietic system can be reproduced only if they have the capacity to link closure and openness. For biological systems this does not require an awareness of, or knowledge about, the environment. For meaning-based conscious and social systems, a system relates to its environment to the extent that the environment is posited as having a function within the system. To this extent, the autopoietic mode of meaning gives the possibility of 're-entry', that is, of presenting the difference between system and environment within the system. This re-entered distinction structures the elementary operations of these systems:

> In social, i.e., communicative systems, the elementary operation of communication comes about by an 'understanding' of the distinction of 'information' and 'utterance'. Information can refer to the environment of the system. The utterance, attributed to an agent as action, is responsible for the autopoietic regeneration of the system itself. In this way information and utterance are forced into unity.
>
> (Luhmann, 1990: 12)

By this synthesis, the system is forced into looking for possibilities of mediating closure and openness. In Luhmann's words,

> communication is an evolutionary potential for building up systems that are able to maintain closure under the conditions of openness. These systems face the continuing necessity to select meanings that satisfy these constraints.
>
> (1990: 13)

Meaning-based systems thus arise in a series of recursive, iterative positionings or new states of informedness.

A related interpretation of communication as a system or code has been put forward by Baudrillard. In his view, the ills of contemporary culture can be attributed to an unfortunate excess of negativity. This is a negativity which derives from the tendency towards realisation, a technologically induced suspension of disbelief regarding the necessity of any limitation on the realisation of possibilities (or selections in Luhmann's terms). For Baudrillard, *every* possibility is given the potential of being realised in a great technological loop, in which the possible and the real are collapsed in what he calls the high resolution space of real time. This integrated circuit performs what Baudrillard (1995) describes as 'the automatic writing of the world'; in the case of false memory syndrome, it is as if the unconscious of the psychoanalytic code is being inscribed in the circuits of global communication.

One possible consequence of this process is that the individual may be rendered unnecessary altogether. Indeed, Baudrillard suggests that developments in the technologies of communication have resulted in the realisation of a pure and minimal form of identity: 'I exist, I met myself.' In possession of this identity, in which the possible short-circuits the real, the subject-less subject feels a little responsible for other possibilities: as Baudrillard wryly comments,

> we always feel a little responsible for films we haven't seen, for desires we haven't realized, for people we haven't answered, for crimes we haven't committed, for money we haven't spent.
>
> (1995: 103)

From this point of view, 'we' may even feel a little responsible for memories we haven't had. Such a subject is comforted that there is a machine that can deal with all these possibilities, can stock them (a data bank), filter them (an answer machine), watch them (a video recorder), on behalf of the subject, freeing him or her of his or her own will, enabling his or her own disappearance. There is then a possible construction of false memory syndrome in which the subject disappears in a spiral of negativity.

Alternatively, however, the individual may, as a consequence of the successful management of re-entry, emerge as a self-legislating system; this is the ideal, I would suggest, that is proposed in the contemporary edicts of lifestyle as the privileged route to 'life itself' described by Featherstone (1991), Maffesoli (1991), Strathern (1992) and other commentators on consumer culture.[12] Mark Seltzer's analysis of the relationship between the market and lifestyle in relation to body–machine complexes is interesting in this respect (although he adopts a slightly different interpretation of the relationship between possessive individual and the market to that proposed here[13]) for he argues that the animism of the pan-intentionalism that appears in the understanding of things as prosthetic extensions of the self serves as something of an antidote to the disciplinary individualism of machine culture. And even Wright seems to recognise that it is lifestyle that most frequently opens up the photographic instant of choice in the

12 Indeed, Baudrillard himself comments, 'We have interiorized our own prosthetic image and become the professional show-men of our own lives' (1995: 97).

13 Seltzer argues that

> the tension between possessive and disciplinary styles of individualism is . . . complicated. Machine culture progressively redraws the vague and shifting line between the animate and inanimate: rewriting the opposition between life and death in terms of the calculation of degrees of aliveness and rewriting the opposition between reproduction (sexual, biological) and production (mechanical) in terms of an experience of reproduction without gender (though not without its own erotics).
>
> (1993: 102)

culture of prosthetics, that is, that the desire to draw a boundary, to fix a frame, is most strenuously put to work in the creation of distinctive lifestyles.

The general point to be gained from this discussion though is that it is not simply the filling in of the gaps in the individual's (auto)biography in the great mirror of the technological order that explains the emergence and take-up of experimental individualism. Rather there has to be a political environment in which this self-identity makes sense and the enclaves or lifestyles of consumer culture may be seen to provide such an environment for here the individual is always somehow insufficently free, employing a choice whose volition is always insufficiently pure. Indeed, the identification of this insufficiency has been facilitated by the rise of cultural intermediaries expert in what Baudrillard, Bauman, Deleuze[14] and others have called the stylisation of everyday life – therapists, advertisers, designers, critics, self-help enthusiasts, publicists and media personalities. (The number of these stylists is said to have grown as part of a market-driven tendency towards the demonopolisation of knowledge, leading to the spread of knowledge characterised by hyper-reflexivity, anti-foundationalism and polycultural 'tolerance' [Featherstone, 1991].) The identification and classification of the insufficiency of will by these intermediaries is what provides the very *raison d'être* of the trials, tests or experiments of lifestyle, the globalised pursuits of escapism as managed risk-taking or strategic daring in the activities of not only tourism, sport, recreation and leisure, but also health, sex, love and work. Autopoiesis can thus be seen as a survival strategy in Bauman's sense in this global culture.

The ideal that the 'normal' consumer aspires to achieve in the enclaves of lifestyle is the ability to experience 'moderate' swings from being in control to being out of control and back again. According to one market researcher,

> These swings, because they can be appropriately monitored and responded to, create a feeling of diversity-within-sameness that is comfortable and comforting to most people. Their lives are balanced between feelings of completeness and incompleteness – the warp and woof of the life experience.
>
> (Hirschman, 1992: 173)

The need implied here for constant self-monitoring and response (or self-observation) demonstrates how the assumption of an insufficiency of will can be mobilised as the source of the dynamism of the experimental individual.[15]

In this wider context, false memory syndrome can thus be seen as an instance of identity politics in which the comfort the technological order offers the

14 Deleuze comments that neurosis has acquired the power of 'propagation by contagion: "I will not let you go until you have joined me in this condition"' (1993: 108).

15 It may be the reason Baudrillard argues that

> we are all animals, and laboratory animals, whom one continually tests in order to extort their reflex behaviors, which are like so many confessions of rationality in the final moment. Everywhere bestiality must yield to reflex animality, exorcising an order of the indecipherable, of the savage, of which, precisely in their silence, animals have remained the incarnation.
>
> (1994: 130)

helpless is aligned with a stylised instrumentalism:[16] in this contemporary reworking of the myth of autogenesis, the subject is reborn with the fundamental right to individuality and is given a new biography in the selection of experiences according to their a/effectivity (Taylor, 1992).[17] However, Wright, whilst recognising the potential of autopoiesis to act as a model of self-identity, is unwilling either to see the opportunities of lifestyle or to uphold it explicitly as an ideal for the individual. That he does not do so, I suggest, is a consequence of his own positioning – as a 'reporter at large' – in the struggles within an internally divided media.[18]

In Wright's representation of recovered memory, input from the (internal and external) environment takes place through the selection and utterance of expert knowledge claims or bits of information in the media; it is through this 'communication' that the system is reproduced. However, Wright, the reporter at large, cannot understand the basis on which this selection is made. All he can see is the endless technical duplication of possibilities, the meaninglessness of the chart, a spatial continuum viewed from any one or rather all of a number of positions. He cannot overcome the fear that recovered memories are not in the control of the individual: for Wright, such memories are produced, both 'without thinking' and in an informed way, by a chaotic system that is not only both defensive and aggressive, but also multiplying out of control,[19] producing itself in an

16 In her discussion of a disputed case of multiple personality syndrome, Stone quotes a psychologist who claims, 'There's an awful excess of attention being paid to MPD these days. You know, in many ways, it's being grossly overdiagnosed. And people are being channeled into it . . . it's like your most recent designer disease' (1995: 48).

17 The novelist Fay Weldon criticises therapists on the grounds that they 'tell stories badly': 'Most of them are failed novelists . . . . If you create the right narrative, you sweep away the doubt and, like a priest, you absolve them of guilt.' She further describes therapy as contributing to 'a kind of Thatcherism of the soul. You think of yourself, your own rights' (quoted in Freely, 1994: 4). In contrast to Weldon's emphasis on (bad) narrative, Eve Sedgwick highlights the use of techniques of temporal fragmentation in therapy, including 'the highly existential "one day at a time" that severs every moment of choice (and of course they are infinite) from both the identity–history and the intention–futurity that might be thought to constrain it' (1994: 134). The question of how the image refigures narratives of self will be taken up again in chapter 8.

18 In a review of a recent clutch of books on false memory syndrome (including Wright's), Frederick Crews makes explicit his own hostility for the media (of which he and Wright are a part). He writes,

> There was nothing exceptional about the Ingram family's prelapsarian make-up or the Olympia scene in general. Apparently, a community steeped in Biblical literalism on the one hand and *Geraldo* on the other needs only a triggering mechanism to set off a long chain reaction of paranoia. Yet such a community epitomizes a good portion of North America. The potential for mass havoc from 'memory'-based accusations is no smaller today than it was in the seventeenth century. In fact, it is incomparably greater, thanks to the power of our sensation-seeking media to spread the illness instantaneously from one town or region to another.
> (1994 : 59)

19 In the United States the growth of the phenomenon of false memory syndrome has been facilitated by the setting up of a number of 'self-help' groups, including VOCAL (Victims of Child Abuse Laws) and FMSF (False Memory Syndrome Foundation), supported by a newsletter, *The Retractor*, which publishes the so-called retractions of women 'returners', women who claim that their memories were fantasies encouraged by their therapists. In the United Kingdom, ACAP (Adult Children Accusing Parents) has recently been formed.

apparently arbitrary series of relations between individuals and an ever-increasing number of environments or worlds through the arbitrary mediation or communication of the media. In short, Wright remains, at heart, the 'reporter at large', unwilling to see that

> the world itself has taken on a 'photographic face'; it can be photographed because it strives to be absorbed into the spatial continuum which yields to snapshots.
>
> (Kracauer, 1995: 59)

Wright's ambivalent representation of false memory syndrome can thus be seen as *both* a wishful longing for a return to a time in which the links between the nation, the individual citizen and memory were secured through their lodging in a mythical political body,[20] *and* a fearful projection of a world in which the individual and the profession to which Wright belongs disappears in the ebbs and flows of the marketing of mediated global space.[21] Ironically this means that although Wright fears the demise of a society which itself arose as a specifically masculine fantasy of the self-controlled, individualised self, he seems unable to accept that a new autopoietic order might be premised upon a mode of self-

20 Jonathan Boyarin (1994) provides an account of the mythical political body of the nation state that supports this interpretation of Wright's inability. He argues that the mythical political body of the modern nation state was secured through two complementary yet paradoxical means of legitimation. The first is a rhetoric of kinship and community that mobilises an assumption of common interest rooted in a putative memory of common origins. The second is the state's self-representation as a guarantor of the individual's rationality and freedom from the shackles and demons of the pre-modern or primitive past. This self-representation, evident in Wright's adoption of techniques of journalistic impartiality, conspires to make the tentacles of state power and knowledge appear to be discrete, disinterested and diffuse. The combined effects of these two techniques, so Boyarin argues, is to create an image of the state as freeing the social from the political intrusions characteristic of the feudal past by keeping its hands off the body of its people; it is an image exemplified in the mythical figure of 'the reporter at large', distant, but always ever vigilant in defence of the purity of the political body of the nation state.

Boyarin further argues that these state ideologies rested upon an appeal to organic experience and commonsense dimensionality. Those who elaborated and maintained such ideologies of nation and body dictated both the contents of appropriate memory – tradition – and the proper spatial boundaries of the collective – territory. The nation rallied allegiance to its sovereign power by dramatising the threat to its integrity from alien bodies and 'primitive' impulses. The suggestion being put forward here is that this threat takes ever new forms, not all of which can be contained by national boundaries, and some of which come from previous allies, producing internal divisions within the apparatuses of the state such as journalism.

21 As Bea Campbell writes,

> Sexual crime provokes a crisis of belief, of procedure and prosecution, and of course it challenges the way we think about the nature of crime and punishment. More than that, it demands the feminisation of the police and the judiciary. Sexual abuse of children now presents society with the ultimate crisis of patriarchy, when children refuse to protect their fathers by keeping their secrets.
>
> We know the alternative – that children put their fathers' pain before their own and protect them, as they always have with silence. Until now all the institutions of the state and civil society have conspired to protect the men in general and fathers in particular and keep their secrets.
>
> (1988: 71)

identification that is also masculine. For, so I would suggest, the recursive, experimental or enterprising reflexivity that Luhmann assumes can be seen as masculine in so far as it presumes the need to maintain closure (even if this is through openness). This means that while false memory syndrome can be seen as a challenge to masculinity, it also contains the potential for the emergence of new forms of masculine self-identity and should be seen not just as a defensive response but also as a more aggressive reaction to contemporary sexual politics.

To sum up the argument developed so far, here and in the preceding chapter, Wright's account moves between the fear of a feminine mimesis and a masculine fantasy of autogenesis afforded by the new order of the autopoietic system (a masculine perversion of mimesis). It can thus be seen as an example of a convergence between neurophysiology, philosophy and aesthetics at the end of the twentieth century, a convergence that is producing a culture of prosthetics that is highly gendered in its implications for self-identity. However, it does not signal the end of sexual politics; simply, a new twist in a continuing story, as the third alternative to seeing photographically outlined below seeks to show.

GENDER, THE BODY POLITIC AND GLOBALISATION

The fearfulness that Wright displays is widespread.[22] There is, for example, a widely held anxiety that a draining of time is being effected through the use of computers and data storage banks, and public concern that an unregulated media has taken on a socialising role comparable to, and perhaps in conflict with, those of the family and the state (Huyssen, 1995), giving rise to novel configurations of self- and collective identity, experience and information. This is not surprising; the spatio-temporal relations of familial and national security are being radically redrawn as newly emerging mnemonic techniques disembody memories, and cut them loose so that they no longer seem to have clear individual or territorial boundaries. However, so this section will suggest, neither the fear expressed by Wright nor the fantasy expressed by Luhmann exhaust the possibilities of prosthetic culture. There is another way of seeing photographically.

22 In the article on serial killers noted above, Mark Seltzer points out that

> it has become something of a commonplace . . . to posit a connection between murder and imitation or mimesis – most visibly in the notion of 'copy-cat killing' and in the notion that serial killing may in fact be an artifact of 'a media-feeding frenzy'.
>
> (1993: 94)

He suggests that this contention is a consequence of a

> radical uncertainty about the relation between repetition and representation – between the passive action of acting addictively and serially and the active passivity of deriving identity from repeated processes of identification.
>
> (1993: 95)

In this way – through a consideration of the 'internal competition between repetition and representation' (1993: 94) – he makes it possible to see the challenge posed by mimesis to the subject of representation.

In his discussion of 'How to see (photographically)', Régis Durand suggests that photographs should not be seen as illustrations; instead, he argues, they are

> like a rebus, a code which, even though it is no simple translation or figuration, must have some affinity, some sense of a connection with the original impulse.
>
> (1995: 149)

He continues,

> There lies something, in the photograph, of unconscious desire, but hardly anything on its surface can lead back to its source – except precisely the sense of its having come from *a* source, and of the ensuing transformation and loss.
>
> (1995: 149)

In this analysis, I would suggest, there is a recognition of the mimetic character of the photographic image and its capacity to make visible 'some sense of a connection with the original impulse', but there is also simultaneously an assumption that no specific source can be identified; instead, the photograph can only provide, so Durand asserts, 'the sense of its having come from *a* source'. In this assertion, the mimetically derived specificity of a particular source is lost and replaced by the awareness of '*a* source', which, in turn, is associated with 'transformation and loss'. Indeed, 'It is in this manner', Durand claims, that the photographic process 'leads back to itself rather than to the object it purports to represent' (1995: 149).[23]

The argument is thus not simply that seeing photographically makes 'loss' visible, but, or so Durand also seems to imply, it does so in such a way that is itself also a loss – 'hardly anything on its surface can lead back to its source'. The specificity of the source is lost; while the effects of an object are depicted, the cause or origin is not identifiable. It has been suggested here, however, that two of the most likely consequences of adopting the view of seeing photographically as necessarily involving a loss to either the individual or the nation are the attempts either to deny it or to in-fill it. These options might be described as fear and fantasy; in the first, the masculine subject of representation is reasserted, while in the second, the articulation of autopoiesis both produces and mantains the masculine need to maintain closure of self- and collective identities through a perversion of mimesis.

Alternatively, however, it is possible to suggest that 'hardly anything' is not necessarily no-thing; indeed, it is, rather, from some (if not all) points of view, some-thing. From these points of view, while the seeing photographically that is part of false memory syndrome does indeed lead back to itself, that is, to its capacity to show 'that really was', this capacity is, from some points of view, also 'the object it purports to represent' (that is, sexual abuse), for, as has been well documented, the posing of the question of the reality of sexual abuse has been

23 There is here, I think, a recognition of the way in which seeing photographically makes possible the displacement of the referent that is part of the constitution of the syndrome as a problem.

integral to the obligation to know that has defined modern society as such to and for itself. Or, to put this the other way around, seeing photographically makes it possible to see that the ways of knowing (and these include techniques of remembering and of forgetting) which have defined the mythical political body of the nation state are unavoidably gendered.[24]

This way (or ways) of seeing photographically recognises the feminine specificity of mimesis and does not produce total recall; rather, it leads to partial remembrance. In this way of seeing photographically, it is recognised that 'what you see is *not* what you get' and that this is because of 'the insufficiency of the decontextualised image' (Jay, 1994: 163). However, this insufficiency is not an absolute loss or a lack; it is, rather, the reinstatement of gaps. Approaching the photograph as a mirror which reflects what is to be seen when no one is there (the inverse of the object that is seen from every point of view) can lead the observer to refuse to look at all (fear), or to believe that everything can be seen (the fantasy of indifferentiation and outcontextualisation). But seeing photographically can encourage another way to do what Barthes advises, that is, 'to look away or close your eyes' (quoted in Robins, 1995: 42).[25] While 'looking

24 If further proof is needed of this, consider Jane Caputi's analysis of the ways in which the popular representation of the threat of nuclear war in contemporary popular culture – popular films, novels, visual images – is intricately inter-twined with the theme of incestuous fatherhood. As she and others note, the father was employed as a figure of protection in the metaphors of male birth and fatherhood adopted in the language of the Manhattan Project, the US government's mission to develop the atom bomb. This device has continued in contemporary representations of nuclear armament. So, for example, in order to persuade Americans to place their trust in the Strategic Defense initiative or the real life 'Star Wars', Ronald Reagan promised that his plan would offer a 'new hope for our children in the twenty-first century' (quoted in Caputi, 1994: 105). But in many of these representations, the bomb, while purportedly protecting, actually threatens. Similarly, the nuclear father as found in comic books, popular films and novels from *The Simpsons* to *Star Wars* (1977) to the novel *The Mosquito Coast* (1982) is valorised *and* turned into a figure of fear. This is evident in both the publicity given to murderous fathers in press reports (who are likened to machines) and the description of fictional father figures such as Leland Palmer in *Twin Peaks* (1989–1990), De-Fens in *Falling Down* (1993) and Freddy Kruger in *Nightmare on Elm Street* (1984). As Caputi points out, these representations of the benign and the threatening aspects of paternal power come together in the figure of the nuclear father:

> Affirming the connection of the personal to the political, and in subliminal recognition of the often apocalyptic experience of American family life, the phrase 'nuclear family' established itself firmly in the national vernacular by 1947.
>
> (1994: 105)

In these ambivalent representations, Caputi argues, the vocabularies used to describe incest and nuclear power reveal a number of parallels: the desecration of the future; the betrayal of trust; the cult of secrecy and denial, aided by the psychological defences of numbing, repression of memory and splitting in both 'survivor' and perpetrator; and the reification of 'survival'. The implication of her analysis is that the authority of the nation state is tied to assumptions about the integrity of the family, and that as one is revealed as being the site of conflict so will the other be called into doubt, and that the ethos of survivalism discussed in chapter 4 is a highly gendered phenomenon.

Caputi gives as an example of this convergence of vocabulary in representations of incest and nuclear war the popular portrayal of General Curtis LeMay, who oversaw the Hiroshima bombing and the creation of Strategic Air Command, as 'more machine than man'. He himself is reported as recalling that when he flew bombers over Germany,

⇒

away' is undoubtedly sometimes a synonym for the willed absence of the embodied self altogether – as is evidenced in the account offered by Wright discussed in the previous chapter – it is not always such a 'turning away'; rather, it may be a process of recontextualisation,[26] of letting the imagination catch sight, of 'creating new relationships both to others and to oneself'.

This is illustrated by, for example, Bea Campbell's discussion of the disputed interpretation of the visual evidence at issue in the so-called Cleveland case investigating sexual abuse. She writes,

> What is the body of the child in the evidential picture saying to us? It jolts the viewer because the child is bereft of its environment, its toys, its potty, its teddy, its friends, its parents, the domesticity (not the assumed asexuality) that defines the context of childhood. The effect of the banishment of all the banal bits and pieces that fill the child's universe is compounded

> his imagination had caught a picture of a little girl down below, horribly burned and crying for her mother. 'You have to turn away from the picture,' he said, 'if you intend to keep on doing the work your Nation expects of you.'
>
> (Quoted in Caputi, 1994: 115)

In this view from above, the previously convergent ideologies of nation and family shear apart. As Kracauer writes,

> For the first time in history, . . . the inert world presents itself in its independence from human beings. Photography shows cities in aerial shots, brings crockets and figures down from Gothic cathedrals. All spatial configurations are incorporated into the central archive in unusual combinations which distance them from human proximity.
>
> (1995: 62)

General Leslie Groves, who was the military chief of the Manhattan Project, initiated a policy of 'compartmentalization of knowledge'. This policy ensured that 'each man should know everything he needed to know about doing his job and nothing else' (quoted in Caputi, 1994: 115). I suggest that putting the knowledge of all these men together might produce a map such as the diagram of the investigation of false memory syndrome produced by the Olympia police department (Figure 5.1 above).

25 This opportunity is not taken up by Baudrillard in his consideration of the televisual representation of the Holocaust. He writes,

> Forgetting extermination is part of extermination, because it is also the extermination of memory, of history, of the social, etc. This forgetting is still too dangerous, it must be effaced by an artificial memory (today, everywhere, it is artificial memories that efface the memory of man, that efface man in his own memory). . . . One no longer makes the Jews pass through the crematorium or the gas chamber, but through the universal screen and the microprocessor. Forgetting, annihilation, finally achieves its aesthetic dimension in this way – it is achieved in retro, finally elevated here to a mass level.
>
> (1994: 49)

Perhaps this pessimism is a consequence of Baudrillard's adoption of the position of 'one' – anyone or no one – rather than some-one. His position may thus be usefully contrasted with that proposed by Haraway, who argues for the necessity of 'views from somewhere' (1991: 196).

26 The recontextualisation that has been developed here is motivated by feminist analyses of sexual abuse: Campbell (1988); *Feminist Review* (1988); Kelly (1988, 1994); Scott (1988); Driver and Droisen (1989); Hall and Lloyd (1989); Hacking (1991); Kelly *et al.* (1991); Bell (1993); Lee (1994). MacLeod and Saraga's work (1988) is of special interest in relation to the approach adopted here because of their discussion of the implications of the adoption of what they call 'family systems theory' for girls and women who have experienced sexual abuse.

> by another absence – the rest of the child's body, its fingers and its face. The child is not playing with itself, and so what we do not see is the child's sexuality as existing in and for itself. . . .
>
> The evidential photographs of abused anuses and vulvas are more than painful – and that they are: they are troubling. They are sexual because they are defined not just by the child's body but by the invisible presence of the perpetrator. *They are difficult pictures to see because what they show is not only a body but a relationship.* They may cause you grief or they may work on your fantasies, but either way, you have to work out who you are as you watch, if you are to know what you think.
>
> (1988: 81; my emphasis)

Seeing photographically may contribute to a need for the in-filling of total recall, the unrealisable desire to fill in a loss that can never be made good, but it may also provoke a looking away, and, in doing so, create new gaps that require the viewer to take up a (new) position. Consequently, it is a vision that may not only comprise the identification of a specific source but also produce a situated or recontextualised knowledge; indeed, in this way of seeing, one would be impossible without the other.

What this suggests is that in order for the changes wrought in mimesis by prosthetic culture to be seen as a transformation and not just decay (as Benjamin advises), changes should be seen not only in the capacity to produce similarities, but also in the ability to recognise or perceive them. This ability – not only to look at the photograph, but to interpret the look of the photograph – is brought into being and sustained by the politicisation of the contexts within which we see photographically (for further discussion of these, see Hearn, 1990; King and Trowell, 1992; Stainton Rogers and Stainton Rogers, 1992; Wattam, 1992; Kelly, 1994; Lee, 1994). To do so is to acknowledge the changes in perceptibility that are part of prosthetic culture, for, as Benjamin writes, 'To perceive the aura of an object we look at means to invest it with the ability to look at us in return' (1970: 190). For this reason, the seeing photographically that is part of the phenomenon of false memory syndrome should not be seen independently of either the ongoing struggles to politicise the issue of child sexual abuse that are taking place in a wide range of contexts today or debates about the nature of visual evidence.[27] In this sense, false memory syndrome is at the heart of debates about what has been called situated knowledge.

Situated knowledge, or objectivity in Donna Haraway's terms, is not about the transcendence of limits,[28] and is thus not about total recall, but rather about

27 However, as Grosz (1995) points out, Caillois does not believe that mimesis is a survival mechanism.

28 Indeed, she argues that

> Relativism is a way of being nowhere while claiming to be everywhere equally. The 'equality' of positioning is a denial of responsibility and critical enquiry. Relativism is the perfect twin mirror of totalization in the ideologies of objectivity; both deny the stakes in location, embodiment, and partial perspective; both make it impossible to see well.
>
> (1991: 191)

Haraway thus provides here a critique of the possibility of 'total recall', describing it as a god-trick.

the drawing of boundaries or frames in ways that make us accountable for what we learn how to see. Arguing against the claim that the development of technologies of visualisation necessarily contributes to the dematerialisation of reality, she suggests that prosthetic culture can lead to a greater recognition of the active, generative capacity of the objects that it makes visible. She believes that the experimentation made possible by such technologies of visualisation has the potential to produce an object of knowledge that is neither a resource nor the fixed determination of what can count as objective knowledge (indeed, she claims the objects so revealed have shattered the mirror stage of vision), but is rather an active, meaning-generating axis of production. She writes,

> Boundaries are drawn by mapping practices; 'objects' do not pre-exist as such. Objects are boundary projects. But boundaries shift from within. What boundaries provisionally contain remains generative, productive of meaning and bodies.
>
> (1991: 201)

In response to developments in technologies of visualisation, she suggests, we must learn how to see in compound, multiple ways, in 'partial perspectives', with 'passionate detachment', adopting the eye of a travelling lens.[29] She writes, as I noted at the beginning of this chapter,

> The 'eyes' made available in modern technological sciences shatter any idea of passive vision; these prosthetic devices show us that all eyes, including our own organic ones, are active perceptual systems, building in translations and specific *ways* of seeing, that is, ways of life.
>
> (1991: 190)

She calls for a vision that initiates, rather than closing off, what she calls the 'generativity' of images, producing copies that require contact; this is a mimetic vision that both requires and makes possible a feminist embodiment or being in the world of 'significant prosthesis'. Prosthesis, she argues, is thus a fundamental category for understanding our most intimate selves. It promises a 'critical vision consequent upon a critical positioning in inhomogeneous, gendered social space' (1991: 195). The fate of this critical vision in contemporary Euro-American societies is the subject of the following two chapters.

CODA

Jonathan Boyarin argues that memory is neither individual nor abstractly collective, for it is not superorganic. At the same time, it is not simply technological; nor, moreover, is it simply representational. It is, rather, embodied in specific bodies, immersed in networks of technologies and modes of signification. The tain of the great mirror of these technologies is no longer (if it ever was) invisible, but its acknowledgement does not taint the mirror's ability to make images;

29 She rejects the notion of standpoint, arguing that 'our maps require too many dimensions for that metaphor to ground our visions' (1991: 196).

rather it is what makes it possible. False memory syndrome is no more and no less than an instantaneous response to a situation in which the constitution of both collective groupings and specific personal identities occurs in relation to rapidly changing techniques of self- and collective identity, including those made possible by the reflexive eye of the camera. It is the result of the reinforcement of some (rather than other) memories as differently positioned members contest and create limits and links, (silver) backings, boundaries and connections among themselves. At the very least, as a photographically informed profane illumination, false memory syndrome provides a recognition that the order of things is necessarily provisional, that 'the valid organization of things remains unknown' (Kracauer, 1995: 63). And at best, the image of false memory syndrome makes it possible to see the forgetting of the specifically sexual violence[30] that is a source of the nation's mythical political body in the camera's eye. This is necessarily a partial remembrance.

Seeing false memory syndrome photographically, looking *away* from mnemonic convulsions, not simply *at* them, demonstrates the continuing power of mimesis, and, in particular, the power of mimesis as a relationship (or what Haraway calls a 'webbed connection') in which the specificity of the 'source' is not necessarily lost, in which something in the object that is 'hardly anything' can be something. Or at least can be something from some points of view. As Hubertus von Amelunxen puts it, 'In photography, the things which we see have disappeared from their representation. This [is] *renunciation* – and not *failure*' (1994: 21). Seeing photographically can both illuminate 'loss' and yet not itself be lacking. Seeing in this way is not not lacking because it is without gaps, for gaps are there; rather it is a way of viewing gaps as requiring of a relationship with the viewer.[31] It is a call for the value of the atopic here and now of situated knowledge, rather than the ubiquitous now/here of global culture; what Deleuze and Guattari call 'the now of our becoming'. Its unformed happening makes possible an inconceivable differentiation (rather than, or as well as, indifferentiation) (Oosterling, 1995).

While it does not thus make use of the force of total recall, it is not without its own violence. As Haraway cautions: 'Vision is *always* a question of the power to see – and perhaps of the violence implicit in our visualizing practices' (1991: 192). However, if it is recognised that these practices are not only autopoietic,

30 The specificity of this recognition does not preclude – indeed, rather requires – an acknowledgement that these contests are linked to race. The use of metaphors such as the 'dark side' of individual psyche and the 'primitive' condition of the national character make visible the race-ing of gender and gender-ing of race which are at the heart of the nation's body. It is no coincidence that the colours of 'truth' and 'falsity' are 'white' and 'black'. See Driver and Droisen (1989) for a discussion of the inter-relationship of issues of race and gender in relation to sexual abuse. See Taussig (1993) for a discussion of 'the intimate relationship' between primitivism and the new theories of the senses circulating with the new means of mechanical reproduction – specifically the phonograph and the camera – in colonial practices at the turn of the century.

31 Consider, for example, the possibility that the space or gap within the photographic phenomenon of recovered memory might be filled by what Deleuze, following Bergson, calls recollection-image (see the next chapter).

but also mimetic, then questions of bio-politics will not be reduced to matters of lifestyle and we will 'see anew the spell of the natural where the reproduction of life merges with the recapture of the soul' (Taussig, 1993: 2). The question the photographic phenomenon of false memory syndrome forces us to address is, 'With whose blood were my eyes crafted?' (Haraway, 1991: 192).

7

MOVEMENT AND THE BODY OF PHOTOGRAPHY

> Man's interest in getting to know the whole world has been enlarged by the feeling of being – at every moment – in every situation – involved in it.
>
> (Lazló Moholy-Nagy, 1969: 15)

INTRODUCTION

In this and the next chapter, the question of the changing relationships between the consciousness, memory and embodiment in prosthetic culture will be further explored. Once again, the focus will be on how photography informs and motivates the relations between these aspects of the modern person. A particular emphasis will be placed on the subject-effects of the introduction and development of computer-aided photography and the processes of digitalisation and their implications for the emergence of what will be called 'non-dimensional' personalities. In order to situate this development, a brief account of the historical relation between vision, the body and subjectivity will be presented. In the more recent stages of this history, the unconscious has been defined in relation to the incommensurability of the relations between the human body, its senses – including vision – and the components of consciousness including memory. Photography will be presented in terms of its ability to intervene in this incommensurability as perceptual prostheses. This, in turn, will lead to a discussion of the optical unconscious of prosthetic culture and a consideration of the notion that the perceptual prostheses of photography are a source of potential for the experimental individual.

While the focus is on photography, the consideration of its subject-effects in prosthetic culture cannot be separated from a more general discussion of the discourse of aesthetics. As Susan Buck-Morss (1991, 1992) argues, even in the development of anaesthetics at the beginning of the twentieth century the role of art was ambivalent because the definition of art as a sensual experience that distinguishes itself precisely by its separation from reality was becoming increasingly difficult to sustain. By the early twentieth century much of what had been the specialised sphere of activity, art, had already entered into the phantasmagoric field as entertainment, as part of the commodity world, bringing with it the possibility of changes in modes of identification signalled by a renewed concern with mimesis, distraction, fantasy and day-dreaming. By the end of the twentieth century, it has been widely argued, this process of de-differentiation has been extended yet further through the aestheticisation of everyday life, what Guattari (1992) calls 'subjectivity's entry into the machine', and the transformation of reality into images and vice versa, the production of virtual realities.

There is a set of inter-related processes at work here. It is argued, for example, that figural regimes of signification now emphasise images which draw on primary rather than secondary processes in the (psychoanalytic) unconscious, promoting the investment of the viewer's affect or desire in the object rather than the maintenance of distance in relations of identification (Lash, 1988; Lyotard, 1991). The aestheticisation of everyday life, in turn, is said to contribute to de-distantiation or instantiation, that is, pleasure from immersion into the objects of contemplation (Featherstone, 1991). Moreover, the individual develops the capacity to view and take pleasure in objects and experiences usually placed outside the range of institutionally designated aesthetic objects; he or she encounters the immediacy of the everyday object, is immersed into the experience through the investment of affect. It is no longer a matter of a pause for reflection before purchase, no longer a question of *just* looking (Bowlby, 1985); rather 'looking' is now a technique of instantiation, of immersion in the object. As Lyotard writes,

> as the new technologies are now invading public space and common time (invading them in the form of industrial objects of production and consumption, including 'cultural' production and consumption), on a planetary scale, it is what we might call the most 'intimate' space–time, in its most 'elementary' syntheses, which is attacked, hounded and no doubt modified by the present state of technology.
>
> (1991: 47)

And yet the entry of subjectivity into the machine does not simply lead to an attack on the intimate; it is also simultaneously a reconfiguration of the matter of bodies:

> It isn't enough for these machines to simulate the results of vision or of writing fairly well. It's a matter (to use the attractively appropriate locution) of 'giving body' to the artificial thought of which they are capable.
>
> (1991: 17)

FROM THE *CAMERA OBSCURA* TO THE *CAMERA LUCIDA*

Art historian Jonathan Crary (1988, 1989, 1990, 1994) has argued that there was a radical break in the mid-1800s between classical and modern conceptions of observation. This break is associated with the collapse of what he calls the *camera obscura* model of vision, and its displacement by radically different notions of what an observer was and of what constituted vision:[1] a physiological optics. I

1 Crary prefers the term 'observer' (from the Latin *observare*) to the term 'spectator', which has dominated film and photography criticism, because he believes it does not connote the passivity of onlooking but rather the disciplined activity of observing codes of vision, of conforming to a prescribed set of possibilities and conventions.

will suggest that one interpretation of this second model is outlined by Roland Barthes (1981) as the *camera lucida*.[2] The thesis proposed here is thus that photography and cinema are not (only) the modern inheritors of the logic of the *camera obscura*, but, rather, are (also) the consequence of philosophical and scientific tendencies to conceptualise vision as a function of the human body.

According to Crary, the classical model of vision which was dominant from the late 1500s to the end of the 1700s made use of the structural and optical principles of the *camera obscura*, both for the observation of empirical phenomena and for reflective introspection and self-observation. It provided a model of vision in terms of a geometric optics, that is, a model of an incorporeal relationship between the perceiver and the object of perception, a process undertaken by a free, sovereign, but isolated individual with clear boundaries between inside and outside, observer and observed, existing within a stable space and continuous time. Crary writes,

> The secure positioning of the self with this empty interior space was a precondition for knowing the outer world. Its enclosedness, its darkness, its categorical separation from an exterior incarnates Descartes's announcement in the Third Meditation, 'I will now shut my eyes, I shall stop my ears, I shall . . . disregard my senses.'[3]
>
> (1988: 32)

The monadic viewpoint of the individual was thus legitimised by the principles of the *camera obscura*: the subordination of that individual's sensory experience to an external and pre-given world of objective truth. There was no matter in Cartesian vision.

In modern observation, in contrast, Crary argues, vision became a bodily process, and came to be understood in terms of physiological optics: 'The body which had been a neutral or invisible term in vision now was the thickness from which knowledge of vision was derived' (1988: 43). The observer is thus plunged into a newly corporealised immediacy of sensations. Crary cites Goethe's *Theory of Colours*, published in 1810, as a work crucial for the articulation of this model of subjective vision in which the body is introduced, in all its physiological density, as the ground on which vision is possible. Crary suggests Goethe is the first of many researchers studying processes which had previously been seen as deficiencies, such as the retinal after-image and its chromatic transformations, who defines how

2 In introducing the *camera lucida* into this history of photography, I am not intending to resurrect an archaic artisanal practice; rather it is an attempt to highlight the existence of a particular counter-practice and its sensory space. David Tomas, who also makes use of the same 'spatio-temporal transposition', that is, 'relocating the *camera lucida* in the late twentieth century', writes,

> The contact and clash of old and new sense ratios, their respective imaging cultures and mode of graphic or electronic imaging 'draws' attention to what Michel de Certeau once described as 'non-discursive practices' – activities, in other words, which have 'not been tamed and symbolized in language'.
>
> (1995: 263)

3 The use of the notion of 'darkness' here, as in the discussion of false memory syndrome in the preceding two chapters, is a further indication of the complex ways in which seeing has been bound up with knowing and modern classifications of genre including race.

vision is an irreducible amalgam of physiological processes and external stimulation. In this reconceptualisation of vision, the observer is repositioned in an undemarcated terrain where the distinction between the internal sensation and external source is irrevocably blurred and the body of the observer is constructed as a surface of inscriptions on which plays a promiscuous range of effects.

Crary traces a further reorganisation of the understanding of the observer during the nineteenth century, pointing to an increasing *embodiment* and *subjectivisation* of vision. He also shows that subjective vision was found to be distinctly *temporal*, an unfolding of processes within the body. These findings had great significance socially, since, as Crary notes, for the new sciences in the nineteenth century, the body was *a priori* a productive body: it existed to be set to work. And its characterisation in this new optics was to inform novel ways in which it could be so employed. Crary focuses in particular on the way in which the relocation of perception into the thickness of the body was adapted in more general models of vision as a component of new machinic arrangements. So, for example, he takes the work of the scientist Helmholtz in the mid-nineteenth century as central to this change in the conceptualisation of vision. Helmholtz compared the nerves in the human body to telegraph wires, which, irrespective of the nature of the stimulus, respond in the same way. The observer was understood as a neutral conduit, a kind of relay station among others, capable of making multiple connections with other agencies and machines.

Moreover, the increasingly quantitative study of the eye, including convergence and accommodation in binocular vision, the relation of image to retinal curvature, and the speed of nerve transmission, heightened the sense of a temporal disjunction between perception and its object and suggested new possibilities of intervening externally in the process of vision. As Crary writes,

> Clearly this study of the eye in terms of reaction time and thresholds of fatigue and stimulation was not unrelated to increasing demand for knowledge about the adaptation of a human subject to productive tasks in which optimum attention span was indispensable for the rationalization of human labor.
>
> (1988: 37)

Furthermore, in this, the first major scientific theorisation of the separation of the senses, there was not simply a heightening or isolation of the optical, but also a notion of an observer for whom vision is conceived without any necessary connection to the act of looking at all. This is what Crary describes as the 'visionary' capacity of the body to produce sensations divorced from referents. What the eye of the observer sees is not simply an object but vision's own subjective perceptions. This capacity meant that the vision was now understood to operate not in response to reality, but independently of any specific referent. Crary writes,

> The theory of the specific nerve energies presents the outlines of a visual modernity in which the 'referential illusion' is unsparingly laid bare. The very absence of referentiality is the ground on which new instrumental

> techniques will construct for an observer a new 'real' world . . . . The issue was not just how does one know what is real, but that new forms of the real were being fabricated and a new truth about the capacities of a human subject was being articulated in these terms.
>
> (1988: 40)

As an attribute of the subject, vision was separated from the realm of the referential and was rendered open to deliberate individual and social manipulations.[4]

So, for example, in his discussion of the stereoscope (a viewing device which achieved the illusion of three dimensionality by superimposing two slightly discrepant images of the same object in an approximation of binocular vision), Crary argues that while it has often been understood as a further perfection of the *camera obscura*, it actually plunges the observer into a disunified field of different subjective intensities. He suggests that depth is rendered as a series of planes in which objects are separated into strangely flattened layers, creating an insistent sense of the 'in front of' and the 'in back of'. Individual elements appear not as round volumes but as cut-out forms arranged in receding planes. In contrast to the *camera obscura*'s centred illusion of depth, the stereoscope offers a derangement of conventional optical cues that challenges the unified, homogeneous space of the *camera obscura*. Significantly, the eerie paradox of tangibility, the illusion of an accessibility to touch, the sense of the proximity of object to viewer, are the most important visionary effects of the stereoscope. Indeed, Crary further argues[5] that the stereoscope shattered the scenic theatrical relationship between viewer and object that reigned in the *camera obscura* by collapsing the separation of the interiorised viewer from the exterior scene of representation into 'a paradoxical form of ocular possession' (1990: 127).

He further argues that this rethinking of vision was linked to concern about the human capacity for synthesis amid the fragmentation and atomisation of a cognitive field. As the philosophical guarantees of any *a priori* cognitive unity collapsed, the problem of 'reality maintenance' became a function of a contingent and merely psychological faculty of synthesis, whose failure or malfunction was linked with psychosis and other mental pathologies. He notes, for example, that for institutional psychology in the 1880s and 1890s part of psychic normality was the ability to synthetically bind perceptions into a functional whole, thereby warding off the threat of dissociation. What is being addressed here, so Crary argues, is a growing concern with the problem of attention, a concept that was fundamental to the emergence of new models of synthesis involving 'the binding of immediate sensory power with the creative forces of memory' (1994: 23).

However, Crary suggests that what he calls the 'opacity or carnal density' of the observer loomed so suddenly into view that its full consequences and effects could not be immediately realised. Nevertheless, as he points out, the continuing scientific exploration of the embodied, temporal relationship between stimulus

4 This development in the study of vision can thus be seen to prefigure some aspects of the conception of the nervous system in neurobiology discussed in the previous chapter.

5 For an interesting critique, see Williams (1995).

and sensation provided much of the knowledge that informed the increasingly calculative management of the relationship between the observer and reality in new regimes of distraction and attentiveness. The development of film and photography was undoubtedly inseparable from the experimental technologies of reality and the self that emerged in relation to this conception of vision,[6] although their role was paradoxical since they helped re-create the myths that vision was incorporeal, veridical and 'realistic':

> if cinema and photography seemed to reincarnate the *camera obscura*, it was only as a mirage of a transparent set of relations that modernity had already overthrown.
>
> (1988: 43)

Nevertheless, as Crary also points out, the ongoing articulation of a vision as non-veridical, as lodged in the body, was a condition of possibility not only for new forms of domination but also for the artistic experimentation of modernism (1988: 43; 1994).

PHOTOGRAPHY, THE BODY AND MOVEMENT

Indeed, in many ways, the techniques of artistic modernism can be seen as an exploration of the dense or thick vision of the embodied eye.[7] Here (as in the contemporaneous writings of Freud and Bergson) temporality was a central issue. And while many uses of photography in modernism as elsewhere contributed to the mirage of the vision of the *camera obscura*, other uses, including those developed by the surrealists, adopted and problematised the technological enhancement that the camera offered to an embodied eye.

In her discussion of 'Photography in the service of surrealism' (1986a), Rosalind Krauss identifies specific examples of such practices. As noted in chapter 4, Krauss argues that surrealism created a photographic frame for an

6 Crary writes,

> For attention is not just one of the many topics examined experimentally by late nineteenth century psychology. It can be argued that a certain notion of attention is in fact the fundamental condition of its knowledge. That is, most of the crucial areas of research, whether of reaction times, of sensory and perceptual sensitivity, of reflex action, of conditioned responses – all of these presupposed a subject whose attentiveness was the site of observation, classification, and measurement, and thus the point around which knowledge of many kinds was accumulated. . . . Anyone familiar with the history of modern psychology knows the symbolic importance of the date 1879 – the year when Wilhelm Wundt established his laboratory at the University of Leipzig. Irrespective of the specific nature of Wundt's intellectual project, this laboratory space and its practices became the model for the whole modern social organization of psychological experimentation around the study of an observer attentive to a wide range of artificially produced stimuli. To paraphrase Foucault, this has been one of the practical and discursive spaces within modernity in which human beings 'problematize what they are'.
>
> (1994: 24)

7 Crary himself identifies two powerful countervailing tendencies: one is a binding together of vision, while the other is a logic of psychic and economic exchange, of equivalence and substitution, of flux and dissolution.

opening in space in which the temporal, embodied nature of vision could be recognised. In surrealist photography, she argues, an internal convulsion of reality, an inter-leaving of nature and culture, was conveyed through the fracturing of space. This fracturing was achieved through a number of techniques, including the use of solarisation, in which photographic paper is briefly exposed to light during the printing process. This has the effect of altering in varying degrees the relationship of light and dark tones, introducing elements of the photographic negative into the positive print. This creates

> a strange effect, of *cloisonné* which visually walls off parts of a single space or whole body from one another, establishing in this way a kind of testimony to a cloven reality.
>
> (1986a: 28)

Negative printing, with the momentarily unintelligible gaps that it creates within objects, promotes the same effect. Doubling, of objects, exposures and images, however, is the formal photographic technique which Krauss identifies as most clearly demonstrating the 'two-step that banishes simultaneity' by transmuting presence into succession, and opens the original to deferral, to one-thing-after-another-ness. For Krauss, this is the technique that exemplifies 'the formal rhythm of spacing' characteristic of surrealism. In making visible this rhythm, it provides the conditions within which the metamorphosis that sparks what Barthes calls the *punctum* may be recognised.

In other artistic uses of photography, too, the manipulation of the temporality of the camera's eye was tied to a recognition of the mobility of being, to movement in the world. The work of Lazló Moholy-Nagy provides an important example here since it offers unexpected and divergent conceptions of the camera's role in extending the vision of the human eye; in this way, it offers a valuable example of the ambivalence to be found in the early stages of the development of a prosthetic culture. For Moholy-Nagy, photography is concerned with the element of representational composition in optical creation, and this composition is explicitly tied to a *social anatomy* of the human body. So, Moholy-Nagy claims that it is motivated by

> relationships of elements imitatively derived from without, objective elements with associational contents, . . . this is the composition of systems dependent upon climate, race, temperament, education, rooted in association and experience.
>
> (1969: 8)

As such its expressional law is to be understood in terms of 'its rootedness in the life of a collective entity' (1969: 16). Painting, in contrast, is said by Moholy-Nagy to be concerned with colour composition, and has a *biological* basis:

> We must assume that there are conditions of colour relationships and tensions, light values, forms, positions, directions which are common to all men and determined by our physiological mechanisms . . . . Biologically

> conditioned expression of these relationships or tensions – be it conscious or unconscious – results in the concept of absolute painting.
>
> (1969: 13)

Thus, for Moholy-Nagy, the principles of both photography and painting are tied to the body, but this is a body understood not only individually (the artist's body) but also collectively, and with both social and biological (or natural) attributes.[8]

Moholy-Nagy further argues that photography, as a 'newly invented optical and technical instrument', offers 'the creator valuable suggestions': 'among other things they give us light painting side by side with painting in pigment, kinetic painting side by side with static' (1969: 9). These suggestions offer the possibility of extending 'the limits of the depiction of nature and the use of light as a creative agent: chiaroscuro in place of pigment' (1969: 7). Most importantly, they offer the possibility of depicting movement beyond that afforded by the human eye; as such, they offer the basis for a new grammar of movement:

> The visual image has been expanded and even the modern lens is no longer tied to the narrow limits of our eye; . . . nor should we regard the ability of the lens to distort – the view from below, from above, the oblique view – as in any sense merely negative, for it provides an impartial approach, such as our eyes, tied as they are to the laws of association, do not give.
>
> (1969: 7)

Moholy-Nagy illustrates his argument with photographs of motion immobilised – a woman jumping, caught in the air, a motor-bike cyclist racing out of the photographic frame, and a flash of lightning rooted in the sky.

The conclusion Moholy-Nagy draws is that 'the photographic camera can either complete or supplement our optical instrument, the eye' (1969: 28). This is a striking statement of the camera as perceptual prosthesis – a technical intervention into the relationship between the observer and reality – but it is also clearly ambivalent about the implications of this intervention. On the one hand, it can be seen as a statement that the camera is a tool that will contribute to the development of a theoretical, abstract, conception of vision; this is a notion of the camera as in-filling, completing or making good the gaps or deficiencies of human vision. On the other hand, it also suggests that the camera offers the possibility not simply of revealing hitherto hidden aspects of movement, but of transforming the very conditions of movement, opening out a new grammar of motion; this is the camera as making possible a (prosthetic) relation of supplementarity with the eye.

Certainly, for Moholy-Nagy the camera provides the possibility of changing the previously existing laws of association: with the assistance of the camera, human vision can develop in line with what he calls 'objective vision':

8 In this sense, these aesthetic principles participate in the creation of what Strathern (1992) calls a plural society (see chapter 2).

> Everyone will be compelled to see that which is optically true, is explicable in its own terms, is objective, before he can arrive at any possible subjective position. This will abolish that pictorial and imaginative association pattern which has remained unsuperseded for centuries and which has been stamped upon our individual vision by great individual painters.
>
> (1969: 28)

This claim would appear to support the first of the interpretations indicated above, but at other points Moholy-Nagy relates this so-called objective vision to a historically specific social anatomy, thus appearing to suggest that new facts or a new objectivity are brought into being by an embodied, technically enhanceable vision that intervenes in, but still maintains, the incommensurability of the relations between perception, consciousness and the body. It thus both presumes and requires a new 'body', while recognising that this new body is never, in itself, complete or completely present to itself.

Moholy-Nagy argues, in terms not dissimilar to those of Benjamin, that vast social changes have been necessary to equip humanity to recognise the camera's potential for the transformation of vision. These conditions include '[t]he vast development both of technique and of the big cities' which have 'increased the capacity of our perceptual organs for simultaneous acoustical and optical activity'. He writes,

> Everyday life itself affords examples of this: Berliners cross the Potsdamer Platz. They are talking, **they hear simultaneously:**
>
> > the horns of the motor-cars, the bells of the trams, the tooting of the omnibuses, the halloos of the coachmen, the roar of the underground railway, the shouts of the newspaper sellers, the sounds of a loudspeaker, etc.
>
> and can keep these different acoustical impressions separate from one another. Whereas a provincial, recently found quite disorientated in this Platz, was so greatly confused by the number of impressions that he stood as though rooted to the spot before an oncoming tram.
>
> (1969: 43)

For Moholy-Nagy, the development of human vision beyond that afforded by the eye is thus connected to the social and biological capacity to participate *in* representation.

Similarly, representation itself, while sometimes attributed to an abstract concept of light, is, on other occasions, understood in relation to temporality:

> The essence of the reflected light play is the production of light–space–time tensions in colour or chiaroscuro harmonies and (or) in various forms by kinetic means, in a continuity of motion: as an optical passage of time in a state of equilibrium.
>
> The newly emergent impulse of time and its ever expanding articulation here produce a state of increased activity in the observer, who – instead of *meditating upon a static image and instead of immersing himself in it and*

> *only then becoming active – is forced almost to double his efforts immediately in order to be able simultaneously to comprehend and to participate in the optical events.*
>
> (1969: 23–24)

Moholy-Nagy's preferred way of achieving his new vision was by exploiting the light-sensitivity of the photographic plate, fixing upon it 'light phenomena' – moments from light displays – composed by the 'photographer'. This, he suggests, can be done with or without a camera, in the latter instance it results in the 'photogram'. What fascinated him was the aperspectival picture-space which could be obtained through this technique; indeed, he argues that the photogram was concerned not simply with 'light instead of pigment' but the space–time continuum itself. 'The photogram enables us to grasp new possibilities of spatial relationships' for what appears in the photogram is no more than the effect of the various exposures and of the distance of the source of light from the objects, which means that 'the photogram literally *is* the space–time-continuum' (quoted in Stelzer, 1969: 149).

Moholy-Nagy identifies a further possibility as well: constructing new cameras on new principles:

> first of all using the camera obscura, secondly eliminating perspectival representation. Cameras with systems of lens and mirrors which can encompass the object from all sides at once and cameras which are constructed on optical laws different from those of our eyes.
>
> (1969: 32)

For Moholy-Nagy, the development of such techniques will lead to the emergence of new uses of photography: not just 'records of situations of reality', but also the 'combination, projection of images on top of one another and side by side'; 'penetration; compression of scenes to make them manageable; super-reality, Utopia, and humour (here is the new wit!)', 'creative means for photo-books, i.e., photographs in place of text; typophoto', 'creative means for two- or three-dimensional non-objective absolute light-projections' and 'simultaneous cinema, etc., etc.' (1969: 36). In short, Moholy-Nagy seems to believe that this kind of practice will lead to revised (and revisable) understandings of movement, and transformed (and transforming) conceptions of the relation between the viewer and his or her senses, body and the environment, producing a seemingly organic super-reality. This is a vision underpinned by a conception of the human body motivated by insatiable senses that reach out for more new experience every time they take something in, a vision in which the human eye is subordinated to the 'photo eye' (Franz Roh, quoted in Stelzer, 1969: 146).

Furthermore, Moholy-Nagy distances himself from the *Gesamtkunstwerk*, the concept of a total work of art, associated with the De Stijl Group located in Holland, and part of the first period of the Bauhaus. He argues that the *Gesamtkunstwerk* was important at a time when specialisation was recognised to be especially intense: 'With its ramifications and its fragmenting action in every field, specialisation has destroyed all belief in the possibility of embracing the totality of all fields, the wholeness of life' (1969: 17). But he is not satisfied with this, since he sees it as only 'an addition', 'alongside and separated from which life flows by' (1969: 17); in its place, he wishes to see emerge *Gesamtwerk*, the unity of life itself:

> a synthesis of all the vital impulses spontaneously forming itself into the all-embracing Gesamtwerk (life) which abolishes all isolation, in which all individual accomplishments proceed from a biological necessity and culminate in a universal necessity.
>
> (1969: 17)

In developing this concept of *Gesamtwerk*, Moholy-Nagy thus puts forward a view of the composition of the human as the synthesis of functional mechanisms. He writes,

> the man of a given period is most perfect when the functional mechanism of which he is composed – the cells as much as the complex organs – is being used to the limits of its biological capacity.
>
> (1969: 30)

In this view, art (including photographic art) brings this about by establishing 'new relationships between the known and the as yet unknown optical, acoustical, and other functional phenomena so that these are absorbed in increasing abundance by the functional apparatus' (1969: 30). Here art arises out of 'a basic fact of the human condition', that is, that the 'functional apparatus craves for further new impressions every time a new exposure has taken place' (1969: 30). This craving, however, must be met by creativity, rather than mere virtuosity; only then will 'unity be produced by conceiving and carrying out every creation from within its fully active and therefore life-forming propensity and fitness' (1969: 18). For Moholy-Nagy, art will lead to the realisation of 'the unambiguousness of the real, the truth in the everyday situation . . . for all classes'; as such photography is a mechanism by which 'the health of the visible is slowly filtering' (1969: 38).

It is easy to see how the functional and organicist underpinning of this new vision came to be reconciled (and recuperated) with an emphasis on the individual artist's sensibility in the interpretations of Moholy-Nagy's work which sprang up around him following his exile to the United States (as well as offering a powerful precedent for the representational vitalism that animates 'The Family of Man'). And, without doubt, it has been this reconciliation that has been influential in mainstream histories of photography, being fixed by, among others, Henri Cartier-Bresson in his formulation of *The Decisive Moment* (*L'instant décisif*). In terms not dissimilar to Moholy-Nagy, Cartier-Bresson writes of 'the organic co-ordination of elements seen by the eye', continuing,

> In photography there is a new kind of plasticity . . . [the] product of the instantaneous lines made by movements of the subject. We work in unison with movement as though it were a presentiment of the way in which life itself unfolds.
>
> (Quoted in Ritchin, 1989: 423)

While this, so far, is a story which Moholy-Nagy might have told, it is given a different conclusion, for

> inside movement there is one moment at which the elements in motion are in balance. Photography must seize upon this moment and hold immobile the equilibrium of it.
>
> (Quoted in Ritchin, 1989: 423)

This 'decisive moment' is the moment when form briefly takes on an essential meaning. The individual artist's ability to capture this moment is not, however, as for Moholy-Nagy, an 'objective' fact at a specific moment, brought into being by specific social and biological circumstances, but is, rather, outside time. Decontextualised in this way, the decisive moment has been used to provide an individualist rationale for a visual coherence or equilibrium within fragmentary instants; as such, it has formed the basis of a highly celebrated genre of photography.

In a recent interview, Cartier-Bresson formulated this theory again, saying that what he looks for in photography is

> to be there, watching and unknown and, quick, disappear. Never quite touch. To live in the moment, for only that exists: the instant. The future runs away just like the line of a horizon when you go forward.
>
> (Quoted in Feaver, 1994: 2)

The ability to recognise such moments is naturalised as an 'intuitive gift' for knowing precisely when to push the button, a gift of the individual: 'That instinct is essential to great photography. You cannot learn it. You cannot fake it. You have to be born with it . . . ' (Cartier-Bresson, quoted in Manchester, 1989: 11). Nevertheless, although critics such as Sontag (1977), Phillips (1988) and Solomon-Godeau (1991)[9] are undoubtedly correct to emphasise the importance of an increasingly abstract and individualistic modernism in the history of photography, it is clear that there was also a concern with the temporality and embodied nature of perception in the work of not only Moholy-Nagy but also many other photographers of the period.

Moreover, it is possible to identify in Moholy-Nagy what might now be described as a conception of a cyborg. This is a being both organic and mechanical, a 'functional apparatus', created in a process in which the efforts of the observer are doubled (in Krauss' sense) in the comprehension of and participa-

9 As Solomon-Godeau notes, the potential for this approach to be developed in terms of an idealisation of the individual artist's creativity was identified early on by writers such as Walter Benjamin. In the following extract, Benjamin seeks to separate out the work of Renger-Patzsch from what he saw as the progressive practices exemplified by Moholy-Nagy, Sander, Blossfeld and Krull:

> Where photography takes itself out of context, severing the connections illustrated by Sander, Blossfeld, or Germaine Krull, where it frees itself from physiognomic, political and scientific interest, then it becomes *creative.* The lens now looks for interesting juxtapositions; photography turns into a sort of arty journalism. . . . The creative in photography is capitulation to fashion. *The world is beautiful* – that is its watchword. Therein is unmasked the posture of a photography that can endow any soup can with cosmic significance but cannot grasp a single one of the human connexions in which it exists . . . .
>
> (Quoted in Solomon-Godeau, 1991: 68)

tion in an optical event, an extension of the possibilities of what it is to be human beyond the limits of the body of the individual. And this recognition of the productive potential of technical intervention in a temporal and embodied process of perception has not been entirely absent in the history of photography. Indeed, as discussed in chapter 4, Barthes's discussion of the working of photography in terms of a *camera lucida* provides an example of the theorisation of this recognition in which seeing photographically engages a tactility or recontextualisation which is activated by (not targeted by) the image.[10] This is the anticipation of vision discussed in relation to Barthes in chapter 4.

The *camera lucida* is an optical tool (first adopted in the early nineteenth century) that allows the eye to perceive the image of a scene or 'view' virtually superimposed onto a drawing surface in such a way as to allow the viewer to produce a more or less accurate delineation of the scene. As Tomas argues, it is thus an instrument that 'links hand and eye through an embodied economy . . . [it] resurrects the body's corporeality as a prerequisite for the forging of a laboring relationship (as defined in the act of drawing itself) betweeen the eye and the hand' (1995: 262). He argues that the *camera lucida* makes visible the role of the body as sensory transducer in the production of images: 'it is at this point that one realizes the extent to which a body's presence can be sensuously transferred and even remapped onto the surface of a second skin, a piece of paper, through the humble medium of a simple pencil' (1995: 262). Furthermore, so Tomas argues, the *camera lucida* is more than a simple optical interface; it enables a recalibration of the ratios between the senses of vision and of touch. In Barthes's interpretation, I suggest, the (technologically enhanced) body itself is the object's medium of recalibration:

> Photography is literally an emanation of the referent. From a real thing, which was there in that specific place, came radiations which ended up reaching me, here in this specific place. The transmission time is of no importance; the photograph of the missing being, as Sontag says, will touch me like the delayed rays of a star. A sort of umbilical bond links the physicality of the photographed object to my gaze: light, although impalpable, is here a carnal medium, a skin I share with anyone who has been photographed.[11]
>
> (1981: 80–81)

10 Crary argues that the new optical regime he describes contributed to the 'dissociation of touch from sight', an 'unloosening of the eye' from references to tactility and thus from a cognitively unified field. Linda Williams, however, argues that while the mobile eye dissociates itself from

> the stable frame of references offered by the *camera obscura* and thus from the centering of the observer's body as unified perspective on a scene 'out there', this mobile body of modernist (and certainly postmodernist) vision is not disembodied; touch is not dissociated from sight; sight engages carnal density and tactility, as well as gender and sexuality, precisely because it is decentered and 'unloosened' from a unified field.
>
> (1995: 15)

11 Margaret Morse describes 'second skins' in the following terms:

> In this reversible logic, in which subject and object are not clearly differentiated, rather than being eaten one can try to become the other by 'getting into someone else's skin'. That is, the

⇒

Barthes identifies here a notion of the *camera lucida* as a visual instrument that facilitates a non-differentiated semiosis in which the body participates.[12] It takes the viewer 'outside its frame, and it is there that I animate this photograph and that it animates me' (1981: 59).

This notion – of non-differentiated semiosis – is a theme which has been taken further by Deleuze in his investigation of the writings of Bergson (1988) and his analysis of cinema (1986, 1989) and by Lyotard (1991) in his discussion of matter and time.[13] In Deleuze's interpretation, Bergson had an ambivalent response to cinema, suggesting that it contributed to a misconception of movement to the extent that it operates in the same way as natural perception (that is, presumably, according to the *camera obscura* model of vision). Deleuze writes,

> For Bergson, the model cannot be natural perception . . . .The model would be rather a state of things which would constantly change, a flowing

> cannibalistic fantasy of introjection has a counterpart in the reverse gesture, that of covering oneself with the other as a means of self-transformation.
>
> (1994: 165)

She goes on to describe societies where ritual has involved human sacrifice, in which the 'skin ego' or envelope of identity and self could literally be transferred by flaying a human victim and wearing his or her skin. A related notion of shared skin draws more upon what Elaine Scarry calls a 'consensual materialism', in which,

> We make material artifacts in order to interiorise them: we make things so that they will in turn remake us, revising the interior of embodied consciousness.
>
> (1994: 97)

12 On the basis of his analysis of spirit possession among the Hauku in West Africa, Paul Stoller argues that the power of mimesis 'derives from its multisensorial affecting presence' (1995: 195). He points to parallels between the spirit medium among the Hauku and the spectator in Euro-American societies:

> The body of the spirit medium is invaded by her or his spirit; the body of the spectator is invaded by mechanically reproduced images. In both cases, bodies are physiognomically transformed which heightens possibilities for sociocultural and political change.
>
> (1995: 195)

13 An alternative example of a non-differentiated semiosis is brilliantly described by Hosokawa in his description of 'the walkman effect'. He locates the development of the walkman in the context of Lyotard's understanding of the postmodern era, in which

> The *self* is small, but is not isolated: it is held in a texture of relations which are more complex and more mobile than ever before.
>
> (Lyotard, 1984, quoted in Hosokawa, 1984: 166)

In this context, Hosokawa argues, the walkman *is* the autonomy-of-the-walking-self; as such, it 'is an effect-event in the pragmatic and semantic transformation of the urban' (1984: 166). It enables musical listening to be more occasional, more incidental and more contingent – that is, in Deleuzian terms, it is singular, rather than individualising. It has no meaningless context; at the same time, however, no context is strictly appropriate to it. Rather, every context (or no context) can be justified, appropriated and legitimated by its singularity. Or to put this in another way, in a double process, the singularity of the walkman in use decontextualises the given coherence of the urban landscape, and at the same time, contextualises every situation whether or not it seemingly coheres with it. Hosokawa further argues that the walkman is to the auditory domain what the polaroid is to the visual domain: 'If walkman is an ocular polaroid: polaroid is an optic walkman' (1984: 170); both complete the process of 'the deconstruction of meaning which is inevitably coupled with its construction' (1984: 171). ⇒

> matter in which no point of anchorage nor center of reference would be assignable. On the basis of this state of things it would be necessary to show how, at any point, centers can be formed which would impose fixed instantaneous views.
>
> (1988: 58–59)

Then, in a move that extends the phenomenological approach adopted by Barthes, Deleuze argues that the image is not only movement, but a movement that can always *reverse* itself in life:[14]

> My body is an image hence a set of actions and reactions. My eye, my brain, are images, parts of my body. How could my brain contain images since it is one image among others?
>
> (1988: 58)

In a process of unending modulation,

> External images act on me, transmit movement to me, and I return movement: how could images be in my consciousness since I am myself image, that is, movement?
>
> (1988: 58)

Photographs, in this view, are but temporary points of anchor: 'Photography, if there is photography, is already snapped, already shot, in the very interior of things and for all points of space' (Bergson, quoted in Deleuze, 1988: 60). Alternatively, as Kracauer puts it,

For Hosokawa, the singularity the walkman effect evokes is radically different both from being individual and from being personal: it is, rather, anonymous, impersonal and nomadic. Yet it is not synonymous with isolation and separation from reality; instead, in only an 'apparent' paradox, it is indispensable for the process of self-unification in singularity:

> Walkman users are not necessarily detached . . . from the environment . . . , but are unified in the autonomous and singular moment – neither as persons nor as individuals – with the real.
>
> (1984: 170)

The double process of singularity is realised in the walk-act, a term taken from de Certeau (1988). In the walk-act, Hosokawa argues, it is difficult to say whether it is the walkman that charges the body or whether, inversely, it is the body that charges the walkman. The walkman works as a built-in part of the body, 'an intrusion-like prosthesis' (recall Benjamin's likening the process of opening the optical unconscious to the surgeon's hand entering the body and cautiously feeling its way around the organs):

> The walkman holder *plays* the music and listens to the sound come from his [*sic*] own body. When we listen to the 'beat' of our body, when the walkman intrudes inside the skin, the order of our body is inverted, that is, the surface tension of the skin loses its balancing function through which it activates the interpenetration of Self and world: a *mise en oeuvre* in the body, through the body of the body. Through the walkman, then, the body is opened; it is put into the process of aestheticisation, the theatricalisation of the urban – but *in secret*.
>
> (1984: 176–177)

14 Stiegler too suggests that we have to consider the following hypothesis: 'life (*anima* in respect of the mental image) is and always has been cinema (cartoon in respect of the image-object)' (1995: 252).

> If it is only the photograph that endows these details [those of the appearance of the subject] with duration, it is not at all they who outlast mere time, but, rather, it is time that makes images of itself out of them.
>
> (1993: 424)

This suggests that the question of time, of temporality or rhythm, is important: that the time of images (or the images that time makes of itself) is not regular or orderly. Deleuze, following Bergson, argues that the recollection-image fills the gap between a received image and an executed movement, an action and a reaction, a stimulation and a response, a perception-image and an action-image. However, this is not an in-filling or indifferentiation; rather, it fills this gap not through movement, but by returning to perception: 'It makes full use of the gap, it assumes it, because it lodges itself there, but it is of a different nature' (Deleuze, 1988: 47). It is a perceptual prosthesis that is not (only) complementary but (also) supplementary. Indeed, Deleuze suggests that in doing so subjectivity takes on a new sense, which is no longer motor or material, but temporal or spiritual: 'that which "is added" to matter, not what distends it; recollection-image, not movement-image' (1988: 47). This is what Deleuze, once again following Bergson, calls attentive recognition, an oscillation in which not only the object is perceived anew, but so are 'the ever-widening systems within which it may be bound up' (1988: 46, Deleuze is quoting Bergson, 1939: 127–128). Indeed, according to Deleuze, attentive recognition informs us to a much greater degree when it fails than when it succeeds:

> When we cannot remember, sensory-motor extension remains suspended, and the actual image, the present optical perception, does not link up with either a motor image or a recollection-image which would re-establish contact. It rather enters into a relation with genuinely virtual elements, feelings of *déjà vu* or past 'in general' (I must have seen that man somewhere . . .), fantasies or theatre-scenes (he seems to play a role that I am familiar with . . .). In short, it is not the recollection-image or attentive recognition which gives us the proper equivalent of the optical–sound image, it is rather the disturbances of memory and the failures of recognition.
>
> (1988: 54–55)

In a similar vein, Lyotard writes that an essential feature of the overturning of Cartesian optics is the 'preeminence of time in the analysis of the relation of body to mind' (1991: 39). He too quotes Bergson, this time recalling Leibniz: 'One can consider every body as a mind that is instantaneous but deprived of memory' (1991: 39). Indeed, in Lyotard's interpretation, every monad, every material point, is for Bergson an 'image'. Lyotard further suggests that everything, 'the whole world', is reflected in each material point, each image, but can only be inscribed if the material point has the capacity to assemble and conserve a lot of information at once: 'Otherwise the recording can take place but remains unknown' (1991: 39–40). The implication of this is there is but a difference of degree between mind and matter, depending on the capacity to gather and conserve: 'there is a continuum from the instantaneous mind of matter to the very gathered matter of minds' (1991: 40). In the latter, immediate reaction is delayed, prevented even, and this inhibition explains the indeterminancy and unpredictability of human action. In Lyotard's terms, the 'mirror' gets more complicated, and the influx on its way out can be 'filtered down many paths' (1991: 42).

The human body conceived in this way 'doesn't stop changing its mass, and has real and exact unity only through its difference, its "point of view", itself determined by its "form", i.e. its ability to gather up the actions exerted upon it' (1991: 40). This difference is one of rhythm. Lyotard elaborates Bergson's explication of shock to make this clear:

> In an 'instant' of conscious perception, which is in fact an indivisible block of duration made of vibration, 'memory condenses an enormous multiplicity of shocks, which appear simultaneously to us although they are successive' (*Matière et Mémoire* [Bergson, 1939], p. 73). In order to get back to matter from a consciousness, it would suffice to 'divide ideally this undivided thickness of time, and distinguish in it the desired multiplicity of movements' (ibid.).
>
> (1991: 42)

As the notion of the two-step in Krauss's interpretation of surrealism and Moholy-Nagy's doubling of vision indicates, some modern uses of photography have begun to identify the 'desired multiplicity of movements'. Computer-aided photography and digitalisation, however, enormously extend the calculative possibilities offered by division and in doing so raise the question as to whether it is now being subordinated to the abstract principle of indifferentiation, of complexification, or whether there is still the possibility of the two-step, a deferral or suspension.

INDEXICALITY AND TIME

In *Camera Lucida*, Barthes's central question is 'what does my body know of Photography?' (1981: 9). To investigate this knowledge, Barthes elucidates what he describes as the *noeme* of the photograph: 'that really existed'. The specificity of this *noeme* is, he argues, a consequence of indexicality – the camera's defining mode of signification:

> It is often said that painters invented Photography (by passing on the notion of the frame, Alberti's perspective and the optics of the *camera obscura*). But, I say, no, it was the chemists. For the *noeme* 'That really existed' only became possible the day a scientific discovery – that of the photosensitivity of silver haloids – made it feasible to capture and print directly the light rays emitted by an object possessing areas of light and shade.
>
> (1981: 80)

As Metz notes, indexicality can be described as 'an actual contiguity or connection in the world: the lightning is the index of the storm' (1990: 156). It is this indexicality that 'leaves room for iconic aspects, as the chemical image often looks like the object' and 'leaves much room for symbolic aspects as well' (1990: 156). Indexicality 'stubbornly points to the print of what *was*, but no longer *is*', and makes possible the functioning of photography as 'past presence'. Indeed, it is as an index of the passage of time that it is possible to speak of the photograph as an 'interface', in Lyotard's term for it is as such that it is capable of 'memorizing, in a fashion inaccessible to us, vibrations naturally beyond our ken' (1991: 43). In the terms developed here it is a prosthesis, an extension of the subject's capacity to memorise, an indication that there is no necessary break between mind and matter.

However, if, as Metz claims, what is indexical is understood as 'the mode of production itself, the principle of taking', the emergence of computer technology will be construed as a threat to the authority of the photograph as a document. Indeed, given the argument presented in chapter 4, in which the potential for mimetic relations to arise in relation to a photograph is held to be a consequence of its indexical character, it might be thought that computerisation will also take away the functioning of photography as past presence, and its ability to make the presence of parts (as well as the whole) visible. However, just as Barthes writes of the chemical process of development that what it 'develops is undevelopable, an essence (of a wound), what cannot be repeated under the instances of the insistence (of the insistent gaze)' (1981: 49), so it is possible to see digitalisation too as a complement to the frailty of human vision. This possibility will be explored here in relation to the notion of *passage* or the *time of exposure*.

Metz argues that immobility and silence underpin the authority of photography; he speaks of the timelessness of photography, which, he suggests, derives from the immediacy of the photographic *take*: this is the 'instantaneous abduction of the object out of the world into another world, into another kind of time' (1990: 158). Metz himself is probably referring here to what he believes to be the significance of the time of the Freudian unconscious in the relation of indexicality, rather than a reference to the instantaneous time of the decisive moment as formulated by Cartier-Bresson. However, as the discussion of Tagg's psychoanalytic interpretation of Barthes in chapter 4 suggests, time is often ignored in psychoanalytically informed analyses of photography. More widely too, as Paul Virilio (1994) notes, the authority of the photographic image has conventionally been assumed without any reference to temporality, or with the presumption that instantaneity is no time at all. Typically, its authority has been made explicit as a material motivation conceived in terms of reference space alone, that is, in terms of the question of interference with some kind of paper or celluloid support surface. (Although, as noted above, other understandings of material motivation, while not foregrounded in dominant histories of photography, have none the less been articulated in many photographic practices.) But the development of computerised photographic technology makes it apparent that this authority is, and was, dependent not only upon the space of its support surface, but also upon *time*: the time of the exposure that allows or edits seeing (Virilio, 1994). As Stiegler puts it,

> The imprint of luminances on the photo-sensitive surface – on which the

> globality of what the object picks up settles immediately, as on a retina – is replaced in the analog–digital context by a deferral: the storage time taken by the break-up of the spectographic elements, before the processing that will lead to the printing of something other than the photonic ectoplasm of a 'that really existed'.
>
> (1995: 234)

Interpretations of instantaneity which take it at face-value ignore the role of memorisation, and of time, in the 'immediate' perception of the photographic 'take'. They fail to see the importance of time as a dimension of the indexicality of the photograph, and thus ignore its specific resistances, capacities, blurrings and 'blind spots'. Similarly, interpretations of the capability of the techniques of digitalisation to enter and modify the rectangle of the image at will, in an apparently limitless technical extension of the perception of the decisive moment – presenting computerised photography as an overcoming of the temporal dependence of human vision – fail to see that what might be called its reverse motivation (see below and chapter 8) may be a radical exploration of that dependence.

THE INDIVIDUAL AND THE TIME OF EXPOSURE

The analogue–digital photograph is the result of computerised pictorial alteration. This involves translating a photograph into digital information which can be read by computer. An image then appears as the sum total of pixels, tiny squares or picture elements, each of which represents information as to the brightness and colour of that sector of the image (Mitchell, 1992). Once digitalised, an image can be modified, pixel by pixel. Renaud writes,

> Digitalization opens a subtle and, in the mathematical sense, catastrophic gap in the functioning and the paradigm of the inherent formal development of this kind of image.
>
> (1995: 182)

The image can be altered in a number of ways according to the application of algorithms, culminating in what Renaud calls 'the informational absorption of photography' (1995: 182), as its former visibility (as shape and imprint) is converted into a pure readability in the 0/1 dimension. As Druckrey comments, 'Images have never before possessed the potential to sustain so much information or, perhaps, meaning' (1994: 6).

In the 0/1 dimension, the constitution of space is discretionary: colours can be changed, the focus sharpened, some elements can be taken out, others replicated, and images can be combined. Alternatively, an image can be subjected to what Fred Ritchin (1990) calls 'reverse cropping', the extension or cloning of the edge of an image. This, like its long-established counterpart, cropping, can be seen as a *space-related* technique. Other developments too change the terms of the material or spatial authority of photography: with the use of still video cameras, there is no need for either a permanent negative or a print. Ritchin writes, 'there is no archival document that can be with certainty called an "original" photograph' (1990: 35). In addition, however, it is now also possible to make a horizontal image into a vertical one, and vice versa; this can be seen as a change in the terms of the photograph's *temporal* authority.

In a much publicised case in 1982 discussed by Ritchin, the magazine *National Geographic* modified a picture of the pyramids at Giza from a horizontal to a vertical image for one of its covers. Several years afterwards, the magazine's editor, Wilbur E. Garrett, described the manipulated image as one that the photographer might have taken were he to have stood a few feet to the side, a kind of retroactive repositioning of the photographer. For Ritchin, this is a 'modification in time'; he writes,

> the photographic image is no longer time specific, the result of the momentary and privileged meeting of subject and photographer. Now, time is not fleeting. The editor's revisionist ability can extend to interfering even with the already completed relationship of the photographer to his or her subject. One can reach backward in time, repudiating the photographer's judgement, to 'rephotograph'.
>
> (1990: 30–31)

For Ritchin, this is disturbing in so far as the creativity, judgement and decision-making power of the photographer as (authorial and/or editorial) subject are erased in this repositioning. He wishes that the relationship between observer and observed could always remain confined in the 'already completed' temporal relationship of chemical photography. But for Virilio, the introduction of computerised technology simply makes visible what had been assumed: the fleeting time of exposure in 'instantaneous' perception.

Virilio is suggesting not that the introduction of computerised technology inaugurates a time of exposure into photography,[15] but rather that it makes that time newly visible, and, importantly, newly productive. He writes that in retrospect we can see that even the

> most instinctive, least-controlled glance is first a sort of circling of the property, a complete scanning of the visual field that ends in the eye's choice of an object.
>
> (1994: 61)

This is the editing time of instantaneous perception or the decisive moment, the time of the contract. Its brevity is not in question – as Ritchin points out, the four hundred photographic images which document the work of Magnum photographers over four decades in *In Our Time: The World as Seen by Magnum Photographers* 'were most probably taken in a total of some four seconds – one

15 Lyotard's analysis of cinema (1993) highlights what he calls 'the political economy of movement in film'. Mainstream cinema, he argues, is the process of selection and elimination of movements: movements which contribute to the production of a meaningful whole ('productive movements') are included, whereas movements considered 'useless' for the whole, which do not contribute to the progress of the narrative, which do not conform to the principles of the composition of the frame or the logic of the sequence ('sterile movements'), are excluded. It is thus at the expense of the aberrant movement that the norm is established and maintained.

second, more or less, per decade' (1989: 417); but its new productivity makes it clear that the space of modern sight is not Newton's space, absolute space, but Minkovskian event-space, relative space. However, as Virilio makes clear, this is still a space which is made in and helps make a visual memory:

> it is not only the dim brightness of these stars that comes to us from out of the distant past, out of the mists of time. The weak light that allows us to apprehend the real, to see and understand our present environment, itself comes from a distant visual memory without which there would be no act of looking.
>
> (1994: 62)

Moreover, computer technology makes it possible to see that Newtonian space was conceived in an instant that was 'no-time-at-all'; a space that was inhabited by an individual whose actions, while, or perhaps because, occurring in the time of the decisive instant, were capable of being subject to a contract. It is no coincidence that Cartier-Bresson's elevation of the decisive moment achieved its status as a principle of photographic aesthetics in part because of the commercial success of the Magnum cooperative agency and its insistence that photographers, rather than the publications in which their images appeared, would retain the rights to photographs.[16] This insistence provided them with control over the editorial use of their photographs, including, crucially for the internationalisation of this school of photography, sales to other countries, to magazines like *Berliner Illustrierte Zeitung*, *Paris Match* and *L'Epoca*.[17] It was through such social practices that the photographing eye's circling of the visual field, its choice of an object, was legalised as an act of momentary appropriation or instantaneous possession in the subjective memory of the photographer-artist as an individual. Computer technology opens up the possibility of new modes of possession in relation to the camera's potential time. While diverse interests are currently at work in setting the terms of its appropriation, the uses of photography are no longer so easy to consolidate[18] in the author(is)ed biography of the possessive individual.

16 Nor, I suggest, is it any coincidence that Cartier-Bresson suppresses the desire to touch; as noted above, he wishes 'photography to be there, watching and unknown and, quick, disappear. Never quite touch.'

17 Romeo Martines, a historian of photography, writes of another of the founders of Magnum alongside Cartier-Bresson, Robert Capa, that he

> was driven by a single notion, which proved to be the healthiest idea in the history of photography: a reporter is nobody if he doesn't own his own negatives. The cooperative was the best form of organization to preserve his rights and to insure the news reporters' freedom of action. In other words, Capa and his friends invented the photographer's copyright. Had they accomplished nothing else, they had at least set their trade free and transformed simple employees into artists who ruled their own lives.
>
> (Quoted in Lacouture, 1989: 48)

See also Sandeen (1995).

18 So, for example, the British Association of Picture Libraries and Agencies argues that its materials are increasingly subject to a piracy which it cannot even recognise. Other bodies are adopting a wide range of strategies to protect their interests: ⇒

Indeed, with the introduction of computerised technology and the development of techniques of topographical amnesia, Virilio suggests that 'we are looking at the rapid collapse of mnemonic consolidation' (1994: 7). In the same moment, however, we are seeing the emergence of new technologies of remembering which are themselves in the process of being, if not consolidated, then legitimated in what have been called here prosthetic biographies.[19] In other words, at the same time that we are seeing a process of topographical amnesia, new configurations of the space–time continuum are enabling other kinds of memory and other kinds of biography to emerge.

For Virilio, then, seeing has always been and continues to be a question of memory: the rise of computerised photography has brought about not simply a loss but rather a transformation in mnesic choices. This transformation is a consequence of the fact that because the observer's moment of perception is no longer in synch, no longer integrated into the time of exposure, his or her instantaneous or topographical perception and the memorisation processes which are part of it may instead be subject to technological mediation in the time of exposure. This mediation is the new relation – which might be called *reversed motivation* – in which the indexicality of photography, the copy and contact of mimesis, continues to take place. In this way mimesis may be recharged in prosthetic culture.

LIFE IN THE 0/1 DIMENSION

For Virilio, then, contemporary memory is not spatial, but temporal: 'the depth of *time* of electro-optical teleology displaces the old depth of *field* of topology

> Sony's . . . purchase of CBS, complete with back catalogue, may point to a future in which hardware giants make wholesale copyright or purchases in order to head off legal restraints to an expanding market for their samplers and scanners. New technology needs content on an enormous scale. Kodak bought rights to the largest image library in the world in 1991, and is set to launch High Street digital scanning and compositing . . . . Professional societies within photography are discussing the setting up of 'collecting societies' in order to reap the benefits of multiple secondary uses of copyright images in the new media of CD-ROMs, laser disks, and fibre optic networks.
>
> (Cameron, 1991: 6)

19 Moreover, there is also the possibility that such memories may be consolidated not in an individual biography, but in a collective biography. Consider, for example, the comments reported by members of the public following the investigation of the murder of James Bulger. According to Sarah Kember, some of the anger aroused by this crime was directed at the inadequacy of the recorded images.

Journalists wrote about 'heartless security video cameras' and 'the demonstrable fact that such "security" devices are clearly anything but'. Another reports on the reactions of one particular local resident speaking on behalf of others:

> We are totally frustrated. James Bulger didn't belong to his mother, he belonged to the people of Liverpool. Why are those video pictures so crap? Why didn't they go into Dixons and buy one of those home videos [*sic*] machines?
>
> (1995: 119)

Kember suggests that this kind of feeling is evidence that the technology of surveillance – and its powers of recall – may be claimed as the property of a collective body.

(1991: 31). This may seem to be at odds with the analysis developed in the last chapter, where it was suggested that what is significant about the camera's vision for memory is that the photograph captures or fixes an object as it would be if seen from anywhere and everywhere, that is, in relation to a spatial continuum. However, this apparent contradiction is more apparent than real. For what Virilio is in fact suggesting is that the very concept of physical dimension has lost its meaning, and, as a consequence, analogical comparison – what Strathern calls partial analogy, the merographic capacity – has been displaced by digitalisation:

> And suddenly the ancient distinctions among the dimensions disappear. The dimensional dissection of classical geometry – where the point cut the line, and the line cut the plane, which then cut through the solids – has lost a critical part of its practical utility. . . .
>
> The last 'dissection' is not so much a fact of physical dimensions as it is a fact of the selection of speeds of perception and of representation, slowed down or sped up, that cut up the depth of time, the only temporal dimension. . . .
>
> What becomes noteworthy, then, is the recuperated importance of the point in the electronic image, as if the 0 dimension suddenly retrieved its numerical significance, at the expense of the line, plane, solid – obsolete analogical dimensions all.
>
> (1991: 32–33)

Depth of space, understood as depth of the field of surfaces available to direct observation, is replaced by the depth of time of the 0/1 dimension available to computerised observation. This is the medium of situated knowledge. Its standard of measurement is light.[20] Virilio writes:

> The morphological irruption no longer spares either the extension of the thickness of matter in the name of the so-called whole dimensions. But, again, since more-or-less dense mass and more-or-less large distances are functions of speed, according to Einstein, this apparent rupture of the continuum does not result from measured, analyzed space. It is an effect of celerity understood not as 'acceleration' so much as '*illumination*' – less speed than subliminal light, the light of the velocity of light that illuminates the world, in the instant in which it offers up its representation.
>
> (1991: 62)

20 After the last evaluation of the speed of light in 1972, a definition was proposed in which a metre would be 'the length crossed by light in a vacuum in 1/299,792,458 of a second' (Virilio, 1991: 41). In this number, Virilio identifies the consolidation of light as a standard of measure for the earth, and thus as a supreme referent. He writes,

> in the new representations of the form-image of the sensible world, the 'point of light' replaced the vanishing point of perspectivists. The luminous point became the vanishing point of the speed of light, the non-place of its acceleration, a photon, electron acceleration that contributes to the present formation of the dimensions of infinite space, just as the point without dimension of ancient Greek geometry served to establish the dimensions of the finite world.
>
> (1991: 43)

Transferred into the eternal present of a relativity whose topological and teleological thickness and depth belong to this final measuring instrument, the speed of light possesses 'only one direction, which is both its size and dimension' (1991: 63–64).

To a great extent, so Virilio suggests, the adoption and development of computerised photography has led to the reduction of the visual field to the line of a sighting device. Indeed, this development is widely seen to be contributing to the subordination of all sensory experience to the visual and the collapse of the human body into an assemblage of its optical effects. It is described by Barbara Stafford (1993), for example, as part of a trend towards 'automated spectralization'. However, as Virilio points out, this trend is not emerging without contest. In the first place, the recognition of the productivity of the time of exposure is not new. So, for example, the photographer Jacques-Henri Lartigue called his camera his memory's eye, abandoning focusing altogether, knowing without looking what his Leica would see: 'even when holding it at arm's length, the camera becoming a substitute for both eye and body movements at once' (quoted in Virilio, 1994: 13). Furthermore, what Renaud describes as the automation of vision – an image 'made by and for an eye *belonging to no body*' (1995: 202–204), and what Virilio describes as the reduction of the human visual field to a sighting device, is not simply technically determined. The newly visibly mnesic choices of photography are being elaborated, investigated, even turned against themselves, in the practices of some photographers who seek to make productive the notion of the temporal dependence of the human eye in a reflexive awareness of the implications of investigating the contradictions of the memory of the moment of exposure.

So, for example, Ritchin (1991) notes that some photo-reporters, such as Raymond Depardon, have begun explicitly to insert their own, biographical time into their photo-reportage. The effect of this is that the irregularities of biographical time are made explicit, providing a principle for the exploration of the potential for movement between speeds of perception made possible by computerised vision. Depardon's work in Beirut and Afghanistan was compiled in a small book called *Notes*, combining diary-like texts with a reporter's captions and photographs. Alternately, other photographers, such as Danny Lyon, have fictionalised the photographer himself, treating him like a character in a novel. (Ritchin himself suggests that it may become useful to label photographs as fiction or non-fiction, as is done with words.[21]) In these ways, it seems that while a grammar of photography is being developed, the articulation of image object and the image is open to debate.

Moreover, as Kevin Robins argues, it is important to recognise the multiplicity and diversity of contemporary images and the possibilities that this offers for the shifting and blending, the layering of images:

> There is a sense in which 'we are now beyond the image' (Bellour, 1990: 56); a sense in which it is now more productive to think in terms of the

21 Some newspapers are thinking of adding an M to the credit line accompanying any image that has been digitally manipulated.

> hybridity of image forms. We must come to terms with new ways of 'seeing' through what might be called an-optical technologies.
>
> (1995: 46)

In this argument, there is a recognition of the productivity of 'the proliferation of "*passages*" or "contaminations" between images, in which the creative interdependence of time and space may be explored, leading to 'the materialisation of linkages in time and space that enhance understanding' (1995: 46; quoting the artist Esther Parada). Stiegler too argues that, in its de-composition of the continuous, digitalisation allows the observer to subject the 'that really existed' to an analytical breaking-up, opening-up the possibility of 'new insights – artistic as well as theoretical and scientific – into the image' (1995: 242).

Robins's use of the notion of passages recalls that of Lyotard. In '*Logos* and *techne*, or Telegraphy', Lyotard describes 'passing' as what happens when technology is turned not on itself, that is, to purposes of appropriation and expansion, but against itself. He suggests that the new technologies of communication may make it possible to recall what could not have been forgotten because it was not inscribed. They may be instruments of anamnesic resistance. He writes,

> The whole question is this: is the passage possible, will it be possible with, or allowed by, the new mode of inscription and memoration that characterizes the new technologies? Do they not impose syntheses, and syntheses conceived still more intimately in the soul than any earlier technology has done? But by that very fact, do they not also help to refine our anamnesic resistance?
>
> (1991: 57)

He further argues that it makes sense to try to recall something which has not been inscribed if the inscription of this something broke the support of the writing or the memory. This something is 'a presence the mirror cannot reflect, but that breaks it to smithereens' (1991: 55).

However, despite the work of photographers such as Depardon, Lyon and Parada, and Lyotard's 'vague hope', both Virilio and Stiegler suggest that the grammatical operative that will be confirmed is technology itself – by which they mean the consequence of the contingent discovery of such-and-such a shape-recognition algorithm, for example, rather than the result of specific (aesthetic or political) decisions taken by grammarians.[22] Furthermore, the adoption and adaptation of specific algorithms is fought over, in the main, in 'industrial strategies and the current battles over standardization' (Stiegler, 1995: 250). That this is happening is a consequence, as Renaud notes, of the fact that the digital trans-

22 For further discussion of 'technology itself', see Eleftheriotis (1995), who contrasts two of the understandings of technology in Heidegger: enframing and poiesis. The former is an ordering revealing that produces the world as a 'standing reserve' and nature as a totality of calculable forces which are at the disposal of man to be tamed, mastered, ordered and exploited. In the latter, objects 'look upon man' rather than being produced by him in an ordered form of visibility.

formation of photography is taking place within a broader context of the regulation of the visible order, or, more precisely,

> the practical and theoretical adaptation of the visible to the desires and capacities of a neo-industrial urban social group whose development (unlimited social exchange) demands the severing of all its links with terra firma, with the ground it stands on.
>
> (1995: 216)

Indeed, it is for this very reason that Stiegler urges

> the artistic and intellectual community to be ready to seize its opportunities and to involve itself in the choices to be made regarding future research and development trends.
>
> (1995: 250)

The speed-limits of the movement of perception on the information superhighway, Renaud, Stiegler and Virilio all believe, are being set by the development of hyperbolic simulation systems, virtual realities or virtual environments, ambient milieux and individuated lifeworlds. And certainly the 'movement industries' are already producing 'grammars' and 'dictionaries' in the form of libraries of moving objects – through, for example, the development of techniques such as interpolation, morphing, cloning, inlaying, capturing in the simulation of animation in chemistry, physics and astrophysics, and the rapidly expanding fields of biotechnology, virtual reality, shape recognition and artificial intelligence, life and death. In short, at the same time that attempts are being made to recognise the productivity of the time of exposure in ways which subvert the meaning of what it is to be an individual, the transition from vision to visualisation being promoted by electro-optical corporations is fixing new ways of seeing and is contributing to revisions of the norms of seeing, remembering and forgetting through its standardisation of procedures. The body, its movements and the unconscious of the subject of vision are being subjected to processes of mathematical, commercial and legal as well as aesthetic regulation.[23] However, so it will be suggested in the next chapter, the status of the 'being' constituted through these processes of visualising is by no means fully determined – no one, for example, really knows if consciousness will be legally

23 Dimitris Eleftheriotis notes,

> 'The Digital Image Stabiliser' is a popular feature of many of the new camcorders – it operates through a digital analysis of each frame which detects and eliminates 'abnormal' movements. In a similar fashion, visual surveillance technology depends upon the identification of 'abnormal' or 'irregular' movements which disrupt the 'normal' flow of people in a street, a shopping centre or supermarket – research currently undertaken looks for ways in which the detection of abnormal movement can become an automaton built into the system.
>
> (1995: 105)

This regulation of the movement of the social body is not new: as many commentators have noted, those who 'loiter' have often been excluded from the private–public spaces of contemporary culture. In *Picturing Time: The Work of Étienne-Jules Marey, 1830–1904* (1992), Marta Braun provides a valuable historical study of the inter-relationship between developments in visual technology and the scientific study of movement.

recognised or no longer be co-extensive with self-identity or whether a being which is defined by an apparent inability to forget will – or should – be acknowledged as alive.

As Stiegler argues, the analogue–digital image is acting as the trigger for a methodical decomposition and recomposition of the (embodied) image, and of movement in particular:

> In its decomposition of the continuous [the indexical], digitalization allows us to subject the 'that really existed' to an analytical breaking-up. The essentially synthetic viewer–image relationship – as demonstrated, for example, in the spontaneous synthesis of the 'that really existed' – thus also becomes an analytical one.
>
> (1995: 242)

In this process, Stiegler believes, there will be a revision of the rules of movement, as 'the evolution of technical synthesis implies the evolution of viewer synthesis' (1995: 250) via the definition (the decomposition and recomposition) of the optimal conditions for the replication of movement. In this respect, he claims, the digital cartoon, the art of synthesised, artificial movement, will have the effect of producing a defining grammar of movement for the subject; the cartoon, he claims, is 'the essence of movement translated into image' (1995: 250). The cartoon's description of movement will be its transformation. This possibility is the focus of the next chapter. In this way, the chapter seeks to address the implications of the analytical intervention into the spatio-temporal relation of the future perfect of the photographic image made possible by the 'last dissection' of digitalisation.

CODA

According to Hardt, there are two relations of being at issue for Deleuze in the development of contemporary visual technologies. These are the possible and the real, and the virtual and the actual. The process of realisation is guided by two rules, resemblance and limitation, while the process of actualisation is guided by difference and creation. In relation to the first process, the real is in the image of (thus resembles) the possible that it realises:

> it simply has existence or reality added to it, which is translated by saying that, from the point of view of the concept, there is no difference between the possible and the real.
>
> (1988: 97, quoted in Hardt, 1993: 17)

Furthermore, Deleuze argues, not all possible realities can be realised, with the consequence that the realm of the possible is greater than the realm of the real. There must therefore be a process of limitation that determines which possibilities will pass into reality. In short, reality pre-exists itself in the 'pseudo-actuality' of the possible and only emanates through a limitation guided by resemblances. This process is the reduction of vision to a sight line (in Virilio's terms).

In contrast, in order for the virtual to become actual, it must create its own terms of actualisation. The actual does not resemble the virtual that it embodies; there is a difference between the virtual and the actual which requires that the process of actualisation be a creation. For Deleuze, the movement of being needs to be understood in terms of the virtual–actual relationship, rather than the possible–real relationship, and he thus advocates 'actualisation' over 'realisation', virtual actuality over possible reality. According to Deleuze, the contemporary extension of things thinkable subordinates descriptions of space and movement to the functions of thought: in doing so, it enables a prosthetics which is not necessarily defined by the movements of technology as such (or by the archive of images on which it may draw), but by the mental connections that can be made by perceptual prostheses. As such, there is always the potential that prosthetic culture may question, respond, object, provoke, hypothesise, experiment or even make a joke or two in accordance with an open list of conjunctions: 'therefore', 'if', 'because', 'actually', 'although' and not just 'either/or'.[24] Similarly, Lyotard writes in his discussion of thinking-machines,

> If you think you're describing thought when you describe a selecting and tabulating of data, you're silencing truth. Because data aren't given but givable, and selection isn't choice.
>
> (1991: 18)

24 In cinema, for example, Deleuze suggests, the situation (the environment, externality) may not be extended directly into action: it may no longer be mediated by the sensory-motor, as in realism, but primarily by the optical and in sound, invested by the senses, before action takes shape in it, and uses or confronts its elements:

> Everything remains real in this neo-realism (whether it is film set or exteriors) but, between the reality of the setting and that of the action, it is no longer a motor extension which is established, but rather a dreamlike connection through the intermediary of the liberated sense-organs.
>
> (Deleuze, 1989: 4)

8

HUMANS, NON-HUMANS AND HEROES

> Where once photography offered the eye depth – the density of a material trace within which each layer could be distinguished and analyzed (this is how photography constructs the image it generates and objectively defines it as a true *geological memory*) – there now reigns a depthless surface on which a host of messages are offered to the vision-automaton and on which they are displayed: a space-invaders game! Abandoning its terrestrial foundations, . . . photography finds itself transmuted, converted into a completely different space on the game board . . . via an impetus that produces at the same time a totally programmatory adaptation of memory. And so can we still speak of photography in the strict sense of the term?
>
> (Renaud, 1995: 194–196)

INTRODUCTION

At the same time that the movement of being is being redefined through the development of the new grammar of infomatics, so too are personality, memory and the unconscious. Indeed, Virilio argues that we are seeing the formation of an optical imagery with no apparent base, no permanency beyond that of mental or instrumental visual memory. What he calls a grid memory[1] sometimes seems to exist independently of a body or subject of vision at all. At the same time, so some writers suggest, the human body or subject is being robbed of its memories: the informational function of the media is such as to make us forget, the media exhaustion of news incites historical amnesia. Others, however, suggest that new beings are emerging, although they may as yet be hard to recognise since they are 'hybrids on the far extent of knowledge' (Legrady, quoted in Diamond, 1993: 11).[2] And while Virilio's grid is undoubtedly in the process of being fixed, current modes of regulation seem, at present, to be inadequate in the face of its contemporary manifestations – the combination of the exhaustive retrievability and inability to remember that is random access memory, for

1 The use of the term 'grid' here recalls Rosalind Krauss's use of it to describe the universalisation of the general condition of form or *gestalt* in the condition of synchrony, which she describes as a privileged mode in modernism's mapping of space.

2 Elaine Scarry (1994), for example, would locate the cyborg in relation to the history of what she calls consensual materialism. This history, she argues, is characterised by a desire for the automaton's volitional positioning, a positioning that has been achieved through 'the labour of animation'. See Gary Lee Downey's analysis of 'Human agency in CAD/CAM technology' (1995) for further discussion of the notion of positioning.

example. In describing the potential being-effects of digitalisation and computer animation, Richard Wright comments, 'the medium has now surrendered, it offers little resistance to the desires of the user and overwhelms us by its aimless potential' (quoted in Diamond, 1993: 11).

THE REVERSAL OF MOTIVATION

The cyborg is perhaps the most widely recognised example of a hybrid creature on the 'far extent of knowledge'. As such, its apparently aimless potential is the object of much recent theorising (Haraway, 1985; King, 1989; Stone, 1992; Gray with Figueroa-Sarriera and Mentor, 1995). According to Barry King, for example, who develops his analysis through an investigation of the computer-animated figure or cartoon, the cyborg is a figure whose principal mechanisms of coherence, rather than referring 'to a state of external being', relate 'to a state of self-sufficient knowing or textuality' (1989: 122). It is a figure which lives at 'a new level of representation in which textuality [i]s triumphantly divorced from context' (1989: 122). While cyborg beings are inscribed into a system of representation or symbolic field much like their human counterparts, they are, King argues, inscribed in a condition of complete inclusiveness.[3] And rather than being aimless, not only do they have an aim, they are effectively targeted images.

How is this absolute inclusivity or effective targeting achieved? And what implications does it have for subjectivity, personality or the individual? As King points out, the cinema has long made use of metaphorical and metonymic devices as substitutes for character and such substitutes often play on the indices of presence in real life: examples include close-ups of personal property, portraits, photographs, letters, voice-overs in interior monologues, and so on.[4] But, according to King, cartoons and computer animation, even if operating such conventions, compound this process of substitution by rendering character itself as an intrinsic textual event as opposed to a textually recoded performance.[5] From the perspective of the politics of performance, the range of variation of voice, gesture, posture and dress that an actor may deploy to recode a character is rendered by computer animation an absolute function of the text

3 Alternately, this might be described as closure through openness in autopoietic terms.

4 As King (1985) notes in another article discussed later, Metz also remarks on the capacity of film to substitute inanimate objects for the actor as a signifier. Adorno also makes a similar argument at a more general level. He argues,

> The late emergence of film makes it difficult to distinguish between technique and technology as clearly as is possible in music. In music up to the electronic period, the intrinsic technique – the sound structure of the work – was distinct from its performance, the means of reproduction. Film suggests the equation of technique and technology since, as Benjamin observed, the cinema has no original which is then reproduced on a mass scale: the mass product is the thing itself.
>
> (1991: 155)

However, he goes on to suggest that the 'movement of interior images' may disturb the equation of technique and technology.

5 Although he notes that motivation is determined in the last instance by what he calls collective conventionalism – 'the cultural frameworks in which it inheres' (1989: 130).

(code or algorithm).[6] This means, King claims, that the potential for 'a negative dialectic between the totality of the text and the particularity of the performance is obliterated' (1989: 138). But is this so? Does the inclusiveness of the grid make not simply dimensionality, point of view and perspective redundant, but also any non-conventional, singular or actual (rather than real in Deleuze's terms) being at all?

Computer-generated images are widely held up as paradigmatic examples of the hyper-real:

> this is the reconstruction – or even the construction *ex nihilo* – of an object or phenomenon, in terms of its various parameters (shape, colour, lighting, texture, positioning, possible transformations and so on), on the basis of a digital model. . . . The computer-generated image is the visual outcome of a process – modeling, algorithmic development, display, etc. – at the end of which digital data are transformed into an *image*, made up of *pixels*, on a screen.
>
> (Renaud, 1995: 178–180)

For King and others, however, this is not, as one might have thought, the death of meaning, but the moment of its authoritarian reinscription. King quotes Teresa de Lauretis:

> The sign aims to be the thing, to abolish the distinction of reference, the mechanism of replacement. Not the image of the thing, its plaster cast. Its double in other words.
>
> (de Lauretis, quoted in King, 1989: 128)

Hyper-reality, in this account, is one consequence of the modern tendency identified by Crary for signifiers to exceed their referent,[7] in this case by pushing the conventions of 'realism' to a point where the relations of motivation between the referent and the signifier are *reversed* (King, 1989: 129). In this view, any figure of the hyper-real, such as a cyborg, is a super-reversed/resolved signifier that, while referring to some, for example, historical figure or event, is marked by an ambition to replace or reincarnate the 'thing' it represents. (It is thus pre-medi[t]ated

6 Benjamin describes the emergence of radio and film as having contributed to a kind of cultural selection process in which only the most performatively adept survive:

> Radio and film not only affect the function of the professional actor but likewise the function of those who also exhibit themselves before this mechanical apparatus, those who govern. Though their tasks may be different, the change affects equally the actor and the ruler. The trend is towards establishing controllable and transferable skills under certain social conditions. This results in a new selection, *a selection before the equipment* from which the star and the dictator emerge victorious.
>
> (1970: 249; my emphasis)

7 Baudrillard describes this tendency in terms of 'the race for the real'. He suggests that there is no escape from this race, because while 'an object is exactly like another, *it is not exactly like it, it is a bit more exact*' (1994: 107). There is thus always the motivation for an escalation in the production of a real that is more and more real 'through the addition of successive dimensions' (1994: 107). However, he also argues that there 'is never any similitude, any more than there is exactitude' (1994: 107); he is thus less pessimistic than King in this respect.

murder; as such, it deliberately incites the shudder of which Barthes speaks [see chapter 4].) For King, then, the cyborg does not abolish the referent but relies, rather, on its mathematical inherence, pan-conventional inclusion, to render intelligible what, in Moholy-Nagy's terms, are its parodic, caricatural or utopian effects.

Indeed, in the next stage of his argument, King suggests that as a consequence of reverse motivation, the hyper-real figure – the cyborg – is able to represent the space or environment of which it is in fact the creation, as its own invention or possession, as inhering in its own capacities. King uses the example of the computer-animated figure Max Headroom to make the details of his argument clear, suggesting that

> Max Headroom presages the power of the electronic media to produce, via a synergy of developments such as high definition television and computer animation, signifiers that subordinate their referents in the external world.
>
> (1989: 137)

He argues that in so far as Max is not simply a representation of a cyborg but a hyper-real figure of representation, his semiotic function is to redescribe the principle of systematic control as an existential statement emerging from the particulars of a concrete personality.[8] In Max Headroom's case, this 'personality' is constituted in a dazzling display of skill in interpersonal relationships. In this respect, King suggests, Max redescribes the life experience and social horizons of the 'new' professional middle classes who make their living through the sale of these and other communication skills (1989: 127).[9]

More generally, according to King, what is essential to the cyborg as the emblematic figure of the hyper-real is not that he/she/it behaves in a particular kind of way or is a particular kind of character, but rather that the cyborg represents all behaviour as goal-oriented or targeted, that is, as a programme or a form of work. In Max's case, for example, he argues, the doing of interpersonal relationships is depicted in this way, and is rendered as a set of skills that are a form of work.[10] He himself redescribes the cyborg's powers of redescription in terms of the 'contours of a post-modern sensibility' in which

> the perception of the arbitrariness of codes, the emphasis on manipulating cultural forms and contents (pastiche, parody) and the corresponding emphasis on simultaneity and the evacuation of history . . . can be

8 The cyborg can thus be seen as an instance of what Seltzer describes as 'self-destruction for fuller self-possession' (1993: 112).

9 Along similar lines, Andrew Ross argues that Max's irony redescribes the attitude of the baby boomer audience, offering it 'a way of reconciling its own dissident youthful past with its professional-managerial present' (1990: 149). Both their analyses can be located within what Umberto Eco (1984) calls 'neo-television', a mode of television less concerned with the 'outside world' than with sustaining an 'interactive' relation with its viewers.

10 This is an interpretation of interpersonal behaviour as work that has obvious parallels with the notion of earned competence or trainability identified by Emily Martin (1994) as part of the emerging requirement of flexibility in the individual in contemporary Euro-American society.

> discerned [to have] . . . a specific social base [the ethos of the new middle classes] . . . . One might go further and suggest that such a sensibility (if generationally diffused) is concretised and rendered pragmatic for those individuals whose education – in art schools and the polytechnic sector, in cultural and media studies – and current or future employment prospects rest on the application of cultural and art historical knowledge to production *per se.*
>
> (1989: 133–134)

In other words, in the reversion of the relationship between signifier and referent that makes possible the depiction of interpersonal and communication skills as intrinsic to the personality of Max Headroom – a cyborg being whose memory is that of the data bank of images of television – King sees a 'psychologistic denial of the role of environmental or contextual factors in human thought processes' (1989: 127). In this way, for King, the figure of Max, in 'his restive radical chic', both conceals and reveals that 'those who oversee the production of cybernetic entertainments are ruled by their own creations and, by extension, those who consume them' (1989: 138). He concludes,

> As such, Max's delinquent personality is not the incursion of carnival as much as a carnivalesque gloss – a playfulness with codes that valorises the capacity of neo-television to sustain itself through self-reflexivity.
>
> (1989: 136–137)

More generally, Margaret Morse describes the age of information in terms of its simulated visibility – 'If it could be seen, this is what it might look like' (1990: 226–227) – while Timothy Druckrey describes the cyborg age as one in which 'Images appear as indexes of a world mediated through TV'. During the second half of the twentieth century, he argues,

> Media icons supplanted political ones – or the distinction between the two collapsed as the 'space' of the print media was being transformed by the 'space' of the television screen. The site of assimilation of social content was shifting toward the immaterial and the programmed, toward the illusory power of the medium as the message. The 'space' of knowing and the 'space' of perception were merging.
>
> (Druckrey, 1994: 6)

BACKSTORIES AND DEPTH OF CHARACTER

This analysis of the cyborg as a self-enclosed and self-sufficient creature is persuasive, and there is much evidence to support it. However, it is worth exploring the precedents for such a figure and considering its implications for self-identity. To do this, I want to return to an earlier article by King in which he describes the competing claims of acting styles, arguing that impersonation (in which the personality of the actor should disappear into the part) has recently been challenged by personification (in which the performance of a part is subsumed by the actor's persona), for this provides a basis from which to evaluate his claim that, with the cyborg, text and performance are flattened out. In impersonation, 'good' acting is based on some concept of intentionality, or even authorship. Indeed, this concept is so powerful that the 'process of character representation through impersonation entails that the actor should strive to obliterate his or her sense of identity in order to become a signifier for the intentionality inscribed in character' (1985: 31). King notes that much of an actor's training is oriented to this end:

> The regime of exercises that constitute an actor's training, while certainly increasing his or her adaptability in respect of casting for specialised skills like juggling, dancing and so on, are nevertheless intended to increase the conscious mastery of the actor over verbal, gestural and postural behaviour. The objective of the control installed through practice is to reduce behaviours like these to a state of automaticity so that they are summonable at will in relation to consciously formulated expressive purpose. In a similar way, versatility of accent, posture, walk and other markers of difference, is intended to enable the actor to 'naturalise' such exogenous behaviours . . . as his or her own for the duration of the performance in order to be convincing 'in character'.
>
> (1985: 29)

King argues that both Method[11] and Broadway/repertoire styles of acting have been effective strategies of realising (and capitalising upon) this conception of performance as impersonation. However, while Method and Broadway acting may both be effective strategies, what is especially interesting about Method acting in relation to the argument being developed here is that it draws attention to the process by which the convincing-ness of the actor's performance is related to his or her ability to make a matter of will, deliberation or intention aspects of the character's behaviour which are commonly understood to be out of an individual's will or self-control. So a recent newspaper feature on the Method actor Harvey Keitel begins:

> Harvey Keitel has never done nudity. He hasn't done a violent film, either. You might suppose you clocked him butt-naked in *The Piano*, wagging his wienerwurst in *Bad Lie[u]tenant* or blowing cops away in *Reservoir Dogs* – but you're wrong. Like Joan of Arc, or the Yorkshire Ripper, there's something inside him that makes him do these awful things. It's called the character. The character, Harvey Keitel insists, takes him places where the real Harvey Keitel would hesitate to go.
>
> (Pulver, 1996: 4)

King, however, identifies a number of limits that he believes to be inherent to impersonation that restrict the places the character can take actors such as Keitel, including the pre-performance selection process of type-casting, which has what he calls a 'persistent tendency towards self-fulfilment – *only actors who look the part get the part*' (1985: 37; my emphasis). He suggests that the actor is tied

11 This style of acting requires that actors do considerable work upon the 'backstory' of their characters before playing a role.

to his or her looks by a kind of biological and social destiny: 'the actor as a member of [a] host culture – with a given hair colour, body shape, repertoire of gestures, registers of speech, accent, dialect and so on – always pre-signifies meaning' (1985: 37).

Keitel, however, may be 'luckier' than some other actors in this respect in that his 'ethnic background has always been one of [his] ambiguities – he plays Jewish gangsters (Mickey Cohen in *Bugsy*) and Italian cops (Vince LaRocca in *Sister Act*) with equal facility' (Pulver, 1996: 4). In other words, it seems that Keitel has been able to escape the fate of which King speaks in so far as his biological and/or social origins are seen to be ambiguous. If these origins can be left visually indeterminate, then the process of self-fulfilment is not limited to the generic narrative of the type-cast actor. Instead, the actor may be seen to profit from a prosthetic biography; that is, *a biography mediated by the spatial and temporal specificities of the image* for this enables him or her to extend the range and variation of characters s/he is able to act convincingly. Indeed, it may be for this reason that Keitel's reputation has increased in recent years, for it suggests that he is able to lay claim to the intentionality associated with impersonation at the same time as the effects of personification.[12] The latter is the term King gives to the style of acting which he argues has largely displaced impersonation and is associated with what he calls hypersemioticisation (an enhancement in the scale of observation leading to an intensification of investment of meaning in the actor 'as a signifying mass') and the displacement of interiority. From this point of view, Keitel's 'ambiguous' looks have contributed to his ability to capitalise on his body as 'a signifying mass'.

This combination of impersonation and personification is by no means easy to sustain since, as King argues, the routine practices of mainstream cinema have tended to shift the frontier of control away from the actor towards the director, and while some directors are willing to share authorial intentionality, by no means all are.[13] In Keitel's case, for example, while some directors may praise him because 'He's gonna go where the character goes. He's not afraid – he's an ex-Marine, for Chrissake' (Abel Ferrara, quoted in Pulver, 1996: 4), others simply stop working with him. So, for example, Francis Ford Coppola is said to have 'ejected' Keitel after a fortnight's location shooting on *Apocalypse Now* because of his refusal to play the part as directed; the journalist writing the piece discussed here explains, 'for the one time Marine, the issue was about not surrendering freedom and control under extreme conditions' (Pulver, 1996: 5).

Moreover, just as there may be disputes between actor and director, so there

12 As King points out, Robert de Niro is similar in this regard 'since he appears, paradoxically, to combine to a stunning level of virtuosity the capacity for impersonation with a drive, role by role, to transform himself physically into the substance of the signified, e.g. Jake La Motta in *Raging Bull*' (1985: 43).

13 It is interesting to ponder whether, as King claims, the twinned processes of hyper-semioticisation and displacement of interiority do indeed lead to the situation in which the actor is increasingly confined to 'being a bearer of effects that he or she does not originate' (1985: 45). While I agree with King's analysis, I do not share his conclusion since, as the analysis of prosthetic culture developed here would imply, I do not agree either that the actor will not be able to lay claims of ownership to the effects of personification or that origins are inevitably tied to intentionality.

may be disputes between writer and actor, especially when, as is reported and recommended in a how-to scriptwriting book (Seger, 1990), writers too are encouraged to adapt the techniques of Method acting and write out a biography for the character they are creating. (This recommendation is provided with the intention of creating 'unforgettable characters'.) Sometimes the backstories actor and writer create may be in synch, retrospectively created from within the 'same' decisive instant or origin as it were. So, for example, one scriptwriter is quoted as saying, 'What you need to know about the characters is what the actors need to know to play the scenes' (Seger, 1990: 49), and claims,

> What is important are the sense memories. It is not important what happened to them but how they felt about it . . . . What you want to ask the characters is, 'What was your most embarrassing moment? Did you ever feel like a fool? What are the worst things that ever happened to you?'
>
> (Seger, 1990: 49)

Yet at other times, there may be a disjuncture, especially if the backstory is realigned in relation to the momentary exigencies of the ongoing plot.[14] (The actor who plays Mark Fowler in the soap *EastEnders* is reported to have said 'How long have I got?' when told that his character was to find out that he was HIV positive.[15]) Another author is quoted as saying,

> What counts is the story you're telling. The backstory has to accommodate itself to your story. As I'm going along, I'll think I know what the past is, but something may happen in the present, and I'll say, 'No, I have to change the past.'
>
> (Seger, 1990: 55–56)

And another is cited to the same effect:

> When I work with backstory, I fill in the background of all the characters as I go along. Backstory information is not important – until you need it! It's crucial to understand that something happened earlier, that some past event has explained motivation in the present. But you do not proceed chronologically.
>
> (Seger, 1990: 56)

Or again,

> One season we discovered that David [a character] had been married. It was a discovery that made sense and was usable to construct a particular episode. Most of the backstory unfolded as we worked on it.
>
> (Seger, 1990: 57)

The author of the manual for aspiring writers from which these examples come concludes:

14 This disjuncture is often the topic of attention elsewhere in the media, including especially the press.

15 I am indebted to Mary Cutler for her illuminating comments on soap opera for many of the points made in this section.

> Finding the backstory is a process of discovery. The writer needs to work back and forth constantly – asking questions about the past to further understand the present.
>
> (Seger, 1990: 62)

In the cases described here, the narrative-linked or topographical perception and the insight of depth of character which arise in this perception are displaced by a perception pre-mediated in the time of exposure and the depth of character it produces. This is a depth of character that is revealed in the speed at which the backstory cross-cuts the continuity of the present. The closing still image of the actor at the end of each episode of many soap operas – notably *Dallas* – is an exemplary image of this pre-mediated depth of personality. As the moving image of the character is brought to a stand-still, his or her present is seen by the viewer to contain multiple backstories and origins (as if in a spatial continuum). As one television critic notes,

> Part of soap's power is the *blindness* of the action. In a self-contained play or film, performance or writing or direction in early scenes will inevitably tend to hint at the outcome, signal the significance of characters. Soap is open-ended.
>
> (Lawson, 1995: 7; my emphasis)

While with the next episode the viewer will see which viewpoint has been chosen as the starting point or origin for the resumption of narrative, the personality's depth is a function of the extent to which this multiplicity is acknowledged in the actor/character's ongoing performance. This open-endedness is not, however, aimless; rather, it is the outcome of negotiations between scriptwriters, actors, directors and producers. For example, in one account of the development of the character Sue-Ellen in *Dallas*, the actor Linda Gray claims to have created a larger role – greater depth for her personality – by building on a closing still of her face on the brink of tears. Moreover, there is not always such a symbiotic relation between actor and personality (as the viewer often comes to recognise on viewing repeats):

> Playing those pilot scenes, Larry Hagman has no idea whether he will survive the spring 1978 ratings war, let alone go on to world superstardom and a liver transplant caused in part by his need to be drunk to get through the increasingly feverish scripts of the later years.
>
> (Lawson, 1995: 7)

Thus while the personalities of reversed motivation are not aimless, they do not always reach their target either.

The examples given so far are those of realistic characters, that is, those that conventionally have been defined as 'the most dimensional', given depth by subjective consistency over time by a narrative biography, complex psychology, attitudes, values and emotions. However, the reversal of motivation described here seems to be leading to a redefinition of psychological realism more generally: as the productivity of the moment of exposure is increasingly made available (even decisive) in the process of the development of the character or individual's personality, it leads to a loss of the depth of space, that is, interiority, and is replaced by depth of time, that is, (super-)resolution. Indeed, this pre-mediation can be seen as one aspect of the creation of a prosthetic biography: the reversal of prophecy – in which action *precedes*, rather than *follows*, intent – is retrodictively productive of the after-life of personality. And, not surprisingly, the pre-mediated nature of the depth of time in personalities is even clearer in relation to so-called non-realistic characters, that is, those who are said to be 'determined by their limits, by their context, and by the associations and responses that the audience brings to each' (Seger, 1990: 174).[16] Here the aim is not simply that the actor's topographical perception be replaced, but also that of the audience. That is, the aim is that the audience's perception, while not 'already completed' in the sense that Ritchin argues was the case in chemical photography, is to be already completed in the character's image as a consequence of pre-mediation.

THE DEPTH OF NON-REALISTIC CHARACTERS

One widely recognised type of non-realistic characters is symbolic characters; they are defined as 'one-dimensional'. Indeed, 'They are not meant to be dimensional. They personify one quality.' Another accepted type is the non-human character, a type including 'the fantasy character', who may be defined by physical exaggeration, by magical powers, or by being 'supergood, or superresourceful, or superbad' (Seger, 1990: 183). The non-human character, it seems, is without any dimension at all, as the following contrast between non-human and human characters reveals:

> A human character achieves dimensionality by adding to, and emphasizing, its human characteristics. But emphasizing the nonhuman aspects of a character will rarely strengthen a nonhuman character. Emphasizing a dog's doglike characteristics (such as a louder bark or running faster to the food dish) is not going to make the dog more endearing to humans.
>
> (Seger, 1990: 178)

16 Allucquère Rosanne Stone also points to some similarities between cyborgs and non-dimensional personalities; she writes,

> As Sherry Turkle first suggested, an 'absent structure of personality' is also another way of describing the peculiarly seductive character of that vague but palpable sentience, the computer. Turkle characterizes this aspect of computer interaction as producing the quasi-personality complex that she calls the 'second self'. Danger, the sense of threat as well as seductiveness which the computer can evoke, comes from both within and without. It derives from the complex interrelationships between human and computer, and thus partially from within the human; and it exists partially within the simulation. . . . The quality of mutability that virtual interaction promises is expressed as a sense of dizzying, exciting physical movement occurring within a phantasmatic space – again an experimental mode psychoanalytically linked to primal experiences. It is no wonder, then, that inhabitants of virtual systems seem to experience a sense of longing for a space that is simultaneously embodied and imaginary, such as cyberspace suggests. This longing is frequently accompanied by a desire, inarticulately expressed, to penetrate the interface and merge with the system – what I have humorously referred to elsewhere as 'cyborg envy'.
>
> (1992: 619)

So how is a personality for the one-dimensional, non-human character to be created? Can the desired degree of resolution be secured? Will the aim reach its target?[17] According to Seger, the processes for achieving a one-dimensional personality include, first, 'carefully choosing one or two attributes that will begin to define the identity of the character' (1990: 178), a process which one might have thought would tend to make the character human, by adding dimensions: significantly, though, Seger announces that the attributes of the non-human (unlike those of the human) never change.

In this context, Eco's comments on the temporality of the character of that well-known one-dimensional personality, the superhero, are illuminating. According to Eco, the 'positive hero' embodies to 'an unthinkable degree the power demands that the average citizen nurtures but cannot satisfy' (1983: 107). Yet the exercise of this power is made difficult since, because he must combine the predictability of the mythic figure with the novelty required of a contemporary cultural product, he cannot *accomplish anything*. If he were to act, he would 'consume himself', since he would have 'taken a step toward death': 'he has gotten older, if only by an hour; his storehouse of personal experience has irreversibly enlarged' (1983: 111). If this were to happen it would contravene his aesthetic and commercial responsibility, and, in this contravention of cyborg ethics, challenge the terms of his legal personality. Eco writes of Superman that he

> must remain 'inconsumable' and at the same time be 'consumed' according to the ways of everyday life. He possesses the characteristics of timeless myth, but is accepted only because his activities take place in our human and everyday world of time. The narrative paradox that Superman's scriptwriters must resolve somehow, even without being aware of it, demands a paradoxical solution with regard to time.
>
> (1983: 111)

The paradoxical solution adopted by Superman's scriptwriters has been to subject his character to a process of iteration, of repetition, of action or adventure outside of everyday time, resulting in the creation of Superman as a model of heterodirection (for he takes action in the 0/1 dimension of the spatial continuum of which he is a creation) (Figure 8.1). The stories so produced occur in a kind of 'oneiric climate', where what has happened before and what will happen after appear extremely hazy.

Furthermore, even without any possible reference to spatial dimensionality, the backstory may be manipulated in relation to an eternal present, and in this relation elements from a past that was never present (what Stiegler calls 'Hades, the kingdom of the dead, the underground' [1995: 232]) are brought to life:

> It occurs, then, that along with Superman stories, Superboy stories are told, that is, stories of Superman when he was a boy, or a tiny child under the name of Superbaby. At a certain point, Supergirl appears on the scene.

17 I would tentatively suggest that such non-dimensional characters have many similarities with brands, what advertisers describe as the 'unique essences' of products.

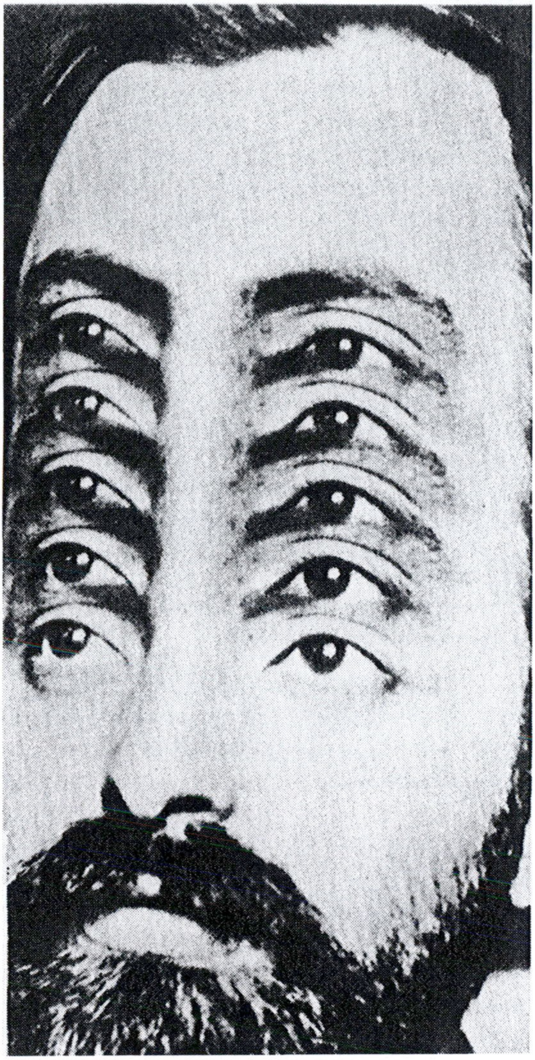

Figure 8.1 Superman or the tree of eyes

> She is Superman's cousin . . . . All of the events concerning Superman are retold in one way or another in order to account for the presence of this new character (who has hitherto not been mentioned, because, it is explained, she has lived in disguise, awaiting puberty, at which time she could come out into the world . . .) . . . . One imagines, using the solution of travel through time, that Supergirl, Superman's contemporary, can encounter Superboy in the past and be his playmate; and even Superboy, having broken the time barrier by sheer accident, can encounter Superman, his own self of many years later.
>
> (Eco, 1983: 114)

The scriptwriters of this exemplary positive hero, or non-human character, have also, according to Eco, adopted the strategy of telling *Imaginary Tales* and *Untold Tales*, the latter being stories that concern events already told but in which 'something was left out', so they are told again as if from another point of view within the spatial continuum.

The model of Mickey Mouse provides an alternative solution to the narrative paradox identified by Eco: a personality in which the law of time itself is included in the text of the figure's very shape or logo:

> In the Disney World, Mickey is the first and last image of permanence, he is the all-encompassing, self-contained law.
>
> (Dorfman and Mattelart, 1975: 3)

As Stephen J. Gould (1979) has argued, the figure of Mickey Mouse has undergone a process of juvenilisation in the course of his 'lifetime'. As Mickey has got older, he has been made to look younger: his nose has been made shorter and thicker, his ears were moved back to give him the appearance of having a rounded rather than sloping forehead, his eyes have become bigger, and his limbs have been made softer and puffier. According to Gould,[18] this animated juvenilisation can be understood in terms of the human fascination with neotony, the retention of youthful characteristics in the adult form. This process has occurred in tension with the iteration which is a characteristic feature of Mickey's cartoon escapades (and Superman's adventures), and underpins his recurrence, across media, as a symbol of youthfulness. Their combination explains the allure of Mickey's persona in products associated with time, including, quintessentially, the Mickey Mouse watch. (In 1935, two million Mickey Mouse watches were sold in a single eight-week period.) Mickey is both outside time and simultaneously includes it within the very contours of his shape; he is a figure in which time makes images of itself.[19]

18 For an illuminating explication of this thesis, see the comic strip by Francis Masse, 'Two in a balcony: the mausoleum of natural history' (1991). I would like to thank Daniel Welch for this reference.

19 One example of a contemporary artist who can be seen to be aiming to produce images according to a similar principle is Nancy Burson, best known for her digitalised composite portraits. She holds a patent (with Tom Schneider, an MIT engineer) on a computer system that simulates ageing in adults and children. The simulated ageing process interpolates between an older and younger person by means of a database that stores templates of typical wrinkling and ⇒

The second and third suggestions offered by Seger in relation to the creation of personality for non-human figures are also revealing. The second suggestion is to emphasise 'the associations that the audience brings to the character in order to expand on this identity'. This can be seen as a strategy to tap into the viewing subject's 'instantaneous' or topographical perception, and the memorisation processes which are part of it, and, through the mechanism of reverse motivation, attribute the capacities accruing in this perception to the figure (that is, to transform the features of the environment recognised by a viewer into the attributes of the personality). Virilio appears to concur that this possibility may be realised in his suggestion that what he calls the phatic image can force the viewer to look; that is, it 'radically reverses the dependent perceiver–perceived relationship'.[20] This is because

> it is already more than a brief memorandum, more than the photographic memento of a more or less distant past. It is in fact *will*. The will to engage the future . . . and not just to represent the past.
>
> (1994: 61)

According to Virilio, the instrumental will that harnesses not only the 'this-has-been' but also the multiplicity of the 'this-might-have-been' (or, rather, the these-might-have-beens) has the advantage of surprise, the power of prospective observation, although it is also prey to a sort of 'panic anticipation that commits the future' (1994: 66). Indeed, as Ross wryly observes, 'in a technocracy proper, there is no future shock; the future arrives by increments, every twenty minutes or so' (1990: 146).

muscle-softening patterns. In an additive process, the computer determines facial type based on such considerations as gender, weight and facial structure, and, using this information, can be made to simulate ageing. In 1983, Burson exhibited her portraits of the British royal family in the year 2010.

She has participated in a number of missing child cases using a related composite process, and taking a percentage of features from an older family member and adding that to the last known picture of the child to produce a 'real-time' image. Bertillon, who, as discussed in chapter 3, declared that the problem of classifying the criminal is, 'at bottom', the same as that which forms 'the basis of the everlasting popular melodrama about lost, exchanged and recovered children' (quoted in Sekula, 1986: 34), would no doubt have been pleased to have his ideas confirmed.

Burson also uses a simple, plastic Diana camera to photograph children born with craniofacial conditions or progeria (a rare condition which means a child will age a lifetime during a few years and die before adulthood), children considered to be difficult to look at, although Burson herself describes them as having 'unusual, very special faces' (quoted in Busselle, 1994: 73). Using digitalised information from these photographs, she has developed what she calls her computer 'anomaly machine' in which a subject's face can be programmed to resemble some of the conditions depicted in her photographs.

20 In his discussion 'How to look at television', Adorno makes a similar point. He argues that the 'handling' of the audience that is part of mass culture may be described in terms of 'psychoanalysis in reverse':

> The implication is that somehow the psychoanalytic concept of a multilayered personality has been taken up by the cultural industry, and that the concept is used in order to ensnare the consumer as completely as possible and in order to engage him psychodynamically in the service of premediated effects.
>
> (1991: 143)

But how is this possible? According to Virilio, with digitalisation has come a standardisation of ways of seeing, resulting not just in synthetic images but also in synthetic perception, the automation of perception. In relation to synthetic images, he writes that, 'Thanks to work on animal conditioning . . . a new certainty was born' (1994: 13–14). This was the belief that 'to retrieve a specific target attribute, it was no longer necessary to activate a whole array of attributes, any single one of them being able to act independently' (1994: 14). He goes on to suggest that the 'parasitic persistence' of 'geometric brand-images, initials, Hitler's swastika, Charlie Chaplin's silhouette, Magritte's blue bird or the red lips of Marilyn Monroe' cannot be explained merely in terms of the power of technical reproducibility, but needs to be understood in terms of a system of message-intensification and the brightness of these phatic images. They are targeted, and force the viewer to look, holding his or her attention.[21] They are the result of an 'ever-lighter illumination, of the intensity of its definition, singling out only specific areas, the context mostly disappearing into a blur' (1994: 12).[22] The recent move by the makers of Pepsi-Cola to identify their product with the colour blue, in contradistinction to the red of their rivals, Coca-Cola, would seem to me an obvious example of how this approach is being taken up and adopted for commercial ends.[23]

The third suggestion identified by Seger is the apparent opposite, it is to create 'a strong context to deepen the character' (1990: 178–179). Here is the

21 As part of his analysis of the Hauku noted above (chapter 7, fn. 12), Paul Stoller writes,

> Sympathetic magic consists of copy and contact. Sorcerers make a copy of that which they want to affect. Through its magical power the copy acquires the properties of the original, which, in turn, implies the sorcerers' mastery and power over the object. Songhay sorcerers, for example, sometimes make copies of magic arrows and bows, which are associated with the arrows and bows of a particular spirit in the Songhay pantheon. On rare occasions they will speak to these replicas from their hearts, naming a victim. Then they take the bow and shoot the arrow in the direction of the victim's dwelling or village. The replica falls harmlessly on the ground in the sorcerer's compound, but the 'inner' arrow flies through the night air. And if a sorcerer's aim is good – if the power pulsing in his veins is greater than that of his enemy/victim – the 'inner' arrow strikes its victim. Victims will wake up in the middle of the night, screaming, with pain shooting up their legs. Once struck, they become progressively weaker. And if they don't seek a cure, they will most certainly die from an invisible (inner) wound. This is an example of what Taussig and Benjamin mean by corporeal knowing.
>
> (1995: 41)

22 Yet the compulsion to look required by the phatic image is neither necessarily effective nor adaptative. Cybernetic systems are premised on interaction with a concrete user, and that interaction requires conformity with a set of procedures and rules (algorithms) if certain, predefined, concrete goals are to be realised. Such systems, therefore, do not merely offer a way of knowing, but have inscribed into their functioning an idealised mode of behaviour. This idealised mode of behaviour may be achieved by the viewer/user of the system, but, in achieving it, the viewer/user may, in Barthes's terms, undergo a metamorphosis. The question arises, what kinds of subject, with what kinds of experience, are produced and reproduced by interaction with cybernetic systems, since interaction, or practice, makes the person, or rather, practitioner, according to Rabinow (1992: 243).

23 There have recently been a series of legal cases which have sought to establish the legal ownership of certain colours through trademark law.

invitation to create the space of which the character is the possession, a space or context which is then made to seem a function of the character (thus resolving the apparent contradiction with the second strategy): so, for example,

> Everything related to war can be found in the context of Mars.
>
> (Seger, 1990: 175)

This third suggestion is, it is suggested here, coming to be especially important in the creation of personalities defined by exposure, the depth of time.

THE SURFACE SPACE OF CARTOONS

In order to see how this possessive relation between personality and context or environment might be created, it is helpful to consider the distinctive spatial organisation of cartoons, since they are one of the most well-developed media in which non- or one-dimensional characters have been developed. Russell George (1990) provides a way of exploring this in his fascinating study of the classical cartoon, in existence from 1928 to 1965.[24] Central to isolating the cartoon's operational field, George argues, is the demand made upon the camera as the instrument of the inscription of the image. The camera is positioned facing and parallel to a flat surface with a drawing or painting upon it, so that this surface occupies the total field of the lens. This position, being a constant within certain parameters, becomes invisible; a prerequisite. As such, it sets the constraints within which the formal spatial mechanisms operate across the substantive elements (such as jokes, story, plot, and so on) of the cartoon:

> The cartoon as a 6 or 7 minute – usually comic – short film is more than its scopic field alone; but too extended a deviation from the basic camera set-up [described above] undermines its status as a member of the category 'cartoon'.
>
> (1990: 298)

As George points out, in terms of the camera there is a sense (formally if not substantively) in which the cartoon consists of only one 'camera angle'. As a consequence, the cartoon is conceived as a flat surface. Indeed, George goes so far as to argue that the cartoon is premised on the nature and status of the presence of the surface. He claims that this surface presence – even in its general 'invisibility' – is always constitutive in the organisation of space in cartoons. This is what he calls 'the surface-based predication of the cartoon' (1990: 303). For George, it has the result that cartoons organise themselves around an illusory matrix; they are premised both on the absence of illusory depth – the 'original' drawing – and also on its presence – the two-dimensionality of both the 'original' drawing and the cinema screen. The imputation of an illusion of 'realistic' depth is 'eliminated' (1990: 299), at the same time that an awareness of depth is 'managed'. The action is premised never on its actual, virtual or 'real' incidence (as, for example, is the

24 The production of the classical cartoon was dominated by seven or eight cartoon studios in this period; they included Warner Bros, MGM, Disney, Fleischer, Lantz, Famous and UPA.

case with pro-filmic events in a real set),[25] but on its relation to the cinematic absence of depth and the presence of the cinema or television screen.

This co-existence of the absence and presence of illusory space manifests itself in the cartoon as *play*. Because a flatness is already there in the cartoon, it does not, relatively speaking, have to de-emphasise perspective; rather, it may either create it (1990: 301)[26] or play with its freedom from photographic perspectival criteria in terms of layout. George writes,

> the cartoon, more even than the slapstick comedy or the musical, retains full-figure, external staging, and thus flaunts its perspectival liberty just as live-action deemphasizes its perspectival restrictedness.
>
> (1990: 302)

The organisation of space in cartoons thus becomes a substantive feature of the shot; one of the various paradigmatic options for the construction of *mise-en-scène* in its particularity, rather than *mise-en-scène* being a pre-existent system within which space is to be organised.

The playfulness of the cartoon in relation to the organisation of space is further enhanced by the different status of the frame in the cartoon as opposed to the live-action film. For example, in cartoons focus is uniform within the frame, in contrast to live action, in which, given normal focus and a centred construction (around, for example, a figure), the edges of the frame are de-emphasised. In the cartoon, then, there is typically a greater uniformity of centre and edges of the frame than in live-action film.[27] One might say, even, that in comparative terms, the frame is *decentred* in the cartoon, and this, George argues, further facilitates the 'graphic play' of the cartoon. Moreover, if the cartoon plays with its flatness, then to that extent, this flatness no longer needs to be 'managed' by the spectator, and the onus of this managing operation is therefore less upon the disparity between binocular and monocular images (as is the case in live-action film) and more upon the disparity between the (projected) 'presence' and the actual absence of the image – the index of which is the frame. As George notes, 'it is what lies beyond the boundaries of this frame that constitutes the cartoon's reaction to and play with this disparity' (1990: 305). In this respect, the cartoon calls up, and plays upon, the relation between the continuousness of the referent and the cut of the frame (a characteristic which Metz [1990] himself describes as more typical of the photograph than of the live-action film of cinema, and which, as noted in chapter 4, Barthes emphasises in his discussion of

25 However, it has recently been suggested (Curtis, 1995) that 'special effects' is a kind of animation which has become acceptable to adults. It certainly fulfils a similar function in attracting attention to the spectacular contrivances of cinema.

26 In contrast, whereas since a camera processes light in a uniform way and produces a perspectival illusion, if live-action wants to construct spatial composition which emphasizes certain graphic or pictorial elements not only over or above but as distinct from an illusion of depth, then that composition must be constructed against the constant perspectival interpretative function of the camera.

(George, 1990: 300)

27 It should be noted, however, that seeing through lenses tends to diminish depth, flattening the object field. This is especially visible in television.

the third meaning or *punctum* of the photograph. It is this 'cut' or wound which, it is suggested here, offers an alternative context of being for the cyborg, for it does not necessarily open into the already completed inclusivity of the text that King identifies but into a 'beyond'.)

In general, it is within the *mise-en-scène* provided by the background that the action of a cartoon – that which is animated – unfolds. As George notes, it is possible that any part of the screen may be used or moved in the diegesis of a cartoon, but it is typically the figure that proves to be the diegetic locus of movement – it moves, uses props, and is the agent of narrative progression.[28] Nevertheless, as noted above, the organisation of space is typically a feature of the shot, and George explores a number of graphical possibilities in terms of their consequences for the diegetic figure: lateral movement, synthetic perspective, double perspective through time, double perspective with intermediate space, and decentred space. Just one of these will be explored here, the last of those mentioned. George writes,

> A perspectivally centred composition offers a static view of an ordered space; a decentred composition offers a less 'static' and therefore potentially more 'mobile' view . . . by failing to emphasize a fixed vanishing point these compositions emphasize the edges of the frame and what potentially lies beyond them.
>
> (1990: 310)

This can be the case with the use of a scroll-background. Here, a decentred, indeterminate perspective carries the burden of the action (usually a chase at speed) to such an extent that it is not felt necessary to let the objects depicted have any other function than their formal graphic role of being objects being passed. The relationship between design and scene is not simply one of relative difference but of a veritable divorce; the image is not designed to communicate the existence of its constituent objects, but, rather, chooses to signify speed by destroying the signification of non-inconsistent space. As George wryly points out, the description of these cartoons as 'limited animation' is particularly apposite; the cartoon 'limits its acts of signification, even if this means isolating the signifier from its proper place in the structure of spatial articulation' (1990: 311). Typically, the cartoon achieves a comic effect through its play with the disparity between the laterality of its movement and the often different diegetic location of the depicted space.[29] This comedy can thus be seen as the outcome of a cut in

28 In an interview with Barry Curtis, Irene Kotlarz comments that

> People who make animated films tend to be really dedicated. There is an obsessive and almost childlike interest in making things move – which often starts in early childhood. It is essentially different from other media in that respect. Like film, it develops narratives, but unlike it, doesn't mistake the photographic for the real. It creates characters that move and often the characters participate in producing or disturbing the illusions which create them.
>
> (Quoted in Curtis, 1995: 25)

29 Kotlarz notes that

> One of the persistent gags [in animation] is the distortion or separation of parts of the body: the infinite malleability that is implied in the connections of 'stretch and squash' – in which

the spatial continuum, sometimes, I suggest, rupturing the textual inclusivity of the cartoon figure or personality.

Moreover, as George goes on to show, this cut may be effected in different ways according to different animation styles, some of which tend to emphasise poses, others stressing movement, and others still a total seamlessness where pose and 'fill' movement are indistinguishable. George writes,

> Pose-oriented animation can use extremes in outrageous, 'impossible' ways . . . or, conversely, for the punctuation of moods and 'looks' which are closely analogous to live-action . . . . Similarly, movement-oriented animation can emphasize impossible physical distortion . . . or general stylistic plasticity – [so-called] 'smear' animation . . . or else 'grace' and 'realistic' pseudo-photographic movement.
>
> (1990: 318–319)

As a consequence, George argues, the cartoon figure exemplifies the problematic of representation itself and the relation of cartoons to live-action film. Indeed, he believes there is a sense in which 'the cartoon figure is *an index* of the issues of representation' (1990: 319; my emphasis).[30]

At the same time, this indexical relation is also one in which the personality of the cartoon figure is created.[31] George writes,

> The later Daffy Duck, exemplified in genre parodies like *Duck Dodgers in the 24(1/2)th Century* (Jones, 1953), is obsessed with asserting control and mastery over a situation. He tries to be something he patently is not, a project at least analogous to the cartoon enterprise.
>
> (1990: 319)

However, the disarticulation between the decentred space and the figure is frequently depicted as a function of the movement of the figure, and in this way the space of which it is the creation may be depicted or redescribed as the figure's possession. In other words, the effect of these techniques may be such that the figure appears to motivate the animation of the picture; indeed, the way in which this reverse motivation is made visible defines the specific personality of the figure. So, for example, some characters confront issues of identity and environment by virtue of an apparent mastery, as is the case with Bugs

> bodies and things react excessively to contact, pressure and tension. It's interesting that animation is a process of bringing together individual moments in time, backgrounds and foregrounds and the work of specialized individuals. Perhaps this incessant sundering which is a feature of the films is a reaction to this determined synthesis.
>
> (1995: 27)

30 Kotlarz writes:

> so many of the concerns of animation have been with the unfilmable, or with aspects of the imagination which are hard to represent in other media. Movement itself can be rendered in evocative ways, objects and people can be deformed, metamorphosed and dismembered.
>
> (Quoted in Curtis, 1995: 25)

31 This is in line with Caillois's view that '[t]he feeling of personality' may be 'considered as the organism's feeling of distinctness from its surroundings, of the connection between consciousness and a particular point in space' (1988: 70).

Bunny's ability to be 'always in command, even in the face of gravest danger'. Others, such as Daffy Duck, confront the same issues by their inability to control events. George notes that when Bugs and Daffy are brought together in *Duck Amuck*, the competition between their characters for the ownership of space has predictable but disastrous consequences. From the beginning it is clear that the entire world of the cartoon is *not* inside the frame: every time Daffy exits and enters past the frame lines, he is forced to make repeated costume changes in a futile effort to match the constantly changing background environments. Finally,

> Bugs is revealed as the enunciator/animator, manipulating the unreal cartoon; whilst Daffy is threatened and humiliated by this very unreality – transformed into a bizarre flower-monster, he is on the margins of existence, something that is and is not Daffy.
>
> (1990: 319)

In short, the cartoon character – a figure existing on the border between person and non-person, as exemplified by the 'cartoon animal' – personifies itself through its relation to space or its environment, a mode of identification which, whilst characteristic of most comedy, is highlighted in the cartoon as a consequence of the disparity between 'actual' surface and diegetic depth.[32]

The disparity between actual surface and diegetic depth so expertly outlined here by George in relation to the classical cartoon has always been and continues to be subject to manipulation and refinement via the continuing development of animation techniques. So, for example, with the use of multiplaning, 'the surface is both fragmented and distended' and, as a consequence,

32 And it is the manipulation of this mode of identification which provides the basis for critical distinctions between not only animations but also their directors; consider, for example, the following contrast between Tex Avery and Chuck Jones:

> Avery violates the sanctity of the forward motion of a cartoon and of the frame lines with crazy arrogance – characters running out of the frame, or hauling the title back into the frame after it's passed; Jones violates the reality of the frame only as an exercise in precise logic (Daffy – and ultimately Bugs in *Duck Amuck* [1953]).
>
> (Thompson, 1980: 220)

Jones's logic is epitomised by the Road Runner series, starting in 1948 and continuing until the early 1960s, which are all about a single character, Wile E. Coyote:

> The Coyote has a self-defeating obsession: to exercise his will over the actions of a force of nature, a demiurge, an occasionally seen Road Runner bird. . . .
>
> The dichotomy of natural force (Road Runner) and active character (Coyote) is reflected at the grosser levels of *mise-en-scène*. . . . The operations of the film are effected through the Coyote. He thinks, thus he loses, doomed by his own intellectuality. He resorts to increasingly complex technology in his efforts to trap the bird, and clearly reaches a point at which his fascination with clever machinery rivals his passion for the bird. . . . Jones presents these mechanical schemes as balletic essays on the unforeseen aspects of the principles of the lever, the wheel, the inclined plane, gravity, trajectory, velocity, Newton's Laws, and Archimedes's idea that if he had a lever and a place to stand, the Coyote could make the earth fall on himself.
>
> (Thompson, 1980: 221–222)

> The irregular variation of the different planes force the spectator to abandon awareness of a specific, unitary space, and thus to embrace other explanatory frameworks – the normal photographic and, more importantly, the diegetic spatial possibilities.
>
> (George, 1990: 314)

With the advent of computer animation and the realism it makes possible, multi-planing results in 'a spectacular exhilaration' for the spectator precisely because the resulting spatial fluidity is not normally expected in a cartoon (1990: 316). But does this exhilaration mean that the cartoon animal, superhuman character or cyborg being is necessarily perceived as the owner of the space of which it might otherwise be seen as the invention? Does the spatial/textual organisation in relation to which the personality of the cyborg being is defined make impossible a negative dialectic between the totality of the text and the particularity of its performance? In short, are individuation and individualisation made one and the same in the cyborg or transformer? And does the reverse motivation of the hyper-real or super-resolved always result in the subsumption of the actual to the real (in Deleuze's terms)?

THE OPTICAL UNCONSCIOUS

A synthesis of the analyses presented in this and the previous chapter suggests that cyborg beings are figures whose personality is given by the (technologically mediated) exaggeration of ordinary and extraordinary senses to an unlimited extent. The realisation of their personality is given not so much by narrative development, which requires the ability to lay a claim of ownership of depth of character over continuous time and perspectival space, but through the ways in which figures (or shapes, or logos)[33] are able to lay claims of ownership to the

33 The following account of the creation of the licensing document for Donald Duck (the first such document to be commissioned by Disney outside the United States) indicates some of the complexities involved in the management of logos:

> Pentagram [the firm who were given this 'honour'] began with a mass of material, the product of a year-long exercise in Disney's Paris office to develop licensing ideas especially for Europe. Disney refined just who Donald was, right down to what he would do in his spare time and the colour ways of his clothes. With the global boom in licensing, it is easy to understand why such care is taken: Donald and all his Disney chums essentially exist as licensing concepts, to be applied so much more broadly than through the simple existence they once had in animation.
>
> Pentagram matched the Disney licensing ambitions with its own multi-disciplinary team . . . perhaps most important of all, the team had on hand the animator Dean Roberts, who had direct experience of working with Disney characters and was able to sketch and interpret just how Donald would look in any given situation.
>
> The resulting That's Donald manual has six themed folders packed full of artwork, patterns and product ideas. The sections take a key fact of Donald's life and interests – such as romance or sport – and lay down precise rules and parameters for licensees.
>
> 'At every stage we tried to make it interesting to use,' comments Weil. 'It would be a terrible thing for other designers to have to work with if you had somehow taken all the fun out of Donald . . . after all, we are exploring a common experience.'
>
> (Blackwell, 1995: 33, 35)

surface spaces of which they are an invention in the no-time of the decisive moment. That they may be able to do so at all is because of the technically enhanced ability offered by digitalisation to allow multiple analytic interventions into a space that is created in the disruption of temporality by the 0/1 dimension. However, these interventions are typically represented as the realisation of the exaggerated senses of personalities; the potential of prosthetic culture is here realised in the performance of the figures themselves. In this way, the reversed motivation of digital imagery makes possible an attribution of personality to the cyborg. The personality of such figures is not manifest in biographies as such, but rather is made visible in figures or images[34] through a process of technically enhanced resolution. Indeed, cyborgs can be seen as emblems of 'the drive towards perfectibility or super-resolution in the image, its hyper-reality' (King, 1989: 127). But is this personality, as the consequence of super-resolution, without interruption, disturbance? Can it alternatively be seen as performance in transition, as a *passage*?

One consequence of super-resolution would seem to be not simply the loss of dimensionality but also the absence of an unconscious which might interfere with the drive towards perfectibility. So, for example, for King, the being of the cyborg – its intentionality – does not, apparently, predate its entry into the symbolic, but is, rather, constituted without a repressed, a residue or an outside, *ab initio*. (As Ross [1990] notes, Max Headroom's first sounds – 'Mama . . . mama . . . mama . . . max' – suggest that he is an infant whose life can only begin when his cries for a mother are transmuted into a self-reference.) This existential completeness, his self-envelopedness, serves to underpin the fact that the cyborg is a creature of organised (logical) thought. Such thought may be reductive, King observes, but it is complete within its own parameters.[35]

34 Logos or image-properties are exemplary instances of their manifestation.

35 To further support his point that cyborgs do not have an unconscious, he gives the apparent contra-example of the cyborg figure, Robocop, who has a 'repressed' unconscious; but this unconscious, as King (1989: 126) points out, is not original to cybernetic being: it is constituted in relation to the memory of its human raw materials, Police Officer Murphy. A similar line of argument could be used to explain how it was that some of the witnesses to the abduction of James Bulger acquired post-traumatic stress counselling *after* they had viewed what they had previously witnesssed by accessing the memory banks of the shopping mall cameras which had recorded his abduction. In his discussion of the issue of representation in relation to television, Stephen Heath suggests a possible explanation for this by identifying the way in which television constitutes 'viewers as audience as receptive capacity'. He argues that it is a mistake to think of this receptive capacity in terms of traditional notions of the individual subject. Instead viewers as receptive capacity need to be seen as part of 'the achieved distribution of a network'. He quotes from the description of the audience participation method developed by the producer and presenter of the West German *Aktenzeichen XY . . . Ungelost* (from which *America's Most Wanted* and Britain's *Crimewatch UK* both derive):

> The method used is reminiscent of the operation of an electronic data-bank from which extraordinarily precise information can be called up in an extremely short time. . . . And the receptive capaciy of millions of human minds, which can be checked at one and the same time with the help of the television screen, could be considerably greater than that of an equally powerful electronic robot.
>
> (Quoted in Heath, 1990: 277)

While King recognises that Max Headroom has a memory, this memory is found wanting; it is only a 'data bank memory'; it is a storehouse – an archive even – of already completed backstories, prosthetic biographies, already given arcs or movements between past and present.[36] Max does not suffer, as Lyotard (1991) requires, from 'the burden' of his memory. More generally, King argues, the forms of cultural production in contemporary conditions tend to take as their aesthetic principle an echoic play on the codes and formats of the image memory bank of Hollywood and its satellites:

> It is as though the process of commercial concentration within the industry itself, evidenced by the rise of conglomerates, had somehow entailed a similar concentration in the area of the symbolic. The creation of derivative and multi-media products is a function of the same movement: the popular TV film is a spin-off of a popular movie; the plaything or the phonograph record continually reawakens a chain of association, definitively blurring the division between infrastructure and superstructure in a vast syndrome of repetition.[37]
>
> (Mattelart, quoted in King, 1989: 136)

Thus, for King, Max Headroom's memory is within the text too; it is not constituted in relation to an unconscious.[38] There has been no repression in relation to

Heath continues his analysis by considering the remarks of the presenters of *Crimewatch UK*, who assert that 'for some extraordinary reason [but then not so extraordinary] . . . people only believe their experiences when they see something on *Crimewatch*'. Heath wryly points out that 'of course, what you see on *Crimewatch* is primarily television: a quarter of a million crimes are reported per month in Britain, but "it is remarkably difficult to find three crimes worthy of reconstruction"' (1990: 277). This last remark suggests that the distinction between human and network memory is not as clear-cut as King implies.

36 As another commentator notes,

> Another characteristic of animators and animation is an acute and expert awareness of the archive. Animation studios tend to keep libraries of diverse material for reference. . . . One of the tasks of commercial animation is to animate ideas which often start out as highly subjective and personal – finding a kind of identikit for vague perceptions and propositions. This is often an aspect of the development of character which can incorporate existing cartoon characters or real people; the history of animation is full of anecdotes of the incorporation and transformation of people into cartoons. It can also involve lengthy deliberations with agents, witnesses, or self over how some imaginary entity looked or moved.
>
> (Kotlarz, quoted in Curtis, 1995: 26)

37 The Getty family recently purchased the Hulton Deutsch Collection (owned for the past thirty years by the BBC), one of the world's most famous photographic portfolios. Mark Getty is reported to have said, 'We are committed to building a major international business as providors of high quality visual content. The Hulton will enhance the group's ability to satisfy the growing demand for imagery which is being accelerated by developments in global communications' (quoted in *The Irish Independent*, 3 April 1996, p. 1). The purchase brings Getty Communications into competition with Bill Gates, the computer billionaire, who is the owner of the Bettmann Archive, based in New York. On purchasing the archive, Gates announced plans to adapt photographs ranging from the *Hindenburg* disaster to Marilyn Monroe's billowing skirt to a 'pay-per-view' system for home computers.

38 Stephen Heath and Gillian Skirrow (1977) have argued that television operates as the 'absence of memory' in its continual stress upon the 'nowness' of its own discourse – unlike film, which tends

which repetition might be understood in a psychoanalytic sense. The moment of photographic exposure, as it were, is not drained of its presentness by the interrupted durations of a past which cannot be included. There is nothing of its past which the cyborg cannot recollect, nothing exteriorised by a boundary or frame. There is nothing irrecoverable in this act of repetition. Or as Morse notes, 'Benjamin might say that the loss of aura associated with electronic reproduction is a function of its inability to *endure*' (1990: 227). At the same time, however, this inability is precisely its limitless potential, its all-inclusiveness; it is what ensures the aim meets its target (even if that target is moving).

Further doubt on the possibility of a cyborg unconscious is provided by Rosalind Krauss's discussion of Walter Benjamin's notion of the optical unconscious in relation to surrealism. She suggests that 'we' will 'of course' be struck by the 'strangeness of the analogy' between the optical and the psychoanalytic unconscious (1994: 178). She asks, 'Can the optical field – the world of visual phenomena: clouds, sea, sky, forest – *have* an unconscious?' (1994: 179). She is, just about, willing to accede to an interpretation of the unconscious which presupposes a collective rather than an individual being (although she recognises this possibility as an element of Benjamin's thought, she herself does not seem to give the notion of a collective unconscious much credence), but not an unconscious that does not clearly originate in or belong to an entirely organic subject at all. She writes,

> If it [the optical unconscious] can be spoken of at all as externalised within the visual field, this is because a group of disparate artists have so constructed it there, constructing it as a projection of the way that human vision can be thought to be less than a master of all it surveys, in conflict as it is with what is internal to the organism that houses it.
>
> (1994: 179–180)

It seems that it is the unconscious of the 'I'/eye of psychoanalysis that Krauss identifies here in the 'writing' in the texts of surrealism:[39] her use of language, of 'externalisation', of 'projection' and 'the organism', indicates that, for her, the (optical) unconscious can only be located in relation to a desiring, bounded (albeit internally divided) sentient being or organism, not a cyborg.

The strangeness, for Krauss, of the analogy between the optical unconscious and the psychoanalytic unconscious seems to stem from her view that the unconscious is a structure that presupposes a sentient being – an organism – within which it operates, and with whose consciousness it is in conflict. In this respect, Krauss appears to insist upon the bodily unity, integrity and incorruptibility of the bearer of the (optical) unconscious. The organically embodied being

towards instantaneous memory ('everything is absent, everything is *recorded* – as a memory trace which is so at once, without ever having been before'). The recorded material television uses, they suggest, is instituted as actual in the production of the television image *vis-à-vis* a generalised fantasy of 'live broadcasting'.

39 Krauss begins her book with a line from Jules Laforgue – 'The optical arts spring from the eye and solely from the eye': the question her argument raises is with what 'I' is this 'eye' constituted in a metonymic relation?

provides the basis, for her, of the only conceivable subject of representation. However, this is also a subject which, as discussed in the previous chapter, is premised upon the refusal of the possibility of mimesis – a process which would have to be interpreted by Krauss as an instance of the image's ability to deceive the (already given) subject of representation. (In the incredulity she expresses in relation to the possibility of an optical field having an unconscious, Krauss seems to display a fear of the image as somehow inherently deceptive. In her fear of the power of the image, she lets a universalising conception of the subject as already complete slip in [Doane, 1985].) Consequently, Krauss's conception of the optical unconscious, as she herself notes, is 'at an angle' to Benjamin's.

Is it possible to identify other ways of theorising the I/eye of the optical unconscious? For Virilio, what characterises the replacement of the depth of space by the depth of time afforded by digitalisation is a splitting of viewpoint, the sharing of perception of the environment between the animate (the living subject) and the inanimate (the object, the seeing machine). The vision of this viewpoint, its visualisations, are 'what is already there' in the eye of cameras installed in banks, leisure centres, at traffic lights, alongside motorways, in shopping malls, remaining in 'a state of *latent immediacy* in the huge junk heap of stuff of memory, wanting to reappear, inexorably, when the time comes' (1994: 43). Its images are not in suspense, but have the status of surprise; they are what Virilio calls an 'accidental transfer' (1994: 64), a consequence of 'drift' (Barthes, 1981). But what does it mean to say that these transfers are accidental? That they do not necessarily follow the pathways of displacement and condensation of the unconscious of the psychoanalytic subject (although it should be noted that Freud referred to Francis Galton's composite images in explaining his notion of condensation) does not necessarily mean that they do not operate in relation to the workings of an unconscious at all.[40] As Edward Casey writes,

> What is memory-laden exceeds the scope of the human: memory takes us into the environing world as well as into our individual lives.
>
> (1985: ix)

Perhaps, then, the latent immediacy of memory banks has the capacity to disturb the pre-mediation of the already completed personality.

To explore this possibility, it is worth considering the passage in the essay 'The

40 Adopting another 'angle' to that taken by Krauss, it is interesting to note that, for Benjamin, the being which the optical unconscious presupposes is not entirely an organism, but may be a body – of sorts – innervated by technology. As Miriam Hansen records, whether or not Benjamin took the term 'innervation' directly from Freud or from French psychoanalytic discourse of the period, his use is clearly related to Freud's adoption of the term to describe a 'physiological process: the transmission, generally in an efferent direction, of energy along a nerve pathway' (quoted in Hansen, 1993b: 56). However, in his use of the term, Benjamin extends these pathways, in line with Helmholtz's description of nerve pathways as telegraph lines, to include technology as 'an organ of the collective' (quoted in Hansen, 1993b: 38). It is in relation to this technological extension of the body that an optical unconscious other than that of the psychoanalytic subject may be identified.

work of art in the age of mechanical reproduction' in which Benjamin introduces the notion of an optical unconscious in some detail. He writes,

> Our taverns and city streets, our offices and furnished rooms, our train stations and factories appeared to have us locked up beyond hope. Then came film and exploded this prison-world with the dynamite of one-tenth seconds, so that now, in the midst of its far-flung ruins and debris, we calmly embark on adventurous travels. With the close-up, space expands; with slow motion, movement is extended. Thus it becomes evident that it is a different nature that speaks to the camera than speaks to the naked eye. Different above all, because an unconsciously permeated space substitutes for a space consciously explored by human beings . . . . [The camera] introduces us to the optical unconscious as does psychoanalysis to unconscious impulses.
>
> (1970: 238)

As Miriam Hansen (1987) points out, the object of such revelation is at once redemptive for Benjamin – in enscripting the mundane milieux of everyday life – and critical – in destroying the conventional perspectives that have reified natural and social arrangements. Moreover, it seems that, in Benjamin's view, film not only makes visible a space which has hitherto been invisible to the human eye (the infinite space which the super-resolved cyborg claims as its own), it also registers aspects of psycho-perceptual reality that only emerged, historically, with modern technology.[41] Perhaps, by adopting, adapting and extending Benjamin's perspective, the cyborg – an exemplary hybrid being – can be seen as the bearer of an optical unconscious?

This possibility may be explored by reconsidering the nature of the performance that is brought forth by reverse motivation. Hansen points out that in an early version of the famous 'work of art' essay, Benjamin elaborates on the changes that the mediation through the cinematic apparatus has visited upon the phenomenology of performance. In a significant respect, he takes a position diametrically opposed to the later version which has become better known: in the screen actor's confrontation with the apparatus, the audience is constructed as identifying not with the testing, critical, impersonal attitude of the camera (as in the later version), but with the actor as 'their stand-in, as a representative of their own daily battle with an alienating technology who takes "revenge in their

41 Another example of this in Benjamin's work is to be found in his discussions of surrealism. In an interesting discussion of this work, John McCole highlights what he sees as the difference between Benjamin's notion of the optical unconscious and the unconscious of psychoanalysis:

> Among the quintessential surrealist experiences was the perception that certain objects, configurations, and places in the waking world sometimes appear to be surrounded by a mysterious shimmer, a haunting quality that hints at a deeper reality, a 'sur-reality' . . . in pursuing such experiences, Benjamin asserted, the surrealists were 'following the traces not so much of the soul as of things' themselves. . . . Paradoxical though it may sound, he looked to the surrealists for a nonpsychological concept of dreamwork. In Benjamin's conception, dreams were not keys to individual psychic conflicts; rather, they were a medium in which an essential dimension of the transpersonal human relationship to the object world was enacted.
>
> (1993: 215)

place"'. In this mimetic identification, gestures and emotions are enlarged the way reality is enlarged by the camera lens:

> The actor's forced self-alienation in front of the camera, microphones, and klieg lights, the extreme presence of mind required in the absence of the aura of live performance, shows the masses how 'one's humanity' (or whatever may appear to them as such) can assert itself in the face of the apparatus.
>
> (Benjamin, quoted in Hansen, 1993a: 43)

As Hansen comments, Benjamin appears to be suggesting here that what humanity, being human, means in the twentieth century can be redefined through the performance of self-alienation, a self-alienation which is mediated by the apparatus of cinema: 'in the representation of human beings through the apparatus human self-alienation has found a most productive realization' (Benjamin, quoted in Hansen, 1993a: 43). For Benjamin, then, the performance of character in the camera's I/eye is neither completely inscribed in the text (as King implies), nor is it located in the sentient organism (as Krauss would appear to suggest), but rather is constituted in a two-way (reversible, reciprocal but not symmetrical) relation of mimesis between the image and the viewer.

This possibility is also given some support by Barthes's analysis of 'the photographic look', by which he means the look in the eyes of whoever is being photographed, not the viewer's gaze; in other words, the gaze is entrusted to the operation of the photographic apparatus. Barthes writes,

> One might say the Photograph separates attention from perception, and yields up only the former, even if it is impossible without the latter; this is that aberrant thing, *noesis* without *noeme*, an action of thought, an aim without a target. And yet it is this scandalous movement which produces the rarest quality of an air.
>
> (1981: 111)

Or again, this time in relation to a specific example, he writes,

> It is because the look, eliding the vision, seems held back by something interior. The poor boy who holds a newborn puppy against his cheek (Kertesz, 1928), looks into the lens with his sad, jealous, fearful eyes: what pitiable, lacerating pensiveness! In fact he is looking at nothing; he *retains* within himself his love and his fear: that is the Look.
>
> (1981: 113)

The look, then, is the presence within the photograph of that which addresses me without seeing me. This is a look that has an aim, but is without a target; it is not the targeted gaze of a sight-line. It is a way of seeing that does not make the visible. It holds the viewer but does not arrest him or her. It is the result of a retention, latent immediacy, an 'intense immobility' (1981: 49), an implosion of the photograph within itself, an index or trace of the optical unconscious.

In order to explore this 'impossibility' further it is worth returning to Barthes's description of the *punctum* yet again. As noted earlier, Barthes describes the *punctum* as a 'tiny detail' that 'has, more or less potentially, a power of expansion. This power is metonymic' (1981: 45), a power which stems from what, in his early writings on photography, Barthes calls the third meaning of the photograph. This is created when the denotative or continuous message of the photograph is cut into by its connotative message (1977: 19–20). It is not the always already filled meaning of reverse motivation 'which comes ahead' but is created in the metonymy of accidental transfer as it opens *obtusely* 'onto the field of meaning totally, that is, infinitely' (1977: 55). This third meaning of the *punctum* 'can accommodate a certain latency (but never any scrutiny)' (1981: 53). It may take the form of 'the scandal, the supplement, the drift' (1977: 54). Defining obtuseness variously as blunted, rounded in form and greater than the 'right angle' of meaningful narrative, Barthes hints here at the open productivity of the 0/1 dimension of time. As Jay writes in his thoughtful interpretation of Barthes,

> Resisting metalinguistic translation, outside the circuits of semantic exchange, not a copy of anything in the real world, obtuse meaning was visual counternarrative: 'disseminated, reversible, set to its own temporality . . . counterlogical and yet "true"'.
>
> (1994: 444)

The *punctum* is a cut in the spatial continuum, time travel in the 0/1 dimension with no expectation of return, 'an aim without a target'. It resounds with 'exhausted time', a time which knows neither present nor future, neither a turning away nor a getting there; a meeting 'not forgotten, not recollected, but gathered into forgetfulness, yet without becoming one's own' (von Amelunxen, 1994: 21).[42]

In these ways, then, both Benjamin and Barthes allow for the possibility that reverse motivation produces not simply a self-referential system,[43] but a cyborg

42 A complementary notion of time is offered by John Berger in his interpretation of Cartier-Bresson's photographs. He writes,

> Think of taking a corner fast on a bike. You lean into it. Imagine that time, instead of flowing straight, takes corners too. Nobody usually notices. The corners are invisible. But Cartier-Bresson's great photos are about time banking, leaning over as it takes corners. The way he makes us see round the side of time.
>
> (1995: 20)

43 The cyborg is thus not only the outcome of self-reference or testing. As Adorno remarks, the notion of 'testing' that Benjamin sometimes advocated can seem pseudo-scientific. In Adorno's view, this indicates that Benjamin did not reflect deeply enough on how some of the categories he proposed are imbricated with the commodity character his theory opposes. However, Benjamin does not always lose sight of their interconnection. In a footnote to the essay 'The work of art in the age of mechanical reproduction', he writes,

> the expansion of the field of the testable which mechanical equipment brings about for the actor corresponds to the extraordinary expansion of the field of the testable brought about for the individual through economic conditions. Thus, vocational aptitude tests become constantly more important. What matters in these tests are segmental performances of the individual. The film shot and the vocational aptitude test are taken before a committee of experts. The camera director in the studio occupies a place identical with that of the examiner during aptitude tests.
>
> (1970: 248)

being with an optical unconscious that is neither that of the machine of vision nor, indeed, that of the embodied individual. The cyborg being is the effect neither of internalisation and inclusivity of the object-image identified by King, nor of the relations of transference, projection and externalisation of a desiring subject described by Krauss, but of a relation between the two, of co-mingling, of contact and copy, of mimesis. For Benjamin, as Gertrude Koch argues, the immobilisation of time in the spatial image allows a corpus to emerge 'out of the anthropologically untenably constructed body, explosively liberated into the image of the "heavenly" from the space of the "optical-unconscious"' (1994: 213).[44]

CYBORG HUMOUR

The mimetic character of the technological animation of the corpus of the cyborg described by Benjamin is not so surprising if one considers Freud's discussion of innervation in relation to the comic. As Rey Chow has pointed out, for Freud the problem of the comic exists 'quite apart from any communication'. It is a quantitative matter, a question of energy, of movement. In the following

44 An alternative response by Benjamin to the question of the being appropriate to the modern world is 'the destructive character'. This 'character' is one who has accepted the mimetic invitation offered by nature to the artificial:

> The destructive character knows only one watchword: make room; only one activity: clearing away. His need for fresh air and open space is stronger than any hatred.
>
> (1985: 157)

Benjamin describes here the faceless model of a positively conceived characterlessness, since as Wohlfarth notes, the 'destructive character' is no 'character' in the psychological sense – it has no personal character traits; rather, character is one of its targets.

> What the inverted commas around the 'destructive character' mark off is less a literal quotation – the phrase is not a standard one – than a summary translation of prattle into language calculated to reduce it to silence. . . . An older notion of character is cited in order to clear away misconceptions. The *bourgeois* character had flourished between the eras of the old subject and the new predicate. Their conjunction marks its withering away. The destructive character expropriates 'possessive individualism'.
>
> (Wohlfarth, 1994: 159)

The destructive character not only has 'no interest in being understood' but 'being misunderstood cannot harm him. On the contrary he provokes it' (Benjamin, 1985: 158).

Benjamin suggests that the destructive character is 'always blithely at work', but does not need the inspiration of vision, since his tempo is dictated by nature, indirectly at least, 'for he must forestall her. Otherwise she will take over the destruction herself' (1985: 157). This, then, is blind imitation or destructive mimesis: 'The destructive character sees nothing permanent. But for that reason he sees ways everywhere' (1985: 158). There is no guarantee, however, that the individual, once rid of inwardness, will, instead of becoming a hollow person, 'let go of himself . . . in the right way' (Wohlfarth, 1994: 171). There is only the destructive character's secret: he can continue to clear space because he never fills up:

> The destructive character is young and cheerful. For destroying rejuvenates in clearing away the traces of our own age; it cheers because everything cleared away means to the destroyer a complete reduction, indeed, eradication, of his own condition.
>
> (1985: 157)

long quotation, Freud outlines his view that the comic is an 'ideational mimetics' that involves 'somatic innervation'. He suggests that as one tries out the very shape of perception in one's own body; the physiology of the body is driven by percepts, and even ideational activity, not only perception, involves such embodying – hence 'ideational mimetics':

> In 'trying to understand', therefore, in apperceiving this movement [the comic], I make a certain expenditure, and in this portion of the mental process I behave exactly as though I were putting myself in the place of the person I am observing. But at the same moment, probably, I bear in mind the aim of this movement, and my earlier experience enables me to estimate the scale of expenditure required for reaching that aim. In doing so I disregard the person whom I am observing and behave as though I myself wanted to reach the aim of the movement. These two possibilities in my imagination amount to a comparison between the observed movement and my own. If the other person's movement is exaggerated and inexpedient, my increased expenditure in order to understand it is inhibited in *statu nascendi*, as it were in the act of being mobilized. . . . ; it is declared superfluous and is free for use elsewhere or perhaps for discharge by laughter. This would be the way in which, other circumstances being favourable, pleasure in a comic movement is generated – an innervatory expenditure which has become an unusable surplus when a comparison is made with a movement of one's own. . . . The comic effect apparently depends . . . on the difference [*Differenz*] between the two cathectic expenditures – one's own and the other person's – as estimated by 'empathy' – and not on which of the two the difference favours. But this peculiarity, which at first sight confuses our judgement, vanishes when we bear in mind that a restriction of our muscular work and an increase in our intellectual work fit in with the course of our personal development toward a higher level of civilization. By raising our intellectual expenditure we can achieve the same result with a diminished expenditure of our movements. Evidence of this cultural success is provided by our machines.
>
> (Freud, 1963, quoted in Chow, 1992: 111–112, 106)

This seems to suggest that for Freud the comic is that which makes apparent a human being's dependence on bodily needs and social situations, the mimetic response to which is a discharge of the unutilised surplus of energy left over from the difference between the 'cathectic expenditures' of the observer and the observed, between estimating or aiming at and meeting the target. Machines or technology are another response to this dependence in so far as they are also a manipulation of the discrepancy of the two cathectic expenditures. (In this context, Moholy-Nagy's claim for the comic potential of photography – its new wit – and the presence of humour in cartoons are unsurprising developments.) But technological development does not necessarily have as its function the aim of diminishing our level of expenditure or overcoming the difference between human and machine – prosthesis as completion; it may also be developed to increase that expenditure, to make productive or intensify those differences –

prosthesis as supplement. Cyborg humour does not depend on which of the two – one's own or the other person/machine's – the difference favours.[45]

However, machines are intimately tied not only, as Chow points out, to the comic, but also to the hierarchical structuring of relations between observer and observed, spectator and spectacle, for the moment of visualisation/realisation has historically coincided with the production of the automatised body as spectacular excess. She writes,

> the moment the 'human body' is 'released' into the field of vision is also the moment when it is made excessive and dehumanized. This excess is the *mise-en-scène* of modernity *par excellence.*
>
> (1992: 107)

Chow further argues that this hierarchical structuring has been gendered in so far as the automatised mobility of the spectacularised other has been organised within a frame of scopophilia which produces a psychic density for the male subject.[46] She argues that this masculinity is presumed and shared by Freud in that he adopts a view of the camera as a mechanised eye. Benjamin, as noted above, however, shifts his analysis between the two, from the actor or spectacularised other to the camera or mechanised eye.

Furthermore, Benjamin also believes that in the historical task of making self-alienation productive, the cartoon figure – exemplified by Mickey Mouse – has certain advantages over the screen actor. While the actor remains (less and less!) tied to a realistic imaging of the human shape and thus can be naturalised and fetishised in the cult of the star, the cartoon figure does not lend itself, in principle at least, to a false restoration of the aura. According to Hansen, the appeal of the animated creature for Benjamin owes much to its hybrid status, its blurring of human and animal, two-dimensional and three-dimensional, corporeal and neuro-energetic qualities (1993b: 44). However, as Hansen goes on to point out, this was not a view shared by Adorno; indeed, it was not a view of which Benjamin himself was entirely convinced. For Adorno, the identification encouraged by the cinematic star, whether living or animated, was one in which the subject takes pleasure in his or her own mutilation, yet without consciousness, identifying with the sadistic principle operating in alienated technology. It is the 'iron bath of fun' administered by the culture industry.[47] And certainly the possibility that digitalisation may allow the creation of a cyborg being that has its own optical unconscious does not undermine the force of King's arguments in rela-

45 For an illuminating explication of cyborg/cartoon humour, see Bruno Latour's analysis, 'A door must be either open or shut: a little philosophy of techniques' (1995).

46 See Linda Williams's discussion of 'Corporealized observers: visual pornographies and the "carnal density of vision"' (1995) for an interesting historical analysis of the gendered dimensions of the erotic uses of the interchange between the body and the machines of vision at the end of the nineteenth and the beginning of the twentieth centuries.

47 As Seltzer notes,

> At the end of *Beyond the Pleasure Principle* in which Freud retells the story of the *fort–da* game, he adds a 'reminder' which, as he puts it, 'is of no use for our purposes'. . . . The useless reminder concerns the 'artistic play and artistic imitation carried out by adults': 'these scenes, aimed at an audience, do not spare the spectators (for instance, in tragedy) the most painful

tion to the likely development and uses of this technology. Disney's press agents, for example, coined the term 'imagineering', which carries its own associations of imagination and engineering, of art and mechanics.

Nevertheless, while Chow acknowledges the historical significance of the structuring of the cinematic gaze at the automated body, she also recognises that it does not have necessarily to be either gendered or hierarchical. Indeed, she argues that feminists working in the First World, such as Kristeva and Haraway, seek to animate the automaton by seeing it through their eyes. She writes of First World feminism that

> It retains the notion of the automaton – the mechanical doll – but changes its fate by giving it life with another look. This is the look of the feminist critic. Does her power of animation take us back to the language of God, a superior being who bestows life upon an inferior? Or is it the power of a woman who bears the history of her own dehumanization on her as she speaks for other women? The idealism of First World feminism would have us believe the latter. The mythical being of this idealism is the 'cyborg', that half-machine, half-animal creature, at once committed and transgressive, spoken of by Donna Haraway.
>
> (1992: 110)

Chow is both supportive and critical of this view,[48] indicating that it must be put to work in tandem with other women, who are the automatons (and have their own looks) as both object and subject, observer and observed.

CONCLUSION

The thesis proposed in this chapter is that the emergence of prosthetic culture has been enabled by the widespread use of seeing photographically to facilitate a re-entry into the continuum of space as an environment of the possessive individual's choosing; not only to move between immersion in and distantiation from the object but to experiment with the effects of so doing. This re-entry is focused through a specific temporality, that is, retrodictive transformation or reversed motivation in the 0/1 dimension of time. These are the visual components of the contemporary manifestations of the processes of outcontextualisation and indifferentiation described in the first and second chapters. As noted in these

experiences and can yet be felt by them as highly enjoyable'. The attraction to scenes of violence 'aimed at' the spectator is for Freud an 'aesthetic' matter (its consideration 'should be undertaken by some system of aesthetics') and is no way 'beyond' the pleasure principle, since 'there are ways and means of making what is itself unpleasurable into a subject to be recollected and worked over in the mind'. But it is perhaps the ways and means of making unpleasurable things into a subject, in the other but here pointedly revoked sense of the term, that the subjection to scenes of imitation and representation intimates.

(1993: 95)

48 Chow argues that the idealism of First World feminism needs to be moderated by Third World feminists, who argue that it is not a question 'of asserting power as women alone, but of showing how the concern for women is inseparable from other types of cultural oppression and negotiation' (1992: 111).

chapters, prosthetic culture is that culture whose members – whether these be individuals, systems, parts of whatever kind – are constituted by their ability to lay claim retrospectively to the effects of 'how to' knowledge or technical competence as if it was their own. In this last chapter, it has been argued that the temporality of the photographic image has acquired an increasing significance in extending the terms of these claims as a consequence of digitalisation; prosthetic culture is thus held to be in danger of being reduced to the dimension of the present in which we live the future of hindsight.

However, while this hindsight is not aimless, is does not always meet its target; the future is not only the past perfected. Cyborgs may be constituted in a reversed motivation, but this may be an imitation that is blind, having no 'latent perfection-seeking homeostasis'; cyborgs may return our gaze with a blinking stare, rebel, somehow, against the coming of the future perfect. Their likeness may be the consequence not of an all-inclusive performance, but of an 'uninhibited polyphenomenality of display' (Rabinow, 1992: 249).[49] It may be helpful, furthermore, in elaborating the notion of the optical unconscious revealed by the technologically recharged faculty of mimesis, to return to the issue of temporality. As noted earlier (in chapter 1), for Benjamin, mimesis, the perception of similarity, always occurs in a flash: 'It slips past [and] can possibly be regained, but cannot really be held fast, unlike other perceptions. It offers itself to the eye as fleetingly and transitorily as a constellation of stars' (quoted in Taussig, 1993: 40). As a consequence of the optical unconscious, the image projects a meaning forwards without a target towards a future that is still open, incomplete. Whereas, for Freud, flashes of recognition, dreams and symptoms refer to truths about the waking world, these truths lie in interpreting past conflicts. In contrast, for Benjamin, the flash of recognition is to come in a future moment of awakening; in this flash, the power of the image, the 'action of thought', will be recognised.[50] As McCole writes,

49 Paul Rabinow draws on Dagognet, a French philosopher of the sciences, to argue that Euro-American societies continue to be constrained by a residual naturalism, an imitation of nature that misleadingly venerates nature because as 'that which is' it is believed to contain an internal principle of generation (indeed, I would suggest that it is this veneration which underpins the current adoption of homeostatic models in the notion of autopoiesis). Nature itself, however, is not natural in this sense; rather, it is a blind bricoleur. Rabinow writes,

> Once [nature is] understood in this way, the only natural thing to do would be to facilitate, encourage and accelerate its unfurling – thematic variation, not rigor mortis.
>
> (1992: 249)

Rabinow continues by quoting Dagognet: 'Either one adopts a sort of veneration before the immensity of "that which is" or one accepts the possibility of manipulation' (1992: 249). Nature's malleability demonstrates an invitation to the artificial; and, as Rabinow suggests, that this invitation – to take after nature – contains both the will to dominate and to discipline as well as the urge to 'unfurl' is inevitable. As Elaine Scarry observes,

> To be sure, some instances of bodily inscription *are* negative. But it cannot be the fact of inscription itself that is the problem since this describes all of culture. If our artifacts do not act on us, there is no point in having made them.
>
> (1994: 97)

> Freud came to believe that any release from the compulsions of the past remains tentative, fragile and conditional. For Benjamin, the ties of historical continuity were already being irrevocably broken; this rupture was a social given, a point of departure rather than a willful act of psychic repression. He may have sought out tentative moments of awakening in the past. But he felt sure that if the relationship between past and present was to become anything more than the permanence of catastrophe, it would have to take the form of a break or reversal as dramatic as waking from sleep.
>
> (1993: 295)

What this chapter has sought to suggest is that the reversal of motivation made possible by digitalisation does not necessarily take away but may rather enhance the possibility of the power of the image to produce such a break, such a reversal, such a future. The photograph may yet 'give the moment a posthumous shock' (Benjamin, quoted in von Amelunxen, 1994) or, as Barthes would have it, waken intractable reality.

50 As Barthes writes,

> the *punctum* should be revealed only after the fact, when the photograph is no longer in front of me and I think back on it. I may know better a photograph I remember than a photograph I am looking at.
>
> (1981: 53)

Deleuze adopts a related view when he argues that

> Culture endows consciousness with a new faculty which is apparently opposed to the faculty of forgetting: memory. But the memory with which we are concerned here is not the memory of traces. This original memory is no longer a function of the past, but a function of the future. It is not the memory of the sensibility but of the will. . . . It is the faculty of promising, commitment to the future, memory of the future itself. Remembering the promise that has been made is not recalling that it was made at a particular past moment, but that one must hold to it at a future moment.
>
> (1993: 246)

9

THE ETHICS OF SEEING PHOTOGRAPHICALLY

> I am the reference of every photograph, and this is what generates my astonishment in addressing myself to the fundamental question: why is it that I am alive *here and now*?
>
> (Roland Barthes, 1981: 84)

POTENTIAL AND PROSTHETIC CULTURE

This book has introduced the idea that we are seeing the emergence of a prosthetic culture, a culture in which *potential* is a defining relation of self-identity. However, the aim and direction of this potential are not defined in advance of the identity they make possible. Rather, the converse is true, that is, aim and direction are determined in retrospect on the basis of a successful claim to some event or action as the outcome of potential. (In this sense, potential can be seen as a temporally and spatially specific form of capability.) Furthermore, it is not necessary, for this claim to the ownership of potential to be successful, for it to refer to the subjective dimensions of the self or to be tied to the articulation of intended aims or desires. Potential is thus not to be understood in relation to an enduring set of personal characteristics, the subjective depth, interior qualities or intentionality of the individual as made possible by the adoption of narrative techniques of the self. Rather it is the retrospective claiming of the effects of actions that are the outcome of the *extension* of self by means of others, an extension that may involve both humans and non-humans, subjects and objects, things and ideas. The notion of extension is thus at the heart of prosthetic cultures and the self-identities it makes possible.

The book has sought to explore how one set of extensions may function to create self-identities such as the artefactual person (Seltzer, 1993) by focusing on photography. The assumptions here were that photography, more than merely representing, has contributed to the emergence of a way of seeing, and that this way of seeing informs contemporary self-understandings. Indeed, it was argued that it is a consequence, in part, of the adoption of this way of seeing that capability has come to be disassociated from intention, consciousness and embodiment and made available for possession on new terms. So, for example, in the discussion of contemporary portraiture (chapters 3 and 4) it was noted that the processes of individualisation and individuation have become ever more closely intertwined, and that as 'willful artifice' is made into 'necessary contrivance' (Wills, 1995), technologically mediated likeness has become a resource to be used in the display of 'interiority without intimacy' (Barthes, 1981) and is manipulated in projects of self-identity that are evaluated in terms of a/effectivity.

Two processes were identified as especially important in this role of the photographic image as perceptual prosthesis: *outcontextualisation* and *indifferentiation.* The first is a consequence of the way in which the recognition of the frame that is part of seeing photographically has encouraged a view of the object as if in a spatial continuum, that is, as if it could be seen from all positions at once. This promotes a perception of the object as not simply decontextualised but as outcontextualised. In short, the power of the photographic image is such that it has encouraged an arbitrary relation to context (Hayles, 1987). Indifferentiation is the term adopted here to describe the filling in of the gap of motivation between cause and effect, subject and object, made possible by the photograph's freezing of movement. It is recognised in our everyday confusion as to whether what it is that the photograph depicts is best described as its subject or object. This freezing – made aesthetically productive in Cartier-Bresson's notion of the decisive instant – produces the 'no-time-at-all' in which the camera's aperture may, as it were, be held open and its holdings be made available for manipulation, transformation and appropriation. In the context of the genre of portraiture, the decisive instant is thus the entry point into the loop in time that inaugurates what Barthes (1981) describes as the advent-ure of the self-as-other.

Indeed, this loop was identified as the key locus of advent-ure for the self who sees photographically, and is what provides a complex twist to the possibilities of capability, risk or daring-do that are part of what has been called reflexive modernisation (Beck *et al.*, 1994). The successful circumnavigation of this loop both requires and makes possible the emergence of what was described as the experimental individual. This is the individual who, in making decisions, is made by them. It was also argued (in chapter 4) that the adoption of this loop as a locus of experimentation has been facilitated by the emergence of a survivalist ethos (Bauman, 1992) in which death itself is represented as a matter of decision-making. This ethos makes it possible to believe that an answer can be found to the question Barthes is forced to ask by the photographic image: 'why is it that I am alive *here and now*?'

In chapters 7 and 8, it was argued further that because digitalisation enables a more systematic exploitation of this moment or decisive instant, it has greatly expanded the significance of seeing photographically for self-identity. It opens up the 0/1 dimension of capability for projects of self-identity. Digitalisation has, in turn, aided the development of the survivalist ethos in so far as it adds to the persuasiveness of a notion of utopia, the perfect future, as the past perfected (for it seems to offer the possibility that the photograph's defining tense 'this will have been' can be mobilised to perfect the future via a process of super-resolution). Some aspects of the character development of the experimental individual were explored in the later chapters. So, for example, in chapter 8 it was argued that the experimental individual – as exemplified by the figure of the cyborg – is not simply well prepared to make decisions (that is, resolute), but is typically super-resolved.

In more general terms, it has been argued that experimental individuals display non-dimensional personalities which enable them to occupy the space of which they are a possession as if it were their own by virtue of their ability to intervene in the 0/1 dimension of time that has been opened up by seeing photographically and expanded by digitalisation. This is the spatial and temporal specificity of their capability. It was suggested that super-heroes provide one attempt to realise this potential in a single figure, logo or phatic image. However, it was also noted – building on arguments in chapters 4, and 6 – that the loop in time that seeing photographically makes possible is not always self-fulfilling, that is, it does not necessarily produce a non-dimensional, experimental individual, but may rather lead alternatively to either the dissolution of the individual,[1] the proliferation of multiple personalities or the emergence of an optical unconscious. It was argued that the 'illogical conjunction' between the 'here–now' and the 'there–then' that Barthes (1981: 44) identifies as characteristic of the photographic image cannot always be subsumed by the spaces of now/here that are currently being created by the institutions of scientific knowledge and the flows of global culture, but may instead make possible the practices of situated knowledge. In both scenarios, however, the very notion of decision-making is itself being transformed, and with it our notions of character, agency and responsibility for self and others. This transformation is the subject of the remainder of this chapter.

THE ETHICS OF CAN-DO

In 'Detraditionalization, character and the limits to agency', Colin Campbell argues that the modern age as a whole might well be described as a culture of character. In doing so, he employs a distinction between personality and character, arguing that the latter refers to the moral and ethical aspect of an individual's personality. The nature of an individual's character is understood as 'the summation of all those qualities judged to be capable of being controlled by will' (1996: 153). By describing the modern age as a culture of character he thus means something more specific than either that this age has seen a process of individualisation or that we are seeing the emergence of a risk society: he is describing the project of turning 'the whole person into a rational agent'. This project – of which the experimental individual can be seen as a contemporary manifestation – is at the heart of many long-standing moral and ethical concerns in Euro-American societies, related as it is to issues of autonomy, responsibility and self-control.[2]

1 Rob Shields (1996) adopts the phrase 'failed individuals' to describe this outcome; however, I prefer not to define this possibility in relation to the norm of the individual.

2 For a useful collection of essays on this topic, see *The Category of the Person* (Carrithers *et al.*, 1993), especially the piece by Charles Taylor. In his essay, 'The person', Taylor argues that the person is 'an agent-plus'. To consider what this 'plus' might be, he contrasts what he calls the representative ⇒

Drawing on the work of Max Weber, Campbell goes on to identify some of the limits he believes to be inherent in this process, that is, in the exercise of agency or the imposition of will by an individual. They include the existence of 'respondent behaviours which are intrinsically resistant to willed control' (1996: 157); a consequence, he explains, of the fact that actors 'are not gods, but biological organisms' and the dysfunctional effects of reflexivity itself, 'which can actually inhibit an individual's ability to perform natural respondent behaviours at will' (1996: 158). These behaviours include those that lead to states such as sleep, contentment, happiness and spontaneity, what Campbell, quoting Elster, calls 'by-product states', so called because they are 'out of reach of intentional action'.[3] Recognising these limits, Campbell suggests, prompts the unavoidable conclusion that 'reflexivity – in the sense of a continuous monitoring of one's own behaviour – is necessarily a self-defeating practice, something which merely serves to impair an individual's power of agency' (1996: 159).

Here, to return to the vocabulary of Marilyn Strathern's argument introduced in chapter 2, is a further exemplification of how the individual has been construed – in its very nature – as partial. That is, the individual is deemed by Campbell to be both more or less than, similar to and different from, more or less determined by society and nature, which themselves are similarly, partially, related to each other and to the individual. The partial analogy is what both enables and constrains self-determination, agency or the exercise of will for the individual; it is what draws the line between character and personality and thus sets limits to capability. And, so Campbell implies, the acceptance of this line is what makes for the good life. However, while Campbell believes that he has identified limits that will protect this way of life, as the summary above indicates, much of this book has sought to show that the terms of the functioning of this analogy are currently being reorganised in what Strathern calls postplural society.[4] Indeed, what has been suggested here is that the very distinction between character and personality is being refigured in the contemporary relations to the self made possible by prosthetic culture. In the refiguring that produces the experimental individual for example, many of the limits to (subjective) agency

view, in which the 'plus' – self-awareness, valuation and choice – are thought to be 'the powers of the individual' (1993: 276) with his own definition in which the 'plus' is 'inseparable from being open to different significances, the specifically human ones, which can't be reduced to the vital and the sentient' (1993: 276). This distinction is useful in so far as it problematises the normalcy of the individual as proprietor of him- or herself, although it may presume the nature of the 'plus'. Interestingly, Taylor argues that the rise of the representative view is linked to the 'unification' of the spaces of disclosure of significance (this makes possible the modern conception of a unified personality) and the interiorisation of personhood. When these two processes come together, he suggests, 'the space of disclosure is considered to be *inside*, in the "mind"' (1993: 277). My argument, however, suggests that these two processes have not come together as easily as he implies, and consequently the mind is not the privileged source of personality in contemporary culture.

3 Interestingly, Niklas Luhmann suggests that honesty and sincerity might be states which the individual faces similar problems in communicating. He writes, 'Anyone claiming to be honest would at the same time give off the impression that there might be doubts about it' (1994: 27). He might like to take the quiz for (in)sincerity described in chapter 2 to check this out.

4 For a related argument, see Bauman (1991).

identified by Campbell are either overcome or rendered unimportant through claims of ownership on the abstract potential that is capability.

In order to consider the implications of this refiguring, it is helpful to return to the terms in which the distinction is made by Campbell. However, before doing so it is worth noting some important qualifications. First, as has been pointed out a number of times during the course of this book, it should not be forgotten that some persons could not be, and have never been, recognised in terms of this distinction at all; in particular, it was pointed out that, historically, women have not generally been fully recognised as individuals. In addition, it is important to note that the gendered nature of the distinction between character and personality has been the subject of much debate in feminism (not least because it is often assumed, adopting this distinction, that women are less ethical than men), with many writers arguing that the individual so defined is inherently masculine. Indeed Carol Gilligan (1982) has famously tied her redefinition of the moral realm to a concept of self that challenges the autonomous self of what she perceives as a masculinist tradition.

However, let me return to Campbell, who draws attention to Weber's initial formulation of this contrast: 'action is conceived as "all human behaviour when and in so far as the acting individual attaches a subjective meaning to it" ', as opposed to 'merely reactive behaviour to which no subjective meaning is attached' (1996: 153). This contrast makes explicit the initial assumption of subjective meaning – intention – and its corollaries of consciousness, memory and embodiment for the distinction between character and personality. However, so it has been argued here, the relation between these three aspects of the self are not as fixed as the taken-for-granted narrative conventions of self-identity may have led us to believe. More specifically, through an exploration of the significance of seeing photographically, it has been argued that the inter-relationship and relative significance of these aspects of the self have recently undergone profound changes. In particular, it has been argued that the distinction between, on the one hand, behaviour to which the individual attaches subjective meaning and, on the other, reactive behaviour is increasingly inadequate in the face of outcontextualisation and indifferentiation. It was pointed out that these changes have significant implications not only for understandings of self-identity and the replacement of generic categories of variety such as gender[5] by those of diversity, but also – as Campbell's argument would imply – for ethics.

In general terms, it was argued that prosthetic culture involves not simply the increasing absorption of personality by character (to use Campbell's distinction), that is, not simply the extension of the remit of intention or an overall increase in the strength and provenance of an individual's will-power, but rather a refiguring of the boundary between them as the relations between will-power, the senses, memory and embodiment themselves are redrawn. In this process the relations between consciousness and the unconscious are also transformed. This

5 So one of the many differences between the approach adopted here and that by Gilligan is that she tends to focus on self-identity as a function of narrative, although her later shift to the language of music to describe moral development, of themes, melodies repeated in different keys or notes heard in relation to other notes, is very suggestive.

refiguring is a function of the frame, and, as Stephen Heath points out in his discussion of its etymological history, 'the frame' is and always has been an ethical issue:

> In frame: the place of image and subject, view (in early French catalogues a film is called a *vue*) and viewer; frame, framing, moral attitude, the correct position . . . the frame is the reconstitution of the scene of the signifier, of the symbolic, into that of the signified, the passage through the image from other scene to seen; it endures distance as correct position, the summit of the eye, representation.
>
> (Heath, 1981: 11–12)

A principal thesis of the book has been that the contemporary development of photography has made the endurance of distance as 'correct' position explicit and in doing so has not only disturbed the workings of representation but also made the frame visible as a *practice* of the self. It thus draws attention to the interrelationship of ethics and aesthetics in the politics of self-identity. Indeed, it was to acknowledge the history of this relationship that the radical potential of the Barthesian conception of the *camera lucida* and Moholy-Nagy's notion of optical hygiene were explored in chapter 7. In these practices, the subject is not all there is to the self for the relations between consciousness, memory and embodiment are technologically extended. Consequences include the recalibration of the senses in experience – producing the astonishment of which Barthes speaks – and the emergence of an optical unconscious.

More generally, however, it has been argued here that the subject-effects of this reframing have been such as to make less and less meaningful the very distinction between character and personality, between merely reactive behaviour and that to which subjective meaning is attached by the acting individual. Indeed it is for this reason that the experimental individual, rather than acting, has been described here as *performing*. However, this is not to say that there are no limits to an individual's capability in prosthetic culture (that we have, in Campbell's terms, become gods), or, indeed, that there is no variation in the ability of people to lay claim to this transferable potential – to perform – and thus be constituted as individuals at all. In other words, it is suggested that while there may be more to the self than the subject, the subject does not disappear (although as Hayles [1993] points out, there is a tendency, at least in literary imaginings of cyberspace, for point of view or 'pov' not simply to emanate from the self but to replace the self).

In this respect, it is once again important to restate some of the qualifications that have been made at earlier points in this argument. In describing the emergence of prosthetic culture, I have not sought to suggest that the earlier forms of hierarchy and exclusion associated with synthetic culture, including those arising in generic classification, do not continue to exist; rather they both exist alongside and in new combinations with the forms of exclusion and division characteristic of prosthetic culture. The suggestion is that particular modes of performance have helped contribute to new forms of survivalism; in other words, the practices of experimentation may operate as the mechanisms of 'natural selection' after nature, or in what Rabinow (1992) describes as bio-sociality. The ethics of this selection for survival were discussed at some length in the consideration of false memory syndrome presented in chapters 5 and 6, and since this phenomenon illustrates some of the ethical complexities that arise in the emergence of a prosthetic culture I will briefly return to the topic here. However, before doing so, let me make one further clarification: I have not meant to imply that these changes in the notion of the individual indicate that those people who understand themselves to be individuals are in any sense any more independent of what has been understood as natural and social determination than in the past, simply that what it is to be an individual makes it possible for them to think and act as if this was so.

BLIND IMITATION

In chapters 5 and 6 I suggested that the phenomenon of false memory syndrome illustrates some of the possible subject-effects of the power of the image or seeing photographically, including the refiguring of the relationship between consciousness, memory and embodiment. I argued that the attempt to recuperate – or reterritorialise – memories in the naming of this phenomenon as false is an indication of the level of anxiety – even fear – provoked by this refiguring. This response was seen as a refusal to acknowledge the existence of prosthetic culture, an indication of a widespread unwillingness to relinquish the previous distinction between character and personality, subjective intention and objective response, control and responsibility, and with it not only the prevailing codes of ethical and moral conduct but also the hierarchical division between men as individuals and women as something 'other'. This response is perhaps the most common in media representations of false memory syndrome despite the widespread and influential political critique of child abuse instigated by feminist and other activists and the complexity of the more philosophical problems it raises in relation to notions of consent and coercion, fantasy and reality, autonomy and relationality.

However, alongside this expression of fear, I also identified a fantasy of the self in the phenomenon of false memory syndrome which I described in terms of autopoiesis. (As I noted in chapter 6, autopoiesis has been defined by one of its advocates as a theory which is meant to answer 'what could well be the most important question about the universe. This is *the nature of potential and the processes by which potential is realized*' [Boulding, 1981: xiii; my emphasis].) Here the refiguring of consciousness, memory and embodiment outlined above is adopted and adapted in particular ways. Most significantly, there is a recognition of the ways in which what was previously naturally or socially determined – including some of the limits of which Campbell speaks – is now being constituted as a matter of potential or technologically assisted choice or rather the 'natural selection' of experimentation. Indeed, it appears, in this fantasy, that there are no limits at all other than those imposed by the individual him- or herself.[6] Autopoiesis is thus a particular organisation of what I have called indifferentiation and outcontextual-

6 More specifically, I suggested that there is a perversion of mimesis in so far as the system produced in autopoiesis is held to be the outcome of the interaction of its own products.

isation in which 'openness' takes place through the self-productive closure of self-observation and self-description. As Luhmann explains in a description of memory,

> All structures of social systems have to be based on [the] fundamental fact of vanishing events, disappearing gestures or words that are dying away. Memory, and then writing, have their function in preserving – not the events, but their structure-generating power.
>
> (1990: 9)

In the autopoietic system, the gap between cause and effect, behaviour and event, is in-filled without remainder and memory is redefined in terms of its structure-generating power: total recall. When used as a model for self-understanding, as I suggested is the case in some constructions of false memory syndrome, the model of autopoiesis can thus be seen to describe a closed individual for whom paradoxically there are no externally given limits. In this process, the individual or system's closure is achieved by defining difference between the individual or system and its environment (including the past) as a difference *from* or *within* the individual or system.[7]

If this fantasy is taken as reality, so Luhmann argues elsewhere, it must be accepted '*that the values of functional systems are not moral values*' (1994: 29). This withdrawal of morality from the coding of functional systems is, he argues, 'morally justified and justifiable' (1994: 30). However, so it was suggested in chapter 6, this withdrawal is not a critique of the inadequacy of contemporary understandings of morality, but rather a masculinist refiguring of the possessive individual in which the sighting/siting of the line between will and reaction, action and behaviour, itself is being redefined as a matter of personal choice.[8]

It was further noted that the model of autopoiesis is powerfully being put to work in the contemporary creation of distinctive lifestyles, where the individual is reconstituted in the possession of this system-producing power or potential. In the context of the stylisation of life afforded by these lifestyles, the subject produced is, as Tyler argues,

> an effect of impersonation or 'mimicry' which results from and expresses an alienating identification with something outside it ... the subject is only retroactively the cause of what it brings into being, an imitation of a reflection or copy of which it 'will have been' the original (so that there can be a copy at all).
>
> (1994: 218–219)

It is in the practices of lifestyle in particular then that the merging of aesthetics and ethics described by writers such as Maffesoli (1991) comes into play. The

7 For Luhmann, meaning denotes that selection of reality which refers to and continually concretises further possibilities of individual experience and action in the face of the infinite variety of possible experiences and actions.

8 For a fascinating discussion of the psychopathology that can take over those whose identity projects go awry, see Shields (1996). He argues that 'Shame and despair come to stand in for identity which exists only in the past tense as a recollected failure' (1996: 5).

boundary between character and personality is refigured and the conventional concerns of responsibility for self and others are reworked with reference to notions of style, originality and creativity.

As noted in chapter 2, the implications of this merging of ethics and aesthetics are a concern of Marilyn Strathern, who argues that what fuels the auto-construction of choice that characterises postplural culture is a style which has no origin, an imitation that is not of but, rather, after nature: to repeat once again, she writes,

> Styles appear to imitate other styles, replicating them by an inner momentum that is contained in the very notion that style itself is an imitative act. Not the imitation of nature or of more noble ages, as it might have been a century before, but imitation of versions of itself.
>
> (1992: 171)

One of the key ethical issues that arises in the analysis of prosthetic culture, then, is whether imitation in this sense is all there is to mimesis and whether or how it is understood in terms of an original and the copy. Of particular concern here is the role of technology, especially the newly emerging visual technologies associated with digitalisation and computer-aided photography discussed in chapters 7 and 8, for, as noted above, they can be seen to extend the potential of technology to anticipate, acting as perceptual prostheses. In these chapters it was argued that while the development of such technologies has been largely subordinated to the requirements of what Barbara Stafford (1993) describes as the quest to make visible the unseen, it is still possible to identify other ways of seeing.

It will be remembered that in his description of contemporary society discussed in chapter 2, Baudrillard claims that the prosthesis does not simply modify the body, but is being imposed as the 'original' model of which the individual is a copy: 'The individual is no longer anything but a cancerous metastasis of its base formula' (1994: 100). In relation to the adoption of autopoiesis as a model of self-understanding, this account of 'a point of no return' or 'moral minimalism' (Bellah *et al.*, 1985) may indeed be an appropriate description. However, it was argued in chapters 6, 7 and 8 that mimesis should not be reduced to this notion of imitation. For what is ignored in this reduction is the sense in which mimesis does not necessarily confirm or construct the notion of a relation between an origin and the copy at all. It is a relation of being similar, not a relation of likeness in which something (the copy) is similar to something else (the original). Nor is it a relation in which the real or the original is similar or secondary to the copy. The relation at issue here cannot be contained within a closed system *whichever direction of motivation* is privileged (as it was argued in chapter 8 seems to be assumed in some definitions of the simulacrum and the cyborg), for its reversibility is not symmetrical; it is not necessarily a relation of either reflection or transparency. It is a blind imitation that makes possible situated knowledges.

Although blind imitation might not sound promising as the basis for redrawing the line between behaviour and action, or, rather, behaviour and performance, it provides a basis for a revised ethics, in so far as it does not presume the (gendered) individual; nor does it tie ethics to the related notion of subjective meaning. Rather, it enables a consideration of what Haraway calls 'significant prosthesis' in the redefinition of ethics. In this way of seeing photographically, the image – as perceptual prosthesis – may, but does not necessarily, lead to the experimental individual, the closed individual who knows no limits. It neither assumes death as an end or exit nor predicts a future without death, the future as the past perfected. Instead, it may – in an encounter that has been anticipated but has not yet happened – cause the viewer astonishment, and continue to provoke the question, 'why is it that I am alive *here and now*?' (Barthes, 1981: 84).

BIBLIOGRAPHY

Abbas, A. (1989) 'On fascination: Walter Benjamin's images', *New German Critique*, 48, pp. 43–62.

Abercrombie, N., Hill, S. and Turner, B. (1986) *The Sovereign Individual*, London: Allen and Unwin.

Adkins, L. and Lury, C. (forthcoming) 'The labour of identity'.

Adorno, T. (1991) *The Culture Industry: Selected Essays on Mass Culture*, London: Routledge.

Adorno, T. and Horkheimer, M. (1982) *Dialectic of Enlightenment*, trans. J. Cumming, New York: Continuum.

Arbus, D. (1996) *Untitled*, New York: Aperture.

Bachofen, J. J. (1954) 'Oknos der Seilflechter' (first published in 1923), in *Gesammelte Werke*, Vol. 4, Basel: Benno Schwabe.

Back, L. and Quaade, V. (1993) 'Dream utopias, nightmare realities: imaging race and culture with the world of Benetton advertising', *Third Text*, 22, pp. 65–80.

Ballard, J. G. (1992) 'Project for a glossary of the twentieth century', in J. Crary and S. Kwinter (eds) *Incorporations,* New York: Zone, MIT Press, pp. 268–280.

Barker, P. (1991) *Regeneration*, London: Viking.

—— (1995) *The Eye in the Door*, New York: NAL Dutton.

—— (1996) *The Ghost Road*, London: Viking.

Barthes, R. (1972) 'The great family of man', in *Mythologies*, trans. A. Lavers, St Albans: Paladin, pp. 100–102.

—— (1977) *Image–Music–Text*, selected and trans. S. Heath, London: Fontana.

—— (1981) *Camera Lucida: Reflections on Photography*, trans. R. Howard, New York: Hill and Wang.

Baudrillard, J. (1994) *Simulacra and Simulation*, trans. S. F. Glaser, Michigan: University of Michigan Press.

—— (1995) 'The virtual illusion: or the automatic writing of the world', *Theory, Culture and Society*, 12: 4, pp. 97–109.

Bauman, Z. (1991) 'The social manipulation of morality: moralizing actors, adiaphorizing action', *Theory, Culture and Society*, 8: 1, pp. 137–153.

—— (1992) 'Survival as a social construct', *Theory, Culture and Society*, 9: 1, pp. 1–36.

Beard, G. M. (1881) *American Nervousness: Its Causes and Consequences*, New York: Putnam's.

Beck, U. (1992) *Risk Society: Towards a New Modernity*, trans. M. Ritter, London: Sage.

Beck, U., Giddens, A. and Lash, S. (1994) *Reflexive Modernization: Politics, Tradition and Aesthetics*, Stanford: Stanford University Press.

Bell, V. (1993) *The Interrogation of Incest*, London and New York: Routledge.

Bellah, R. H., Madsen, R., Sullivan, W. M., Swidler, A. and Tipton, S. M. (1985) *Habits of the Heart: Individualism and Commitment in American Life*, Berkeley: University of California Press.

Bellour, R. (1990) 'La double hélice', in R. Bellour, C. David and C. van Assche (eds) *Passages de l'image*, Paris: Centre Georges Pompidou.

Benjamin, W. (1970) *Illuminations*, trans. H. Zohn, London: Fontana.

—— (1979) 'Doctrine of the similar', *New German Critique*, 17, pp. 65–69.

—— (1985) *One Way Street and Other Writings*, trans. E. Jephcott and K. Shorter, London: Verso.

Bennett, C. (1994) 'The satanic verses', *The Guardian Weekend*, 10 September, pp. 12–20.

Berger, J. (1980) *About Looking*, London: Writers and Readers Publishing Co-operative.

—— (1995) 'Henri Cartier-Bresson', *Aperture*, 138, pp. 12–24.

Bergson, H. (1939) *Matière et mémoire: Essai sur la relation du corps à l'ésprit*, Paris: PUF.

Bhabha, H. (1990) 'The third space', in J. Rutherford (ed.) *Identity: Community, Culture, Difference*, London: Lawrence and Wishart, pp. 207–221.

Bhabha, H. (ed.) (1993) *Nation and Narration*, London and New York: Routledge.

Biddick, K. (1993) 'Stranded histories: feminist allegories of artificial life', *Research in Philosophy and Technology*, 13, pp. 165–182.

Bing, S. (1995) 'Are you a master of (in)sincerity?', *Fortune*, 13 November, pp. 49–50.

Blackwell, L. (1995) 'Duck tales', *Creative Review*, May, pp. 32–35.

Borch-Jacobsen, M. (1988) *The Freudian Subject*, trans. C. Porter, Stanford: Stanford University Press.

Boulding, K. E. (1981) 'Foreword', in M. Zeleny (ed.) *Autopoiesis: A Theory of Living Organization*, New York: North-Holland, pp. xi–xiii.

Bowlby, R. (1985) *Just Looking: Consumer Culture in Dreiser, Gissing and Zola*, New York and London: Methuen.

Boyarin, J. (1994) 'Space, time and the politics of memory', in J. Boyarin (ed.) *Remapping Memory: The Politics of TimeSpace*, Minneapolis: University of Minnesota Press, pp. 1–39.

Braidotti, R. (1991) *Patterns of Dissonance: A Study of Women in Contemporary Philosophy*, trans. E. Guild, Cambridge: Polity Press.

—— (1994) *Nomadic Subjects: Embodiment and Sexual Difference in Contemporary Feminist Theory*, New York: Columbia University Press.

Braun, M. (1992) *Picturing Time: The Work of Étienne-Jules Marey, 1830–1904*, Chicago: University of Chicago Press.

Breuer, S. (1985) 'Adorno's anthropology', *Telos*, 64, pp. 15–31.

Buck-Morss, S. (1991) *The Dialectics of Seeing: Walter Benjamin and the Arcades Project*, Cambridge, Mass.: MIT Press.

—— (1992) 'Aesthetics and anaesthetics: Walter Benjamin's artwork essay reconsidered', *October*, 62, pp. 3–41.

Burgoyne, P. (1995) 'BA's new route', *Creative Review*, May, pp. 27–28.

Busselle, R. (1994) 'A defining reality: the photographs of Nancy Burson', *Aperture*, 136, pp. 73–75.

Butler, J. (1990) *Gender Trouble: Feminism and the Subversion of Identity*, New York and London: Routledge.

—— (1992) 'Contingent foundations: feminism and the question of "postmodernism"', in J. Butler and J. W. Scott (eds) *Feminists Theorize the Political*, New York and London: Routledge, pp. 3–22.

—— (1993) *Bodies That Matter: On the Discursive Limits of Sex*, London: Routledge.

Butler, K. (1994) 'You must remember this', *The Guardian Weekend*, 23 July, pp. 6–12, 53.

Caillois, R. (1988) 'Mimicry and legendary psychasthenia' (first published in 1935), in A. Michelson, R. Krauss, D. Crimp and J. Copjec (eds) *October: The First Decade, 1976–1986*, Cambridge, Mass. and London: MIT Press, pp. 58–76.

Cameron, A. (1991) 'Digital dialogues: an introduction', *Ten-8*, 2: 2, pp. 4–5.

Campbell, B. (1988) *Unofficial Secrets: Child Sexual Abuse: The Cleveland Case*, London: Virago.

Campbell, C. (1996) 'Detraditionalization, character and the limits to agency', in P. Heelas, S., Lash and P. Morris (eds) *Detraditionalization*, Cambridge, Mass. and Oxford: Blackwell, pp. 149–171.

Caputi, J. (1994) 'Unthinkable fathering: connecting incest and nuclearism', *Hypatia*, 9: 2, pp. 102–123.

Cardinal, R. (1992) 'Nadar and the photographic portrait in nineteenth century France', in G. Clarke (ed.) *The Portrait in Photography*, London: Reaktion Books, pp. 6–25.

Carr, D. (1986) *Time, Narrative and History*, Bloomington: Indiana University Press.

Carrithers, M., Collins, S. and Lukes, S. (eds) (1993) *The Category of the Person: Anthropology, Philosophy, History*, Cambridge: Cambridge University Press.

Casey, E. S. (1985) *Remembering: A Phenomenological Study*, Bloomington: Indiana University Press.

Chow, R. (1992) 'Postmodern automatons', in J. Butler and J. W. Scott (eds) *Feminists Theorize the Political*, New York and London: Routledge, pp. 101–121.

Clarke, G. (1992) 'Public faces, private lives: August Sander and the social typology of the portrait photograph', in G. Clarke (ed.) *The Portrait in Photography*, London: Reaktion Books, pp. 71–94.

Clifford, J. (1988) *The Predicament of Culture*, Cambridge, Mass. and London: Harvard University Press.

Coombe, R. (1991) 'Objects of property and subjects of politics: intellectual property laws and democratic dialogue', *Texas Law Review*, 69: 7, pp. 1853–1880.

—— (1993) 'The properties of culture and the politics of possessing identity: native claims in the cultural appropriation controversy', *Canadian Journal of Law and Jurisprudence*, VI: 2, pp. 249–285.

Cornwall, J. (1995) 'True lies', *The Sunday Times Magazine*, 14 May, pp. 20–28.

Crary, J. (1988) 'Modernizing vision', in H. Foster (ed.) *Vision and Visuality*, Seattle: Bay Press, pp. 29–51.

—— (1989) 'Spectacle, attention, counter-memory', *October*, 50, pp. 97–107.

—— (1990) *Techniques of the Observer: On Vision and Modernity in the Nineteenth Century*, Cambridge, Mass.: MIT Press.

—— (1994) 'Unbinding vision', *October*, 68, pp. 21–44.

Crews, F. (1994) 'The revenge of the repressed', *The New York Review*, 17 November, pp. 54–60.

Crossley, N. (1995) 'Merleau-Ponty, the elusive body and carnal sociology', *Body and Society*, 1: 1, pp. 43–63.

Csikszentmihalyi, M. (1990) *Flow: The Psychology of Optimal Experience*, New York: Harper and Row.

Curtis, B. (1995) ' "In betweening": an interview with Irene Kotlarz', *Art History*, 18: 1, pp. 24–36.

de Certeau, M. (1988) *The Practice of Everyday Life*, trans. S. F. Rendall, Berkeley and Los Angeles: University of California Press.

Deleuze, G. (1986) *Cinema 1: The Movement Image*, trans. H. Tomlinson and B. Habberjam, London: Athlone Press.

—— (1988) *Bergsonism*, trans. H. Tomlinson and B. Habberjam, New York: Zone Books.

—— (1989) *Cinema 2: The Time-Image*, trans. H. Tomlinson and R. Galeta, London: Athlone Press.

—— (1993) *The Deleuze Reader*, ed. C. V. Boundas, New York: Columbia University Press.

Diamond, S. (1993) *Angles of Incidence: Video Reflections of Multimedia Artworks*, Banff, Alberta: International Council for Computer Communication and the Banff Centre for the Arts.

Diprose, R. (1994) *The Bodies of Women: Ethics, Embodiment and Sexual Difference*, London: Routledge.

Doane, M. A. (1985) 'When the direction of the force acting on the body is changed', *Wide Angle*, 7: 1–2, pp. 42–57.

—— (1990) 'Information, crisis, catastrophe', in P. Mellencamp (ed.) *Logics of Television: Essays in Cultural Criticism*, Bloomington and London: Indiana University Press and BFI, pp. 222–240.

—— (1993) 'Technology's body: cinematic vision in modernity', *differences*, 5: 2, pp. 1–23.

Dorfman, A. and Mattelart, A. (1975) *How to Read Donald Duck: Imperialist Ideology in the Disney Comic*, trans. and intro. D. Kunzle, New York: International General.

Downey, G. L. (1995) 'Human agency in CAD/CAM technology', in C. Hables Gray (ed.) *The Cyborg Handbook*, New York and London: Routledge, pp. 363–371.

Driver, E. and Droisen, A. (eds) (1989) *Child Sexual Abuse: Feminist Perspectives*, London: Macmillan.

Druckrey, T. (1994) 'Introduction', in G. Bender and T. Druckrey (eds) *Culture on the Brink: Ideologies of Technology*, Seattle: Bay Press, pp. 1–15.

Durand, R. (1995) 'How to see (photographically)', in P. Petro (ed.) *Fugitive Images: From Photography to Video*, Bloomington and Indianapolis: Indiana University Press, pp. 141–152.

Eco, U. (1983) *The Role of the Reader: Explorations in the Semiotics of Texts*, trans. W. Weaver, London: Hutchinson.

—— (1984) 'A guide to the neo-television of the 80s', *Framework*, 25, pp. 18–27.

Edelman, B. (1979) *The Ownership of the Image: Elements for a Marxist Theory of Law*, trans. E. Kingdom, London: Routledge and Kegan Paul.

Eleftheriotis, D. (1995) 'Video poetics: technology, aesthetics and politics', *Screen*, 36: 2, pp. 100–112.

Ermacora, B. (1994) 'Orlan', *European Art Photography*, 56, pp. 15–19.

Faludi, S. (1992) *Backlash: The Undeclared War Against Women*, London: Chatto and Windus.

Featherstone, M. (1991) *Consumer Culture and Postmodernism*, London: Sage.

Feaver, W. (1994) 'Still living for the moment', *The Observer Review*, 20 November, pp. 2–3.

Feldman, M. D. and Ford, C. V. (1996) *Patient or Pretender? Inside the Strange World of Factitious Disorders*, New York: Wiley.

Feminist Review (1988) Special Issue: Family Secrets. Child Sexual Abuse, no. 28.

Foster, H. (ed.) (1988) *Vision and Visuality*, Seattle: Bay Press.

Foucault, M. (1971) *Madness and Civilisation: A History of Insanity in the Age of Reason*, trans. R. Hammond, London: Tavistock.

—— (1976) *The Birth of the Clinic: An Archaeology of Medical Perception*, trans. A. M. Sheridan, London: Tavistock.

—— (1980) *Power/Knowledge: Selected Interviews and Other Writings, 1972–1977*, ed. C. Gordon, Brighton: Harvester Wheatsheaf.

—— (1989) *The Order of Things: The Archaeology of Human Sciences*, London: Routledge

Franklin, S. (1995) 'Life itself', *Encyclopedia of Bio-Ethics*, New York and London: Macmillan.

Frazer, J. G. (1911–1935) *The Golden Bough: A Study in Magic and Religion*, London: Macmillan.

Freely, M. (1994) 'A suitable case for treatment', *The Guardian*, 9 February, pp. 4–5.

Freud, S. (1953) 'Family romances', in J. Strachey (ed.) *The Standard Edition of the Complete Works of Sigmund Freud*, 9, London: Hogarth Press and the Institute of Psychoanalysis, pp. 235–241.

—— (1963) *Jokes and Their Relation to the Unconscious*, trans. and ed. J. Strachey, New York and London: W. W. Norton and Company.

Friedland, R. and Boden, D. (eds) (1994) *NowHere: Space, Time and Modernity*, Berkeley and Los Angeles: University of California Press.

Friedman, J. (1994) *Cultural Identity and Global Process*, London: Sage.

Gaines, J. M. (1992) *Contested Culture: The Image, the Voice and the Law*, London: BFI.

Game, A. (1991) *Undoing the Social: Towards a Deconstructive Sociology*, Milton Keynes: Open University Press.

Gasché, R. (1986) *The Tain of the Mirror: Derrida and the Philosophy of Reflection*, Cambridge, Mass. and London: Harvard University Press.

—— (1994) 'Objective diversions: on some Kantian themes in Benjamin's "The work of art in the age of mechanical reproduction"', in A. Benjamin and P. Osborne (eds) *Walter Benjamin's Philosophy: Destruction and Experience*, London and New York: Routledge, pp. 183–205.

George, R. (1990) 'Some spatial characteristics of the Hollywood cartoon', *Screen*, 31: 3, pp. 296–321.

Gergen, K. (1991) *The Saturated Self: Discourses of Identity in Contemporary Life*, New York: Basic Books.
Gerrie, A. (1993) 'The accused', *Options*, June, pp. 46–49.
Giddens, A. (1991) *Modernity and Self-Identity: Self and Society in the Late Modern Age*, Cambridge: Polity Press.
Gidley, M. (1992) 'Hoppé's impure portraits: contextualising the American types', in G. Clarke (ed.) *The Portrait in Photography*, London: Reaktion Books, pp. 132–155.
Gilligan, C. (1982) *In a Different Voice*, Cambridge, Mass.: Harvard University Press.
Gould, S. J. (1979) 'Mickey Mouse meets Konrad Lorenz', *Natural History*, 88.
Grant, L. (1993) 'A past imperfect?', *The Guardian*, 24 May, pp. 10–11.
—— (1994) 'Tricks of the memory', *The Guardian*, 25 April, pp. 8–9.
Gray, C. Hables with Figueroa-Sarriera, H. and Mentor, S. (eds) (1995) *The Cyborg Handbook*, New York and London: Routledge.
Grosz, E. (1995) *Space, Time and Perversion: Essays on the Politics of Bodies*, New York and London: Routledge.
Guattari, F. (1992) 'Regimes, pathways, subjects', in J. Crary and S. Kwinter (eds) *Incorporations*, New York: Zone, MIT Press, pp. 16–36.
Hacking, I. (1991) 'The making and molding of child abuse', *Critical Inquiry*, Winter, pp. 253–288.
—— (1994) 'Memoro-politics and the soul', *History of the Human Sciences*, 7: 2, pp. 29–53.
—— (1995) *Rewriting the Soul: Multiple Personality and the Sciences of Memory*, Princeton: Princeton University Press.
Hall, L. and Lloyd, S. (1989) *Surviving Child Abuse: A Handbook for Helping Women Challenge Their Past*, New York: Falmer Press.
Hammond, M., Howarth, J. and Keat, R. (1991) *Understanding Phenomenology*, Oxford: Blackwell.
Hansen, M. (1987) 'Benjamin, cinema and experience: "The blue flower in the land of technology"', *New German Critique*, 40, pp. 179–224.
—— (1992) 'Mass culture as hieroglyphic writing: Adorno, Derrida, Kracauer', *New German Critique*, 56, pp. 43–73.
—— (1993a) 'Of mice and ducks: Benjamin and Adorno on Disney', *The South Atlantic Quarterly*, 92: 1, pp. 27–61.
—— (1993b) ' "With skin and hair": Kracauer's theory of film, Marseille 1940', *Critical Inquiry*, 19, pp. 437–469.
Haraway, D. (1985) 'A manifesto for cyborgs: science, technology, and socialist feminism in the 1980s', *Socialist Review*, 80, pp. 65–107.
—— (1991) *Symians, Cyborgs and Women*, London: Routledge.
—— (1993) 'Modest witness@second millennium: the female man meets OncoMouse', conference paper, UCLA.
Hardt, M. (1993) *Gilles Deleuze: An Apprenticeship in Philosophy*, London: UCL Press.
Harvey, P. (1996) *Hybrids of Modernity. Anthropology, the Nation State and the Universal Exhibition*, London: Routledge.
Hayles, N. K. (1987) 'Text out of context: situating postmodernism within an information society', *Discourse*, 9, pp. 24–36.
—— (1993) 'Virtual bodies and flickering signifiers', *October*, 66.
Hearn, J. (1990) 'Child abuse and men's violence', in the Violence Against Children Study Group *Taking Violence Seriously*, London: Unwin and Hyman, pp. 62–85.
Heath, S. (1981) *Questions of Cinema*, London: Macmillan.
—— (1990) 'Representing television', in P. Mellencamp (ed.) *Logics of Television: Essays in Cultural Criticism*, Bloomington and London: Indiana University Press and BFI, pp. 267–303.
Heath, S. and Skirrow, G. (1977) 'Television: a world in action', *Screen*, 18: 2, pp. 7–61.
Helman, C. (1988) 'Dr Frankenstein and the industrial body: reflections on "spare part" surgery', *Anthropology Today*, 4: 3, pp. 14–17.
Hewitt, A. (1992) 'A feminine dialectic of Enlightenment? Horkheimer and Adorno revisited', *New German Critique*, 56, pp. 143–170.

Hilton, T. (1994) 'Mann's family and other animals', *The Independent on Sunday*, 29 May, p. 26.

Hirschman, E. C. (1992) 'The consciousness of addiction: toward a general theory of compulsive consumption', *Journal of Consumer Research*, Vol. 19, September, pp. 155–179.

Holland, P. (1992) *What is a Child? Popular Images of Childhood*, London: Virago.

Homberger, E. (1992) 'J. P. Morgan's nose: photographer and subject in American portrait photography', in G. Clarke (ed.) *The Portrait in Photography*, London: Reaktion Books, pp. 115–132.

Hosokawa, S. (1984) 'The walkman effect', in R. Middleton and D. Horn (eds) *Popular Music, Volume 4: Performers and Audiences*, Cambridge: Cambridge University Press.

Huyssen, A. (1993) 'Fortifying the heart – totally: Ernst Jünger's armored texts', *New German Critique*, 59, pp. 3–23.

—— (1995) *Twilight Memories: Marking Time in a Culture of Amnesia*, New York and London: Routledge.

Ihde, D. (1995) 'Image technologies and traditional culture', in A. Feenberg and A. Hannay (eds) *Technology and the Politics of Knowledge*, Bloomington and Indianapolis: Indiana University Press, pp. 147–159.

Irigaray, L. (1993) *An Ethics of Sexual Difference*, London: Athlone Press.

Jameson, F. (1992) *Postmodernism or, The Cultural Logic of Late Capitalism*, London and New York: Verso.

Jardine, A. (1985) *Gynesis: Configurations of Women and Modernity*, Ithaca and London: Cornell University Press.

Jaroff, L. (1993) 'Lies of the mind', *Time*, 29 November, pp. 56–61.

Jay, M. (1993) 'Unsympathetic magic', *Visual Anthropology Review*, 9: 2, Fall, pp. 79–82.

—— (1994) *Downcast Eyes: The Denigration of Vision in Twentieth Century Thought*, Berkeley and London: University of California Press.

Jenks, C. (1995) *Visual Culture*, London and New York: Routledge.

Kelly, L. (1988) *Surviving Sexual Violence*, Cambridge: Polity Press.

—— (1994) *Sexual Abuse in Childhood*, London: Sage.

Kelly, L., Reagan, L. and Burton, S. (1991) *An Exploratory Study of the Prevalence of Sexual Abuse in a Sample of 16–21 Year Olds*, Polytechnic of North London: Child Abuse Studies Unit.

Kember, S. (1995) 'Surveillance, technology and crime: the James Bulger case', in M. Lister (ed.) *The Photographic Image in Digital Culture*, London and New York: Routledge, pp. 115–129.

King, B. (1985) 'Articulating stardom', *Screen*, 26: 5, pp. 27–50.

—— (1989) 'The burden of Headroom', *Screen*, 30: 1–2, pp. 122–138.

King, M. and Trowell, J. (1992) *Children's Welfare and the Law: The Limits of Legal Intervention*, London: Sage.

Koch, G. (1994) 'Cosmos in film: on the concept of space in Walter Benjamin's "The work of art in the age of mechanical reproduction"', in A. Benjamin and P. Osborne (eds) *Walter Benjamin's Philosophy: Destruction and Experience*, London and New York: Routledge, pp. 205–216.

Kracauer, S. (1993) 'Photography' (first published in 1927), *Critical Inquiry*, 19, pp. 421–436.

—— (1995) *The Mass Ornament: Weimar Essays*, trans. T. Y. Levin, Cambridge, Mass. and London: Harvard University Press.

Krauss, R. (1986a) 'Photography in the service of surrealism', in R. Krauss and J. Livingston *L'Amour Fou: Photography and Surrealism*, London: Cross River Press, pp. 15–57.

—— (1986b) 'Corpus delicti', in R. Krauss and J. Livingston *L'Amour Fou: Photography and Surrealism*, London: Cross River Press, pp. 57–115.

—— (1994) *The Optical Unconscious*, Cambridge, Mass. and London: MIT Press.

Krauthammer, C. (1993) 'The molestation of normality', *The Guardian*, 18 November, p. 16.

Kuhn, A. (1991) 'Remembrance', in J. Spence and P. Holland (eds) *Family Snaps: The Meaning of Domestic Photography*, London: Virago, pp. 18–25.

—— (1995) *Family Secrets: Acts of Memory and Imagination*, London: Verso.

Lacey, H. (1994) 'The dangers of memory', *The Independent on Sunday*, 16 January, p. 23.

Lacouture, J. (1989) 'The founders', in W. Manchester (ed.) *In Our Time: The World as Seen by Magnum Photographers*, New York and London: W. W. Norton and Company, pp. 47–65.

Lasch, C. (1978) *The Culture of Narcissism: American Life in an Age of Diminishing Expectations*, New York: Norton.

Lash, S. (1988) 'Discourse or figure? Postmodernism as a "regime of signification"', *Theory, Culture and Society*, 5: 2–3, pp. 311–337.

Latour, B. (1995) 'A door must be either open or shut: a little philosophy of techniques', in A. Feenberg and A. Hannay (eds) *Technology and the Politics of Knowledge*, Bloomington and Indianapolis: Indiana University Press, pp. 272–282.

Lawler, S. (1995a) ' "I never felt as though I fitted": family romances and the mother–daughter relationship', in L. Pearce and J. Stacey (eds) *Romance Revisited*, London: Lawrence and Wishart, pp. 265–279.

—— (1995b) 'Mothering the self: a study of the mother–daughter relationship', PhD thesis, Lancaster University.

Lawson, M. (1995) 'Nights at the opera', *The Guardian*, 4 December, pp. 6–7.

Lee, N. (1994) 'Child protection investigations: discourse analysis and the management of incommensurability', *Journal of Community and Applied Social Psychology*, 4, pp. 275–286.

Leys, R. (1992) 'The real Miss Beauchamp: gender and the subject of imitation', in J. Butler and J. W. Scott (eds) *Feminists Theorize the Political*, New York and London: Routledge, pp. 167–215.

Luhmann, N. (1986) *Love as Passion: The Codification of Intimacy*, Oxford: Polity Press.

—— (1989) *Ecological Communication*, Cambridge: Polity Press.

—— (1990) *Essays on Self-Reference*, New York: Columbia University Press.

—— (1994) 'Politicians, honesty and the higher amorality of politics', *Theory, Culture and Society*, 11, pp. 25–36.

Lury, C. (1993) *Cultural Rights: Technology, Legality and Personality*, London and New York: Routledge.

—— (1997) 'The objects of travel', in C. Rojek and J. Urry (eds) *Touring Cultures*, London: Routledge.

Lutz, C. A. and Collins, J. L. (1993) *Reading National Geographic*, Chicago and London: University of Chicago Press.

Lyman, C. M. (1982) *The Vanishing Race and Other Illusions: Photographs of Indians by Edward S. Curtis*, New York: Pantheon Books.

Lyotard, J.-F. (1984) *The Postmodern Condition: A Report on Knowledge*, trans. G. Bennington and B. Massumi, Manchester: Manchester University Press.

—— (1991) *The Inhuman: Reflections on Time*, trans. G. Bennington and R. Bowlby, Cambridge: Polity Press.

—— (1993) 'Acinema', in A. Benjamin (ed.) *The Lyotard Reader*, Oxford and Cambridge, Mass.: Blackwell, pp. 169–180.

McClintock, A. (1995) *Imperial Leather: Race, Gender and Sexuality in the Colonial Contest*, New York and London: Routledge.

McCole, J. (1993) *Walter Benjamin and the Antinomies of Tradition*, Ithaca and London: Cornell University Press.

MacFarlane, A. (1978) *The Origins of English Individualism: The Family, Property and Social Transition*, Oxford: Blackwell.

—— (1994) *On Individualism*, Lancaster University: CSCV.

MacLeod, M. and Saraga, E. (1988) 'Challenging the orthodoxy: towards a feminist theory and practice', *Feminist Review*, 28, pp. 16–56.

McNeil, M. (1991) 'Making and not making the difference: the gender politics of Thatcherism', in S. Franklin, J. Stacey and C. Lury (eds) *Off-Centre: Feminism and Cultural Studies*, London: HarperCollins, pp. 221–240.

Macpherson, C. (1962) *The Political Theory of Possessive Individualism: Hobbes to Locke*, London: Clarendon.

Maffesoli, M. (1991) 'The ethics of aesthetics', *Theory, Culture and Society*, 8, pp. 7–20.

Mailer, N. (1961) *Advertisements for Myself*, London: André Deutsch.

Malcolm, J. (1996) 'Aristocrats', *The New York Review of Books*, XLIII: 2, 1 February, pp. 7–8.

Manchester, W. (ed.) (1989) *In Our Time: The World As Seen by Magnum Photographers*, New York and London: W. W. Norton and Company.

Martin, E. (1994) *Flexible Bodies: The Role of Immunity in American Culture from the Days of Polio to the Age of AIDS*, Boston: Beacon Press.

Masse, F. (1991) 'Two in a balcony: the mausoleum of natural history', in *Raw: High Culture for Low Brows*, 2: 3, New York: Penguin, pp. 4–9.

Maturana, H. R. and Varela, F. J. (1980) *Autopoiesis and Cognition: The Realization of the Living*, Dordrecht and Boston: D. Reidel.

——(1984) *The Tree of Knowledge*, Boston: Shambala.

Mellencamp, P. (1990) 'TV time and catastrophe, or *Beyond the Pleasure Principle* of television', in P. Mellencamp (ed.) *Logics of Television: Essays in Cultural Criticism*, Bloomington and London: Indiana University Press and BFI, pp. 240–267.

Metz, C. (1990) 'Photography and fetish', in C. Squiers (ed.) *The Critical Image*, Seattle: Bay Press, pp. 155–164.

Mihill, C. (1995) 'Psychologists guarded on "false memory" of abuse', *The Guardian*, 13 January, p. 8.

Miller, C. (1994) Review of *Sally Mann: Immediate Family*, *European Photography*, 15: 1, pp. 64–65.

Mitchell, W. J. (1992) *The Reconfigured Eye: Visual Truth in the Post-Photographic Era*, Cambridge, Mass. and London: MIT Press.

Moholy-Nagy, L. (1969) *Painting, Photography, Film*, London: Lund Humphries.

Montgomery, S. L. (1995) 'Through a lens, brightly: the world according to *National Geographic*', *Science as Culture*, 5: 22, pp. 6–45.

Montrose, S. (1993) 'Phototherapy', *Elle*, December, pp. 57–60.

Morse, M. (1990) 'Information, crisis, catastrophe', in P. Mellencamp (ed.) *Logics of Television: Essays in Cultural Criticism*, Bloomington and London: Indiana University Press and BFI, pp. 193–222.

—— (1994) 'What do cyborgs eat? Oral logic in an information society', in G. Bender and T. Druckrey (eds) *Culture on the Brink: Ideologies of Technology*, Seattle: Bay Press, pp. 157–191.

Morton, J. (1994) 'Let's not make up our minds', *The Guardian*, 14 May.

Newhall, B. (ed.) (1980) *Photography: Essays and Images*, London: Secker and Warburg.

Nickols, F. W. (1995) 'Feedback about feedback', *Human Resource Development Quarterly*, 6: 3, pp. 289–296.

O'Neill, J. (1992) 'Horror autotoxicus', in J. Crary and S. Kwinter (eds) *Incorporations*, New York: Zone, MIT Press, pp. 264–268.

Oosterling, H. (1995) 'No(w)here as the ideal place: on the relations between concepts, percepts and affects', *Art and Design*, 10: 5–6, pp. 20–26.

Orbach, S. (1993) 'When is abuse not abuse?', *The Guardian Weekend*, 26 June, p. 18.

—— (1994) 'Through the past darkly', *The Guardian Weekly*, 14 May, p. 52.

Otis, L. (1994) *Organic Memory: History and the Body in the Late Nineteenth and Early Twentieth Centuries*, Lincoln and London: University of Nebraska Press.

Pandiscio, R. (1996) 'What you wear and what you want', *Interview*, January, pp. 88–93.

Pateman, C. (1988) *The Sexual Contract*, Cambridge: Polity Press.

Peirce, C. (1991) *Peirce on Signs: Writings on Semiotics*, ed. J. Hoopes, Chapel Hill and London: North Carolina University Press.

Phillips, C. (1988) 'The judgement seat of photography', in A. Michelson, R. Krauss, D. Crimp and J. Copjec (eds) *October: The First Decade, 1976–1986*, Cambridge, Mass. and London: MIT Press, pp. 257–296.

Pinney, C. (1994) 'Future travel: anthropology and cultural distance in an age of virtual reality or a past seen from a possible future', in L. Taylor (ed.) *Visualizing Theory*, New York and London: Routledge, pp. 409–428.

Prigogine, I. and Stengers, I. (1984) *Order Out of Chaos*, New York: La Nouvelle Alliance.

Prince, M. (1910) *The Dissociation of a Personailty: A Biographical Study in Abnormal Psychology*, 2nd edn, London: Longman, Green and Co.

Pulver, A. (1996) 'The art of darkness', *The Guardian*, 29 January, pp. 4–5.

Rabinach, A. (1992) 'Neurasthenia and modernity', in J. Crary and S. Kwinter (eds) *Incorporations*, New York: Zone, MIT Press, pp. 178–190.

Rabinow, P. (1992) 'Artificiality and Enlightenment: from sociobiology to biosociality', in J. Crary and S. Kwinter (eds) *Incorporations*, New York: Zone, MIT Press, pp. 234–254.

Redner, M. (1982) *In the Beginning was the Deed: Reflections on the Passage of Faust*, Berkeley: University of California Press.

Renaud, A. (1995) 'From photography to photology: concerning certain philosophical implications of digital transmutation of the photographic image', in Cypres (ed.) *Art/Digital Photography*, Aix-en-Provence: École d'Art d'Aix-en-Provence, pp. 178–220.

Ricoeur, P. (1984–1985) *Time and Narrative*, trans. K. McCaughlin and D. Pellauer, Chicago: University of Chicago Press.

Riley, D. (1988) *Am I That Name? Feminism and the Category of 'Women' in History*, London: Macmillan.

Ritchin, F. (1989) 'What is Magnum?', in W. Manchester (ed.) *In Our Time: The World as Seen by Magnum Photographers*, New York and London: W. W. Norton and Company, pp. 417–445.

—— (1990) 'Photojournalism in the age of computers', in. C. Squiers (ed.) *The Critical Image*, Seattle: Bay Press, pp. 28–37.

—— (1991) 'The end of photography as we have known it', in P. Wombell (ed.) *Photovideo: Photography in the Age of the Computer*, London: Rivers Oram Press, pp. 8–16.

Robins, K. (1995) 'Will image move us still?', in M. Lister (ed.) *The Photographic Image in Digital Culture*, New York and London: Routledge, pp. 29–51.

Robson-Scott, M. (1994) 'Desperate remedies', *The Guardian*, 9 February, pp. 4–5.

Root, M. A. (1864) *The Camera and the Pencil*, Philadelphia: M. A. Root.

Rose, J. (1986) 'Jeffrey Masson and Alice James', in *Sexual Difference*, Oxford: Oxford Literary Review, pp. 185–192.

—— (1987) 'The man who mistook his wife for a hat', in L. Appignanesi (ed.) *Identity: The Real Me*, London: ICA, pp. 30–34.

Rose, N. (1985) *The Psychological Complex: Psychology, Politics and Society in England, 1869–1939*, London: Routledge.

—— (1989) *Governing the Soul: The Shaping of the Private Self*, London: Routledge.

—— (1996) 'Authority and the genealogy of subjectivity', in P. Heelas, S. Lash and P. Morris (eds) *Detraditionalization*, Oxford: Blackwell, pp. 294–328.

Ross, A. (1990) 'Techno-ethics and tele-ethics: three lives in the day of *Max Headroom*', in P. Mellencamp (ed.) *Logics of Television: Essays in Cultural Criticism*, Bloomington and London: Indiana University Press and BFI, pp. 138–156.

Roughley, N. (1995) 'The post-post-structuralist attitude: remarks on the affective phenomenology of Roland Barthes's *Camera Lucida*', *New Formations*, pp. 108–121.

Sandburg, C. (1993) 'Prologue' to E. Steichen, *The Family of Man*, New York: The Museum of Modern Art (first published in 1953), pp. 4–5.

Sandeen, E. J. (1995) *Picturing an Exhibition: The Family of Man and 1950s America*, Albuquerque: University of New Mexico Press.

Saunders, D. (1992) *Authorship and Copyright*, London: Routledge.

Scarry, E. (1994) 'The merging of bodies and artifacts in the social contract', in G. Bender and T. Druckrey (eds) *Culture on the Brink: Ideologies of Technology*, Seattle: Bay Press, pp. 85–99.

Schade, S. (1995) 'Charcot and the spectacle of the hysterical body: the "pathos formula", as an aesthetic staging of psychiatric discourse – a blind spot in the reception of Warburg', *Art History*, 18: 4, pp. 499–517.

Schnabel, J. (1993) 'The 65 faces of Donna', *The Independent on Sunday*, 24 October, pp. 10–15.
Scott, A. (1988) 'Feminism and the seductiveness of the "real event"', *Feminist Review*, 28, pp. 88–103.
Sedgwick, E. K. (1994) *Tendencies*, London: Routledge.
Seger, L. (1990) *Creating Unforgettable Characters: A Practical Guide to Character Development in Films, TV Series, Advertisements, Novels and Short Stories*, New York: Henry Holt and Company.
Sekula, A. (1975) 'On the convention of photographic meaning', *Artforum*, 13, pp. 36–45.
—— (1981) 'The traffic in photographs', *Art Journal*, 41, pp. 15–25.
—— (1986) 'The body and the archive', *October*, 39, pp. 3–65.
Seltzer, M. (1993) 'Serial killers (1)', *differences*, 5: 1, pp. 92–128.
Sherman, C. (1994) *Cindy Sherman, 1975–1993*, ed. R. Krauss, New York: Rizzoli.
Shields, R. (1996) 'The everyday, cyberspaces and individuals: cyberpunk Cinderella or depressed heroine?', unpublished paper.
Slater, D. (1995a) 'Domestic photography and digital culture', in M. Lister (ed.) *The Photographic Image in Digital Culture*, New York and London: Routledge, pp. 129–147.
—— (1995b) 'Photography and modern vision: the spectacle of "natural magic"', in C. Jenks (ed.) *Visual Culture*, London and New York: Routledge, pp. 218–238.
Solomon-Godeau, A. (1991) *Photography at the Dock: Essays on Photographic History, Institutions and Practices*, Minneapolis: University of Minnesota Press.
Sontag, S. (1977) *On Photography*, New York: Farrar, Straus.
Spence, J. (1986) *Putting Myself in the Picture: A Political, Personal and Photographic Autobiography*, London: Camden Press.
Spence, J. and Holland, P. (eds) (1991) *Family Snaps: The Meaning of Domestic Photography*, London: Virago.
Stacey, J. (1997) *Teratologies: A Cultural Study of Cancer*, London: Routledge.
Stafford, B. M. (1993) *Body Criticism: Imaging the Unseen in Enlightenment Art and Medicine*, Cambridge, Mass. and London: MIT Press.
Stainton Rogers, R. and Stainton Rogers, W. (1992) *Stories of Childhood: Shifting Agendas of Child Concern*, Hemel Hempstead: Harvester Wheatsheaf.
Staples, L. (1995) 'What happens when the edges dissolve?', *Eye*, 18, pp. 6–7.
Steichen, E. (1993) *The Family of Man*, New York: The Museum of Modern Art (first published in 1953).
Stelzer, O. (1969) 'Postscript: Moholy-Nagy and his vision', in L. Moholy-Nagy *Painting, Photography, Film*, London: Lund Humphries, pp. 145–150.
Stiegler, B. (1995) 'Images and after-images', in Cypres (ed.) *Art/Digital Photography*, Aix-en-Provence: École d'Art d'Aix-en-Provence, pp. 220–252.
Stolcke, V. (1993) 'Is sex to gender as race is to ethnicity?', in T. del Valle (ed.) *Gendered Anthropology*, London: Routledge, pp. 17–38.
Stoller, P. (1995) *Embodying Colonial Memories: Spirit Possession, Power and the Hauku in West Africa*, New York and London: Routledge.
Stone, A. R. (1992) 'Virtual systems', in J. Crary and S. Kwinter (eds) *Incorporations*, New York: Zone, MIT Press, pp. 608–626.
—— (1995) *The War of Desire and Technology at the Close of the Mechanical Age*, Cambridge, Mass. and London: MIT Press.
Strathern, M. (1988) *The Gender of the Gift: Problems with Women and Problems with Society in Melanesia*, Berkeley and Los Angeles: University of California Press.
—— (1991) *Partial Connections*, Savage, Maryland: Rowman and Littlefield Publishers.
—— (1992) *After Nature: English Kinship in the Late Twentieth Century*, Cambridge: Cambridge University Press.
—— (1995) 'Potential property: intellectual rights and property in persons', unpublished paper.
Tagg, J. (1988) *The Burden of Representation: Essays on Photographies and Histories*, London: Macmillan Education.

Taussig, M. (1993) *Mimesis and Alterity: A Particular History of the Senses*, New York and London: Routledge.

Taylor, C. (1989) *Sources of the Self: The Making of Modern Identity*, Cambridge, Mass.: Harvard University Press.

—— (1992) *Multiculturalism and 'The Politics of Recognition'*, Princeton: Princeton University Press.

—— (1993) 'The person', in M. Carrithers, S. Collins and S. Lukes (eds) *The Category of the Person*, Cambridge: Cambridge University Press, pp. 257–282.

Thomas, R. Roosevelt (1990) 'From affirmative action to affirming diversity', *Harvard Business Review*, March–April, pp. 107–117.

Thompson, R. (1980) 'Meep-Meep!', in G. Peary and D. Peary (eds) *The American Animated Cartoon: A Critical Anthology*, New York: E. P Dutton, pp. 217–225.

Tomas, D. (1995) 'Art, psychasthenic assimilation and the cybernetic automaton', in C. Hables Gray (ed.) *The Cyborg Handbook*, New York and London: Routledge, pp. 255–267.

Trachtenberg, A. (1992) 'Likeness as identity: reflections on the Daguerrean mystique', in G. Clarke (ed.) *The Portrait in Photography*, London: Reaktion Books, pp. 173–193.

Tyler, C. (1994) 'Passing: narcissism, identity and difference', *differences*, 6: 2–3, pp. 212–249.

Verbeke, W. (1992) 'Advertisers do not persuade consumers; they create societies around their brands to maintain power in the marketplace', *International Journal of Advertising*, 11, pp. 1–13.

Virilio, P. (1991) *The Lost Dimension*, New York: Semiotext(e).

—— (1994) *The Vision Machine*, London: BFI.

von Amelunxen, H. (1994) 'Andreas Müller-Pohle', *European Photography*, 15: 1, pp. 21–23.

Wattam, C. (1992) *Making a Case in Child Protection*, Harlow: Longman.

Williams, L. (1995) 'Corporealized observers: visual pornographies and the "carnal density of vision"', in P. Petro (ed.) *Fugitive Images: From Photography to Video*, Bloomington and Indianapolis: Indiana University Press, pp. 3–42.

Williamson, J. (1983) 'Images of "Woman"', *Screen*, 24: 6, pp.102–106.

Wills, D. (1995) *Prosthesis*, Stanford: Stanford University Press.

Wilson, E. L. (1980) 'To my patrons' (first published in 1871), in B. Newhall (ed.) *Photography: Essays and Images*, London: Secker and Warburg.

Winship, J. (1987) *Inside Women's Magazines*, London: Pandora.

Wittig, M. (1992) *The Straight Mind and Other Essays*, Hemel Hempstead: Harvester Wheatsheaf.

Wohlfarth, I. (1994) 'No-man's-land: on Walter Benjamin's "Destructive character"', in A. Benjamin and P. Osborne (eds) *Walter Benjamin's Philosophy: Destruction and Experience*, London and New York: Routledge, pp. 155–183.

Wright, L. (1993a) 'Remembering Satan – Part I', *The New York Review*, 17 May, pp. 60–81.

—— (1993b) 'Remembering Satan – Part II', *The New York Review*, 24 May, pp. 54–76.

—— (1994) *Remembering Satan: Recovered Memory and the Shattering of a Family*, New York: Serpent's Tail.

Zeleny, M. (ed.) (1981) *Autopoiesis: A Theory of Living Organization*, New York: North-Holland.

Ziff, T. (1991) 'Digital memories', *Ten-8*, 2: 2, pp. 76–78.

Zola, D. (1990–1991) 'Autopoiesis: critique of a postmodern paradigm', *Telos*, no. 86, Winter, pp. 61–80.

INDEX